4–31 Infantry in Iraq's
Triangle of Death

4–31 Infantry in Iraq's Triangle of Death

Darrell E. Fawley III

McFarland & Company, Inc., Publishers
Jefferson, North Carolina

The Department of Defense Office of Prepublication and Security Review cleared this work for publication on 25 January 2019 (Reference number: 18-S-2207). This work and its conclusion are solely those of the author and do not necessarily reflect any position or opinion of the U.S. Army, Department of Defense, or United States Government.

All photographs are from the author's collection.

Library of Congress Cataloguing-in-Publication Data

Names: Fawley, Darrell E., III, 1983– author.
Title: 4–31 Infantry in Iraq's triangle of death / Darrell E. Fawley III.
Description: Jefferson, North Carolina : McFarland & Company, Inc., Publishers, 2020. | Includes bibliographical references and index.
Identifiers: LCCN 2019048841 | ISBN 9781476676050 (paperback : acid free paper) ∞ |
ISBN 9781476638317 (ebook)
Subjects: LCSH: United States. Army. Infantry, 31st. Battalion, 4th—History—Iraq War, 2003–2011. | Iraq War, 2003–2011—Regimental histories—United States. | Iraq War, 2003–2011—Campaigns—Iraq—Baghdad (Province) | Counterinsurgency—Iraq—Baghdad (Province)
Classification: LCC DS79.765.U6 F39 2020 | DDC 956.7044/342—dc23
LC record available at https://lccn.loc.gov/2019048841

British Library cataloguing data are available

ISBN (print) 978-1-4766-7605-0
ISBN (ebook) 978-1-4766-3831-7

© 2019 Darrell E. Fawley III. All rights reserved

No part of this book may be reproduced or transmitted in any form or by any means, electronic or mechanical, including photocopying or recording, or by any information storage and retrieval system, without permission in writing from the publisher.

Front cover images © 2020 Shutterstock

Printed in the United States of America

McFarland & Company, Inc., Publishers
Box 611, Jefferson, North Carolina 28640
www.mcfarlandpub.com

For Sergeant Matt Moran
and all the other Polar Bear soldiers
who have taken their lives since returning from Yusifiyah,
that others may read this and understand
what we did and why it was important

Table of Contents

Preface	1
Introduction	7
1. A Land on Fire	11
2. The Polar Bears Go Marching In	31
3. Mountain Men in a Flat Land	52
4. Into the Heart of Darkness	85
5. A New Strategy?	104
6. The Unceremonious Pyre	130
7. A New Day	140
8. Going Home, Staying Behind	159
9. What It All Means: Theory of Small Unit Counterinsurgency	171
Conclusion	192
Acronyms and Abbreviations	195
Chapter Notes	197
Bibliography	207
Index	215

I believe in the force of a hand grenade, the power of artillery, the accuracy of a Garand. I believe in hitting before you get hit, and that dead men do not look noble.

But I also believe in men like Brandon and Novak and Swope and Kerrigan; and all the men who stood up against the enemy, taking their beatings without whimper and their triumphs without boasting. The men who went and would go again to hell and back to preserve what our country thinks is right and decent.

My country. America!

—Audie Murphy

Preface

When my feet touched down on American soil for the first time after a fifteen-month deployment in the area of Iraq known as the "Triangle of Death," I sure felt victorious. The time between leaving and returning home had been long, at times frustrating, at times fun ... at times a number of things. There were times when I failed to see the logic in my unit's approach, even times when it seemed futile to try anything. But by the time I left the east shore of the Euphrates River, I believed we had done something truly special in a place that felt like hell no matter how biblical it may be.

But the more I talked to others who had deployed with different units and in different areas, the more I read about Iraq, the more I sat in lectures led by other units, it became clear to me that despite perception in the media and among the people, nearly everyone coming home from Iraq hadn't just made progress, they had won. And while by November 2007—when my unit had arrived home—there had been some progress in improving Iraq's security situation, it was unlikely that everyone had been so prolifically successful. Which led to the question *How can one even determine success in such a complex situation?*

Our deployment had been brutally violent; many soldiers died and more were maimed in some manner. When soldiers march off to war, the young are idealistic and the veterans skeptical. As the war drags on and casualties mount, nearly every soldier questions what is happening. *Are we doing the right thing? Should we even be here?* And, ultimately, one question lingers in a soldier's mind: *What does this mean?* I have often wondered just what was the meaning of what we did.

Even before I returned from Iraq, the idea of writing about my experiences came to mind. But writing a memoir of my own experience seemed oddly self-serving for a lieutenant. I also considered writing a book about my unit's deployment but I had no idea how to conduct the research. My undergraduate studies, while filled with research papers, had never taught me something on this scale. But two questions remained in my head for the next ten years: *Were we successful? What did it all mean?*

I came home from my first tour in Afghanistan a few weeks shy of Christmas in 2012, just over five years after returning from Iraq. Three days later, the opportunity presented itself to teach Reserve Officer Training Corps (ROTC) cadets at Ohio University, a school 60 minutes from where I grew up and one from which my father, sister, and brother-in-law had graduated. The school treated my wife and I well, providing us the opportunity to pursue graduate degrees on its dime. During the course of my studies I received the opportunity to take a class in the history department related to modern counterinsurgency that was outside the scope of my standard coursework. It was there, under the tutelage of Dr. Ingo Trauschweizer, that I found not the answers to my questions, but the path to those answers. My term paper for the class focused on my unit's—4th Battalion, 31st Infantry Regiment—counterinsurgency efforts. The process familiarized me with the sources I would need for further research. It was also where I read Peter Mansour's *Surge: My Journey with General David Petraeus and the Remaking of the Iraq War*. While the book is insightful, it was really the format that provided me a guide for writing this book. Mansour is both a participant and an historian in *Surge*. That is the methodology I have adopted here.

I moved from Ohio University to the Command and General Staff Officer Course at the Army's Command and General Staff College (CGSC) at Fort Leavenworth, Kansas. There, as a part of the Art of War Scholars program, I wrote a thesis examining the effect the arrival of General David Petraeus had on units in Iraq using 4th Battalion, 31st Infantry as a case study. This gave me the research foundation I needed to write this book, which is not a continuation or an expansion of that thesis. It is an attempt to answer those two burning questions. My research tells me it is a compelling story of counterinsurgency in a place that seemed at the bottom of Hades. But this is not a story of the men who fought in the Triangle of Death per se; it is a story of how those men fought there.

The tale of the Triangle of Death is not a new one. Journalist Jim Frederick wrote perhaps the best-known book on it, *Black Hearts: One Platoon's Descent into Madness in Iraq's Triangle of Death*. He focuses on the unit my battalion replaced. It is a great case study in ethics and leadership in combat and paints a grim picture of the area. Frederick's book is a worthy addition to the literature of Iraq, but it stops in the summer of 2006, right about the time of the arrival of my battalion.

Three books do cover the deployment of 4th Battalion, 31st Infantry in some fashion. Charles Sasser's *None Left Behind: The 10th Mountain Division and the Triangle of Death* is a nice tribute the soldiers in the battalion but lacks depth in its research. The book focuses mostly on Company D and the battalion commander and is more personality based than anything. Reading the book will not provide much insight into the battalion's counterinsurgency approach. Two memoirs have also emerged. The battalion's chaplain, Captain Jeff Bryan, published *Memoirs from Babylon: A Combat Chaplain's Life in Iraq's Triangle of Death*. The book is a full memoir of Bryan's path to becoming the unit's chaplain and then his time serving the soldiers of the 4th Battalion. Much of the latter part of the book is largely based on his diary. Well written, the memoir accomplishes its purpose and is worthy of its place among the literature of war. (Self-published, the book has a spot on many military library bookshelves.) However, Bryan's book is neither a history of the deployment nor an assessment of counterinsurgency in the Triangle of Death.

The other memoir, *Not in the Wind, Earthquake, or Fire*, is the work of Philip Sharp, a staff sergeant at the time of its writing. It is Sharp's journal mixed with additional commentary providing context. In a few instances, other members of the unit provide commentary as well. Sharp's book is a very honest view of his squad's deployment and provides a glimpse of how a mid-level non-commissioned officer perceived the decisions of those higher up and how he felt during the deployment. Sharp's insight is quite valuable. However, like Bryan's memoir, its usefulness to the questions at hand is limited.

Other books have explored Yusifiyah as part of a larger subject. The anthology *The Strong Gray Line: War-Time Reflections from the West Point Class of 2004* has a few entries from officers who served in Yusifiyah including one who served in my unit. The United States Military Academy's Center for the Advancement of Leader Development & Organizational Learning (CALDOL) published *A Platoon Leader's Tour*, which is a collection of short vignettes designed to help cadets and lieutenants prepare for the myriad challenges of deployments. The book features scenarios from several of 4th Battalion, 31st Infantry's lieutenants. Both of these works provide some insight but are limited to a handful of pages. Lastly, Dale Andrade's *Surging South of Baghdad: The 3D Infantry Division and Task Force Marne in Iraq, 2007–2008* provides some coverage of the battalion as part of a look at the 2nd Brigade Combat Team's role under 3rd Infantry Division, but it is not the focus of the book.

There is also Sue Diaz's *Minefields of the Heart: A Mother's Stories of a Son at War*. Diaz, a writer and reporter, largely focuses on her interactions with her son and longing for communication with him, an infantryman. The book touches on Yusifiyah because her son served there in the 2005–2006 timeframe. However, her book does not offer much beyond what other sources already cover with respect to the subject at hand.

While all of these works contribute to the history of the battalion and help to address the questions that swirled in my mind since returning from Iraq, none are sufficient to serve as a history or an analysis of the unit's counterinsurgency. Had this work sought to be a memoir, it would also fall short. Instead, *4–31 Infantry in Iraq's Triangle of Death* provides an operational history of the 4th Battalion, 31st Infantry, in the Triangle of Death and analyzes its counterinsurgency approach. This book begins with a history of the Yusifiyah area prior to the arrival of 4–31 IN, then follows the battalion from its train up to its return home. This work ends with a chapter considering counterinsurgency at the battalion and lower level. This final chapter is important. Despite a multitude of mid–20th-century works by practitioners of counterinsurgency analyzing their actions, there has been little theory developed regarding U.S. military actions in Iraq and Afghanistan from the works of participants.

Along the way I will offer some leadership and humorous anecdotes for the benefit of the reader. However, many works have sought to tell the story of individuals in the Global War on Terrorism; Sasser's book is a prime example. So while this book will talk about the conditions the men lived through, it will not go into detail about any individuals except where necessary. I have used names only where it is important for the history of the unit or the understanding of the reader. Generally, unless the individual has published on the subject or been featured in a work by name, I have not named him in this work. Two notable exceptions are the brigade and battalion commanders whose names are a matter of public record. All ranks used in this book are those of the individuals at the time of events.

This book uses several sources that other authors have not used that help provide a fuller picture of 4th Battalion, 31st Infantry's time in Yusifiyah. I used several brigade, battalion, and company newsletters that had not appeared as sources before as well as other documents and articles previous authors have not cited. While a fair amount of this book comes from my own experience, I have attempted to use primary and secondary sources to inform my memory. Throughout the deployment I sent many letters and often wrote short documents about my experience. I did not keep a journal but saw these as equivalents. I have drawn on these documents and letters as primary sources to help inform dates and events.

I have used many news articles and press releases as sources due to the fact that many of the unit's records are still classified. Since a large number of these articles were written and published by 4th Battalion, 31st Infantry's parent brigade, they surely strike a favorable tone. The basic facts of these articles are reliable and there is nothing to suggest any information was falsified. However, the authors of these articles often include quotes that favor the narrative the unit sought to advance. Thus, I have taken this into consideration when using these sources. I feel that my experience helps me to be appropriately skeptical when considering sources. However, the work done by Specialist Chris McCann and Staff Sergeant Angela McKinzie in chronicling for the Fort Drum newspaper (at the time *The Blizzard*, but now *The Mountaineer*) provides the frame for this history. Their yeoman's work in writing short articles has allowed me to trace the battalion's operations along with the memoirs of Sharp and Bryan. Not every unit does as good a job writing about its actions as I discovered searching for information on 2nd Battalion, 70th Armor Regiment's time in the Triangle. I hope soldiers are keeping journals and holding on to letters and that one day there will be a central archive for the Global War on Terrorism.

I have endeavored to read as much as has been written about Yusifiyah and consider it. I prefer accounts written or based on notes close to the actual event. Memory has a funny way of changing over time. Not every primary source is more trustworthy than a secondary source. Still, I have looked at what is there and attempted to deduce the most accurate history with the unclassified sources available. In trying to craft a coherent narrative, many actions have gone from draft to cutting room floor. Others never made it to paper to begin with. Unlike Richard Frank, whose *Guadalcanal: The Definitive Account of the Landmark Battle* accounts for combat actions down to the half-minute, this book is not about everything. For those reading this who participated in the events, if you feel I have underplayed your action or an event, I apologize. I have made no attempt to diminish anyone's actions. But this book is about the larger counterinsurgency approach, not the individual skirmishes and raids.

Some notes on naming conventions are in order. First, the main city, Yusifiyah, has been spelled variously as Yusufiyah and Yousefiya, among others. A transliteration of the Arabic word comes to Yusifiyah, which is the standard spelling I will use. One town had three names depending on whom one talked to and what source one looked in. The going in name was Al Taraq, but throughout of the deployment some called it North Hargawi and others Ahmed Suhel. Sources mix this, especially the articles generated by the 10th Mountain Division. Since Al Taraq is what appeared on maps and was the first used, that is what I use in this book. This is simpler and clearer than switching between names. The rest of this book will only use that name. Another area, Qarghuli Village, is alternatively spelled Karghuli, Karghouli, and even Carghuli, in sources. I use Qarghuli here for no reason other than that is how I always spelled it and many sources agree. A final point relates to sources. Since the political district of Mahmudiyah covered the cities in the Triangle of Death, many sources cite Mahmudiyah as the location of things that happened in the Yusifiyah area. Thus, the kidnapping of soldiers in in Qarghuli Village is sometimes referred to as the Mahmudiyah kidnapping and the rape of Abeer Qassim Al Janabi and killing of her family is sometimes referred to as the Mahmudiyah rape and killings. I have placed these events in their proper geographic locations.

The U.S. Army typically capitalizes certain words, such as "soldiers," that are not normally capitalized. Thus, at times, quotes may contain a capitalized form of a common noun. To increase readability, I have left out the [*sic*] designation where this is the case. For any quotes that came from a speech, I have standardized spelling and capitalization if the source uses a different convention than I have. If I quoted written word, I left the spelling as is. I have checked all the quotes. Similarly, for the Marines, if I am referring to the service or a unit within the service I have capitalized the word. However, I have not adopted the Marine Corps' preference for capitalizing the word "marines" when it refers to troops or individuals.

Additionally, while trying to maintain accuracy in doctrine and terms, I realize that the military could speak in acronyms all day long if it so desired. I am reminded of the scene in *Renaissance Man* where Danny Devito, looking down at a set of directions someone has just given him and the eye chart-like nature of it, asks, "Can I buy a vowel?" I have done my best to limit my use of acronyms and tried to only use those that make the prose flow better. For the reader's convenience, there is a list of acronyms included. I have also done my best to limit military jargon.

This work has gone from an inkling to a finished product over the course of more than a decade. There are many I would like to thank starting with my family. My wife, Lindsey, has always been a strong source of encouragement for me and her dedication to education has made it easier to pursue my own. If not for her support, this project would never have gotten off the ground. She allowed me time to write and research and I cannot thank her enough for that. She is every bit my equal, if not more. My parents, Darrell and Annie, have been great role models for me and have supported me every step of the way. We had one computer growing up and they allowed me plenty of time to use it writing stories, which turned me into an effective communicator. My grandfather, Darrell, was my primary motivation to become an Army officer. I am saddened that he was not around to see me graduate from West Point.

Academically, Dr. Ingo Trauschweizer provided me the first forum to explore this topic. Dr. Katherine Jellison and Dr. Marvin Fletcher of the Ohio University history department and Dr. Jason Jolley of the George Voinovich School of Leadership and Public Affairs provided me the opportunity to take his class when it was outside of my graduate programs. Dr. Mark Hull, Dr. Donald Wright, and Colonel (retired) Steve Boylan served on my thesis committee at the Command and General Staff College when I took my education further and explored this topic at greater length. All of these people helped me formulate my ideas and challenged my conclusions. But for them, this would be a much worse project. Further, Dr. Dean Nowoweijski, the Ike Skelton Chair at the Command and General Staff College and director of the Art of War Scholars program, has been a great source of mentorship and has helped convince me this was a worthy project to push forward.

I hope this work reaches three audiences. First, I hope the general American public reads it and gets an idea of what this kind of war my generation has fought is like. It may help them to gain perspective on the first long war our nation has fought where the average citizen was not forced to serve. Second, I hope those that study war, especially those in battalions and below, read it so that they may have an idea of how units conducted counterinsurgency in Iraq. Few books really look at this subject. Lastly, and most importantly, I hope the soldiers in the task force read it. More than I care to count have taken their own lives fighting their demons. Others suffer from their experience. I hope that those surviving can learn the meaning of what they did and that it may give them a renewed sense of spirit and pride and a means to understand what their friends died for or what they risked everything for. Hopefully they will see themselves as successful.

Finally, it is necessary to note that everything I've written here is based on open source information and that any conclusions I've drawn are my own. My assessment and analysis of Task Force 4–31 IN or any other organization or person do not reflect any official or unofficial positions of the Department of Defense or U.S. government nor any of their subordinate organizations.

Pro Patria!

Introduction

Route Malibu, Qarghuli Village, Iraq
12 0444 May 2007

In the still darkness of the early morning hours, two vehicles sat facing in opposite directions on a lonely stretch of road in a forgotten town. It was a quiet night with barely a sound. The vehicles' engines were off and the slow flow of the Euphrates River just to the west made no noise. The spotty electricity in the village was out, meaning the only light was from the stars and a waning crescent moon.

Only a few hundred meters from friendly troops, the eight men might as well have been on an island in a distant sea. Their surroundings were inhospitable. The tribesmen inhabiting the dwellings were indifferent to their fate in the best of cases. In the worst, they were hostile, willing to aid and abet anyone looking to harm the soldiers. The sole barrier between the vehicles and any attacking force was a solitary strand of concertina wire, a minor inconvenience to even a partially determined foe.

The American infantryman is a predator, but, on this night, he was prey. Off in the recesses to the east among a tangle of houses and canals lay a score of a men, watching, waiting. They'd all been here before, two nights ago. On that night, the predators aborted after hearing the engines rumbling, fearing the soldiers were ready to defeat them. But tonight, those engines were off and the gun turrets, facing down the road in either direction, appeared to be unoccupied. To the leader, it appeared all criteria were in place to execute his mission: capture U.S. soldiers.

The terrorists waiting in the wings were not a ragtag group of amateurs. They handled this operation like a military unit would: each man had a role; the leader had issued an order using a diagram of the objective; the unit rehearsed their actions. The teams were set up much like a doctrinal raid: security, breach, assault, command and control. There was no direct fire support element. Instead, a man took video footage of the assault. All that was left was to execute before the sun's first light began to poke up over the horizon.

Slightly more than a quarter to 0500, the two security teams ran up and isolated the objective by placing decoy IEDs to the north and south of the vehicles. The bombs would be obvious to anyone who came upon them and significantly slow any response. At the same time a breach team moved forward and silently clipped a hole in the wire that would allow the assault teams unabated access to the vehicles. As the direct action teams moved forward, they threw explosives in the turrets hoping to disorient the occupants long enough to pull them out of their vehicles and subdue them.

Up to this point, the plan had gone ahead with clockwork precision. But something went wrong. Before the attackers ever got to the soldiers, the trucks were on fire from the inside. Ammunition was cooking off and shooting into the air through the turret. Hoping for hostages, four of the soldiers were on their way to a gruesome death. The rest of the soldiers began to emerge from the vehicles to meet their attackers in close combat. With the fire in their eyes and the dark of the night all around, their aim was wild and ineffective. Better positioned, a second wave of enemy began to fire on the soldiers.

One soldier took off north, flinging off his gear, likely in an attempt to alert his headquarters, less than a quarter mile up the road. Enemy fighters shot him dead. While no radio call ever came from the soldiers, the explosions, rifle fire, and tracers alerted the higher unit to the ambush. Quickly, the platoon leader for the soldiers under attack scooped up the rest of his men and rushed them south while a platoon sergeant for another platoon gathered up a portion of his platoon and proceeded north. The lead elements of both these platoons found the IEDs and halted the vehicle movement. Both response forces then pushed off on foot, weaving amongst the tangle of houses and canals, en route to their brothers. They moved as quickly as possible.

The two forces converged on the flaming hulls at roughly the same time, greeted by a gruesome scene. The stench of burning flesh bit their nostrils. Three American and one Iraqi soldier sat in the vehicles, aflame in an unceremonious pyre. One soldier lay dead in the street.

But that was not the worst of it. As the two elements took stock of what they found, it turned out that three American soldiers were missing. Only a bloody trail leading off to the east provided any clue as to where the soldiers may have gone. Soon, an obscure jihadist organization calling itself Islamic State would claim responsibility for the attack. In the land where everything burns, this was an especially gruesome attack.[1]

* * *

A volcano can be both beautiful and vicious, something that draws people and something that kills them without mercy. Filled with immense destructive potential, it can lay dormant for centuries or millennia, with nary a tremble to remind people it is more than a passive piece of the landscape. But then one day all of that pent up, deadly power erupts without warning and charts a course of devastation no one expected and no one knows how to contain or repair.

In Iraq, there is a small patch of farmland, beautiful to just about any beholder, that went largely unnoticed for several thousand years until it erupted in flames and refused to quit. It went from hardscrabble land to gentry farming to military industrial hub. Then, in the wake of the U.S.–led invasion in 2003, the area devolved into a chaotic land where Iraqi security forces, U.S. soldiers, and Shi'a Iraqis suddenly became *persona non grata*. The coalition ignored the area, but then waded in late in 2004. From the moment U.S. forces clashed with Iraqi insurgents in the region, a fire ignited and burnt bright for years. Though it seemed uncontainable, by the end of 2007, a tenuous peace had emerged.

This land, located at the western apex of the Triangle of Death and known as Yusifiyah, saw just about everything once it burst into international prominence in 2004. A sleepy part of the military-industrial complex and retirement community for Saddam-loyalists before the war, afterword it was a staunch center of sectarian violence. Kidnappings and killings were common place. Five U.S. soldiers alone became temporary captives of Sunni insurgents. The organization now known as Islamic State of Iraq and Syria (or Iraq and the Levant) pulled off a devastating attack against U.S. forces in its infancy. U.S. troops committed one of the worst atrocities of the war, raping a 14-year-old girl, killing her family, and burning their bodies. The same U.S. base twice caught fire. But not all was bad. Three units stayed long enough to enact counterinsurgency approaches that, built upon each other, led to a first-of-its-kind peace deal brokered amongst the tribes. The moniker Triangle of Death was left by the wayside and ISIS, despite its best efforts, was not able to retake the land on the east bank of the Euphrates.

A volcano is an imperfect metaphor. One cannot stop lava from spewing where it may and destroying what it will and only the foolhardy would think they could enact any measure to stop future eruptions. The men who entered the Triangle of Death attempted to do just that. This book is the story of how they did that; it is both about history and counterinsurgency. While focused in depth on the fifteen months that 4th Battalion, 31st Infantry (4–31 IN) roamed Yusifiyah and its environs, this book considers the history of the area in its breadth from just before the 2003 invasion to present day.

Chapter 1 sets the scene, describing the region, the people, and the threat while also telling the story of Yusifiyah from the turn of the century to August 2006 when Task Force (TF) 4–31 IN arrived. Chapter 2 describes the history of the 31st Infantry, the state of Iraq in August 2006, and the training program that TF 4–31 IN used to prepare for Iraq. Chapter 3 describes the opening mission, *Operation Polar Blizzard*, that sought to clear significant swaths of the region and hold key terrain. It further describes initial efforts to consolidate gains. Chapter 4 relays the task force's push into Qarghuli Village and up Route Malibu, an especially dangerous area teeming with hostile Iraqis. Chapter 5 highlights the battalion's approach during the beginning of General David Petraeus' tenure as commander of Multi-National Forces-Iraq. Chapter 6 focuses on the capture of three U.S. soldiers by Islamic State militants and the subsequent efforts to find the soldiers and quell violence in Yusifiyah. Chapter 7 looks into the period of time beginning in the early summer of 2007 when the combination of U.S. missions and firepower, territorial gains by Iraqi troops, and the formation of a neighborhood watch organization in the style of Sons of Iraq dramatically increased security in the area. Chapter 8 focuses on the battalion's return home and the history of the area after their departure and analyzes the battalion's performance in light of the eleven years since they left.

Chapter 9 departs from the linear timeline of the previous chapters and seeks to describe the reasons for success for the battalion that future students of counterinsurgency may use. I hope readers will engage in debate over the conclusions and help build the theory of small unit counterinsurgency. A brief conclusion wraps up the story.

Every author has a bias; I was a member of the battalion during the time covered in this book. I have done my best to analyze the evidence as fairly as possible. I hope the reader will think critically about everything I have presented. This is primarily a book about small unit counterinsurgency in action. It is a subject that has received very little attention since the Surge. I hope to rectify that in a small way.

1

A Land on Fire

What is to give light must endure burning.—Viktor Frankl

In the country of Iraq between the inhospitable desert of Anbar and the unforgiving city of Baghdad, lies a verdant piece of land as lethal as it is luxuriant. Twenty-five miles south of the capital, the Euphrates River gives the area life; terrorists hiding in the ditches and orchards brought death to it. Crisscrossed by canals, dotted with hamlets and villages, and lined with farm fields, the vistas can be quite spectacular. The rising sun shining its light across the land provides a beautiful view to anyone able to gaze upon it. Editor Lawrence Kaplan described it thusly: "On a helicopter flight south from Baghdad to Yusufiyah, a panorama unfolds wholly unlike the polluted and broken capital behind us. The debris of the city quickly gives way to a stunning landscape, with canals and dikes ordering lush farmland into neat grids." Countering the beauty, Sean Smith, a photographer for *The Guardian*, wrote, "when you move through the area, it reminds you of John Boorman's film Deliverance [sic]; you never know what will be around the next corner." Balancing the two, Sean Alfano of CBS News, called it "a river area, lush and green with farm fields and palm trees ... [b]ut even by Iraq's horrific standards, it's an especially lethal area dominated by Sunni insurgents." First Lieutenant Nicholas Ziemba, who served as an advisor to Iraqi Army soldiers, wrote:

> At the apexes of the [T]riangle [of Death] were the small cities of Mahmudiyah to the north, Yusifiyah to the west, and Lutifiyah to the south. These cities, like most across the country, were at times vicious and at others vibrant: overflowing markets full of brilliant spice displays and hanging, fly pestered goat carcasses were equally likely to attract shoppers and suicide bombers. The buildings and streets reeked sourly of raw sewage and were run down with both years of prewar neglect and more recent battle scars, but the people who inhabited these places had, at some point, made the fatalistic decision to keep on living amid the despair.

The land was beautiful and deadly like a female superhero on the pages of a comic book.[1]

Nearly 300 square miles, the area is an amorphous triangle with apexes in the towns of Yusifiyah, Mahmudiyah, and Lutifiyah or Al Iskandriyah (Alexandria) depending on what source one uses (this book recognizes Lutifiyah as the third apex). A smaller triangle within the larger one with points at Yusifiyah, the Jurf As-Sukr Bridge (JSB), and Rushdi Mullah, known as the Shakariyah Triangle, is the primary focus of this book. It is a land that hibernated in obscurity for much of its ages-old existence, like that powerful, long dormant volcano. Ruins of the ancient Hittites, who ruled, among other areas, Upper Mesopotamia (where Iraq is) at their height in the mid–14th century BCE, still dot the area. Alexander the Great must have come through the area in 331 BCE given that his name still adorns one of the region's cities. However, in the ensuing two and half millennia, the area remained free of historical significance. Books on Iraq or Mesopotamia written prior to the 2003 invasion of Iraq generally refer to the area only when discussing archeology of the Hittite ruins. For a patch of Earth that had seen human activity for at least thirty-four centuries, it waited until 2004 to gain any true significance.

Before the 2003 invasion of Iraq, the area around Yusifiyah was essentially a Baathist retirement community with mansion-sized estate homes lining the Euphrates River. President of Iraq Saddam Hussein built many of the canals in order to encourage agricultural production and granted land to loyalists who promised to farm it.

The Euphrates River gave life to the Triangle of Death, but it was a poor barrier against the flow of insurgents and weapons.

Thus, most of the residents around Yusifiyah were Sunni Muslims, even if they were not enthusiastic supporters of the president. It was not uncommon for locals to imbed Baathist symbols in their masonry to avoid any questions of loyalty. In the midst of these large estates were much smaller farm homes and farming communities. Many of the residents were poor farmhands and tradesmen. Due to the almost complete Sunni makeup of the area outside the town proper, sectarian tensions were not a primary concern as they were in other areas. However, tribal differences did create issues.[2] And, there was still tension between the largely Shia Iraqi security forces and the residents.

Yusifiyah itself, the largest town in the Shakariyah Triangle, had a population of roughly 25,000 in a relatively compact area.[3] The residents of the town were mostly Shia who demonstrated a more congenial relationship with the Iraqi security forces than the rest of the population. Yusifiyah was the seat of the political district where the *nahia*, or local council, met. In the area, there were three major tribes: the Janabis, the Zobais, and the Qarghulis. The first two had a more national standing where the Qarghulis were more local.

On the far northwest side of the Triangle lay the unfinished Yusifiyah Thermal Power Plant (YTPP), which was roughly eight miles from Yusifiyah. Russian contractors begun work on the complex in 1989 but halted during the Gulf War. They would not resume work until 2001 but had to suspend operations due to the invasion. At that point, it was not finished by any stretch leaving a sprawling complex frozen in time. Connecting the YTPP and the city of Yusifiyah was the Mullah Fayad Highway, a paved route that ran in a series of curved right angles. (Mullah Fayad was a small town that abutted Yusifiyah.) The aforementioned JSB was the one bridge in the area that crossed the Euphrates into Anbar Province and would become a major focal point for U.S. and Iraqi forces.

Before the U.S. led invasion of Iraq, Yusifiyah was a seemingly innocuous point on a map. But this ostensibly placid setting that would transform into a cesspool of Sunni militants appeared in pre-war intelligence reports. The area around Yusifiyah, which housed a decent portion of Iraq's military-industrial organization, was suspected of housing potential nuclear, biological, and chemical weapons program sites. There were six known weapons facilities in the area which produced a wide array of military material such as mobile launchers, missile fuel, warheads, nuclear parts, and missiles. Inspectors were able to visit some of these cites before Hussein began denying access in the lead up to the invasion. During these visits, inspectors did not uncover anything illegal and it does not appear that the coalition targeted these sites during the invasion. Rick Atkinson, who was embedded with the U.S. 101st Airborne Division (Air Assault), the unit that came through the area now known as the Triangle of Death, does not mention Yusifiyah at all in his book *In the Company of Soldiers: A Chronicle of Combat* and mentions Mahmudiyah twice but only in passing.[4]

While Atkinson did not see enough significance in the unit's time in Yusifiyah to note it in his book, the presence of the Screaming Eagles created some controversy that came to light after *In the Company of Soldiers* went to press. The division's 2nd

Brigade assembled at the Al Qaqaa Weapons Facility during the invasion but they did not seize any material, nor did they stay in the area long (likely only two to three weeks). Later, local residents would tell a reporter for a British newspaper that they pleaded with the brigade's commander, Colonel Joseph Anderson, to take control of the explosives in the compound. Anderson told the same reporter he had never been informed of any munitions at the facility. While it is unclear what Anderson knew, video aired by an ABC affiliate in Minneapolis shows U.S. servicemembers at what appears to be the facility opening containers with explosives in it around the time that the brigade was at the site. Later, Charles Duelfer, a special advisor to the director of Central Intelligence, submitted a 1,000-page report in which he confirmed that up to 350 tons of explosives were missing from the Al Qaqaa Weapons Facility. In the coming years, the Sunni militants would employ a near endless supply of explosives, much of which likely came from Al Qaqaa and other locations overlooked in the invasion.[5]

When 2nd Brigade finally left, they were likely the last coalition unit to venture into the greater Yusifiyah area for nearly a year. There are no reports of any military force in the area until members of the U.S. 82nd Airborne Division ventured into the town on a seemingly frivolous hearts-and-minds mission around the beginning of February 2004. (An unsubstantiated report from Al Jazeera claimed that two soldiers were killed in Yusifiyah in an ambush in June 2003. No reporting corroborates this and the aggregate list of U.S. fatalities maintained at iCasulaties.org shows no June 2003 deaths in the area.) The soldiers passed out school supplies and cash to help with projects. By nightfall, they were gone. There is no indication any of the money they gave out led to any positive change in the area.[6]

It appears that elements of the 82nd Airborne had responsibility for the area, but rarely ventured there. In an interview with the U.S. Army's Combat Studies Institute, two soldiers from 1st Squadron, 1st Cavalry Regiment, 1st Armored Division note they were stationed in Yusifiyah in the late spring of 2004. One, Specialist Stephen Rockhold, said:

> I always thought Baghdad was bad, but I found out Baghdad was a pretty nice place to live compared to this place. This place was the dumps. They had no plumbing whatsoever. They drank out of the main creek area. They would throw their waste out in the street. They had no place to put their trash so trash went out in the street. This place was just bad. Everything you can picture a third world country being, this place had it and then some. It was like, "Wow." The people in Baghdad, they felt like they were entitled to things. But when we went down to Yusifiyah and gave some kids some Charms (a type of candy formerly found in military rations) or whatever out of our MREs (meals ready to eat), they'd just look at us like they were actually grateful. But even then, there were still some kids who were scared to death of you. So you really can't tell (people how Iraq is going) because Iraq is a big country and there are different areas. You can't just base it off of one city because there's a lot more to Iraq than Baghdad or Fallujah or whatever.[7]

The macabre nickname arrived sometime in the summer of 2004. The name "Triangle of Death" first appeared in western media, not capitalized, on 3 October 2004 in a French newswire. Sixteen days later, it appeared in English in a British paper, this time capitalized. However, it was not the Western media nor the coalition that bestowed the *nom de guerre* but locals. Later accounts have provided a plethora of reasons for the name which were likely speculative—one officer claims it was because Americans killed so many insurgents there—but the earliest accounts agree that the title was the result of sectarian and anti-coalition violence in the area. The first American newspaper to report on the area after the bestowing of the title, *The Washington Post* detailed that Shi'a Baghdadis branded the area bounded around Yusifiyah, Mahmudiyah, and Lutifiyah (the "Fiyahs") as the Triangle of Death because, "if a car passes through there, it will burn." Purportedly, Sunni militants would ambush anyone not of their ilk: Shi'a, Iraqi security forces, or coalition soldiers. The bounties for the death of a Shi'a, Iraqi National Guardsman, and American were $1,000, $2,000, and $3,000, respectively. Given that the Triangle sat between Baghdad and the Shi'a holy lands to the west in Al Anbar province, this was a major problem. The population of Yusifiyah proper being mostly Shi'a, it is unclear what status they held in this structure.[8]

But those three categories were not the only targets. In May 2004, Dr. Salamah Al Khafaji, a member of Iraq's Interim Governing Council, was transiting the area from Al Najaf en route to Baghdad when militants attempted to assassinate her. She survived, but up to four people with her (three of them bodyguards) perished in the attack. Her son's body was found in a river (presumably the Euphrates) the next day. The day after that, the body of a Japanese journalist showed up in Yusifiyah. The journalist had been traveling with a colleague and an interpreter when their vehicle was struck by insurgents and caught fire. Then, on 11 June 2004, insurgents traveling in seven vehicles converged on the Yusifiyah police station firing small arms and rocket propelled grenades (RPGs). The police, armed only with rifles and sidearms, fled and called for help from American troops who reportedly did not arrive for five hours. In the meantime, the insurgents rigged the building with explosives and destroyed it before withdrawing. In short, the area desperately needed order and security.[9]

Marines fancy themselves the first men in. While not true for the Triangle in general, they were first to establish a permanent presence in Yusifiyah. Previously, Mahmudiyah had been the limit of reach. Around the time the lush river valley became known as much for death as life, the first enduring coalition forces arrived in the Yusifiyah area. The 2nd Battalion, 24th Marine Regiment (2/24 Marines), a reserve unit known as the "Mad Ghosts," arrived in early fall, placing Company F in a position on the outskirts of town. Possibly in conjunction with this move, on 9 October U.S. forces, Iraqi National Guardsmen, and Iraqi police forces conducted an operation that included a large-scale raid into the town. According to Iraqi Captain Hadi Hatif, more than 60 armored vehicles including tanks and Bradley Fighting Vehicles, backed by fighter jets and helicopters, raided the town arresting 27 gunmen who had documents indicating they were planning an attack. The raid killed six civilians and wounded 18 more. A house and three stores were destroyed in the operation.[10] Hatif's account may be embellished, but it is certain that the coalition was coming to stay.

The Marine battalion commander, Lieutenant Colonel Mark Smith, and a number of the battalion's other leaders were law enforcement professionals in their regular jobs and this shaped their vision of a community policing approach or, as they labeled it, a "zip code offensive." The marines of Company F took over a town "whose deserted streets reek[ed] of sewage," giving an indication of the state of the town in October 2004. John Burns, a *New York Times* reporter who spent time with the unit, reported, "There is little they cannot do, with hard work and improvisation, the battalion's officers say, reflecting the widely varied backgrounds of the men in the Chicago-based unit—doctors, policemen, engineers, teachers, carpenters, truck drivers, lawyers, computer specialists, community counselors, college students, to name a few." Burns' assessment brings to mind French counterinsurgency theorist David Gallula's admonishment, "The soldier must then be prepared to become a propagandist, a social worker, a civil engineer, a schoolteacher, a nurse, a boy scout." Calling it an "improvised war," Burns captured the character of military operations in the area and highlighted one of the great values of reserve forces in a counterinsurgency fight: a diverse range of backgrounds and qualifications not often found in a standard active duty rifle organization.[11]

The Marines began patrolling at all hours to establish a presence and confirm map data. While the idea of "presence patrols" would later be criticized as useless and dangerous (largely because they seemed to lack a purpose and led to soldiers hitting IEDs), the concept likely made sense to these law enforcement professionals. One way many police commissioners and mayors reduce crime and curb violence is by placing more police in an effected area. Thus, rather than being patrols intended to "drive around until we get blown up," as many later critics would refer to presence patrols, these patrols had a clear purpose of increasing security by reassuring the populace and deterring militants. It seems likely that the leadership, whose troops patrolled the Triangle of Death in "suicide wagons" (thin-skinned/unarmored HMMWVs with a truck bed for troops to ride in), would not put their troops on the streets just to attract IEDs.[12]

To outside observers, the marines made an early impact. Reporter James Hider of *The Times* of London wrote a hopeful article detailing the progress of F/2/24 early on. "After two weeks of heavy fighting, Yusufiyah is starting to come under their control: the gangland tribes, religious extremists and full-time guerrillas are being driven back by constant exchanges of mortar fire, allowing Iraqi security forces to resume tentative patrols under the watchful eyes of the American troops."[13]

However, the enemy would soon show it still had the ability to strike hard. On 12 November 2004, the first sustained combat action against the marines took place in Yusifiyah. On that date insurgents conducted a coordinated attack on F Company's position, Forward Operating Base (FOB) Yusifiyah. For six hours, insurgents employed indirect fire and machine guns to advance on the base. Marines, who doctrinally fight in an integrated Marine air-ground task force consisting of ground troops and fixed wing air support, replied with air- and mortar-delivered munitions to fend off the attack with an estimated 70 insurgents killed (the actual number is likely much lower). One marine made the ultimate sacrifice.[14] While the engagement turned out relatively well for the marines, it also proved that the enemy could mass in a company-sized element and conduct, even if imperfectly, small unit maneuver using direct and indirect fires.

Yusifiyah's strategic location meant that nationally focused insurgent groups transited through the area frequently. The area served a quasi-sanctuary for insurgents both in Anbar province and Baghdad. When *Operation Phantom Fury* (the Second Battle of Fallujah) kicked off on 7 November 2004, many insurgents crossed the Euphrates River into the Triangle of Death looking for safe havens. Author Jim Frederick claims thousands of fighters poured across the river at this time, though there is no good estimate.[15]

Of those national groups, the most prominent was Al Qaeda in Iraq led by Abu Musab Al Zarqawi, a former Jordanian thug who had fought in Afghanistan and been named *emir*, or prince, of the organization by Osama bin Laden. Some believe Zarqawi transited the area during this period and U.S. intelligence would later focus on Yusifiyah in its search for the *emir*. The most prominent insurgent confirmed to have crossed was 62-year-old Sheikh Abdullah Al Janabi. A reporter for the *New York Times* claimed that Al Janabi was "rated by American military intelligence as one of the most menacing figures" in the insurgency. It is a hard statement to corroborate—"military intelligence" and "most menacing" are phrases devoid of specificity—but it is clear from other sources that Al Janabi was an important player. In December, the marines of F/2/24 raided his ancestral home, but their search came up dry. He was last seen in January 2014 openly preaching in a Fallujah mosque.[16]

Al Qaeda in Iraq developed a reputation for its brutality and Zarqawi became so extreme he drew rebukes from senior Al Qaeda leadership. Therefore, the infusion of Al Qaeda in Iraq fighters into the hinterlands around the town of Yusifiyah certainty increased the volatility of the area. Further, these enemy troops were not the type who were looking for a better opportunity in Iraq and therefore not susceptible to standard counterinsurgency measures. They were the type of enemy that needed to be dealt with in a lethal manner. This led the battalion commander to declare, "This is now the most dangerous place in Iraq."[17] While the commander is unqualified to make the statement in that he owned a small patch of a large country, events over the next three years would reinforce that few places in Iraq were more dangerous.

While F/2/24 continued its zip code offensive using community policing, it was clear that more offensive action was necessary. This was true not just in Yusifiyah but across the Triangle. In late November, a combined force of U.S., British, and Iraqi troops launched *Operation Plymouth Rock* in the "Fiyahs." Led by the 24th Marine Expeditionary Unit, 2/24 Marines' parent organization, the operation consisted primarily of raids against suspected enemy and cache locations. In Yusifiyah, coalition troops captured 856 projectiles of unreported type.[18]

In December and January, an Army brigade and the marines launched *Operation River Walk*. While most of the operation involved clearing potential cache sites along the west bank of the Euphrates in Anbar province, the marines conducted searches along the east bank. The marines entered the denizens of Qarghuli Village, the largest cesspool in their area, in order to conduct a house-to-house search. Marines uncovered an IED factory with two vehicles rigged for use in an attack and a propaganda factory with computers, presses, and photocopiers.[19]

This operation and subsequent smaller ones no doubt led to progress, but without the ability to stay behind and hold terrain, they amounted to limited objective raids. Despite the marines' best efforts, the enemy remained capable of pulling off significant attacks. On 9 January 2005, a vehicle-borne IED (VBIED) exploded at an Iraqi Army checkpoint in the city killing eleven and wounding 23 others. Two days later, another VBIED exploded in town killing seven and wounding three. Ten days following that, insurgents detonated a third VBIED at a wedding. The attack killed at least ten.[20] The insurgents maintained freedom of movement throughout much of the area of operations.

However, the marines were present for what felt like a momentous day in Iraq. On 30 January 2005, Iraqis nationwide headed to the polls to elect their leader in what was billed as a free and fair election. (Sunnis largely boycotted the election.) F/2/24 secured the Yusifiyah polling site and provided overwatch. On that day, insurgents lobbed at least twenty mortar rounds in the direction of the polling station, but the marines were able to silence the ineffective attacks with counterfire. Reflecting on his battalion's tour as a whole, battalion commander Smith declared success, noting that 71 percent of voters in the Triangle of Death turned out for the election and that enemy generated hostile acts reduced from 12 to 18 each day to roughly one every week. Further, the battalion as a whole claimed to have killed 400 insurgents and detained 1200 more. Smith stated later, "We went in there with the full expectation that we were going to do shit differently, and our goal was to set a standard on how you fight this enemy, this new asymmetric warfare. And you fight it by finding out who they are and killing them. That's it."[21] Smith's statement completely ignores his unit's community policing approach.

While Company F had made progress in establishing the foothold in Yusifiyah, there was a long way to go before long-term change could be expected. In fact, Smith's comments point to why they may have seen success in their time but not lasting success for the region. They focused on killing enemy in the hinterlands without securing the area. Of course, Smith lacked the forces to do much beyond the town itself. Ultimately, as I wrote in a term paper while pursuing a master's at Ohio University, "[Smith] accomplished the mission he was given though it was not the mission needed in the area."[22] At that time, the focus in Iraq for coalition forces was elections and the fulfillment of the United Nations mandate, not the complete pacification of all areas.

Shortly after the election, the marines turned over the Triangle to an active Army tank battalion, 2nd Battalion, 70th Armor (2–70 AR), the "Thunderbolts," commanded by Lieutenant Colonel Leopoldo Quintas, who had commanded the battalion in the invasion. They assumed responsibility in February 2005 with the intent of handing the area over almost immediately to elements the 3rd Armored Cavalry Regiment, led by Colonel H.R. McMaster. However, McMaster received orders to move to Tel Afar in the north right as his 2nd Squadron was arriving at Mahmudiyah.[23]

Information on 2–70's time in Yusifiyah is almost non-existent. The website iCasaulties.org only lists a non-combat related death for the battalion in Yuifiyah. However, on 29 April, the coalition captured Amar Adnan Muhammad Hamzah Al Zubaydi, alias Abu al Abbas, in Baghdad. Al Zubaydi was a facilitator of IEDs, building them at his farm near Yusifiyah and sending them to Baghdad. He also assigned suicide bombers and facilitated the flow of foreign fighters into Iraq.[24]

The Thunderbolts handed over the reigns of the Triangle to the 48th Infantry Brigade of the Georgia Army National Guard at the start of summer. In Yusifiyah, the brigade's Company E, 1st Battalion, 108th Armor Regiment (E/1–108 AR) took control. They moved the base from the outskirts of the city to an old potato factory in a more central location where the unit could better radiate power. The brigade's stay in the Triangle was brief but brutal. By the time an active duty battalion arrived to replace them in October 2005, the unit had seen 21 comrades killed across the brigade's area of operations, four of which occurred in Yusifiyah. From the 48th's perspective, the unit had made progress in the Triangle of Death. However, soldiers from the incoming unit believed they were handed a mess.[25] Of course, that may reflect the inclination toward outgoing units to offer rosy assessments and incoming units to take a pessimistic view. Jim Frederick, however, in his interviews with soldiers saw a much more deep-seated resentment from the new unit.

Like its predecessor, information on the 48th's time in Yusifiyah is scant. The *Atlanta Journal-Constitution* kept a blog on the brigade's deployment updating it as often as every day. However, rarely did the *Journal* report on Yusifiyah outside of human-interest stories more useful to its readership than history. In fact, the most notable article had to do with the unit changing the name of the base in the town from FOB Yusifiyah to FOB Stokley in honor of Specialist Michael Stokely who was killed in the city in an IED strike. Whether this name change was official or not is unknown. It may have just been something the soldiers called it since every unit thereafter would continue to refer to the FOB's name as Yusifiyah. In fact, no other source mentions the name FOB Stokley. There is one article that talks about an engineering project to improve the Yusifiyah water pumping station. However, the article refers to the Tigris River multiple times making it possible that it was another pumping station since the Tigris is a long distance from Yusifiyah.[26]

When the 2nd Brigade of the 101st Airborne Division (Air Assault) returned in October 2005, having last been in the area during the invasion, Yusifiyah proper was the western edge of controlled territory, and only that if you have a loose definition of control. West of that and on to the river was a lawless frontier. In fact, the enemy was in such control that it was "a defensive belt akin to a minefield."[27]

It was not the pacific, idyllic farmland it must have appeared to be in April 2003 when the whole brigade transited through Yusifiyah; this time only Company B, 1st Battalion, 502nd Parachute Infantry Regiment (B/1/502 PIR) came. In addition to FOB Yusifiyah, the company also guarded the Jurf As Sukr Bridge. By this point, the position at the JSB included a platoon sized outpost located at a defunct water treatment plant with two unimproved positions outside the compound generally consisting of one or two HMMWVs. One of the positions overwatched an Armored Vehicle-Launched Bridge (AVLB) over a canal connecting the bridge to the Yusifiyah road network. The 48th had named the position at the AVLB "the Alamo" since it was important and yet manning only allowed a handful of soldiers to guard it at a given time. The Alamo position was precarious and not easily defensible. While the unit could not spare more men, it is possible they could have improved the position in other ways. Still, often during the day two soldiers stood watch while three to four did so at night.[28]

If the position was risky it was also essential; it could not have been abandoned. The enemy would have unobserved access to the AVLB allowing them to destroy or damage it. In that case, the platoon at the JSB would become isolated on an island between a canal and a river, only accessible by helicopter. Of course, they guarded a bridge spanning the Euphrates, but there was not a unit within any proximity to respond rapidly from the west side. The position controlled the most direct means of smuggling men, weapons, and equipment from Syria into Baghdad and it could not be left unguarded. There were other ways to cross the Euphrates in the area, but none allowed such ease and capacity. Needless to say, the Alamo was under attack from the start.

The arrangement of manning the JSB and FOB Yusifiyah, placed one platoon approximately 10 miles from the company headquarters. Company B's 1st Platoon was the first to occupy the JSB after the transfer of authority. It is an axiom of the defense that positions are never done until the fight starts. With that in mind, 1st Platoon began improving positions immediately but had few tools and supplies with which to do the job. The platoon lacked electricity and, at times, was short on water. 1st Platoon's platoon sergeant constantly requested supplies and equipment in an effort to get the position up to snuff.[29]

Soldiers were exhausted from the start, patrolling, building positions, and guarding with no relief. While the battalion commander and command sergeant major visited frequently and implored the platoon leadership to work faster to improve the JSB, members of the platoon felt the two battalion leaders never truly understood how difficult it was for them. They do not appear to have provided additional resources, such as more troops or construction equipment, to speed the task. It is unclear how often the company commander visited. He was known to spend between 20 and 24 hours per day in the company command post at FOB Yusifiyah.[30]

While one platoon occupied the JSB at all times, the other two platoons split time between patrolling Yusifiyah and the surrounding communities and securing the FOB, improving its defenses, and running convoys and a quick reaction unit as needed.[31] Company B shared the FOB with some indigenous forces with whom they ostensibly partnered. According to author Jim Frederick, the unit, 4th Battalion, 4th Brigade, 6th Iraqi Army Division (4/4/6 IA) was widely considered the worst Iraqi unit in the area, though it is unclear how to quantify that.[32] 1/502's headquarters, like the previous battalions, was at Mahmudiyah about 10 kilometers of partially-governed road to the east.

It did not take long for the enemy to engage Company B (or Bravo Company). From the word go, the Alamo and JSB absorbed enemy attacks. On 25 October, 3rd Platoon was on patrol—its third patrol of the day—when they struck an IED. The platoon leader dismounted his platoon to search the site and look for a possible suspect. He found the wires leading to the blast hole and began investigating when a second IED went off. The bomb blinded him and burned his face. While surgery would bring

1. A Land on Fire

his sight back, his war was over less than a month after it began. In a grim way, he would be a trendsetter for Bravo Company's platoon leaders.[33]

Around the time that 3rd Platoon's platoon leader lost his sight, a different IED attack destroyed one of his platoon's HMMWVs. Route Sportster, which connected the JSB and Yusifiyah earned the moniker "the Gauntlet." The route was pock marked with blast craters requiring a deal of maneuvering when driving the road and a degree of luck to make it down the route unscathed. Attacks on the route were a daily occurrence and it seemed to the men on the ground that the bombs only got bigger.

It was time to take action. The company could not ignore the line of communication between its two bases. On 30 October, soldiers from 2nd Platoon occupied a position at the intersection of Routes Sportster and Peggy (which branched east off of Sportster south of Yusifiyah). This position became permanent under the designation Traffic Control Point (TCP) 1. Realizing the strength of a more permanent presence and continuous oversight, the company followed this up with an operation to gain control of the entire route. Ultimately, the company established a total of four TCPs on Sporster.[34]

These positions would generally begin as a HMMWV parked at a location and manned by a few soldiers and then grow into built up positions with defensive control measures and protective obstacles. Later, the battalion would add two more. These positions were labeled TCPs 1 through 6 with numbers reflecting chronological rather than cardinal order. The battalion commander's hope had been to turn these positions over to the Iraqi Army, but they refused. He remained hopeful they would change their minds as the security situation improved and their training increased. Until that happened, the positions would suck a platoon's worth of combat power from Bravo Company and significantly restrict the options available to its commander. Minimally manned and extremely spartan—the company commander described TCP 3 as "a bunch of cinder blocks piled together in an organized manner"—these positions also drained morale.[35]

The first month of the tour had been tough, but thus far the company had not lost any soldiers. November would not be so forgiving. On the second day of the month, two soldiers from the company, Private First Class Tyler MacKenzie and Specialist Joshua Munger, along with another soldier, Specialist Benjamin Smith, were the first of many Strike solders to die in the Triangle. The soldiers, detailed to the battalion commander's personal security detachment, were transiting through the area of operations after a visit to the JSB when an IED obliterated one of the convoy's HMMWVs. Munger and Smith were dead instantly but soldiers responding to the burning wreckage could not find MacKenzie. His body had been blown into a canal where soldiers later found it.[36]

Two days later, a convoy of Company C soldiers was returning from FOB Mahmudiyah where they attended the memorial ceremony for MacKenzie, Munger, and Smith. A vehicle from a U.S. route clearance team, mistaking the Company C convoy for enemy vehicles, opened fire on the convoy killing Staff Sergeant Jason Fegler. Thus, it was Fegler's memorial that soldiers from Bravo Company were returning from when they were traveling down Route Fat Boys, which connected Yusifiyah and Mahmudiyah, on Veterans Day. An IED strike on the convoy exploded on the first sergeant's vehicle setting it ablaze. When the smoke cleared and the fire had been extinguished, all soldiers were alive. However, the first sergeant was suffering from compartment syndrome is his leg requiring seven surgeries to get him to walk (mostly) normal again. Like 3rd Platoon's lieutenant, his war was over shortly after it began.[37]

On Thanksgiving Day, 23 November, a Military Police (MP) platoon from the 170th MP Company of the U.S. 3rd Infantry Division came into the sector to investigate unmarked graves. While driving along Route Caveman which paralleled the Caveman Canal running southeast to northwest from near the Alamo to the Yusufiyah Thermal Power Plant, the platoon hit an IED. Soldiers responding from the JSB could locate the vehicle by the plume of black smoke rising over the reeds. When the responders arrived, they found that the vehicle was on fire and had been blown across the canal. The driver, the convoy commander, and an Iraqi colonel died in the attack with the convoy commander suffering particularly gruesome wounds. The interpreter survived with a broken back and the gunner lived but lost both legs. An Explosive Ordnance Disposal (EOD) unit responding to the scene estimated the weight of the explosives in the bomb to be 2000 pounds.[38] Likely the explosives had come from the Al QaQaa Weapons Facility or another nearby location. The enemy was well resourced and well prepared.

The insurgents displayed an impressive diversity in attacks. A few weeks following the Thanksgiving Day deep buried IED, they employed an insider attack to kill two NCOs at TCP 2. An informant the unit had been using walked into the checkpoint and was greeted warmly when he pulled a pistol from under his clothes and shot Staff Sergeant Travis Nelson in the skull and Sergeant Kenny Casica in the neck. Both NCOs, members of 1st Platoon, would die shortly after being evacuated to FOB Yusifiyah.[39]

Nine days later, the company would lose its third key leader and second platoon leader. On 19 December, 2nd Platoon was traveling east on Route Fat Boy en route to the battalion FOB to retrieve members of their platoon who did not have enough vehicles to convoy back to Yusifiyah. Along the way, the platoon leader's vehicle hit an IED and flipped into a canal running along the road. The driver was severely wounded suffering a lost arm and leg while the gunner was also injured. The platoon leader remained in charge until a quick reaction force arrived, but his arm was broken and you can't lead an infantry platoon with your arm in a cast. By the end of the night, he was on his way home leaving just one platoon leader left in the company and that officer didn't have long to go.[40]

Last of the three was Second Lieutenant Benjamin Britt of first platoon. Three days after the evacuation of 2nd Platoon's platoon leader, on 22 December, Britt was leading his platoon with an Iron Claw route clearance team on a mission to clear Route Caveman. During the patrol, the soldiers came under RPG and mortar fire which disabled one of the route clearance vehicles. After this, the Iron Claw team left. There was a suspected tube that may have remotely fired the RPG (which may have actually been rockets) and the company commander from the company command post ordered Britt to seize the tube. Despite reservation, Britt followed the order.

Britt took a handful of soldiers to investigate. While he and Specialist William Lopez-Feliciano, who had been in Iraq only three weeks, were walking behind two others an IED of several hundred pounds exploded underneath them. Both were killed instantly. The platoon had now lost it platoon leader, a squad leader, and team leader as well as a soldier while also having a soldier return to the States with burns from a non-combat related explosion. The company commander assessed the unit as combat ineffective and informed the battalion commander, who subsequently gave the platoon two days off.[41] Thus closed the books on the three platoon leaders who had arrived in October, likely all hopeful of experiencing combat. Britt was the last to go and the one who went in the worst way. He would be buried in a coffin the Army had provided with his name misspelled.[42] Gone too was the company first sergeant. The company had suffered several critical losses of leaders with three quarters of the tour still staring them in the face.

While much would go on over the next month, it was not until the 1st of February that the next major event occurred. 3rd Platoon's platoon sergeant led a force comprised of members of his platoon along with a fire team from 1st Platoon as well as 1st Platoon's new platoon leader. The patrol moved toward Rushdi Mullah to investigate grids from a captured Global Positioning System (GPS) device. The element came under fire from several places, but the majority from a single house. In order to maneuver on the building, some soldiers breached a hedgerow of sorts that surrounded the building and came into contact with two insurgents wearing suicide vests and a third loading mortar ammunition onto the bed of a Kia Bongo truck. The soldiers killed the two would-be suicide bombers, but had trouble moving on the final insurgent. In the exchange two soldiers were wounded and later evacuated by helicopter.

The two leaders knew there was an insurgent loose in the house but also knew it was risky to enter into a building they had never been inside before. They attempted to walk an AH-64 Apache helicopter onto the target and have it destroy the house. However, the pilot lacked authorization to discharge his Hellfire missile and could only employ his 30-mm cannon. The cannon could not reduce the house to rubble, so the platoon sergeant ordered a three-man team to clear the structure. Entering the unfamiliar building, the team found a confusing layout with four entryways covered by sheets. The insurgent opened fire from one of the entryways, wounding two of the soldiers. The platoon sergeant quickly got another helicopter to evacuate the soldiers, but en route Specialist Anthony Owens died. Soon, another Apache came on station with clearance to fire its missile and thus destroyed the house. The insurgent was dead but the ordeal was far from over.

The leaders decided to take over another house and remain overnight. A relief patrol arrived after dark with needed ammunition, water, and food. The next day, EOD arrived with soldiers from the battalion Headquarters and Headquarters Company (HHC) led by their company commander. EOD was traveling with the HHC patrol and destroyed the suicide vests. The group then came under mortar fire from the direction of Rushdi Mullah as it watched women and children conduct an orderly evacuation of the town. They also saw insurgents in Bongo trucks arrive and set up a perimeter in the village.

Exhausted and without a full complement of ammunition and munitions, the assembled leaders requested relief from the mission. While they may have been salivating at a chance to finally get into a standup fight with these insurgents who fought like ghosts, their cooler heads told them they were in no condition for a sustained fight. After some delay due to a desire from the brigade and division headquarters to stay on site, the battalion commander finally decided to authorize the withdrawal of the forces.[43] It must have been frustrating to quit the battlefield with the enemy in sight, but good leaders know when their units have culminated.

While the Bravo soldiers did not stay to engage the enemy that day, the battalion decided to take a more aggressive stance against Rushdi Mullah, which appeared to be a haven for insurgent activity. Soldiers from the battalion began air assaulting—conducting operations initiated via helicopter insertion—at infrequent intervals and occupying the town for various periods of time in an effort to throw the insurgents off balance.[44]

In the years since the invasion, the Triangle of Death had become known as a place where everything burned. From the time U.S. forces began to permanently patrol the area, insurgents had turned several vehicles into smoldering rubble. However, on 5 February 2006, something caught on fire that was not a vehicle and the cause was not insurgent activity. This time it was the FOB itself. Faulty wiring shorted an already overloaded outlet and set fire to the potato barn that served at once as living quarters, a home for the attached Military Transition Team (MiTT), and Bravo Company's command post. No one was injured, but many soldiers lost personal possessions. Soon the smoke provided an ample target for the enemy, who began lobbing mortars. Shortly thereafter, the ammunition housing area caught fire sending a spew of expended rounds into the air, firing anti-tank rockets off, and setting off minor explosions. One soldier indicated the scene resembled a fireworks display. In the Triangle, everything was hard.

Though potentially demoralizing, the fire almost seemed trivial. According to reporter Sue Diaz, who took the quotes from a 101st Airborne Division (Air Assault) newsletter, Bravo Company's commander stated, "The fire could have been devastating for someone else, but because we've been through so much, we were like 'OK, I guess we'll rebuild and move on.'" Another officer offered, "It was almost comical. We were like, 'Gee, I wonder what I'm going to write in my journal today—oh, wait, my journal burned up.'"[45] With all they'd been through, the men of Bravo would survive this too.

Less than a month after the fire, on 2 March, 2nd Brigade launched an assault into the western hinterlands. Named *Operation Glory Light*, the mission involved the 3rd Battalion, 1st Brigade, 6th Iraqi Army Division and 1/502 PIR arriving via helicopter at the Yusifiyah Thermal Power Plant and clearing the complex. Soldiers from another Iraqi Army Division and more soldiers from the 6th Iraqi Army Division cleared routes to the objective on land. The mission led to seven detentions, a couple caches being discovered, and about a dozen IEDs found and cleared. One commander claimed it to have dealt a significant blow to the insurgents, but it is hard to believe that a formidable enemy losing two caches and seven insurgents would be setback considerably. This is especially true in the light of the fact that the brigade did not leave anyone behind to

1. A Land on Fire

occupy the area. In essence, the operation reflected a continued raider mentality west of Route Sportster. Units would clear but never hold and certainly never build. Bravo Company's role in the operation was to establish a blocking position in Rushdi Mullah, which 2nd Platoon accomplished along with the company headquarters. During the mission, company Radio Telephone Operator (RTO) Specialist Ethan Biggers was on the roof of an occupied building when a shot hit a wall and ricocheted into his skull above the eye. Though Biggers survived the wound, he was in a coma, a state he would remain in for nearly a year before his family decided to remove him from life support.[46]

As the deployment went on, members of 1st Platoon, the unit hit hardest by casualties, began getting more violent than normal with the locals. They had always shown a tendency to "rough up" suspects in the middle of raids, but now seemed to get more forceful with less provocation. Additionally, their drug and alcohol use increased. Though drugs are forbidden in the Army and alcohol is banned in combat operations by General Order Number 1, the soldiers were able to get both with the help of opportunistic Iraqi soldiers. For some of the soldiers, abusing alcohol and drugs increased their deep contempt for Iraqis and enhanced their ingrained personal issues.

One soldier, Private First Class Steven Green, had always had a dark side and began talking about killing Iraqis. His red flags had been ignored or missed for some time. Many of the members of the platoon knew him to be a racist with extreme disdain for Iraqis and he had abused drugs and alcohol in his youth. Some of the other members of the platoon had reputations for being punks. They were Specialists Paul Cortez and James Barker. The three began to talk about raping and killing Iraqis. On 12 March, their bravado turned to action when they decided to leave Traffic Control Point 2 and walk, in broad daylight, to a house where they intended to commit their act. They would bring along Private First Class Jesse Spielman, who was not one of the conspirators, but who went along willingly nonetheless.

Cortez was the highest ranking of any of the soldiers at the TCP—there were no officers or NCOs. He and Barker dressed in their black silk weight cold weather undergarments while Spielman and Green wore stripped down uniforms. Cortez left two privates first class at the checkpoint all alone. The four then walked to the nearby dwelling they had chosen where they rounded up the family. Spielman pulled security. Green took control of the father, mother and youngest daughter, attempting to kill them with the father's AK-47. Barker and Cortez took 14-year-old Abeer Qassim Al Janabi into another room and raped her.

Meanwhile, Green struggled with the family and the AK-47 jammed. He ended up having to use his shotgun to kill the father. Spielman helped clean up shotgun shells. After dispatching the rest of the family, Green entered the room where Cortez and Barker were holding Abeer and he raped her. (Spielman fondled Abeer's breasts but never penetrated her.) They then set Abeer on fire. Before leaving, Green agreed to take responsibility if it got back to them. Amped up, the four returned to base.

Later that day, family members discovered the bodies and contacted the Americans for help. Sergeant Tony Yribe from the same platoon but at a different TCP responded and grabbed Spielman and Cortez en route to the house. He needed them to help him pull security, investigate, and catalog evidence. Spielman acted fine but Cortez could barely function at the crime scene. Yribe found a shotgun shell that was clearly American, but put it out of his mind. However, later in the day Green came straight out and confessed to Yribe without any provoking; at the time, no one suspected U.S. soldiers to be involved. Initially, Yribe didn't believe Green, but Green—who was not part of Yribe's investigative detail—could describe the scene in a way only someone having been there could. Convinced, Yribe decided not to report Green but to threaten him, saying if Green didn't get himself out of the Army, Yribe would. Green took Yribe's advice, convinced a psychologist he was unstable and unfit for combat (which he was), and went home to be out-processed due to mental health. The truth remained hidden for some time. While some Iraqis believed Americans had something to do with the crime, others blamed a host of groups so there was no U.S.–led investigation into the atrocity for several months.[47] But 1st Platoon had clearly hit rock bottom.

There would be no relief for the weary (or morally bankrupt). By April, special operations forces had turned their attention to Yusifiyah and its environs searching for Al Qaeda in Iraq's leader Zarqawi. Task Force 6–26, the Special Operations Task Force commanded by Major General Stanley McCrystal believed Yusifiyah was the location of some important meetings. While Zarqawi would ultimately be killed north of Baghdad, evidence suggests that one raid into the Yusifiyah area missed him by half a mile. In fact, on the day Task Force 6–26 killed Zarqawi, 7 June 2006, McCrystal guessed that the mark drones were following would lead them to the town.[48]

Clearly, he spent time in the Triangle. To protect their leader and maintain their smuggling route, Al Qaeda in Iraq moved their Aeisha Brigade into the area. The brigade specialized in antiaircraft operations. On 1 April 2006, the brigade shot down its first helicopter, an Apache, one mile northwest of Rushdi Mullah. The wreckage lay in a field, smoldering. Both pilots died but U.S. forces recovered their bodies. In a foreshadowing of future tactics, the enemy used IEDs to slow the rescue parties.

A week later, on 8 April, special operations forces conducted an early afternoon raid, entering their objective at 1356, in Yusifiyah. A hail of gunfire greeted them as three would-be suicide bombers rushed them. The commandos killed two and the third detonated early, killing only himself. Six insurgents died and five were detained along with weapons and videos. The team conducted another raid just up the road immediately following the first detaining another dozen. But a week later, on 14 April, another helicopter, this time a special operations forces AH-1 Little Bird, went down in a raid.[49]

By mid–April the battalion could not ignore the festering problem of Rushdi Mullah any longer. Like Route Sporster in late October, they knew the only way to have a chance at taming a place like Rushdi Mullah was to hold it. They established a patrol base in the town and began rotating units in with Companies A (Alpha) and C (Charlie) in the mix with Bravo. Though the area was highly kinetic, the soldiers seemed to enjoy firefights to IEDs. It was the first long term presence in the town by troops, and it was needed. By May the coalition was focusing intelligence and special operations on Yusifiyah as the staging area for suicide attacks in Baghdad; it was also establishing electronic listening bases in the area in search of Zarqawi.[50]

On 15 May, the trend of helicopters falling out of the sky continued. Insurgents shot down a special operations forces helicopter near Yusifiyah in the middle of an engagement. The battle began when troops and aircraft maneuvered on a suspected safe house. The aircraft opened fire on the building and a vehicle outside leading to a series of explosions. The attack resulted in the death of two insurgents and the detention of four others. During the engagement, at least two women were wounded and U.S. forces loaded them onto a helicopter to be evacuated for medical treatment. As the bird was taking off, insurgents who were located in another complex and likely from the Aeisha Brigade, engaged the helicopter and others with machine gun fire and either rockets or RPGs. Fighter jets and other helicopters fired on the enemy positions leading to twenty insurgents killed. Three insurgents tried to break though the ground cordon in a truck, but troops engaged them and prevented their escape. One of the insurgents set off a suicide vest but he only killed himself. A local resident claimed that several civilians were killed and many fled, but the U.S. military denied any civilians died. One U.S. helicopter crashed during the engagement killing both pilots. En route to the helicopter, a rescue patrol encountered 19 IEDs. Insurgents claimed to have shot down four helicopters in the Yusifiyah area, though it is unclear if they meant that day or in the aggregate.[51]

Two days later, some news outlets published a report detailing ruminations of an Al Qaeda operative in the Yusifiyah area who lamented the poor morale of insurgents. The documents, seized in a 16 April raid and written by an unnamed insurgent, detail issues within the organization. Among the insurgent's complaints were that Al Qaeda was "disorganized and lack[ed] a comprehensive strategy," they were "not considered more than a daily annoyance" to the Iraqi government, and their equipment and numbers were inferior to the coalition forces, who were resilient.[52] The report is interesting, if ultimately inconsequential. If anything, it shows that privates in Al Qaeda can be just as frustrated as privates in the U.S. Army.

Even if the report were accurate, the U.S. side was having trouble of its own. While Jim Frederick details the morale problems of B/1/502 PIR, particularly 1st Platoon, the real issue was the need to be so many places at once. Establishing TCPs and patrol bases enabled the battalion as a whole to radiate power and control more terrain, but these positions were manpower intensive. Rarely could Bravo Company provide adequate leadership across the greater Yusifiyah area and the position in Rushdi Mullah extended that stress to the battalion.

So, in June, the battalion determined that it could no longer dedicate the manpower to the Rushdi Mullah position without suffering elsewhere. 2nd Platoon, Bravo Company, drew the task of dismantling it. But even pulling out of an area proved extremely dangerous. Units are especially vulnerable when they are establishing or breaking down positions. As 2nd Platoon was shutting down the base, the soldiers came under fire. Before long a dump truck was barreling toward the gate. A soldier on guard in a bunker began firing on the vehicle with an M240B machine gun. He did not stop the vehicle, but may have altered its path enough to save some troops. Rigged as a suicide-initiated VBIED, the dump truck exploded at the compound wall, collapsing the bunker around the responding soldier and throwing soldiers across rooms and into the air. Though fifteen U.S. soldiers, eight Iraqis, and an interpreter were injured, no soldiers were severely wounded or killed.[53]

That fortune would be short lived. In late May, Iraq's deputy prime minister for security had gone on a political talk show and spoke of security concerns in his country. He noted Yusifiyah as a high-tension area where many kidnappings occurred.[54] It is significant and prescient that the deputy prime minister would single out Yusifiyah. The area continued to be the Wild West. To that point, none of the kidnappings involved U.S. soldiers. That would change.

On 6 June, three soldiers, Specialist David Babineau and Privates First Class Thomas Tucker and Kristian Menchaca, were pulling guard at the Alamo. Babineau was the highest ranking and like the rape and murders, there was no NCO present. At 1949, a group of Iraqi insurgents converged on the Alamo. Babineau was likely out of the vehicle and was not wearing his body armor. He was shot in the back and killed. The other two, who were not wearing their helmets, were drug away, likely bleeding. None of the three fired a shot at the insurgents indicating complete surprise or a lack of preparedness. A later investigation determined the soldiers had been alone for 36 hours without supervision. The investigation also concluded it was likely that Iraqi Army soldiers nearby saw and heard the attack but chose not to respond.[55]

A vehicle responded from TCP 4 and another element rushed from the JSB. However, the unit coming from the JSB encountered a familiar tactic in the form of two oilcans serving as decoy IEDs. This forced them to dismount, buying time for the insurgents to search the vehicle and haul off their two captives. Within the hour, forces from outside the company began converging on the Alamo to search for the soldiers.[56]

After an intensive and exhaustive search, evidence finally led forces to that great bastion of insurgent activity, the lawless and ungoverned power plant. On 19 June, forces discovered the bodies of Tucker and Menchaca, mutilated and booby trapped. Tucker's head had been decapitated. The Mujahadeen Shura Council, an ostensible umbrella group for Islamic terrorists which Al Qaeda in Iraq created to appeal to a wider range, took credit claiming that their leader conducted the killings himself. Later, the council would claim the attack was motivated by the murders and rape on 12 March, but this is unlikely. At the time of the kidnappings, it was not known that Americans had killed the family, and no one knew a rape had occurred.

However, soon thereafter news broke that an investigation into the murders was in progress. The kidnappings led Yribe to mention to Private Justin Watt what Green had told him. Watt dutifully informed Sergeant John Diem who decided it had to be reported so he told the chain of command. An investigation ensued and 1st Platoon was pulled from duties and tasked with security at FOB Mahmudiyah for the rest of the deployment. Ultimately, Green would be arrested and tried in civilian court after leaving the Army. Cortez, Barker, and Spielman were also tried for the rape and murder via the military's judicial process. All were convicted with Green receiving life in prison, Barker 90 years, Cortez 100, and Spielman 90. Private First Class Bryce Howard, who was left on the TCP the day of rape and failed to report the crime, plead guilty to

1. A Land on Fire

obstruction of justice and being an accessory after the fact. He received 27 months. Yribe was charged with several crimes in relation to the cover up, but in exchange for his testimony charges were dropped and he was discharged from the Army under the category "other than honorable." Green attempted to kill himself in 2014. Though he was not successful, complications from the attempt ultimately led to his death in February of that year. Spielman, Cortez, and Barker are all incarcerated at the United States Disciplinary Barracks at Fort Leavenworth, Kansas, as of this writing.

Shortly after the discovery of Menchaca's and Tucker's bodies, reporters Akeel Hussein and Colin Freedman, writing for *The Sunday Telegraph*, reported that a Mahmudiyah based Sheikh named Saba Shukr (possibly actually an imam) told them, "[T]he mujahedeen brought revenge when they kidnapped two American soldiers in Yusifiyah. They are still waiting to kidnap and kill another eight soldiers, as the price for the death of the girl should be the death of 10 Americans. I am sure about this. The mujahedeen promised us revenge."[57] Shukr's statement would prove to be an eerily prescient one bordering on fateful. Only, it would be the fate of the next unit, not the current one.

Yusifiyah continued to vex with its pattern of setbacks and achievements. The same week that soldiers discovered the grim remains of Menchaca and Tucker, the Army reported it had killed Mansur Salayman Mansur Khalif al Mashdani near Yusifiyah proper. Al Mashdani was believed to be the religious emir for Al Qaeda in Iraq. He died from a U.S. air strike.[58]

This pattern would continue in the aftermath of the kidnapping. With 1st Platoon removed from combat duties, it became unsustainable to keep Bravo Company in charge of all of Yusifiyah. Therefore, Charlie Company transitioned a large portion of its area in Lutifiyah to the Iraqi Army and took control of the JSB. The 1/502 PIR did not give up on the area and continued to send forces on patrols and raids. On 5 August 2006, Alpha Company's Private First Class Brian Kubik was killed in a firefight in Rushdi Mullah. Then on 30 August, the insurgents conducted a coordinated attack against fourteen Iraqi Army checkpoints in the area. However well planned the attack was, its execution was rather inept. Not a single soldier was even wounded.[59]

By the end of August, soldiers from the beleaguered battalion would begin to see their replacement from the 10th Mountain Division. The Strike soldiers, like their counterparts in the Marines and National Guard, had paid a high price for the terrain they held. Each unit had extended their lines a little further, but, in the end, much of the Yusifiyah countryside remained an uncontrolled hinterland where insurgents were free to roam. Qarghuli Village remained relatively untouched and the battalion controlled nothing west of Route Sporster. The soldiers knew what needed to be done; they needed to occupy the whole of Yusifiyah. But they were all out of Schlitz in August 2006. They did not have the manpower to go the distance.[60] The final step of gaining control of the land where everything burns would be left to a unit known as the Polar Bears. They, like their forbearers, would pay a heavy price for the ground they would tread.

* * *

In the late winter of 2003, the greater Yusifiyah area was a sleepy farm community that also happened to be home to part of Iraq's military-industrial complex. It was so strategically inconsequential to the coalition that no histories of the invasion mention the area by name. While an Army brigade came through the area, it was not a focus of the post war occupation until nearly a year and a half later. By that time, the various insurgent and jihadist groups vying for power had realized its geographic importance and filled the security vacuum and set the idyllic land on fire.

By mid-summer 2006, the U.S. military had been fighting the raging fire that was Yusifiyah and its environs, paying a heavy price for the ground it gained and held. In 22 months, four different units: a Marine reserve company, an Army tank formation, a National Guard armor company, and an Army air assault infantry company, tried to contain and beat back the blaze. Whether one stood close enough to feel the heat on their face or watch the flames from afar, it seemed the fire was still out of control. But those units had set the stage for a new unit to arrive and have hope of extinguishing the flames.

It was the marines of F/2/24 that seized the foothold in October 2004. The marines fought their way into town and began probing into the hinterlands. They enacted a community policing approach in the town and began conducting operations against the extremist elements out west. They successfully secured the election, though the large national boycott that Sunni's enacted made the results somewhat illegitimate.

In *States and Power in Africa*, Jeffrey Herbst describes the means European colonial powers used in Africa to control areas and population they needed in order to extract natural resources. The ability to control a hub and roads enabled these powers to control what they needed. Essentially, European powers controlled within the limits of their cannon. The soldiers of E/1–108 AR moved the FOB from the outskirts of town into a more central position allowing them to radiate power and B/1–502 PIR established control of the line of communications between the JSB and FOB Yusifiyah through a series of check points known as Traffic Control Points. Like the African states Herbst describes, this left a lawless hinterland beyond the hubs and spokes. However, unlike the European powers, the Americans didn't have the luxury of ignoring what was beyond their control.

So, while the inferno burned bright and hot, the previous 22 months had not been for naught. Like the smoke jumpers that descend into the forest who are not there to extinguish the fire but to contain it, F/2/24, 2–70 AR, E/1–108 AR, and B/1–502 PIR had drawn a line in the sand. This didn't make the task easy for the next unit, but it established the conditions necessary to enact a thorough, methodical approach. The unethical conduct and indiscipline of a handful of soldiers in B/1–502 PIR had set the American efforts in the area back. However, it had not destroyed the hard work of all the others.

The road ahead for the Polar Bears would still be a long one and, in August 2006, time did not appear on their side. The will of the American people was waning and it seemed that the goal was to pull back not push forward. Further, the area needed a dedicated counterinsurgency approach focused on securing the populace, increasing the capacity of national security forces, and enabling local governance, and there was no manual for how to do any of it.

2

The Polar Bears Go Marching In

A gentleman said: "To rely on rustics and not prepare is the greatest of crimes; to be prepared beforehand for any contingency is the greatest of virtues."—Ho Yen-hsi

Iraq was an inferno. Americans had lost their will. Troops commuted to work and then retreated to large bases at night, never truly connecting with the populace. The war was complex, far more so than previous American conflicts save maybe Vietnam. No one knew counterinsurgency; hell, few even knew the military was fighting an insurgency. Yes, Iraq in August 2006 was an unmitigated disaster. Or so the popular narrative goes.

At the macro-level, these claims are hard to dispute. Just the previous month, Lieutenant General Peter Chiarelli, the commander of Multi-National Corps-Iraq (MNC-I), the tactical headquarters for the four-star command, had requested the extension of the 172nd Stryker Brigade Combat Team for four months in anticipation of coming violence. The unit moved from the border into Baghdad. Though it doesn't seem like much, the unit had already sent 300 soldiers home and was in the process of sending the rest behind them. The last-minute extension, which led to Secretary of Defense Donald Rumsfeld visiting with families, certainly fed the narrative.[1]

And Iraq was certainly still quite deadly. In June, 63 servicemembers died, followed by 46 in July and 66 in August. Interestingly, in retrospect these numbers seem tame. Over the next 14 months, no month would pass without at least 70 U.S. servicemember deaths with five of those months seeing more than 100 troops die.[2] If Iraq was bad in August, the Fall and Winter of 2006–2007 would be much worse. Of course, U.S. casualties is only one metric of determining the lack of security of an area and not necessarily the best. But it is the most readily accessible.

This violence and lack of security combined with the continued cost in blood and treasure with no apparent gain seemed to be draining the will of the American people. Signs pointed to a poor midterm election for the Republican party and President George W. Bush. In fact, the Republicans would go on to lose 30 seats in the House of Representatives and six Senate seats along with a number of governorships. It was the first time since 1994 that the Democrats gained control of both houses of Congress. While the war was not the only reason, it was a major factor. So much so that in September, Senate Majority leader Mitch McConnell went to the Oval Office to ask the president to bring an unspecified amount of troops home to stave off the Democratic challenge.[3] Bush refused to do so as he was already considering a troop surge and the Senate would tie 49–49 with two Independents caucusing with the Democrats, effectively providing them a majority. Bush would change Secretaries of Defense in the aftermath.

Ultimately, *The Washington Post* senior Pentagon correspondent Thomas Ricks would conclude of the situation in the summer of 2006,

> while there is a small chance that the Bush administration's inflexible optimism will be rewarded, that the political process will undercut the insurgency, and that democracy will take hold in Iraq, there is a far greater chance of other, more troublesome outcomes: that Iraq will fall into civil war, or spark regional war, or eventually become home to an anti–American regime, or break up altogether. In any of these forms it would offer a new haven for terrorists.[4]

While Ricks was just one observer, few of the journalists covering Iraq at this time would challenge the spirit of his remarks. They may disagree on the scale of the hopelessness, but most agreed that Iraq was in a bad spot.

Below the surface, things were murkier. It does appear that many units lived on large FOBs. In a 2004 letter to Al Qaeda leadership, Zarqawi blasted Americans for avoiding real fighting by holing up on large bases. He called them "the most cowardly of God's creatures."[5] General George Casey, the U.S. Army general who commanded Multi-National Forces-Iraq (MNF-I), Chiarelli's higher headquarters, had recently ordered the closure of small U.S. bases and the consolidation onto larger FOBs. His intent was to reduce the ability of Iraqi troops and policemen to rely on coalition forces and thus not grow. Further, Casey, along with his boss at U.S. Central Command (CENTCOM) Army General John Abizaid and Rumsfeld, was seeking to reduce the U.S. footprint in Iraq and send some units home.[6] Casey was not insensitive or unaware of the violence in Iraq, especially in and around Baghdad, but he and his staff believed that the violence was no longer due to an anti-government insurgency but a sectarian rift and thus it was time to transition. As Casey notes in his memoir, most of the violence was contained in four provinces, however, he omits those were the four most populous provinces.[7]

But in August 2006 none of the 1/502 PIR bases had been closed in favor of consolidation (the base in Rushdi Mullah had closed due to manpower constraints). Other units were still in the business of small bases near the populace as well. In June 2006, Colonel Sean McFarland and his Army 1st Brigade Combat Team, 1st Armored Division had isolated and cleared the city of Ramadi in Anbar province and begun setting up small bases in the city. McFarland's approach would continue beyond August and into the next year. McFarland's method resembled that of Colonel H.R. McMaster in Tel Afar the previous year. In fact, McMaster and McFarland both demonstrated a keen knack for the intricacies of counterinsurgency and how to blend offensive, defensive, and stability operations to accomplish the mission. There has been no formal study on counterinsurgency prior to the arrival of General David Petraeus that takes into account all units (I wrote a monograph looking at McMaster, McFarland, and three other officers).[8] However, it is clear that the U.S. military was aware of the threat of the insurgency and taking steps to mitigate it.

Casey, generally maligned in the journalist-written histories of Operation *Iraqi Freedom*, was the man at the center of much of this. In late 2004 he created a Counterinsurgency Academy in Taji, Iraq, and ordered all company, battalion, and brigade commanders to attend to increase their knowledge of counterinsurgency. He also created the Phoenix Academy to train advisors. Further, he directed a study of 20th century counterinsurgencies which Dr. Kalev Sepp undertook and published in 2005.[9]

Petraeus would gain fame for his oversight of the creation of U.S. Army Field Manual (FM) 3-24, *Counterinsurgency*, which was concurrently published as Marine Corps Warfighting Publication 3-33.5. The manual, issued two months prior to Petraeus' relief of Casey as commander of MNF-I, was released with great fanfare, but while Petraeus' team labored away in August 2006, the Army was not without any doctrine. On 1 October 2004, the Combined Arms Center at Fort Leavenworth (the same organization Petraeus commanded while overseeing FM 3-24) issued FM (Interim) 3-07.22, *Counterinsurgency Operations*.[10] It is fair to wonder, however, how widely distributed this manual was.

The most accurate picture of Iraq and counterinsurgency in the mid-summer of 2006 may well be this: just about everyone knew it was an insurgency but there were divergent views on the nature and therefore the best approach to it and that there was not a singular operational approach nested across all units. Counterinsurgency was not non-existent; but its implementation was anarchic. Rather than radiating from the central authority and implemented at the point of contact with respect to the unique situation of each hamlet and unit, it was implemented according to the faith, knowledge, dedication, and interpretation of the commander on the ground. In Yusifiyah, offense and defense ruled the day and it is unclear that 1–502 PIR made earnest attempts to implement a counterinsurgency approach at all. It is possible they did, but the evidence remains ambiguous. It was into this environment that the Polar Bears would go marching in.

* * *

Prior to the Global War on Terrorism, the 4th Battalion, 31st Infantry had served in only one war. That war was the one in Vietnam that remains so vexing more than five decades from its ending. In the past decade and a half, it has become vogue to label Vietnam a counterinsurgency. While true to some degree, this reduces the complexity of the threat environment significantly. Regardless, 4–31 IN's only war had been, at least in part, one against an insurgent. Of course, none of those serving in the unit in mid-summer 2006 had served a day in Vietnam, so the Polar Bears' experience in counterinsurgency was limited to what members of the unit had learned in Iraq on previous tours.

The unit's current standing is a relatively recent one. It did not exist on the Army's rolls until two years after Operation *Restore Hope* in Somalia. Still, the Polar Bears that marched into Yusifiyah in September 2006 drew their lineage from the storied 31st Infantry Regiment. Like the contemporary unit, the regiment had faced its share of trials and tribulations. Brought into being in August 1916 in the Philippines, the unit was notable for not having served in the United States until after the Korean War. Left in the Pacific during the Great War, the regiment deployed to the Russian port city of Vladivostok in response to the Russian Civil War. There they guarded Allied war stocks and spread out to guard the Trans-Siberian Railway and for this they gained the nickname "Polar Bears." In a conflict whose American involvement few have heard about, the regiment earned 16 Distinguished Service Crosses, the nation's second highest award for valor, and lost 32 soldiers. In 1920, the regiment returned to the Philippines where it would remain until 1932 when it deployed to Shanghai to guard the international settlement.

During the Second World War, the regiment was back at its home garrison in the Philippines. When the Japanese invaded, the regiment fought at Bataan to cover the withdrawal of forces. The soldiers held out for nearly four months but they lacked medical provisions, adequate food, and supplies, their weapons were obsolete for the fight they were in, and their ammunition was poor. Men were starving and dying of disease. Utterly exhausted, the regiment's superior, Major General Edward King, capitulated. Most of the survivors would take part in the infamous Bataan Death March moving 68 miles under a brutal sun and even more brutal occupier. They went into internment on Luzon for three and a half years enduring the oppressive custody of the Imperial Japanese, suffering nearly 800 dead of a total of 1600. Twenty-nine of the regiment's members earned Distinguished Service Crosses. Prior to the Japanese occupation, officers buried the regimental colors (along with a punch bowl and cups purchased during the Shanghai mission). Following their rescue, the officers retrieved the colors and punch ware.

In 1946, the 31st Infantry served in Korea under the 7th Infantry Division. Moving to Japan in 1948, the regiment returned in 1950 as part of the Inchon landings under General Douglas MacArthur. They fought alongside marines at the famous Chosin Reservoir where they were effectively decimated. Although the Americans lost the battle, they made it a pyrrhic victory for the Chinese forces they fought against. The Army reconstituted the regiment and sent it back into the fray where it fought it such battles as Pork Chop Hill, Old Baldy, Triangle Hill, and OP Dale. Five members of the regiment earned the Medal of Honor for their actions in the war. (Clint Eastwood's character Gunnery Sergeant Highway in the movie *Heartbreak Ridge* earned his Medal of Honor with the 31st Infantry in Korea.)

Following the end of hostilities, the 31st remained in Korea making it the only regiment to that point that had never served on American soil. However, as the Army looked to reorganize for the possibility of atomic war, it created the 2nd Battle Group, 31st Infantry, and placed it at Fort Rucker, Alabama, in 1958. By 1967, Army reorganization led to six battalions spread across the globe. The 4th Battalion, the only one on active duty today, stood up at Fort Devers, Massachusetts, in 1965.

2. The Polar Bears Go Marching In

From 1966 to 1971, the 4th Battalion, 31st Infantry Regiment (4–31 IN) served in Vietnam. Originally it served in War Zone D as a subunit under the 196th Infantry Brigade, a separate unit unattached to a division. Later in 1967, the unit transferred to the 23rd Infantry Division, better known as the Americal Division (a contraction of American, New Caledonian Division, in reference to it being created for the defense of the latter during World War II). In 1971, the battalion returned from Vietnam as part of the last brigade to leave and the Army deactivated it. Among the multitude of honors the battalion and its soldiers earned in Southeast Asia were two Medals of Honor awarded in separate incidents at Hiep Duc. The 6th Battalion, 31st Infantry, also served in Vietnam under the 9th Infantry Division starting in 1968. Fighting mostly in the Mekong Delta and the Plain of Reeds, the battalion also helped push communist forces out of Saigon after the May attack of the Tet Offensive in 1968. In 1970, the battalion crossed into Cambodia as part of the Seminole Raid. That same year, the battalion returned to the United States and was, similar to 4th Battalion, deactivated.

For nearly 25 years, the Army went without any permutation of the 31st Infantry. That ended in 1995 when the Army reflagged the 3rd Battalion, 14th Infantry, at Fort Drum, New York, as 4–31 IN, in the 10th Mountain Division's 2nd Brigade, the "Commandos." The brigade as whole would become the most deployed in the Army and the Polar Bears went early and often. A month after the 11 September 2001 terrorist attacks, members of the battalion deployed to Uzbekistan and then into Afghanistan and participated in *Operation Anaconda*. From April to September, the battalion conduct *Operation Polar Harpoon*, sweeping through the Shah-i-Koht valley clearing enemy bunkers and cave complexes. The next year, part of the battalion deployed to Djibouti (Company C) while others went to Iraq (Company B) and Afghanistan (Company A and HHC). In 2004, the battalion deployed with the 2nd Brigade Combat Team to Iraq serving in various areas around Baghdad. Upon returning from that deployment in June 2005, the battalion, with a new commander, set its sights on returning to Iraq and taking the fight to the enemy.[11]

The 31st Infantry Regiment in its various permutations had twice been decimated attempting to hold off a larger, better equipped, and better resourced enemy; it had fought in a few obscure places and obscure wars; it had been called on for some of the toughest missions and done so with little fanfare. The blue collar, service first, no frills culture that had characterized the regiment throughout its first 90 years would carry on with the Polar Bears as they prepared for and then pressed into Yusifiyah. There would be no glory, no pomp, heavy casualties, and a tough job to be done. But first, there was the matter of training for the mission at hand.

* * *

When the Polar Bears came home in June 2005, they returned to Fort Drum, a post with a history of evolving and adapting. In 1908, the Army sent Major General Frederick Dent Grant, son of Ulysses S. Grant, to the Pine Plains region of upstate New York where he determined that the area was ripe for military training. Grant, a graduate of West Point, was no stranger to what it took to train a military force (his mission was to train 2,000 Army regulars and 8,000 militiamen). As a child he'd followed his father during Civil War campaigns and as an officer served on the staffs of William Sherman and Phil Sheridan. In 1935, the area held the largest peace time maneuver in Army history, with 36,500 troops participating. World War II brought expansion and three divisions: the 4th and 5th Armored Division and the 45th Infantry Division. It also housed prisoners from the European Theater of Operations.

Following World War II, the post hosted a number of units throughout the years. In 1951, the Army renamed the post Camp Drum, in honor of Lieutenant General Hugh A. Drum. Drum was an interesting choice as he had lost favor with senior Army leaders during the Carolina Maneuvers, a series of Army exercises held in 1941 to test the Army's preparedness for war, when he was captured by the 2nd Armored Division. In 1974, the Army upgraded the post to a fort and in 1984 began standing up the 10th Mountain Division on the post. The Division, which had fought valiantly in Italy during World War II, had been dormant for 27 years. Fort Drum was seemingly an odd place for a unit with "Mountain" in its name as there is barely even a hill on the whole of the post. But the Division only retained the "Mountain" designation due to its history not its mission. The 10th was a light unit unencumbered by a specialized mission (such as airborne) or equipment thus enabling the Army the deploy it rapidly for a variety of missions. Its latest mission, given to the 2nd Brigade Combat Team, would, like its post throughout history, require adaptation to meet the needs of the Nation.

Colonel Michael Kershaw, who had previously commanded 1st Battalion, 75th Ranger Regiment (1–75) in Afghanistan, took command shortly after the brigade's return. He was the commander of the 1–75 during the raid to rescue Private First Class Jessica Lynch, the first successful rescue of an American prisoner of war since Vietnam. It was up to him and his subordinate leaders to tackle the ambiguous problem of bringing security to whatever part of Iraq it would find itself in. The 4–31 IN also received a new commander, Lieutenant Colonel Michael Infanti, who had been the brigade's deputy commander previous to taking command.

Both commanders assessed the situation in Iraq and understood that their units were facing an insurgency. They knew the complexities of the coming deployment required unique training that incorporated standard infantry tasks as well as counterinsurgency instruction. 4–31 IN trained on its normal progression of weapons training and fire and maneuver, but also held weekly professional development sessions for its leaders. These sessions were a mission-oriented opportunity to teach and discuss with various themes such as history, culture, and counterinsurgency. The battalion had a unique reading program wherein a platoon leader/platoon sergeant team would be assigned a book and then present a distillation of the relevant points of the book to the battalion's leaders. Topics ranged from the Middle East, Arab culture, and insurgency and contributed to the education of the unit. Infanti would use these sessions as opportunities to discuss his intended approach and update the leadership on the area of operations, among other things.

Ultimately, the battalion's training plan largely focused on warrior tasks and drills, small unit operations in an urban environment, and standard training progressions for units preparing to deploy balanced by these academic sessions. It is clear that Infanti saw importance in ensuring that his squad leaders and above had an appreciation for the intricacies of the battle they would soon be in. Being bigger and more powerful than the other guy was still the number one priority; the Polar Bears would be tough and seen as tough. But the nuances of warfare focused on the populace rather than terrain or destruction of an enemy force as the end goal remained a close second.

Kershaw, his staff, and subordinate commanders saw the problem they would face as a "classic counterinsurgency." Their goal would be to secure the populace. They wanted to "drive a wedge between al Qaeda and the locals." This would allow them to separate the insurgent "fish" from the population "water" they swam in (a reference to Mao Tse-tung's dictum that insurgents were fish who inhabit the water that is the people[12]). Further, the leaders saw the development of the Iraqi Army as a decisive measure in their operations. Thus, Kershaw decided to dedicate his artillery battalion, 2nd Battalion, 15th Field Artillery Regiment (2–15 FA), to the task of partnering with the Iraqi Army. Infanti assigned his Company A headquarters a similar task. Kershaw determined that the first step would be to move into the Triangle of Death and establish outposts among the populace thereby allowing the brigade to apply pressure on the insurgents and interdict smuggling routes.[13]

In March 2006, the brigade conducted a training deployment to the National Training Center at Fort Irwin, California, where it would essentially validate its training path. Set in the Mojave Desert, the National Training Center (NTC) was created to prepare U.S. Army brigades to fight against a Soviet-style enemy. It was one of the many post–Vietnam, Cold War innovations that proved invaluable in Desert Storm. (Interestingly, 4–31 IN was one of the original opposing force, or mock enemy, units at Fort Irwin.) After the Soviet Union collapsed, the NTC evolved to train units for the more ambiguous environment of the 1990s where the enemy might employ guerrilla and criminal tactics along with conventional threats.[14]

By 2006, training replicated as best as possible the complexities of Iraq. The opposing force used insurgent tactics, ethnic Arabs acted as role players and spoke Arabic while pretending to be villagers and key leaders, and soldiers faced IED attacks. While there, units had the ability to place their soldiers through additional training and scenarios outside of the whole-unit training environment. This training could be quite involved. An example the Polar Bears faced was a battlefield trauma lane where extra stressors like snipers and angry or excited locals complicated their efforts to conduct first aid.[15] In short, the Army provided the Polar Bears first class, immersive training prior to deploying.

Previewing how the battalion intended to operate in Iraq, the Polar Bears eschewed living on the forward operating bases and instead established positions in mock villages. This forced them to practice the procedure for clearing an area and building up a position. It further forced them to learn how to live alongside villagers and control a town. While there, the battalion conducted patrols with simulated Iraqi Army units in a move that foreshadowed some of their approach.[16] The battalion returned from the rotation on 20 April. While there would be nearly 120 days from the time the battalion left the

NTC and the day it began deploying, the training center rotation was largely the culmination of a year of training to employ a mix of light infantry doctrine with tactics, techniques, and procedures found in counterinsurgency doctrine and theory.

Companies C and D (Charlie and Delta) jumped into live fire training focusing on situations in urban settings.[17] Charlie company's exercise focused on a single compound with a series of challenges. The soldiers entered several rooms, moving through the shoothouse engaging enemy targets and having to restrain from shooting noncombatant targets; they even had to apply first aid. The day iteration was relatively straightforward. During the night scenario, the commander wanted to replicate the unreliable electricity environment of Iraq. Therefore, at times the lights would be off and suddenly turn on forcing the teams to rapidly adjust. At other times, the lights would be on and suddenly turn off.

Delta company's live fires focused on a mock urban objective with multiple buildings where the units were searching for a high-value individual. The mission called for a cordon and search, a type of movement to contact wherein a unit isolates an objective by forming a secure perimeter around it and then moves another element inside either pursuing a particular individual or looking for signs of the enemy. This was reminiscent of a typical mission in Iraq and one that the company would be called on to do repeatedly.

Ultimately, what these two live fire exercises demonstrate is the importance of offensive actions among the populace in a counterinsurgency environment. While urban operations are a normal infantry mission regardless of the type of war, they still have their place in a counterinsurgency environment. The tagline "hearts and minds"—a misleading cliché by the end of combat operations in Iraq—can deceive people into believing that counterinsurgency is all about swaying the populace. While the populace is the ultimate goal, offensive action is necessary to seize the initiative, clear areas, and hold them against enemy counterattack.

And the fundamentals remained important as well. 2nd BCT held Expert Infantryman Badge (EIB) testing. First awarded in 1944 as part of the Army's efforts to distinguish infantrymen from other soldiers, the test requires a soldier to demonstrate proficiency in a number of technical tasks and skills and physical events. Standards have evolved through the years, but in 2006, the requirements included a host of pre-requisites such as achieving a passing score on the Army Physical Fitness Test, completion of a 12-mile foot march in three hours with 35 pounds of gear, expert qualification with a rifle, and completion of day and night land navigation courses. After the pre-requisites, soldiers had to test on more than twenty tasks following exact standards. Soldiers could fail up to two different tasks so long as they retested and passed within an hour. Those who were first time go's on everything were known as "true blue" while those who failed two tasks were known as "blade runners." Needless to say, this took a considerable amount of the training time which demonstrates the importance the brigade's leadership placed on basic infantry tactics in the face of their coming mission.

Infanti set the tone that he expected his platoon leaders to personally ensure the success of the mission. Therefore, he required all platoon leaders to ensure successful completion of the road march within their platoons. That meant marching with soldiers who failed or were unable to do it previously for some reason. I ended up doing the march three times in a span of eight days. One of my fellow platoon leaders had to do the march four times. My company commander pulled me in, along with my fellow lieutenants, and told us, "All good infantrymen earn their EIB; earn yours." It seemed like a tacit means of saying, "Get it or I'll fire you." The company first sergeant's advice was to be inconspicuous; the graders would be extra hard on a lieutenant. Going through with a squad would demonstrate dedication to the unit; going through alone would denote selfishness. Also, we should avoid arguing with NCOs.

While the test itself was great training in attention to detail, calmness under stress, and knowledge of the fundamentals, an unintended consequence provided a truly great development opportunity that would help me down the road. Testing for the badge requires a plethora of NCOs who have earned it before. That meant that all of my NCOs were on the committee except for two enrolled in the Warrior Leader Course, the school for sergeants. Sometimes one of my NCOs was available, but oftentimes it was like a pre–Invasion Iraqi platoon: one officer and a bunch of Joes. It was a great opportunity to interface with the soldiers and learn to lead the platoon without being able to lean on anyone. As for that test itself, I blade ran to success along with two members of my platoon. The company as a whole had the highest numbers of soldiers in the brigade earn the badge and the Polar Bears had the highest total in the brigade, more than all other units combined.[18] All of the company's infantry officers earned the badge.

Charlie Company also participated in an experimental physical training program that would better prepare it for the rigors of combat in farmland. All soldiers participated in a pre-test conducted twice over three days that included a balance test, chin ups, a shuttle sprint with body armor on, an agility drill, max bench press, seated medicine ball throw, sit and reach, vertical leap, and a casualty recovery.[19] In the intervening weeks, we did two days of weight training consisting mostly of squats, presses, and cleans along with pull ups, and two days of jumping, throwing, and agility, often in body armor, plus core strengthening. The middle of the week was reserved for foot marching. I found it to be a much better program and test than the general Army program and I think it prepared our company for the challenges of patrolling in Yusifiyah.

Free training time was scarce, but my platoon was able to carve out some time to train on our own. My medic developed an innovative training program to prepare our guys to respond to wounds under stress. Two-man teams entered a dark room and had to clear it where they found three casualties in various states. In the background, the medic had war movies blaring to create the sounds of battle. It was a great training event that pushed young soldiers to recall their training in a difficult environment and one that would save lives the following February.

Additionally, I took my platoon out on an all-night training event that required squad leaders to set up ambushes. After that, the platoon conducted link up and marched to an objective where each squad had the opportunity to conduct a raid after getting a last-minute order and having to plan on a short timeline. Originally the training event was planned at 24 hours, but the commander, conscious of taking soldiers' time and needing time himself, only allowed us the night after putting families to bed. It was exhausting but good training for me if no one else.

With that done, the battalion only had a couple of pre-deployment tasks to complete. One was to move George, the massive Polar Bear statue, from the current battalion headquarters to the Old Post area where the rear detachment would locate for the duration of the deployment. We foot marched behind a forklift hoisting George to the other side of post, had a small ceremony, and marched back. The other was a brigade-wide deployment ceremony and parade where the announcer rattled off the deployment history of 2nd BCT in the two short decades since its activation. The list was exhausting to listen to and humbling at the same time. It would be tough for this iteration of the Polar Bears and Commandos to make their mark on that distinguished lineage.

In 1927, Captain Curtis Wheeler and Lieutenant Carl Sack were conducting training on aerial support to ground troops by dropping messages to the soldiers below in the vicinity of Pine Camp, present day Fort Drum. Something caused Wheeler to lurch forward and engage the rudder. This caused Sack to lose control of the aircraft. Unable to recover, the plane crashed into the grounds. For their dedication to supporting ground troops, the airfield that supports Fort Drum soldiers through the housing of aviation assets and the deployment gateway bears their name.

So it was that the Polar Bears began their march to war on the tarmac of Wheeler-Sack Army Airfield beginning on 16 August 2006. Many of the NCOs were entering the fray for the second or third time, but most junior soldiers and lieutenants faced their first combat. Among the Joes was a mix of apprehension and resolution. A Charlie Company mortarman admitted being nervous but confident. "It's a lot to take in," he told a reporter, "but I am well trained and know what to do." A machine gunner in Bravo Company said that "the training [he] received was really good." He also noted how he gained confidence from the fact that many of the NCOs were already combat veterans. Kershaw, speaking of the entire brigade, said, "the soldiers are well-trained and prepared for the mission." Staff Sergeant Philip Sharp, a squad leader in Bravo Company and combat veteran, wasn't nearly as confident. His squad had been pieced together toward the end of train up. However, he would make the best of his time in Kuwait awaiting passage into Iraq. Daily, he would drill his soldiers getting them prepared for the mission.[20]

The battalion's first stop in Southwest Asia was an intermediate staging base in Kuwait. A patch of otherwise useless desert, Camp Beurhing served as a sort of way station for units. It provided a place for units to conduct final mission checks and coordination and a spot for the Army to house soldiers until it was ready to move them into Iraq or Afghanistan. The camp, situated 15 miles from the border with Iraq opened in January 2003 as part of the coalition build up prior to the kick off of the invasion. Along with serving as an intermediate staging base, it was a large hub for rotary wing (helicopter) assets. Originally named Camp Udari, the U.S. rechristened it in May 2004 in honor of Lieutenant Colonel Charles "Chad" Beuhring, who was killed in a rocket attack the previous October while serving in Iraq.[21]

While at Camp Beuhring, the battalion was engrossed in what the military calls reception, staging, onward movement, and integration or RSOI. Among the tasks required of the unit were for each soldier to zero their rifle sights, receive briefings on the Law of Land Warfare and the Rules of Engagement, and a brief from the brigade safety officer. In an interesting incident, the safety officer, a military retiree who wore a military uniform with all his badges, showed up thirty minutes late when it came time for him to brief Charlie and Delta Company. Soldiers were naturally a little amped after having to wait and one kept chirping at the safety officer. Eventually, the briefer instructed the soldier to go to the back and report to his first sergeant. The crowd roared when the soldier stood up as it was Delta Company's first sergeant. A fourth event, participating in a simulation munitions clearance of a mock building, was cancelled.

Kuwait initially provided time for the leaders to prepare for the upcoming mission. Daily the platoon leaders and commander of Charlie would gather to discuss the mission and any operations or intelligence updates and then the platoon leaders would split off to their soldiers to brief the mission and talk to subordinate leaders. It was the first time we received useful maps, mostly satellite imagery. In the days before the deployment the battalion issued us several topographical maps that were near useless without relief or an accurate representation of buildings. (Interestingly, I was able to patrol with one of these maps.) So our situational awareness of the mission, the enemy situation, and just what the place looked like increased dramatically in those early days.

About a week after arriving in Kuwait, the battalion remained. The battalion and company commanders moved into Iraq to participate in Casey's COIN Academy. It was another educational experience for the platoon leaders who would often find themselves away from the company headquarters. While soldiers received ample down time to relax before what was sure to be a tough deployment, the unit took the opportunity to continue training. As previously mentioned, squad leaders like Phil Sharp took the opportunity to drill their men in the basics. My first squad leader found a park of abandoned temporary buildings and conducted yet another turn of urban operations training, both outside and inside the buildings.

The company also fell back to universal tasks. We conducted physical training daily. The battalion physician's assistant provided a class on emergency medical aide. (His section on what happens when a bullet shatters a pelvis was quite graphic.) Ultimately, the heavy emphasis on medical care throughout the train up and in Kuwait would save lives and limbs over the next 15 months. Charlie also took advantage of the helicopters stationed at Beuhring. We coordinated to conduct static load training which prepares soldiers to load and unload aircraft in preparation for combat operations. The helicopter would prove an invaluable tool in the farmlands soon enough.

Rumors were swirling about the land we would go into. Sharp wrote that "[Yusifiyah] was painted as a festering inferno of total destruction and absolute anarchy with the chance of death and injury increasing greatly." He told his men that they were going into the land of "moo zeein" (Iraqi Arabic for "no good"). In his journal on 28 August

2006, Sharp wrote, "I predict a major fight within a month to establish control of Yusufiyah. I hope our leadership shows courage and foresight to take the fight to the enemy and not set [sic] passively still while the cowardly enemy blows us up."[22] Sharp's prediction and wish were soon to come true.

We were alerted three times for movement out of Kuwait, each time moving all of our baggage and equipment out of the tent and once getting all the way to Ali Al Saleem Air Base before getting sent back to Camp Buehring. But eventually we made it onto a C-17 cargo plane and headed to Baghdad International Airport (BIAP). It was about 0100 when we landed in Iraq. I had a feeling between thrill and disappointment. I'd been anxious to get to Iraq since the buildup began in 2002 and now in late summer 2006, here I was, standing on an airfield in the middle of the night surrounded by a massive, safe base complex. Also, we stood there getting our identification cards swiped (to track we were in country) while Delta Company boarded CH-47 Chinooks headed for Lutafiyah. We were doomed to another week or two at Camp Stryker. Delta was replacing C/1/502 PIR and would assume responsibility of the JSB and the Alamo.

We bedded down at Camp Stryker on the Victory Base Complex that also housed Camp Liberty and BIAP around 0400 that morning. It was good to have arrived and the reunification with the commander relieved a lot of stress. It had been tough for me being a young lieutenant without a commander, even if for only a short period. Between that and having all my NCOs gone for the Expert Infantryman Badge, I learned a lot and developed an independence that would be a great asset and also something that got me in trouble during the deployment and throughout my career.

Chaplain Bryan arrived a day of ahead of Charlie. In his book, he describes his first look around Iraq while moving from the airfield. The neighborhoods were "littered with razor wire, abandoned guard towers, bullet pocked billboards, and abandoned vehicles. A new level of unease washed over me. The maze of ruined structures testified to how much destruction and disrepair could be brought upon a society by war."[23] And this was just on the complex. His words resonate with me as I think back on our early morning drive from the airport. Whatever his impressions or mine, where we were was prettier than where we were going.

Bravo Company landed a few hours after us and some of their leaders immediately hopped onto a bird and headed to FOB Yusifiyah. They found it a bit scary even for the veterans. Iraqi Army soldiers guarded the towers without any U.S. soldiers mixed in. Americans did guard the front gate, known as the Entry Control Point or ECP, where an M113 armored personnel carrier blocked the entrance. Living quarters were a little better than expected. They consisted of tents lined with wooden walls and concrete barriers ran in between them to provide protection from mortar fire and rockets or recoilless rifles.[24] Bravo would replace B/1/502 PIR which still held responsibility for Yusifiyah and the TCPs along Routes Sportster and the Mullah Fayad Highway which connected the town of Mullah Fayad just south of Yusifiyah with the Yusifiyah Thermal Power Plant.

Back at Camp Stryker, life was busier than at Camp Beuhring. We did physical training in the mornings. We had to inventory and sign for equipment and meet with the unit we were replacing. I wrote a day after that inventory that I was signing for "8 trucks like a fucking armored armada." It is certainly an indication of my rawness, my excitement, and my naivety at the time. Looking back after having commanded two Stryker-equipped infantry companies, my amazement at having eight HMMWVs seems laughable. Despite my education and training at West Point and my graduation from Ranger School, in many ways I was still a bit of a bright-eyed 23-year-old boy.

On 7 September, the officers set out for a reconnaissance of the area Charlie Company would occupy. However, the patrol discovered an IED and EOD would not come until morning, so we returned to base and tried again the next morning after an Iron Claw route clearance team moved through the area. That morning we arrived at Patrol Base (PB) Gator Swamp, a complex of three buildings in a former Baathist neighborhood located between Route Fat Boy, the road that linked Mahmudiyah and Yusifiyah, and Route Earnhardt, a dirt road that ran parallel to Fat Boy on the opposite side of a canal.

Spartan was the best way to describe Gator Swamp. The ground was moon dust, sand fleas ran rampant, there were no facilities for preparing food, and soldiers had to use makeshift urinals ("piss tubes") and outhouses. Journalist Thomas Ricks wrote that it was "a half-ruined house bristling with black dull machine guns and surrounded by green sand bags, shin-deep mud holes, and shadowy palm groves." (Writing of the command post building, he omits mention of the other two buildings.) Describing the medic station, Ricks wrote, "with its bare cots and hanging lightbulbs [it] felt like a scene from World War II." While not much to get excited about, Gator Swamp had one very important mission: keep the enemy contained in the area and not let them or their weapons into Baghdad.[25]

The Swamp was actually outside of the confines of Yusifiyah, being north of the Janabi Run Canal that defined greater Yusifiyah's northern border and it was not in 1/502 PIR's area of operations (nor in the area 4–31 IN would inherit). This area was under the control of Company B, 2nd Battalion, 502nd Parachute Infantry Regiment, 1/502 PIR's sister battalion. At the outset, Charlie would fall under 4–31 IN's sister battalion, the Golden Dragons of 2nd Battalion, 14th Infantry Regiment (2–14 IN).

The platoon sergeants and squad leaders (minus one per platoon left behind to oversee preparation at Stryker) arrived later in the day. That evening one of my West Point classmates took my squad leaders, our commander, another platoon leader and me on a patrol through the southern part of the area of operations. For me, taking the first step outside the wire of Gator Swamp with a round in the chamber was the culmination of more than five years of work. I once feared, as all young cadets do, that the war would pass me by. But here I was.

The patrol itself was relatively mundane, but presented what a typical mission in a counterinsurgency environment may look like. We talked to some local Zaedi tribesmen and visited one of the checkpoints on Route Slipknot, which ran north to south toward the greater Yusifiyah area. We left the squad leaders there to spend the night and learn about operations at the checkpoint. We also spent time talking to the headmaster of a local school who said his teachers were taking competency exams, which seemed to be good news. I remember thinking of my sister who had to take the Praxis as a teacher. It was comforting knowing that there were academic standards, though we would learn finding qualified teachers probably wasn't the biggest problem in education in the area. We also noticed a lot of brand new, red tractors and no one seemed to know where they came from.

War has a steady history of large periods of time trying to kill boredom with short, but exciting periods of time trying to kill the enemy (and not be killed yourself in the exchange). Theater policy prevented more than a handful of new guys going on patrol and the company only had one unit patrolling at a time, so most of the time we sat around. I had figured to be too busy to read or write and left everything behind at Camp Stryker. The base was relatively open, so going outside of a building required you to be in full gear. Just going to urinate was an ordeal. After getting kitted up in body armor, helmet and eye protection, you had to go stand on a box and urinate into a PVC tube with a cut off bottle as a funnel to vector you in. Shaving with a helmet on for those of us without electric razors was no fun either.

Our leaders began to filter back to Stryker, but the lieutenants remained behind. We weren't sure if we were going back. In truth, our platoon sergeants were running the show back there and they could bring our gear out. The company Fire Support Officer and I managed to get out on another patrol. Then at 0230 on 12 September someone alerted us we were moving back to Stryker. We gathered our stuff and loaded up. While I sat in the back of a HMMWV, the truck behind us rammed our bumper sending me lurching forward. All I could think was, "Thank God vehicles don't behave like they do in the movies." In *First Blood*, two deuce-and-a-half trucks collide and explode. That would not have been good. Thankfully, the vehicle was fine and we made it back to Camp Stryker around 0430 and got a couple hours of sleep.

On the eve of formally moving out into sector with the entire platoon, I wrote a letter to my parents. Up to then, my letters were filled with immature ramblings denigrating the servicemembers who served in Kuwait and complaining about how nice non-infantry soldiers had it. But I wrote an interesting paragraph that, reading it eleven years later, seems to have been quite prescient:

> I would say I'm going to become a really good Infantry leader through pain and heartache. I'm going to learn through much error and have to think and make decisions with little guidance. The CO [commanding officer] is just too busy to really mentor us anymore and a lot of times we're running with no guidance at all. It's an awesome situation for a young leader, but stressful. Besides, in the Infantry, no one ever really compliments you. You can work your ass off and do what you think was an amazing job, only to be told "good" or, worse, "fix it." But, that's the nature of the beast. At times, it makes you feel left in the dark or "fucked," but it's important to just take what you have and be a leader. It can be frustrating and it seems that you are expected to perform highly when you don't know what to do.[26]

This letter shows that my commander had to practice Mission Command, the Army's command philosophy that provides flexibility to subordinates, in order to effectively lead the company. The best way to teach a subordinate is to force them to figure things out for themselves. It also reflects the immense amount of tasks a commander in combat has. Subordinate officers that need constant guidance can be a hindrance. Platoon leaders have to grow up fast and my first test wasn't far away.

Our first experience with the friction of war occurred on 14 September as we were preparing to convoy out to Gator Swamp from Stryker. We were up at a 0400 preparing our vehicles to move out but had significant trouble getting our radios properly filled. Even the NCOs from the 101st had difficulty figuring out the issue. Ideally, we would have filled them the night before and worked through all of our issues then, but there was a communications security code changeover that night. Our 0600 departure became a 0740 step off. The company headquarters was with us, but this was my first patrol in the lead. It was relatively innocuous and uneventful and we arrived at Gator Swamp around 0900.

Immediately, we dropped our stuff and went to work. Half the platoon stayed at the patrol base getting after priorities of work such as improving defensive positions and living quarters. The previous unit rotated platoons through the base and thus only used one building for housing. Our commander had decided to place the whole company at the base and that required getting another building ready. The building was on the opposite side of the base from the other living quarters and headquarters building, which housed the command post. About 200 meters of moon dusted motor pool

The building at Gator Swamp that held 1st and 3rd Platoons. Infested with sand fleas, the Polar Bears found human feces in the building when they first moved in.

stood between the other two and the third building. It had not been used for some time other than to man rooftop positions. Occasionally, Iraqi Army soldiers would stay there when on the base, so my platoon sergeant and half the platoon along with third platoon went to work cleaning it and preparing it for living. They found human feces laying on the floor, an indication of the lack of sanitation. Living in the foyer, I would wake up each morning with sand flea bites covering my arms and they would itch terribly. It was a long way from home. But it set the tone early: the company would eschew comfort to be as close to the populace as possible.

The company had five mission divided amongst the headquarters and three rifle platoons: securing the patrol base, overwatching Route Slipknot at the checkpoint, patrolling the area of operations, conducting maintenance operations at Camp Stryker, and securing Route Earnhardt. My platoon took the security rotation on Route Earnhardt first. Cautioned to do as the old unit did until their soldiers were gone—four 101st soldiers stayed back per platoon for a week—we placed vehicles every 400 m to keep security on the route.

The vehicles were minimally manned: driver, gunner, and truck commander. We were fortunate if we were able to see one other truck. Vehicles were exposed and vulnerable. The area surrounding Route Earnhardt was a cornucopia of good terrain for an attacking enemy. Most of the south side of the route was covered with dense housing while the northside consisted of hilly farmland and a few groves. For the brigade that had three soldiers captured all alone in a HMMWV, they seemed perfectly fine with the set up. One soldier would pull security and listen to the radio from the turret. In the nighttime, the other two would sleep. The outgoing platoon leader told me he would sleep with his night vision devices pulled down over his eyes. It was precarious and my commander had resolved to change the method as soon as he could assess the situation. 2nd Platoon went on patrol cycle and 3rd Platoon took responsibility for the check point on Route Slipknot with half the platoon on maintenance and refit back at Camp Stryker. For the first day or so, our set up went well. It was all quiet as we adjusted to our surroundings. But soon the enemy would test us and it would be where we most expected … and feared he would.[27]

Thomas Ricks visited Patrol Base Gator Swamp in late December of 2005. One soldier, an NCO, told him that patrolling in the area was "like trying to track down a bunch of ghosts." Another said he "didn't like anything about being here" and believed that soldiers were leaving the Army because they'd been through so much. A third chimed in and explained morale was down because of the way the soldiers were dying and being maimed—fighting an invisible enemy with progress near impossible to measure. "It makes you wonder what do you gain by sticking around?" But they had stuck around, because, as their commander put it, "the important thing is to keep them fighting here. That's really the crux of the fight."[28]

So we were there on 16 September, the day before the transfer of authority, trying to contain the enemy. We seemed to have figured out our rhythm by then. The enemy had left us alone long enough to do that. We went to twelve hour shifts on Earnhardt and the boys were able to get some sleep between rotations. We had tried six and eight hours on and off, but there was so much to do pre- and post-shift just to get ready and there were so many work priorities that the time off patrol wasn't restful. For a day or two, this was not a big deal but we were staring down eleven more months of taxing work, and we had sentry posts off by their self; the last thing we needed was a set of exhausted soldiers. Through the use of mosquito netting and some bug spray, I had gained an upper hand in my battle with the sand fleas. Things were looking up. The next day, the 101st would be gone and we would be free to adapt to a posture we felt was better.

All was quiet at 1105. I had trudged over to the command post building in hopes of calling home or using the internet for a few minutes. As I sat squeezing peanut butter out of some dipping packets (the MREs had sat in the sun so long the fruit had squeezed out of many of the pouches and thus seemed unappealing) the radio came crackling alive. It was one of my vehicle positions calling the command post to inform them that the gunner had just received one round of sniper fire. The bullet cracked past the gunner's head and impacted into the bullet proof glass beside his helmet. As the vehicle commander provided the report, there seemed to be relief and elation among all involved. The company and the soldiers in the vehicle had survived their first contact of the war. It was close, but it was out of the way.

Then, down the road, an explosion and a burst of flames and before long all that could be seen of the fourth vehicle was a blazing hull. The gunner, who wasn't necessarily in the clear from the sniper, turned to get a better look while the vehicle commander and command post began sending out calls, hoping to make contact There was no way for anyone in the third vehicle to effectively respond to the incident save for driving there and leaving a large section of the road unguarded. Calls continued and continued but there was no response and no visual on the troops. My heart sank into my stomach as the situation came together in my head. We had three soldiers, cut off from the rest of the platoon, unaccounted for. My thoughts were assuredly the same as the others listening to the radio: *DUSTWUN!* Short for Duty Status-Whereabouts Unknown, it was both a code and a status. Menchaca and Tucker, the soldiers from B/1/502 PIR who had been captured were declared DUSTWUN before their bodies were discovered.

My first instinct was to mass on the area. I threw my body armor on and ran across the moon dust covered expanse between the command post and my platoon's living quarters and sounded the alarm. My soldiers reacted quicker than you might expect for a unit of people not prepared to be minutemen. We rushed to the vehicles and lined up at the gate, which was really just a strand of concertina wire. I called on the radio to the command post to report our patrol's exit. I was first or second in line and the commander called me as we were leaving to say he was right behind me (in this case literally the vehicle behind mine). My first reaction was, "What the hell is this guy doing? It's my platoon." But it was his company and this didn't appear to be a small fight. There may be people missing. He needed to be there and I would have done the same thing.

We raced down Earnhardt, counting the other vehicles as we went. The other three were there, intact. We could see the plume of smoke as we went. As we passed the third truck, I could see the flames encapsulating the smoldering wreckage of a vehicle. I'd never imagined a hunk of steel could burn that easily and quickly, but it did. The enemy had welcomed us to the place where everything burns. When I exited my HMMWV, no more than fifteen minutes after the first report, there wasn't much left. I rushed out of the vehicle and looked around. There was no sign of the three soldiers.

As I stood on the dirt road all I could imagine was that there were three soldiers in that truck, trapped and burning. If they weren't in there, they had to have been captured. I tried to get close to the vehicle to peer in, but .50 caliber ammunition from the M2 Browning machine gun was cooking off and spewing randomly around the hull. I was still raw and was unaware of how much danger these burning rounds were to me—likely they could only burn my skin given the massive amount of protective gear we wore, so I decided to sprint past the vehicle and look in as I went, hoping to minimize my exposure. It seemed like an incredibly bad idea, but the best option. As I got to the far side I was surprised to see my radio telephone operator coming up behind me. Amazed someone would follow me in a stupid stunt like that, I asked him what made him do it. He said he was the RTO and it was his responsibility to follow the platoon leader. That was loyalty.

The first sergeant and the company's intelligence NCO moved around to the side standing off about twenty meters and squatted, looking in the vehicle. None of the four of us saw any bodies nor had anyone heard from the soldiers. We converged on the commander and conferred. Our suspicion was that the soldiers had been dragged into the house next the vehicle. There was no evidence for this—no drag marks or blood. But there was proximity and logic. We knew we had to search it and that time was of the essence. If they were in there, who knows what was happening to them. It had to be done now. My RTO went to run something down and the commander, first sergeant, intelligence NCO, and I, under the commander's direction, formed an impromptu four-man team and entered the house alone and unafraid.

I truly believe that to be a good infantry officer, you have to be a good infantryman, not the best, but knowledgeable on the whole gamut. I hadn't trained a lot personally on clearing houses, but I had trained others and watched them do it, so in that moment, never having practiced together and with adrenaline high, the four us cleared the estate house, room-to-room, stairwell to floor, until we converged on the roof. There was no enemy nor was there any sign of our boys. I had imagined for many years what my first combat experience, if this was combat, would be like. I had never imagined this. I had never considered I would take the role of a rifleman in a stack.

Somewhat dejected, we exited the house where my RTO brought us good news. Things were seeming bleak until he informed me that the three had linked up with the third vehicle. They had been together for some time, but the radio net was so clogged the vehicle commander couldn't get the report through. At the time, we were using only one radio net for the company so everyone had to compete for space to communicate. It was quite a relief knowing those guys were okay. We were fortunate it wasn't worse. We had come close to realizing our worst nightmare.

Over the next several hours, we secured the wreckage until a recovery team could pile it onto a flat bed and take it back to Camp Stryker. We also investigated the area. I climbed onto the third vehicle to inspect the sniper bullet and determine the direction it came from. I passed this information on to the commander who developed a theory about where the shooter had been when he engaged the vehicle. We moved to a warehouse to clear it but did not find a rifle or a sniper. Still, the commander's theory was seemingly confirmed when a future sniper attack that occurred on another unit in the area ended in the sniper being captured at his perch. (We had interacted with the captured sniper that day.)

We took the opportunity to talk to locals. The commander held an impromptu engagement with leaders in the area and we attempted to gather intelligence and get to know the people. It was a great opportunity to leave an impression on the locals. We had just lost a vehicle, but had not harmed a single civilian, neither with bullet nor fist. The enemy was our enemy, not every Iraqi. Our response was measured and allowed us to extend a narrative.

We debriefed the three soldiers from the vehicle. The squad leader was standing outside the vehicle when he heard the RPG fired and saw it coming. It is possible the munition was an RPG-7, an anti-tank version. He opened the door as the round hit the HMMWV, attempting to alert the others. One soldier, in the driver seat, felt the impact and lost consciousness for a few seconds. When he woke up, the steering wheel was in his hands, detached from the truck. In the confusion, he tried to drive before the soldier in the gunner seat told him to get out. The squad leader gathered the other two and began movement to a better location, ending up at the other vehicle. The fourth vehicle had been lined up perpendicular to a courtyard wall and the first sergeant believed the enemy gunner had little to do but aim parallel to the wall and await results. Wherever it struck, it did so in a location that caused the vehicle to catch on fire.

Despite the vehicle being utterly reduced to steel rubble, the three soldiers were relatively fine. One had burst eardrums. Another took a small amount of shrapnel in his ankle. The squad leader had a minor burn on his fingers after reaching into the vehicle following the explosion. Aside from placing one soldier on command post duty for a few days to heal his ankle, we lost no man hours to the attack. It was incredibly fortunate.

The soldier in the gunner station reflected on the event and lamented to me that he should have seen it coming. He told me that kids had been playing earlier but had suddenly all disappeared just prior to the attack. He was mad at himself, but I was not. Though it is a warning sign that incoming units are told about, it takes time to observe an area and understand patterns. At that point in our deployment there was no way of knowing that the kids leaving wasn't just a call to a meal or work. Had we been there several weeks it would have been more obvious than it was at a handful of days. Still, that soldier's ability to be self-critical is an admirable trait. Though a Private First Class at the time, he was several years older than the average soldier of that rank and thus much more mature. He had the intellect of an officer, the leadership skill of an NCO, but the rank of junior soldier.

A convoy from 2–14 IN finally arrived to pick up the wreckage. With them was their battalion commander. He asked me what happened and what we had done. Then he informed me it was the first contact in the brigade. I had imagined my first test in combat coming under heavy enemy fire, not in response to a burning vehicle. But it was somehow fitting that in a land where everything burned, I would first come into contact with a fire.

By late afternoon, we sent the previous shift home and those of us who had responded assumed guard. As he was returning to base, the commander told me to come up with a recommendation to change the way we guarded the route. He didn't want soldiers exposed and the next day the brigade would officially assume command of the Triangle of Death. My first squad leader and I got on the roof of the same abandoned house I had searched earlier and decided it would be better to infiltrate soldiers there at night and use it to overwatch the route, so the next night, we did just that. The tall house provided better observation but the tradeoff was a longer response time to any threat. Two vehicles remained down the road in static positions. A day or two later, 2nd Platoon assumed responsibility for the route, and implemented a roving patrol with

Soldiers patrol along the Janabi Run Canal that served as the northern border of the Triangle of Death. 1/502 PIR admonished the Polar Bears not to go south of the canal without a machine gun.

2. The Polar Bears Go Marching In

the two vehicles moving up and down and stopping at infrequent intervals to conduct surveillance. Another squad occupied the building. While the previous way had worked for the company from 2/502 PIR, this aligned better with the commander's intent and our interpretation of the mission.

Our experience was not as bad as what A/2-14 IN and soldiers from the Brigade Special Troops Battalion would experience the following April. In that event, a large IED destroyed two vehicles, killed four soldiers, and wounded two more. But for the rest of our time there, the route, Gator Swamp's only usable lifeline to the rest of the world (that area of Route Fat Boy south of the base was considered black or off limits to vehicles), was secure. Without increasing our manning we increased our security and reduced our risk. It was an efficient move that relied on the brainpower and experimentation of several leaders.

Charlie Company's experience at Gator Swamp and life north of the Janabi Run Canal was short lived. Within ten days of arriving, A/2-14 IN arrived to replace us. We would be reuniting with the rest of the Polar Bears soon. But in that short week and a half, the Triangle of Death had already lived up to its reputation as a place where everything burns. In those opening days at the Swamp, the 101st had repeatedly warned us about going south of the Janabi Run Canal without a machine gun team, at the least. We were about to go there in force … and stay.

3

Mountain Men in a Flat Land

Security may be ten percent of the problem, or it may be ninety percent, but whichever it is, it's the first ten percent or the first ninety percent. Without security, nothing else we do will last.—John Paul Vann

The day after 1st Platoon's HMMWV burned to the ground, the battalion officially took control of the Triangle of Death from 1/502 PIR assuming responsibility for Mahmudiyah, Lutafiyah, and Yusifiyah. At the 17 September ceremony marking the transfer of authority, the battalion uncased its colors. In a speech, Infanti admonished his soldiers. "You own it, you defend it, and you … establish an Iraqi government."[1] Once the final members of 1/502 PIR had left, Infanti gathered members of the battalion into a room on FOB Mahmudiyah, where the battalion headquarters initially sat, and said, "Any delay in attacking will be disastrous. We will attack, attack, and continue to attack!" He then told the soldiers to pack their bags because they were moving west into the places where others said they couldn't go.[2]

Kershaw further laid out the brigade's objectives in a letter to the troops published in the brigade's internal newsletter, *The Sandstorm*. Those objectives were

- to build and work hand-in-hand with the Iraqi Army and Police forces and to provide security to the Iraqi people.
- to assist the Iraqi government in providing the essential services, government tools, and economic stability for Iraq to be independent.
- to protect the force.[3]

At the time of transition, Mahmudiyah's mayor, Mouayad Houssen, made a bold and terribly incorrect prediction. "I think the new unit, they can make an easy victory with the people."[4]

The enemy made it clear there would be no time to adjust. The day after the transfer of authority ceremony, a car bomb exploded in the Yusifiyah market. This appears to have been an attempt to harm the economy and drive a wedge between the government and the people. Soldiers from the battalion responded and fire trucks were escorted in from Mahmudiyah to help put out the flames. One of the responding NCOs described the scene: "Driving to the site was like passing through pure desolation. Fires were burning all over. Debris was thrown everywhere. Any window that was intact prior was no longer in tact [sic]. Large amounts of dust still occupied the air." The blast left a hole deeper than six feet. An assistant operations officer for the brigade described the effect of the bombing: "Terrorists are attacking those things that support the people. This market is key to the economic stability of Yusifiyah. [Because of] this action, construction is delayed, which means that jobs are delayed, families are inconvenienced and it will take longer for stability."[5] From the start, things were burning in Yusifiyah.

The next day, the 19th, the battalion struck tragedy when a vehicle from the mortar platoon overturned into a canal near Mahmudiyah. Specialist Bobby Callahan, a squad leader, despite being in danger, ensured his soldiers got out of the vehicle. However, they were unable to get him out before he drowned in the canal. Callahan was on his second deployment. Soldiers remembered him as a quiet leader who led by example and could always make people smile. Callahan, who left behind a wife, received a posthumous promotion to corporal.[6]

At some point in this first week, possibly the same day as Callahan's death, FOB Yusifiyah came under a coordinated attack. An enemy force of about thirty men attempted to storm the ECP (the M113 manned by soldiers) using VBIEDs to breach the wall or kill the guards. The guards engaged the attacking vehicles, preventing them from reaching the ECP and soldiers on base quickly reinforced the rooftop and tower positions. After an initial explosion of fire, the fight settled into a series of small engagements as time wore on. Insurgents hunkered down in a nearby irrigation ditch and soldiers fired high explosive grenades from their rifle mounted M203 launchers to flush them out. Eventually, the enemy withdrew having lost up to seven insurgents. There were no deaths on the coalition side.[7]

After five days of the enemy attacking his formations, Infanti put his battalion on the offensive. On 20 September, elements from Companies A and B, both headquartered at Yusifiyah, began the battalion's thrust into the Wild West. The soldiers pushed northwest along the Mullah Fayad Highway from Battle Position (BP)/TCP 5 and established a new outpost about a half mile up the road. The position was a house and the unit provided the owners time to move as well as a claim card to receive just compensation for their home. Despite enemy attempts to dislodge them with RPG and rifle fire, the combined unit was able to string wire around the compound through the night and establish vehicle obstacles on the road.[8] Bravo Company started calling this position the Alamo and soldiers from Delta began referring to the site at the AVLB as the AVLB. (Henceforth, references to the Alamo will be in regard to the position on the Mullah Fayad Highway.)

Shortly after the establishment of the new Alamo, Charlie returned to Camp Stryker before moving to FOB Mahmudiyah which had one time been FOB Saint Michael after the patron saint of warriors. Along with the battalion headquarters, Charlie shared the space on the FOB with 2-15 FA, which maintained a hot firing battery to deliver artillery in support of operations on top of their partnership mission. Charlie was preparing to begin patrolling the town, but soon was alerted to a mission change. As the hot month came to an end, Infanti's convoy struck an IED wounding him for the second time in his career, both times in his present rank.⁹ The enemy had had a fun filled September exploding car bombs, destroying vehicles, attacking bases, and, now, wounding the battalion commander. Historian Kimberly Kagan described the depth of initiative Al Qaeda had at this point:

> Al Qaeda operated almost freely in a pendulum-like arc south of Baghdad, swinging from the Euphrates to the Tigris. They traveled southeast along the Euphrates River, often by boat, from Fallujah to Sadr al Yusifiyah. They followed the roads that link Sadr al Yusifiyah, Yusifiyah, and Mahmudiyah.[10]

It was time now for the Polar Bears to go to bat and take the fight to the enemy. The shaping operation on 20 September had just been batting practice.

* * *

Zarqawi was dead; dead as Marley. That was for sure. The United States military and intelligence apparatus had spent years making sure that happened, but his movement didn't die with him. The organization he left behind set about transforming itself to better align with their founder's goal: a pan–Islamic caliphate in the Middle East. And though Zarqawi himself had left the area before being killed, many of his adherents remained behind. So, in October 2006, the main insurgent group in the area was a direct descendant of Al Qaeda in Iraq, an organization whose simple title referred to its grandiose objective: Islamic State. (Islamic State officially took form on 12 October 2006.)

Also fighting in the area were the 1920 Revolutionary Brigade, primarily Qarghuli tribesmen loyal to the former regime, and Jaysh Al Islami. The groups were competing against each other as well as the coalition, but at times could come together to fight against Iraqi and American armies. Islamic State was the most hardnosed. They were extreme fundamentalists who had coerced women into marrying their members, forced locals to emplace IEDs, and restricted smoking for religious reasons.[11] Islamic State had a coercive grip on the population and it was the Polar Bears' task to break that hold and provide hope to the people.

While Islamic State was the most dominant and the 1920 Revolutionary Brigade and Jaysh Al Islami were the other prominent groups, smaller anti-government, anti–Shia, and fundamentalist insurgent groups controlled the hamlets like an urban gang may control a city block. These organizations would work together to accomplish common objectives, but one could not pass through another's territory without permission. As First Lieutenant Nick Ziemba, a Polar Bear officer attached to the artillery battalion for advisor duty, described it "sociopathic bands of terrorists, not to be confused with romanticized freedom fighters, roamed the countryside, killing entire families, blowing up mosques, and targeting well-intentioned coalition and Iraqi security patrols with ever-increasing volumes of explosives."[12] This presented a significant challenge for the Polar Bears. There was not a single enemy to concentrate on nor was there a single cause or desired end state among those enemy. Fighting what was at best a confederacy of insurgents would require careful consideration. The advantage was that each group required some support from the populace even if it was passive or coerced

3. Mountain Men in a Flat Land

and each required space to operate. This meant that focusing on the terrain and populace would help mitigate the need to counter myriad insurgent narratives. With that in mind, the Commando Brigade and Polar Bears began planning their first steps to knocking the enemy back, gaining territory, and securing the populace.

There was a palpable sense of foreboding among the 101st soldiers regarding the area south and west of Yusifiyah proper. Soldiers in 2/502 PIR told us not to enter without a machine gun. At Mahmudiyah, soldiers warned incoming Polar Bears to stay away from Qarghuli Village. According First Lieutenant Doug Livermore, then serving as a battle captain, soldiers described the village "as a veritable 'Heart of Darkness' into which no sane man would dare travel, much less attempt to subdue." When visiting one of the battle positions before the handover, a soldier staring down the Mullah Fayad Highway from TCP 6 told Chaplain Bryan, "If anyone goes past this [concertina] wire, they're going to die. Anybody that tries to drive up the rest of the road will never live to see the other end." That soldier and another troop related stories of catastrophic IEDs with the second soldier surmising that there was an IED buried every few feet.[13] There may be some hyperbole in the reporting, but it was clear that the area remained

Staring down the Mullah Fayad Highway from the Alamo. Soldiers warned of IEDs every few feet and that no one could go down that the road and come back alive.

a terrible place. The 101st soldiers had reason for their feelings; they had faced hardship over a tough twelve months. Although Jim Frederick's book *Black Hearts* details one platoon (1st Platoon, Bravo) out of control, for the most part those soldiers had acquitted themselves well. But there was still a long way to go before the Triangle of Death was no more.

The Polar Bears were now up to bat. On 1 October, Charlie Company moved to FOB Yusifiyah and the company commander issued an operations order detailing the unit's role in a brigade-level mission known as *Operation Commando Hunter*. The purpose of the operations was "to deny the terrorists safe sanctuary near Yusufiyah." The battalion's piece of the mission was titled *Operation Polar Blizzard*.[14] *Polar Blizzard* would be a three-company, multi-pronged and multi-modal assault into the heart of the hinterland. The main effort, Bravo, would air assault two platoons in via UH-60 Black Hawk helicopters along with a unit of Iraqi soldiers with partnered members of Alpha. Their objective was to clear Rushdi Mullah and establish a patrol base. Their remaining rifle platoon would escort supplies in via the Mullah Fayad Highway once the road was clear. Charlie, the first shaping effort, would conduct a ground assault into Al Taraq, a village of about 50 homes between Mullah Fayad and Rushi Mullah that commanded a 90-degree bend in the Mullah Fayad Highway thus allowing the movement of supplies and equipment into Rushdi Mullah. 1st Platoon and an Iron Claw route clearance team would move from the Alamo clearing the route of IEDs all the way to Rushdi Mullah. 1st Platoon would walk along the road searching for command wires that could initiate IEDs while the Iron Claw team inspected the roads. 2nd and 3rd Platoons with company headquarters would move into Al Taraq and clear the town after 1st Platoon had moved past it. Alpha and partnered Iraqi Army units would move down Route Peggy and establish a new battle position south of the FOB. It was an ambitious plan, but in a place like Yusifiyah, it was better to cannonball in than dip a toe.

Around midnight heading into 2 October, 1st Platoon and the Iron Claw team, having conducted pre-combat checks and inspections and having done mission briefings, left for the Alamo, arriving at 0030 where they parked inside the perimeter and soldiers tried to get a little sleep. 1st Platoon was down seven soldiers from our assigned strength. One soldier helped guard detainees in Baghdad, another served on the battalion's personal security detachment, one was attached to another element due to his expertise with a particular combat system, and we had to leave four back at FOB Mahmudiyah to secure the base including our weapons squad leader, so we were 29 in number, possibly less.

The night was still and dark as the moon had set shortly after midnight. Disturbing the quiet, the combined team of 1/C and the Iron Claw platoon started their engines and pulled out of the Alamo and onto the Mullah Fayad Highway, heading into the lawless frontier. A contingent of my soldiers and I dismounted and spread out along the line of departure on either side. The air was warm. It was 0330 and the first moving pieces of a complex machine were on their way.

I moved on the south side of the road to the left of the vehicle fleet while my platoon sergeant controlled the element on the north side of the road. We moved in what

3. Mountain Men in a Flat Land

is known as an inverted V formation. This provided us flank protection and gave us a better opportunity to detect wires further from where the IED most likely was: the road side. As we trounced through the fields, tripping over the minor ridges, the Iron Claw team crept behind us, offset by a few hundred meters. Following them were 1st Platoon's vehicles.

While the night's hibernation continued amongst the residents, the roads and skies around Yusifiyah were coming to life. A steady stream of vehicles exited the entry control point of FOB Yusifiyah, passing the lone M113 and turning left down the access road toward Route Sportster: Charlie Company Headquarters, 2nd and 3rd Platoons, Charlie, 3rd Platoon, Bravo, the EOD element, and more. Bravo Company headquarters with its 1st and 2nd Platoons and an advisor element from Alpha with partnered Iraqis had boarded Black Hawk helicopters at BIAP and were approaching on their air access of advance.

As the battalion roared forward, my infantrymen led the way in front of heavily armed and armored vehicles. We were the skirmishers out front ready to detect any threat to the trucks that would prevent them from accomplishing their mission. In this case, there were three missions stacked up behind each other. The first mission was to clear the Mullah Fayad Highway and open a line of communication from the Alamo to the soon-to-be established patrol base in Rushdi Mullah. The second mission was to clear Al Taraq and seize control of the 90-degree turn in the road. The final mission, which belonged to 3rd Platoon, Bravo Company, was to deliver necessary supplies and equipment to Rushdi Mullah. From the lead engineer vehicle to the final HMMWV there were 53 vehicles stretched out over more than a mile.

As we inched forward, Black Hawk helicopters moved in from the north in two waves aiming for a pair of landing zones (LZ). At 0400, the helicopters began to touch down one mile south of the Rushdi Mullah objective, depositing 1st Platoon, Bravo with its attached Iraqi's and advisers. Around that time, 2nd Platoon and its contingent began landing approximately a mile southeast of the objective. The elements consolidated and began moving out. Bravo Company had bifurcated Rushdi Mullah, assigning 1st Platoon the west side of town while 2nd Platoon took the east side.

Now there were three elements picking their way through the uneven farmland in the dark dealing with friction. Movement proved difficult under night vision as the devices used to improve visibility hindered depth perception. Compounding this was the soft, muddy soil. The friction of war also showed itself in the form of communications issues. My element on the left side of the road could not raise our element on the right side via the radio (nor could the engineers) despite them being only a couple hundred yards from us. After moving to my platoon sergeant, my RTO was able to fix their radios. However, observing the terrain on their side, I pulled them to the south of the road and we pushed on as one unit. There was little threat of a command wire on that side and they were restricted to 30 m from the road to a parallel canal.

The element Bravo Company led was moving closer to their objective having a relatively smooth movement. The lead element approached an intersection of the dirt farm roads that crisscrossed the countryside when the quiet erupted. An advisor to the Iraqi Army, or someone near him, stepped on a pressure plate setting off an IED. The blast threw the officer into the air but no one else around him was wounded. Soldiers moved quickly to stabilize him and they called for helicopter medical evacuation (MEDEVAC) which arrived quickly and loaded him. Soon the officer was in a bird on his way to the Combat Support Hospital (CSH, pronounced "cash") in Baghdad. His war was over. He would survive but lose parts of three limbs. His wounding only served as a temporary setback; Bravo continued on toward the objective.

My platoon was making progress, but the nature of the task was slow. Ideally, by sunrise we would be clear of Al Taraq and the rest of the company would have seized a foothold on the south edge of town, but it was getting later in the morning. Before Morning Nautical Twilight (BMNT), the point where the first faint light crests the horizon, was 0503 that morning. We were not far from Al Taraq at the moment, a little more than a kilometer, which would normally take a platoon in those conditions about fifteen minutes, but between the platoon and the bend in the road were at least three canals of unknown width and depth that would take time to negotiate, and there was always the possibility of finding a command wire.

Those two obstacles came together shortly after the advisor was wounded. Prior to our mission, my company commander had warned me of an intelligence report of sporadic gunfire from the canal near the Alamo. Here we were, but not under fire. It was likely the enemy had no idea 1st Platoon was there. It was still dark and the main show was already in contact down at Rushdi Mullah, but we did have a problem. We had no idea if the canal was crossable and really no way to tell. Before I could ruminate on what to do, my lead team leader grabbed the bull by the horns and waded in with another team leader right behind him. Standing on the east bank, I was about to step in when the call came that the NCOs on the far side had found a wire.

We relayed the information to our engineers who came to the spot where the canal intersected the road. The Iron Claw team found a 105 mm howitzer shell prepared as an IED in the area where the canal ran into the road. They had to call EOD up from the rear of the armada to diffuse of the bomb. While everything worked out all right, it was well after first light that the situation was resolved enough to move on. EOD had been too far away to support in a timely manner. There was palpable frustration on the command net with the delay as we began moving on.

Down in Rushdi Mullah, things were a lot smoother. Although an officer had been severely wounded, the combined element came under no direct resistance. The two elements closed on their objectives and began clearing them without any issues. The enemy had either gone to ground or left on the approach of the helicopters (or the sound of the IED).

Back on the Mullah Fayad Highway, my platoon pushed forward with wet pants and heavy, muddy boots as the rising sun slowly ratcheted up the temperature. It was difficult moving in the muddy fields and I wondered if we would be able to effectively fight if the enemy engaged us. We lacked traction but the roads seemed like death traps. We could at least suppress the enemy from the fields. On the roads we were playing into his plan.

3. Mountain Men in a Flat Land

The canals were worse than the fields. The banks were often steep making it difficult to step into the waist deep water and more difficult to climb to the opposite side. A typical infantry tactic for crossing a linear danger area is to establish nearside security and then push someone across to establish far side security and slowly push across, but the reeds prevented anyone on the nearside from overwatching anyone crossing, so there was a great risk in getting guys across until the first three or four made it.

Less risky, but much worse for those of us on the ground was that many of the canals not only served to irrigate the farm fields but to move sewage. In all the things any of my soldiers or I expected to experience in combat, wading up to our bellies in human waste was certainly not one of the them. The stench was horrible and the thought of whatever germs, bacteria, or disease might be swimming in the water was unpalatable. What leads a man to do it, to not just refuse to go any further, is hard to say, but part of military socialization is accomplishing the mission and doing what your teammates need you to do. Certainly that was part of it.

The canals were annoying and a minor tactical problem, but bigger issues awaited. The engineers in the Iron Claw team spotted a man emerge from the reeds on the north side of the road and dig a hole near the highway. He then dropped something into the hole, moved to the south side, and repeated. They chose not to engage and asked us to interdict the man. We were in the neighborhood of 150 to 200 meters away, and given the conditions of our boots (which felt like cement) and the field, it was a long 150 to 200 meters. We weren't getting to him anytime soon, so the engineers began to move forward to investigate with their specially equipped trucks and we pushed forward crossing a concrete lined canal of pure water. It looked deep, potentially deeper than six feet, so I decided being a pretty good swimmer, I would go first. I handed my armor and rifle to someone and got in to discover it was chest deep on an average sized man like me, so we all pushed through and into an open field just south of Al Taraq.

The plan called for us to halt where we were and wait for our vehicles to catch up. We would take a break and refill our water, but the plan had also believed that by 0700 we would be marching toward Rushdi Mullah. Now, the engineers were occupied and we were exposed in the open. The vehicles provided us our heavy firepower, but they were well behind us. We were all tired and the sun was oppressive. We were either out of water or out of appetite for it. (Knowing the bite valve to my Camelbak had been through human waste meant it wasn't going to my lips.) We kept moving forward but would have to stop soon. Before I made the call, a soldier from 1st Squad found a wire leading back to the road.

My RTO called it up and we established a security perimeter as best one can in an open field. Exposed, we had no good options. Moving forward or to our right put us on the road where we knew at least one IED existed. Though we were in control of the command wire, there could be others. Moving south would further isolate us from our support. It would be another 400 meters to any real cover. Going back would have left the engineers in a vulnerable position to any direct fire engagement. Soon, though, the situation made the decision for me.

Boom! We all lurched slightly forward in reaction and then looked back to see a plume of smoke rising from the other side of the canal. A quick call on the radio confirmed an engineer vehicle was damaged. *Boom!* Another vehicle, moving forward to establish security, was now engulfed in smoke. The vehicles retained communications and firing capabilities but could not move. The road to Rushdi Mullah was sealed with two quick blasts. The canals impaired movement through the fields and the farm roads presented a possibility of IEDs and provided no guarantee they could handle the weight of vehicles moving on them. That strong, imposing armada of vehicles had been stopped by a couple of hastily planted devices that probably cost a few hundred dollars to create.

When I moved my right-side element onto the left side to maintain communications, I left the right flank exposed. I'd made the call because our mission had been to find and report all command wires. Focused on the task rather than the purpose and lacking the experience to think about larger threats, I made the call that made the most sense to maintain control. There was little threat of a command wire on the north side. My decision enabled us to accomplish our task and therefore was not wrong, but with more experience we could have provided greater protection to the element and enabled mission accomplishment.

From where we were, we could see a mass migration out of town to the northwest as residents streamed away from the village expecting a fight to occur. (This is similar to what occurred earlier in the year when the B/1/502 PIR element was approaching Rushdi Mullah.) The engineers asked us to secure the town so they could move recovery assets forward, however, there were some complications with this. We knew there was at least one IED on the road between us and the town and we had no idea what the enemy situation was. It was logical to assume the women and children were leaving, but that the fighters remained. Ultimately, I didn't have the authority. Entering Al Taraq wasn't my call and one of those bombs exploding on us as we crossed the road would render the whole element combat ineffective. The enemy gave me no time to think it through, regardless.

A ping rang out in the distance. Many of the men heard it, but none of them discerned its meaning until an explosion occurred to the west of our position. The round landed harmlessly, about 75 meters away but it was clear the enemy had a decent understanding of how to wield his weapon. It may not be a problem now, but it could become one quickly. There were four bad options: move forward, move back, or move to either side. Moving forward was a non-starter; there was nothing to be gained by rushing into the fire. Moving to our right would take us into town and past the IEDs on the curb. To our left, lay a wide expanse of farmland. There was no cover available nor would we gain any concealment from the enemy. The rear provided us cover in the form of our vehicles and concealment in the form of the reeds along the canal. It left the engineers at the front of the line of march. A team leader suggested a fifth option: move to our two o'clock and into a set of buildings beyond the bend in the road. I nixed that. (We'd later find the curve lined with IEDs and those buildings had no roof.) I gave the order to move to our rear 300 meters where we consolidated and moved to our vehicles.

The enemy had demonstrated a level of sophistication I hadn't believed he had.

3. Mountain Men in a Flat Land

He sealed off the route into town and to Rushdi Mullah and used indirect fire to delay or deter the ground element from maneuvering. Now, his elements were exiting town in force rather than standing and fighting. There was no blocking force at either Al Taraq or Rushdi Mullah which enabled the enemy to escape our grip. Isolation is a key tenant to seizing an objective and we could not achieve it. There were not enough helicopters or forces to go around and the leadership had decided to seize both objectives without blocking forces. To mitigate this, the plan relied on speed, but the enemy and terrain had voted against speed. A less bold plan may have called for the seizure of Al Taraq followed by a subsequent seizure of Rushdi Mullah a week later. This would have boxed in the enemy in Al Taraq, but the real prize of Rushdi Mullah would have been left alone and provided the enemy indication of what was coming. There were tradeoffs to both.

The enemy was active in other parts as well. At some point in the morning, a call came into the Alpha Company command post reporting that Lieutenant Colonel Muhammad, the commander 4/4/6 IA, and the occupants of his HMMWV had been killed in an IED strike. Later, Private First Class Statieon Greenlee, an Alpha Company soldier assigned to the personal security detachment, took a sniper bullet to the head and died. Information on these events is scarce, so it is difficult to place them in time and space. However, it is clear the enemy was prepared to fight, but seemed much more prepared to stop a ground assault than an air assault. Civilian casualties were also making their way to Yusifiyah where the battalion aid station triaged and treated them.

As it reached mid-morning, Bravo Company was in Rushdi Mullah and having an easy go at the clearance of town, but its ground support element was far behind them with no realistic chance of reaching them for hours. The engineers of the Iron Claw team were dealing with the problem of two vehicles being disabled. My platoon was in a staggered column on the Mullah Fayad Highway and the rest of Charlie and others were in line behind us. 2nd Platoon, Charlie, had to return to the FOB. With Charlie Company having done little but sit in their vehicles all morning, the commander was keen to get into town before he lost all opportunity to conduct a meaningful operation. Shortly after arriving at our vehicles, the commander issued the company a fragmentary order (FRAGO)—a short order normally amending an operations order—directing my platoon to take 2nd Platoon's place and for the seizure to commence shortly. Seven hours behind schedule, it was time to seize the initiative.

The shift from a supporting effort walking point for a ground assault to becoming the main effort for a company assault was easier than may seem. Soldiers are naturally flexible when well trained. They drill on tasks often enough as a unit so it allows them to adjust. Obviously, reconnaissance, rehearsals, and planning make things better, but in a pinch soldiers can react with effectiveness. As the platoon leader, it was not difficult either. I had taken part in the planning process and knew 2nd Platoon's mission and had their graphics on me. Certainly, I had been disappointed at not being a direct part of the clearance of Al Taraq, but not letting that prevent me from understanding the mission of my adjacent units and higher headquarters paid dividends.

I went from vehicle to vehicle updating the NCOs on the new plan. It was easier than trying to communicate to seven other vehicles by radio and I could show the graphics to the squad leaders and team leaders as I talked. We switched out a few of the soldiers from ground to vehicle and vice versa, but generally kept the same thirteen on the ground for the movement into the town. The vehicle "tax" hadn't seemed so high when were just walking, but dedicating fifteen or so soldiers to man the vehicles and having seven away from the platoon really put a strain on our numbers now. I split the dismounts into two sections. My 1st Squad Leader would lead one; my 3rd Squad Leader would lead the other. I retained over all control and my platoon sergeant was with our medic prepared to receive any casualties.

We moved into position near my lead vehicle while 3rd Platoon and the company headquarters crossed the canal north of the road and got into formation. We crept forward trying to pace our movement with the element on the north side of the canal. We couldn't see them but had an idea of how long it would take them. Movement was easier in the day light and on drier land. As we passed by the crippled vehicles, we began to see the town. The reed line ended about 20 meters from a canal that ran north to south parallel to the eastern edge of Al Taraq.

The canal was the same one that 1st Platoon had crossed earlier in the mission. The company came online and 1st Platoon established a support by fire position. 3rd Platoon crossed the canal and moved into town. They seized a foothold in the first couple of buildings and established an overwatch position with the commander coming up behind them. Once their position was set, the company first sergeant and a medical team consisting of a physician's assistant and the company's senior medic moved in to establish a casualty collection point. At that point, I ordered my 1st Squad to enter the town while 3rd Squad remained in the support by fire position.

Prior to the mission, the commander or one of his headquarters guys had taken an overhead image of the town and numbered each building for common reference. It makes it easy when reporting information and to keep track of units. However, this imagery was the bird's eye and we infantrymen possessed the cat's eye. There are important differences. We quickly found ourselves encountering buildings not on the imagery and trying to keep the commander abreast of our progress while creating new common numbers. Unlike in the United States, there were no house numbers, no street names … no addresses. In the intervening years, I've seen a big Army trend and tactical unit trend to eschew ground reconnaissance in favor of overheard reconnaissance and surveillance. It's the bird's eye versus the cat's eye all over, but in my experience you need both, so long as the Army operates on the ground, which appears to be the case for the foreseeable future.

The buildings were all locked, which makes me wonder what we would have accomplished had we entered town when the engineers requested. I had been smart to bring the imagery, but I had not considered bringing breaching tools and we had left our shotguns in the vehicles. My RTO reported that the doors were locked and we didn't have our tools. Predictably, the commander directed us to breach anyway; it wasn't his problem we were not prepared. Tired and exasperated, I said, "With what?" I had no intent for my RTO to relay that but he dutifully asked the commander, "With what, over?" Thankfully, the commander didn't take offense or notice, but it was a lesson in clear communication and keeping emotions to yourself.

We found an unlocked garage containing a car in an odd state of repair. My immediate thought was that it looked like a vehicle in the process of being rigged as a VBIED. Many suicide bombers came to Yusifiyah for training and to receive their bombs, so it was possible this was one of the factories. In fact, just days before the operation, the Iraqi government released a video it had captured of a terrorist named Abu-Ayyab Al Masri—whom they credited with the making of over 2,000 VBIEDs—demonstrating his methods. The video had been found in the Yusifiyah area.[15] My RTO reported the finding and we grabbed tools from the garage to help us break locks. We were able to make up for our lack of preparation with resourcefulness. The rest of the buildings in the area yielded nothing significant and we pushed on into the homes careful not to enter the mosque.

After clearing about a quarter of the way up town, we established a security perimeter. I talked to a local we had come across, the only person left in town. He said everyone left when they saw us approaching. Around that time, soldiers from the Iraqi Army linked up with us and they went back through the houses searching them in more detail. Americans were very good at the kinetic part of clearing a building but the Iraqis were much better at searching. Further, there were less cultural issues that arose from one Iraqi searching another's stuff, especially religious and feminine possessions.

At 1500, the commander directed us to move back south and wait for our vehicles. We would resume our push to Rushdi Mullah. My men were exhausted and dehydrated and the thought of walking in that oppressing heat—it reached 102 degrees that October day—with our gear on, and crossing more canals, was less than exciting. Things continued to explode as the day went on, but there was a job to do. This is one of the reasons it is so important that young infantry officers attend Ranger School. You have to learn to lead when your body wants your own mind to take a break or quit and you have to lead men who are exhausted to mission accomplishment. I was mentally fatigued but resolute.

Water hurt us more than anything. We could not drink enough or carry enough and we continued to sweat profusely. Nearly all of our trucks were out of water and the resupply was about a mile behind our trail vehicle. Down at Rushdi Mullah, the delays on the road turned their water situation desperate. Bravo and the Iraqi Army soldiers had cleared the town and begun building up defenses at the new outpost there. They had carried all of their supplies in and worked through the hot sun filling sandbags in full kit. Now, they were critically low on water with their resupply sitting at the tail end of a long, immobile convoy. They would not get a water resupply until the following day and that came by air.

It was another three hours before we were able to get moving again. The sun had already begun to drop below the horizon when it was time to get started again. The engineer platoon we were working with switched out since their primary IED hunting vehicles were disabled, but there was no one to replace us. However, I decided to switch

Vehicles line the Mullah Fayad Highway waiting to move forward during Operation *Polar Blizzard*. More than 53 vehicles lined the road behind a slow moving foot patrol.

around the platoon. Everyone was exhausted. No one had slept much and hours upon hours of standing in a turret in the sun is in no way restful. But the drivers and gunners had fresher legs and it is always good to replace guards often lest they get complacent. Those in the vehicle, mostly 2nd Squad with some members of 1st, 3rd, and Weapons, got out on the ground under my 2nd Squad Leader. We would be in much closer contact in the vehicles due to the large curve in the road.

    I didn't like the idea of searching for IEDs in the dark. It hadn't been fun earlier and wasn't going to be fun now, but there was a real need to get the road open that night. Rushdi Mullah needed supplies. Using our formation, the inverted V, and staying off the road at least 20 meters kept the dismounts relatively safe, but the dark would reduce effectiveness no matter how we aligned and who we put on the ground.

    Fortunately, the mission barely got started before it ended. Within only a few minutes of heading out, they found the command wire we had found earlier. We hadn't done anything about it due to the events that happened between then and now. Almost immediately, 2nd Squad Leader's voice broke over the radio. It sounded like they were in trouble, but it wasn't the enemy. A helicopter coming in to land mistook the infrared strobe on the squad leader's helmet for the marker denoting an LZ and landed almost on top of the soldiers. After that, it was an easy decision to halt for the night. My commander called off the patrol. Everyone was tired, there was a new route clearance platoon that hadn't been part of the planning, and it was dark. Regardless of how hard we went, it was unlikely anything was getting to Rushdi Mullah on the ground until daylight.

Work continued on the defenses of the new outpost in Rushdi Mullah. The company needed to beef up security fast, so they filled sand bags and built positions through the night. They worked feverishly expecting the enemy to attack at any moment. Charlie occupied a house on the southern edge of town and established rudimentary defenses. The engineers pushed into the curve and set up a perimeter for the night integrated with my platoon. My RTO and I went into Charlie's perimeter to confer with the commander. 2nd and 3rd Platoons were there now with headquarters and the small complex was teeming with bodies. There was no room for our platoon.

With the road now unclogged, the battalion pushed forward a tank platoon from Company B, 1st Battalion, 22nd Infantry Regiment, (B/1–22) a mechanized infantry company team attached to the battalion, to help secure the curve. Their mission in the operation had been to secure the 90 degree curve near Rushdi Mullah where the battalion would build a battle position once my platoon and the engineers cleared through. Most of the day they had been stuck behind Charlie Company, but now were forward with us. Since we would all be working together in the morning, the three platoon leaders conferred and planned out security for the night. The terrain around the roads was less than ideal and essentially our vehicles could do little more than space out on the road, but we had a lot of guns and could look in multiple directions, plus the tanks brought thermal sites. What we didn't know is that all around us on the south side of the curve were IEDs lying dormant in the dirt next to the road.

The company was able to resupply us on water, but could only offer us tips to conserve gas. We had left Yusifiyah with full tanks, but now we were well past the point we planned to be complete and there was no fueler nearby nor could we break away and return to Yusifiyah for gas, so we had to go the night without using the air conditioning systems. I briefed the plan moving forward and tried to get some sleep in the front passenger seat, but there is little leg room and no way to recline in a HMMWV. We rotated shifts in the turret and listening to the radio.

As morning came, I went truck to truck rousing the weary from their restless slumber and getting our dismounts ready. The dismounts were primarily those who had started the previous morning. We formed up in the dark, but waited until close to sunrise to get going so we could actually see any command wires we came across. As we stepped off, we found a wire leading to the road and the engineer platoon leader told us to bypass it and keep moving forward. I thought it odd, but we pushed on. My interaction with the new Iron Claw platoon leader led me to believe he was not as strong of a leader as the previous one. He seemed overly reliant on his NCOs and indecisive. It is one thing to listen to your NCOs, another to be dependent. Later we would lead EOD to the wire and they determined it wasn't connected to an IED, but there was no way for him or his platoon to know that at the time.

After the curve at Al Taraq, the road ran north to south until it got to Rushdi Mullah and then curved 90 degrees off to the west again. A canal ran along the east side of the road similar to the one on the north side the day before, so we walked primarily on the west side of the road about 100 meters from the highway. With all the explosions, I figured the hardest avenue of approach for us was the best. Within the first 100 meters we hit another sewage canal, this one smelling worse than any of the other ones. I cringed moving through it, and we joked about it to dull the pain.

October 3 was much less eventful, but still dangerous. The predicted attack on the new base in Rushdi Mullah never came. Bravo fought thirst, but no insurgents that day. The insurgents provided them much needed time to get their defenses up to snuff. Platoons 2 and 3 of Charlie Company were able to clear the entirety of Al Taraq smoothly, unabated. They were complete by noon. For the new team consisting of my platoon, the Iron Claw team, and the tank platoon, there was no direct fire enemy contact.

We were moving south when we came across a major, reed-lined canal that had flooded past its banks. Just getting near it put us up to our knees in water. 1st Squad searched for a break in the reeds, but found none. My Alpha Team Leader in 1st Squad who seemed to always take danger easily, pushed into the water. Suddenly, he said, "I can't feel the bottom." As we turned to look at him, he said about as calmly as possible, "Help." He grabbed one of the reeds, which were pretty strong, and handed his rifle to his squad leader while the latter waded into the canal. The Bravo Team Leader grabbed the squad leader and I grabbed the Bravo Team Leader. Pulling the Alpha Team Leader out looked like Jimmy Bailey and his chain gang rescuing Harry from the frozen pond.

Unable to find a passage to the north, our only option was to cross at the road. I called the engineers to push a vehicle forward that could support us and look for any disturbed earth near the canal. Finally, we crossed the Mullah Fayad at the Rushdi Mullah curve only to hear an explosion behind us. One of the tanks had been struck by an MRE bomb, an IED planted in the wrapper of the Meals Ready to Eat ration. The IED blew part of the track off the tank, disabling it for mobility but not rendering it unable to shoot or communicate. As we reached our limit of advance, I decided we should move back to our vehicles since we were once again exposed in an open farm field. The engineers reported that they suspected up to five IEDs on the road. We got orders to move back to Al Taraq but remain on standby to support the engineers. By now, the tanks were forward and in position where the two battle positions near the curve would go in. The road from Mullah Fayad to Rushdi Mullah was open, but not safe by any stretch.

Bravo Company, which was beaten down from the sun, exhausted from a full night of guard and manual labor, and filled with thirst from having to ration water, began the work of preparing the two battle positions that would help control the 90 degree curve in the Mullah Fayad Highway as well as the access road to the Rushdi Mullah. The two tanks controlled the curve and provided both Bravo and the Iron Claw team with excellent optics and range down the long, straight stretch of road coming into and going out of the curve. Bravo's new positions would be rudimentary to start until better equipment arrived, but the work needed to be started.

Infanti was on the move to inspect the new positions, provide guidance, and visit troops. Chaplain Bryan was in tow and described the drive from Yusifiyah, "Destroyed American vehicles littered the highways leading to the main objective areas, including one semi-trailer supply truck that rested thirty feet in front of its skeletal undercarriage. Doors open and windows shattered, the large vehicle sat deathly still, a mute casualty of a devastating bomb.... We weaved left and right as we sped along the highway, dodging IED craters every few feet...."[16] There may be a bit of exaggeration in this, there could not have been IED holes every few feet, but it provides the reader a glimpse of what the battalion went through to open the route.

Back at Al Taraq, I had worked to secure the commander's approval to go back to Yusifiyah. Our trucks were low on gas and at least two sorely needed maintenance. The Army Jeep may have been reliable, but its replacement, the HMMWV loaded down with extra armor, was not. Primarily, I wanted the guys to shower and change clothes. My main concern was health. We had walked through our share of human waste, and we needed to get clean. The commander said we could go at 1500 and take the military working dogs, who were hot, and out of treats, with us.

But things happen to alter plans and our platoon was called on once again to be flexible, which would be a great skill for the soldiers over the next year. Special Operations Forces tipped the Polar Bears off to a possible cache north of Al Taraq along the Janabi Run Canal. 2nd Platoon went to investigate and found several among the reeds. The commander needed to go get eyes on and catalog the contents. He turned to me and asked, jokingly I hope, if I wanted to finally do something infantry related. Of course I wanted to be a part of the mission, so I grabbed some soldiers and we loaded into three trucks and escorted the commander and his truck. We drove north along the road paralleling the town and linked up with 2nd Platoon.

When we got out of our vehicles, Iraqi Army soldiers were standing around, most without their equipment on or rifles in hand. It was frustrating to see, but I was informed they had found the caches. The caches had been dug into the opposite slope of the canal bank and hidden in the tall reeds that lined the dirt road paralleling the canal. The commander began to log everything and get pictures to send to the battalion intelligence officer, the S2, for analysis.

The sun was starting to dip lower in the sky and dark was not that far off. The commander had a large part of his force in unfamiliar terrain that was not easily defensible due to the dead space (area a gunner could not observe). The company would not be able to move the contents of the caches or have them destroyed until morning when EOD could get relief from clearing IEDs on the route. With the day away, he developed his security plan for the night. He brought additional vehicles onto the canal road and released us to move back to FOB Yusifiyah for maintenance, resupply, and hygiene.

The lead driver had his foot hard on the gas. I'm not sure if he was trying to outrun the IEDs or the possibility of getting another mission. We hit a snag back toward the Alamo where the road was clogged. My driver had to turn the engine off so we could save a few fumes. By the seat of our pants, we made into the gate at Yusifiyah and to the fuel point. Before the night was through, two of our HMMWVs were deemed inoperable. Their crews would be up trying to fix them most of the night.

Commando Hunter would continue for several more weeks, but *Polar Blizzard* had come to an end. The mission was a good one. It was not without its flaws. We had not been able to isolate the towns, we had been slow to get into Al Taraq, and the route, though open, was not safe by any means, but it had been aggressive and seized a foothold deep in Indian country and shown the enemy we weren't there to raid but to control. We had found and cleared 12 IEDs and several more had gone off. It would be another week before all the previously buried IEDs were neutralized. It was a foundational experience for many of the young soldiers and officers experiencing combat for the first time. But there was still work to be done. However, pride was in order. Reflecting on my platoon's piece of the operation, I wrote, "It was a crappy mission to draw, but it was a good one to be a part of."

Polar Blizzard was 4–31 IN's opening salvo in its counterinsurgency campaign and it was almost purely an offensive action. Charlie Company had carried a 5-ton truck full of humanitarian supplies, but due to the mass exodus from town, the company didn't distribute these until after the operation. There was some expectation for civil engagement beyond the passing out of aide, but that never materialized for the same reasons. While not a violent offensive action—there are no recorded direct or indirect fire engagements—it was an aggressive push into the area. In this, the path the Polar Bears and Commando Brigade took was not that different than that of Marine Major General Richard Natonski (*Operation Phantom Fury*: Fallujah II) or Army Colonels H.R. McMaster (*Operation Restoring Rights*: Tel Afar) and Sean MacFarland (Ramadi) who had used a heavy offensive action to seize control of key areas as the prelude to more security and stability-based operations. The biggest difference is that those actions were in large urban areas. The Commando Brigade was applying similar principles but in a rural setting.

Ultimately, the leadership recognized the importance of controlling Rushdi Mullah just as the previous battalion had and the Polar Bears had the manpower to take hold of it as they were not burdened with Lutafiyah or Mahmudiyah anymore. Going in aggressively came with risks. There was a long line of communication from the FOB at Yusifiyah to the base at Rushdi Mullah and two platoons and a company headquarters were now committed on a permanent basis, but the battalion gained the advantage of nearly 12 months to develop the area versus a slow, methodical push into the town. Time would tell if they made the right call.

As early as 3 October, Charlie and the battalion's forward support company began an initial look at where it would emplace a position on the curve to provide overwatch down both stretches of road. They discussed where it might go and what kind of material may be used such as a tower or HESCO (Hercules Engineering Solutions Consortium) barriers. It was clear that the favored area was along the curve as it straightened out on the way to Rushdi Mullah. Those who were part of the ground reconnaissance of this area decided not to incorporate the two unfinished buildings into the position. The final position would be a 30 foot tower manned by two soldiers and two vehicles

3. Mountain Men in a Flat Land

at the base of the tower to provide automatic weapons fire and to protect any enemy attempt to infiltrate the tower. This provided control of the curve, but left the town of Al Taraq in the hands of the enemy.

It was obvious that Charlie could not leave Al Taraq unguarded. As the operation ended, nearly the whole company had congregated in the house which had served as a base of operations on the night of 2 October. There were still rudimentary defenses and guard positions (a single strand of wire not held in by pickets and guards without cover, concealment, or range cards). The commander commanded his company with a radio and a handful of headquarters soldiers and the three platoons competed for room to lie down between missions in the building and courtyard. As yet there was no plan to retain a position in Al Taraq and there were no engineer assets available to help build up defenses if necessary. Just before the operation, Charlie Company took over Bravo Company's command post at FOB Yusifiyah, freeing Bravo to move in force to Rushdi Mullah. Charlie took responsibility for Yusifiyah-proper, but Bravo still retained control of the Alamo. This created an odd situation where one company was responsible for battle space inside another company's area of responsibility. The Al Taraq problem remained.

Regardless, Bravo continued working to build up the position at Rushdi Mullah and fortify BPs 148 and 150 guarding the curve in the highway and the access road to the main position. The roads from Yusifiyah to Rushdi Mullah remained perilous, but supplies could come by land now allowing them to make progress faster. Despite their efforts, nothing was going to be great. BP 148 was "[a] lone connex surrounded by empty hescos [sic] beside a road."[17] The HESCO barriers would get filled as equipment allowed. The work of engineers in this fight has been sorely underappreciated. Most know of the IED hunting teams, the Iron Claw route clearance soldiers conducting a sapper-type mission, but vertical and horizontal engineers were a high demand, low supply industry. There was never enough equipment to satisfy requirements. Filling HESCO barriers by hand was nearly impossible, so units had to wait for bucket loaders to become available. Until the position got stronger, two HMMWVs and an extra rooftop machine gun position provided protection. To give an indication of the life and times of a solider, troops at BP 150 had to cross about 50 meters of unprotected space to squat down onto a toilet seat to use the bathroom in a sunken in enclosure and then bag up their waste and throw it on the burn pit. Again, the Polar Bears eschewed comfort for the sake of the mission.

My platoon returned on 4 October, the morning after going back to Yusifiyah, and immediately went out to assist the soldiers guarding the caches. We brought them some supplies and assisted as needed. Later in the day, while making the same turn onto the canal road we had, the mortar platoon hit an IED, believed to have been initiated by a pressure plate. All the trucks occupants were wounded. The front end of the vehicle was completely blown off, but the soldiers were evacuated. Describing his thoughts while watching the evacuation birds take off, Chaplain Bryan wrote, "The doors lay on the ground and blood splatter covered the cabin of the vehicle. I felt pain for the wounded men who had once occupied it, along with fear that another bomb under the road could explode. It was then I grasped just how intelligent and mobile the enemy really was.... I sensed they were watching us from everywhere."[18] The enemy may have had the IED already in place to guard the cache sites, but had not been able to hook it to the initiation device until the morning of the 4th. Pressure plates need some sort of electrical source and usually can only remain in place for 24 hours before the battery dies. Still, how we never hit it ourselves has remained on my mind all these years.

Bravo had been working feverishly to be ready for the enemy to counterattack and Charlie saw it as only a matter of time, but it was Alpha Company that faced the first real test from the enemy following *Operation Polar Blizzard*. The same day the mortar platoon hit the IED, Battle Position 155 out on Route Peggy—the likely area where Lieutenant Colonel Muhammad's vehicle was hit—came under a heavy enemy assault. Employing three machine guns, the enemy approached from different sides of the building and surrounded 3rd Platoon and the Iraqi Army soldiers posted there. The position, a small building surrounded by farm fields, provided an easy target. The platoon sergeant on site led the U.S. response and coordinated for indirect fire and air-based assets. With the 28 soldiers pinned down in a desperate fight for survival, he crawled on his belly across the roof so that he could get his eyes on the enemy. He identified the location of the worst fighting and called in an Apache strike to destroy the position. Once this occurred, the enemy was beaten back and unable to continue the attack. The enemy had placed a lot of resources into a failed attack and the Polar Bears demonstrated they would not leave easily. For his leadership, the platoon sergeant would be awarded the Silver Star.[19]

If the blow of the failed counterattack on BP 155 wasn't enough, the enemy was taking a huge loss to its logistical base. For Charlie, finding caches was becoming routine. The enemy clearly had built a support zone in the area around the town. Some of the munitions and explosives probably came from the military industrial facilities in the area that the Army failed to secure in 2003. However, a large amount of it likely came through smuggling routes. By the end of 5 October, roughly 48 hours from the time 2nd Platoon and the Iraqi Army discovered the first cache, 2nd and 3rd Platoons had uncovered a total of thirty. That night, the battalion's scouts were out on a mission when they came across something to the east of town that looked like a cache. However, in the dark, they didn't want to investigate too closely lest it be rigged, so they took the grid down and passed it to Charlie. To that point, all of the caches were discovered north of the town along the Janabi Run Canal.

Charlie Company was pretty thin at that point. Anytime someone found a cache they had to secure it until EOD could destroy it or at least a patrol could come pick up the contents. The base required security and the company ran patrols back to Yusifiyah for supplies and fuel. When the commander passed the grid and the mission on to me, there weren't a lot of men available. Most of my manpower was sucked down by security, so I grabbed a handful of soldiers and a junior NCO. Not only were we strung out, we were not as bound by rules. We barely had a squad out with us to operate more than a mile from friendly troops and thought little of it. Times would change.

3. Mountain Men in a Flat Land

It was a hot day, as all October days were, but we were dry and excited. Our platoon had been on the sideline of the cache finding business; we were ready to get in on the action, but we were sorely disappointed. Getting to the grid was easy and certainty there was a cache there. However, there was nothing in it. Insurgents had dug a 55-gallon drum into the side of a mound, but either had never filled it or had removed its contents before we arrived. I was hot and frustrated and thinking with emotion more than reason. *We are not going back without a cache!* I paced around the site for a few minutes looking around, hoping I'd find something. I saw a slight amount of loose dirt where everything else was hard packed and dry. I pointed to the patch of dirt and said, "Dig!"

Someone asked, "Are you serious, sir?"

I said I was. I think they were all skeptical and probably could sense I had nothing more than a hunch. Digging in the heat of Iraq with body armor on is both strenuous and cumbersome, but soldiers follow legal and moral orders. Still, I don't think I or anyone else really thought we'd find anything. It only took two or three thrusts of the shovel to hear a *ping*. Soon, we had a 90-mm rocket with English writing on it. Then

A cache consisting of, among other things, eighty-six 90 mm rockets discovered in October 2006 after the author noticed loose dirt near another cache site.

we found another, and another, and another. One of my soldiers dropped to his knees and just started digging like a prairie dog burrowing, pulling out rocket after rocket. By the time the hole ran dry, we'd found eighty-six 90 mm rockets, one 155 mm shell, and a rocket or round of unknown size that looked like a giant mortar round.

Later that day, while we were guarding the cache, 2nd Squad was on another patrol slightly to the north and west of us. Moving along a reed lined canal, they uncovered three PKM (Pulemyot Kalashnikova) 7.62 caliber machine guns with belts seated in the feed tray and an RPG launcher with two rounds. It was not really a cache but a set of weapons staged for an attack. Given the previous day's attack at BP 155 where insurgents assaulted from three directions with a machine gun each side, it is likely a complex attack on either the temporary command post in Al Taraq or one of the units up on the Janabi Run Canal was in store. The attack never materialized.

Not far from that site, 2nd Squad uncovered two more caches, one with seven 60 mm mortar rounds and another with RPG rounds, ammunition, and a gun that belonged to one of the helicopters that had been shot down by the Aeisha Brigade earlier in the year. By this point, more of the platoon was available and my platoon sergeant had some of the vehicles near 2nd Squad. He started moving the vehicles down the dirt farm road near the canal the squad was searching. However, these banks and edges were not engineered with anything more than a Kia Bongo in mind, if that, so as my platoon sergeant moved the vehicles forward to assist in the collection of the caches, the lead HMMWV slid into the canal and began to sink on one side. Soon, the next HMMWV came up to help pull it out and suffered a similar fate. At the time, I was very frustrated, but by the time I got home the following year, many HMMWVs in other platoons had made their way into canals on these tight farm roads. The commander informed me that it would be until the next morning before an M88 armored recovery vehicle could get to us to pull the vehicles out. We would have to establish a patrol base and guard the vehicles and caches overnight, so we hunkered down for a night of fighting mosquitos and hoping the vehicles didn't slip too far into the drink.

The cache hunting is just one example of the myriad initiatives Bravo and Charlie undertook to deny the enemy the ability to disrupt operations. *Polar Blizzard* was a shock to the enemy system and for the first time he had large numbers in his yard for an extended period of time. Aside from security and improving positions, Bravo and Charlie were spending little time sitting on the bases. Platoons and parts of platoons patrolled constantly, applying pressure and making it hard for the enemy to set the tone. The initiative clearly rested with the Polar Bears. While inspecting the caches on the Janabi Run Canal, Infanti, speaking to a reporter, summed up a simple philosophy for the battalion post–*Polar Blizzard*, "We're attacking all the bad guys who are attacking the guys who want to be left alone…. They're thanking us for providing more security for them."[20]

While things continued to blow up daily on the Mullah Fayad Highway, especially on the stretch from Al Taraq to BP 148, the battalion was in control of most of the line of communication that ran from Yusifiyah to the Yusifiyah Thermal Power Plant, but that place remained open to terrorists. None of the previous operations had done more

3. Mountain Men in a Flat Land

Two of the author's HMMWVs slipped into the canal after a curious platoon sergeant misjudged the strength of the canal road. Scenes like this were not atypical.

than disrupt insurgent activity. Kershaw and Infanti both wanted to wrest control of it from the insurgents as quickly as possible. Kershaw called the power plant "sort of an al Qaeda way point for terrorists moving from the predominantly western part of the country into sanctuaries to attack Baghdad."[21] To both, things had gone well, but that meant striking harder not being satisfied. The brigade began working to get a unit onto the power plant grounds that could stay.

A week following the air assault and the same time Infanti spoke to the reporter, Bravo was still working round the clock to build up Rushdi Mullah. An adage of the defense is that you never stop improving your positions, and Bravo worked hard to be prepared for an attack. The enemy fired mortars at them to disrupt their work but the attacks were inaccurate. Soldiers bounced between guard and filling sandbags if they weren't out on patrol searching for caches, securing the area, and gathering information on the people and environment. The cycle was rough but necessary. Sharp, a squad leader in Bravo Company, compared conditions to a passage from the Book of Nehemiah (4:15–23), which describes half of the men on guard and the other half working while holding their weapons. As Verse 16 states, "From that day on, half of my men did the work, while the other half were equipped with spears, shields, bows and armor. The officers posted themselves behind all the people of Judah who were building the wall. Those who carried materials did their work with one hand and held a weapon in the other, and each of the builders wore his sword at his side as he worked. But the man who sounded the trumpet stayed with me."[22] The men can never go anywhere without their sword and never change clothes, quite apt.

Charlie Company had less manual labor to do. At the time, Al Taraq remained a temporary position so work was mostly focused on immediate defenses and security came more from constant patrolling than hard positions. Thus, cache searching continued in earnest. The enemy had been relatively silent over the previous week and Charlie had something to do with that. On 9 October, we opened up the searching south of town and came across a 120-mm mortar system in a series of caches. First, we found a couple of mortar rounds under some brush and then using a metal detector one of the grenadiers came across some loose dirt and discovered the mortar tube. Just down the way we found the base plate thrown into the canal. We may have been close to coming in contact with the mortar team. Within minutes, Kershaw and his security detachment were on the scene whisking the tube and base plate off for an easy life of being a brigade trophy. The brigade commander provided the solider who'd found the tube a coin and informed us it was the first mortar system captured in the brigade. We later came across some test tubes stuffed with explosives with an artillery fuse on top of them. Neither we nor EOD could truly determine what they were (A homemade hand grenade? A makeshift bouncing betty?). It was interesting handiwork, but EOD said the fuse and explosives were incompatible.

A few days later, 2nd Platoon headed west of town and uncovered a treasure trove of caches to include four mortar tubes, a recoilless rifle, and a suicide belt. After that, Charlie's focus shifted to searching in that area and it proved fruitful. At one point, we had found so many caches that it became routine and it seemed if you came back empty handed, you had done something wrong. A team leader in 3rd Platoon captured the feeling of cache searching pretty well when he said only half-jokingly that it was "… like an Easter egg hunt, only you roll the dice every time you do it."[23] We were very fortunate none of the caches were rigged with anti-tampering devices.

Arwa Damon, patrolling with the company commander and 3rd Platoon on 17 October noted the upbeat attitude of the company. She wrote, "One would never think they were operating under circumstances in which a wrong step, an unlucky jab with a knife into the ground or an insurgent attack could cost them a limb or their lives."[24] This elation probably stemmed from the feeling of winning that came with finding each cache and denying the enemy use of the material. By that point, the equipment to make more than 1,000 IEDs had been captured. It was intoxicating.

Eventually, though, the well ran dry and the trail grew cold. Finding caches in the area became an exception rather than a rule, but the work Charlie Company did significantly hampered the enemy's ability to fight the way he wanted. Not only did Charlie remove an incredible amount of munitions from the battlefield but it also kept up a dizzying presence in the area that made it hard for the enemy to move. Neither Bravo nor Charlie came under any significant contact those October days. Sporadic, short firefights occurred and occasionally a vehicle would hit an IED, but for the most part the enemy could not effectively attack the Polar Bears. He may have been on the run; he may have been significantly disrupted; he may have just been observing. Whatever he was doing, he was allowing the Polar Bears to get their way.

From 3 October to 19 October, Charlie Company removed the following items from the battlefield:

Weapons

Hand grenade, all types	23
RPG launcher	12
AK-47, 7.62 mm rifle	10
82 mm mortar tube	5
Improvised rocket launcher	5
PKM, 7.62 mm machine gun	5
RPK, 7.62 mm machine gun	5
Anti-tank mine	4
DShK, 12.7 mm machine gun	3
14.5 mm anti-aircraft gun	3
Yugoslavian Mauser	3
Iranian HK	3
Machine gun, unknown type	2
SPG-9 73 mm recoilless rifle	1
120 mm mortar tube	1
60 mm mortar tube	1
SKS 7.62 mm carbine	1

Ammunition/Munitions

7.62 mm round, all types	12,955
12.7 mm armor piercing round	3006
14.5 mm anti-aircraft round	676
23 mm high explosive rounds	233
SVD-63 Dragunov round	200
.50 caliber round	200
82 mm mortar shell	171
120 mm mortar shell	162
60 mm mortar shell	161
RPG round, all types	101
90 mm rocket	86
30 mm round	54
Rocket, unknown type	13
130 mm artillery shell	12
105 mm artillery shell	11
90 mm recoilless rocket round	9
155 mm artillery shell	6
122 mm mortar round	5
20 mm rocket	5
Liquid explosive, 55 gallon barrel	4
22 mm rocket	4
500 lb aircraft bomb in shipping crate	2
107 mm rocket	2
120 mm sabot round	1
85 mm artillery shell	1
12 mm rocket	1

IEDs/Explosives

Pound, home made explosive (HME)	455
Pressure plate	50
Directional charge	28
Stick of explosives (TNT, dynamite, HME)	17
MRE bomb	6
Suicide belt	1
Soda bottle bomb	1

Other

Roll/spool of wire/detonation chord	13
Aircraft bomb casing	4
Pipe	7[25]

The above list does not contain everything. Charlie Company found a fair amount of IED making components along with pieces to machines guns and mortar tubes (bipods, spare barrels, etc.) that I have not listed above. The haul is impressive and gives an indication of why the enemy was off balance. Of note are the three anti-aircraft guns that likely belonged to the Aeisha Brigade.

As the cache finding became less frequent, soldiers continued to press the enemy moving through fields and towns by day and night never giving him much breathing room. Charlie had an advantage at the time. Unencumbered by the requirements of manning and building a base, all three platoons minus some for security were available to patrol. Life out at Al Taraq was Spartan. Soldiers generally ate years-old MREs or ready packed meals colloquially known as "Jimmy Deans." Shower and laundry facilities were non-existent, but warm bottles of water were plentiful and most soldiers received steady shipments of baby wipes for hygiene through the mail. Soldiers urinated in a common trough known as a "piss pit" and defecated in a plastic sack filled with a kitty litter–type substance that they spread out over a portable water cooler. Called a Wag Bag, the packet came with an extra sealable bag to hold the waste bag and a wet wipe and small packet of toilet paper (which was actually the napkin from an MRE). Soldiers threw the bag on a fire pit to be burned along with the unit's trash. My forward observer's RTO and my RTO made a hilarious video tutorial on the use of a Wag Bag; as for me, it's still hard to drink water from a yellow and red cooler.

We often slept packed into rooms or under the stars in the courtyard. If it rained, things were extra crowded, but when the weather was clear, sleeping outside could be comfortable if not pleasant. Conditions were similar for Bravo and Delta, though most soldiers in Delta lived in a dusty building and many Alpha soldiers were forward as well under similar conditions. If there was electricity, it came from the unreliable city power for Charlie, which normally amounted to a few hours a day. Regardless, there was no internet and the companies generally had one Iridium satellite phone each, so a soldier may get 10 minutes a week if that to call home.

Soldiers sleep in the courtyard of the compound that would become T147 in Al Taraq. Note the makeshift toilet at left. Soldiers eschewed comfort to live among the populace.

At FOB Yusifiyah, soldiers could get one to two hot meals a day, shower, use a portable toilet, and sleep on a cot and may be able to use fifteen to thirty minutes of slow, spotty internet in a day. Soldiers enjoyed making trips back to the FOB for maintenance or to get supplies so they could enjoy basic amenities for an hour or two. What those at Yusifiyah gained in comfort, if that's what existed there, they made up for in being a target. It was much easier for enemy mortarmen to fire on Yusifiyah than the small bases. Tina Susman, a staff writer for the *Los Angeles Times*, observing the battalion in late May 2007, wrote that "Most [soldiers] ... stay in austere bases that are little more than empty buildings turned into dorm-like dwellings with no running water, plumbing or privacy. They are cold in the winter and hot in the summer, when temperatures rise above 120 degrees. Human and other waste is disposed of in fiery pits that create a smoky stench and add to the searing heat."[26] So life was.

While most of the battalion focused in the western parts of the area of operations, south of Yusifiyah presented another challenge. The roads leading into the town of Abu Habe were classified as "black" meaning no U.S. vehicles were allowed on them. All patrols had to move in by foot. One day in the second week of October, insurgents from the area fired mortar rounds at FOB Yusifiyah. A soldier in the tactical operations center was able to track the mortar team using surveillance equipment and pinpointed the enemy in the area of Abu Habe. Alpha Company drew the mission. The element consisted of a platoon leader, platoon sergeant, a forward observer, a medic, and a machine gunner plus three more for a total of nine Americans and an additional four Iraqi soldiers. As in the Al Taraq region, patrols could be ad hoc and become weird combinations. Everyone needed to be a good rifleman. The mission was to investigate the point of origin of the mortars and attempt to recover the base plate, which the enemy team had left behind in their haste. Additionally, the battalion S2 accompanied the patrol with an eye toward learning about the area and the people.

As the patrol left the FOB, they knew they were entering into an area where every other patrol had come under fire. They also knew that any MEDEVAC was off the table. The air was "red" indicating that the weather was too poor for commanders to risk flying helicopters unless in extreme emergencies. They were almost sure to get into a fight and would have to rely on themselves to get out. At a total of thirteen men, a single casualty would make them effectively unable to perform a combat function rendering the unit *hors de combat*. The terrain leading into Abu Habe was not unlike that of the areas surrounding Rushdi Mullah and Al Taraq. There were several canals that left hiding spots for the enemy.

The patrol started off well. As the makeshift unit arrived on the scene of the point of origin, they discovered a cache of mortar rounds—30 in total—dug into the side of a canal in a manner similar to many of the Al Taraq caches. Continued searching led to two more caches. The first contained computer hard drives, cameras, and video tapes. The second was the biggest of all, a massive cache of homemade explosives.

While the soldiers celebrated their success, they also knew that it put them at risk. They were extremely vulnerable in a known enemy hotspot. No men were around, just women and children, an ominous sign. They had encroached on the insurgents' supply stocks. They had captured more material than they could carry back to the FOB. There was no way they could get a vehicle there and no one was qualified (or prepared with demolition material) to blow the explosive material in place.

The platoon leader and the platoon sergeant decided to establish a base in a house nearby while the S2 attempted to glean information from the women. They debated whether to take what they could back to the FOB or defend in place until a larger force could move to them. Before they could take action, the gun team on the roof spotted enemy activity. As the forward observer was plotting grids, the first rounds started cracking overhead. The M240B leapt into action. The platoon sergeant assigned the S2, the highest-ranking member of the patrol, a position. *Everyone has to be a good rifleman.*

Soon, the assistant gunner was down, hit by an enemy bullet and bleeding. The machine gunner grabbed his assistant and drug him into the stairwell. He turned toward the platoon leader, informing him that the enemy had damaged the machine gun and it wouldn't fire. The platoon leader called in for a MEDEVAC, but he was denied. Air was still red. The medic quickly went to work trying to stabilize the wound. It was serious. The bullet hit the assistant gunner's bicep, passed through the arm, and then settled in his chest above where his protective plate was.

With the machine gun down, the patrol appeared to be in serious peril of being overrun. They could only see one enemy, but the longer they were there, the more time he had to mass. Soldiers busted the windows and began firing back doing their best to maintain their position. Soon, though, the sweet sounds of friendly mortars impacting came to the soldiers' ears. Between the rounds and fire from the building, the enemy called off the attack.

However, there was no opportunity to maneuver and finish off the enemy. Plus, the patrol had a casualty and hadn't brought along a litter. Fortunately, the S2 had found a blanket to secure the hard drives so the soldiers were able to build a makeshift litter—something most soldiers learn in basic training.

The soldiers didn't know if the enemy had been killed, had withdrawn, or was out there lying in wait. Fortunately, it was now dark making it hard for an insurgent to accurately suppress U.S. forces. However, it slowed them down as well. The Iraqis had no night vision. Even for the U.S. soldiers, it is hard to judge depth and the grade of the ground below through goggles. The wounded soldier was stable, but needed better care than the medic could provide in the living room of a farmhouse. They needed to move just shy of mile. They were exhausted.

The patrol came across a ten-foot wide and four-foot deep canal that they couldn't get around. Soldiers had to pull the wet blanket up to their chests to keep the wounded comrade form drowning and then had to move up the steep embankment. Harrowing as it was, they made it across and 90 minutes later, though they had gone only 1500 meters, they arrived at a link up point where they could pass the casualty off to a vehicle so their friend could get help.[27]

While the Polar Bears had moved into the greater Yusifiyah area, makeshift toilets and all, the goal was not a long-term occupation. Soldiers would endure the hardships in the short term, establish a presence, put the enemy on his heels, and build the infrastructure necessary for sustained operations, but the real payoff would come if the Iraqi Army could take control and effectively provide security. (Of course, that had been a goal of the previous unit that never was achieved.) With that in mind, Kershaw updated the families while keeping the focus on the Iraqi Army. In a video teleconference with families back at Fort Drum, a couple of weeks into *Commando Hunter*, Kershaw stressed that the primary role of the brigade was training Iraqi security forces and transitioning them into the lead unit. His plan was to transfer as much battle space as possible to the Iraqis. "Slightly less than half of this [transition] has already been done here (in places outside of Yusifiyah)," Kershaw told the gathered families. "Ideally, whatever unit follows us in would not have to occupy the large sector that we are currently occupying. In that sense, we hope to progress that plan forward to reduce the number of U.S. troops needed in this sector."[28] Many of the soldiers in Bravo, Charlie, and Delta fought to set the conditions and buy time for the Iraq soldiers to get up to speed while Alpha focused on developing the Iraqi Army. Though not always transparent to the line troops, training, advising, assisting, and partnering with the Iraqi Army remained a major theme throughout the tour. In fact, nearly every time Kershaw spoke to someone or wrote something for consumption, he mentioned the development of the Iraqi Army.

Heretofore, the battalion's counterinsurgency approach had largely focused on offensive actions with a subset being security patrols. The companies had begun to establish relationships with locals, but the battalion had not conducted a focused stability operation in the first two weeks after *Polar Blizzard*. Taking advantage of the lack of concentrated enemy activity and seeing an opportunity to open a seam between the enemy and the people of Rushdi Mullah, the battalion hosted a medical clinic on 19 October in conjunction with the Commando Brigade's medical company, Company C, 210th Brigade Support Battalion. The primary goal of the operation was to gauge the medical needs of the local community to inform future operations. The 4–31 IN wanted to see what medical support was available in the community and determine what medical supplies were necessary for the future. It also provided an opportunity to gain information and look the people in the eyes.

The operation started off slow as few Iraqis showed up following a loudspeaker broadcast of the event. Thus, a patrol went out to talk to the populace and inform them of the clinic. Thereafter, turnout increased significantly. Soldiers from Delta Company established temporary traffic control points around the city to prevent insurgents from interfering. The enemy made no overt attempt to disrupt operations.

The Polar Bear battalion's medical platoon leader called it "…a positive step in the war on terror." He saw Iraqis use of the clinic as a sign of trust. To a degree, he was correct. Any collusion with the Americans could make a man a marked target, which it certainly did at times. However, attending such an event was safer than standing by the Americans in other ways. Still, it meant there was at least an opportunity for the government to gain support of the population in an area that had not seen the hand or face of the government in a while. In a statement reflecting Kershaw's, the medical platoon leader said that the goal was eventually to enable the Ministry of Support to conduct these operations. It was a long game, not a quick one. It does not appear that Iraqis—military or government—were involved in the operation, demonstrating there was still a long way to go from the present day where Americans provided for the people to the future where the government did so.[29] However, before the end of October, Iraqi Army soldiers arrived at Rushdi Mullah to live and work alongside the men of Bravo Company.[30]

The enemy had been on his heels for three weeks when he finally fired back on 22 October. As 2-14 IN was preparing to assault the Yusifiyah Thermal Power Plant with the intent to place a company there permanently at a position to be known as PB Dragon, insurgents fired mortars, automatic weapons, and RPGs at Rushdi Mullah. This was the first coordinated attack since *Polar Blizzard* established the position. During a sustained firefight, Specialist Nicholas Rogers, a medic with Bravo Company, was manning a position when the attack occurred. He immediately jumped on the M240B in his position and engaged enemy forces to his front. He would die a hero's death defending his brothers.

At his memorial ceremony, Rogers' squad leader said, "It's an expectation [making the ultimate sacrifice] that some soldiers may shy away from. Specialist Rogers did not. He died defending his men and attacking the enemy." Chaplain Bryan, a soldier's chaplain for sure, encouraged soldiers to be dedicated to duty like Rogers. "He did this not only by giving his life, but by living his life. His life was all about helping others." Rogers left behind a widow and a daughter.[31] He was the second soldier killed in action—and third to die—since the Polar Bears arrived in the Triangle of Death.

Demonstrating the issues that the battalion had in getting sustainment and protection assets to keep pace with the rapid progress, at the time of the attack, Bravo Company had still not received the engineer assets needed to fill their HESCO barriers. Bravo Company's Commander, in a 2012 interview, said "in essence we were defending our control base [sic] with a screen of fabric and sandbags. It was vulnerable in the sense that we didn't have earthen walls or some type of structure outside of the buildings that we were sitting in, but after the attack, we got the engineer assets within a couple of days. It worked out … they were actually going to try and drive a vehicle born improvised explosive device … into us, but one of my guys on the roof, who was manned with a .50 caliber [machine gun] was able to put a few rounds through the windshield of the VBIED, and the driver dumped it in the canal. We were very lucky because if that VBIED had driven towards us it would have just kept going right through the building."[32]

While Rogers died in the attack on Rushdi Mullah, the enemy still hadn't regained the initiative. Soldiers continued to see some progress with locals. Bravo's commander sounded hopeful when telling *Washington Post* reporter Josh White at the time that, "Insurgents are coming in and smacking the locals around, going on their roofs, and they don't like it. I think it's a matter of days before we start getting really good intelligence from them." Also speaking to White, Kershaw added to the company commander's optimism, saying, "We've got them up against the river now, and they don't have many options."³³ However, if anything, the insurgents were rats in a corner, not a vanquished enemy.

Outside of Qarghuli Village, the locals may not have been enthusiastic supporters of the Sunni insurgency, but the legitimate Iraqi forces weren't their horse either. A resident of Mullah Fayad, Juad Kazim, reported that the locals were afraid of Shia militias and the Iraqi Army, which was a Shia dominated force. Rumors circulated that Shia militias would attack their children if they went to school. According to Kazim, only the presence of American soldiers allowed them to feel safe in the presence of Iraqi soldiers. This was not an uncommon sentiment. At the time, anonymous U.S. soldiers in the brigade assessed to White that the Iraqi Army was still "many months" away from being effective.³⁴ So though the development of the Iraqi Army remained a focus and both Kershaw and Infanti dedicated significant forces to the task, it wouldn't be an overnight success story, and the locals may have been in position of fearing both sides and maybe feeling a little better supporting, even if tacitly, the Sunni militants.

If the locals weren't warm to the Iraqi Army, there were signs that they were warming up to the Americans. Bravo's commander reported that locals brought to the base in Rushdi Mullah a girl who had accidently ingested diesel fuel seeking medical attention. After that locals thanked them and would point out suspicious activity.³⁵ After a patrol of Yusifiyah proper on 3 November, 1st Platoon, Delta Company, who at the time served as the battalion Quick Reaction Force (QRF) with the additional task of patrolling the city, reported townsfolk were warming up to them. One soldier, a gunner, said, "[The people] are talking to us a lot more than when we first got here." A squad leader reported, "The locals are coming out more often to see us." In fact, they noted that many kids were on their way to school, which was a good sign in an area like that.³⁶

A week later on 10 November, Charlie Company hosted a medical operation in Al Taraq. The medical operation served at least 58 children, women, and elderly men. The Polar Bear battalion's operations officer (S3) used the opportunity to speak with local leaders about their concerns. Leaders spoke to him about restoring electrical power to the town and gaining access to markets in Yusifiyah and Mahmudiyah.³⁷ That the town leaders were talking to battalion leaders about their issues was another positive indicator of success. It demonstrated trust in the unit. However, as Kershaw acknowledged when talking to the families the month prior, lasting success would ultimately come only when local leaders could come together with Iraqi civil and military leaders to solve their problems. Americans were just a bridge.

The next day, Veterans Day in the United States, Bravo Company counted ninety students and six teachers reporting for school in Rushdi Mullah. It was the largest amount of students reporting to school in the town since the school reopened earlier in the week, making it an early but not definitive indicator of security in Rushdi Mullah.³⁸ Of course, to this point, the preponderance of security was provided by Americans.

In that vein, the battalion moved forward. It moved its tactical command post to Yusifiyah in preparation for a full move of the entire battalion headquarters. Charlie's unofficial occupation of the eastern Mullah Fayad Highway became official in November. The company took control of the Alamo from Bravo, no longer occupying space within Bravo's area of operation. The company moved its forward command post there along with two of the platoons. One platoon remained at the imam's house in Al Taraq which the battalion turned into a walled complex with a motor pool, gym, and burn pit in addition to the improvised barracks. The new position became T147, the T standing for tactical infrastructure. In addition, the battalion finally emplaced a tower on the curve 100 meters down the road to keep eyes on the highway in both directions. To protect that, two vehicles kept eyes on the ground around the tower. In total, this brought standing guard requirements on the road and the position to thirteen with six at the tower, three at the entrance to T147, and three on the roof plus one sergeant of the guard. From the Alamo to T147, Charlie began stringing concertina wire and tangle foot in a triple-strand configuration on both sides of the highway. Eventually, they would begin constructing obstacles toward Rushdi Mullah. The purpose of these efforts was to make it harder for the enemy to get an IED on the road. This, combined

Soldiers string concertina wire along the Mullah Fayad Highway. Though tedious, the emplacement of an obstacle combined with constant patrolling prevented the enemy from placing IEDs on the stretch from PB Siberia to Al Taraq.

with the vehicles facing down that stretch of highway from both positions, provided a good start but wouldn't be the ultimate solution to securing the road. It would take into February to fully complete these efforts. Bravo Company had a complimentary effort down near Rushdi Mullah.

Reeds were also a problem for Bravo and Charlie. They grew tall and lined one side of the road along most of the highway. Cutting them down would take years going reed by reed for four kilometers. They were tough and thick. Burning was the best solution, but they were filled with and surrounded by water. Lighting one did not light the next, as might be expected. In a place where everything burned, reeds generally did not. It required a well-timed combination of dry days, wind, and gasoline, spread through a fuel sprayer. We would douse a reed in fuel and light it and then as the wind picked up spray fuel on the next and hope it lit. It was not fast, and reeds could grow back. Ultimately, it was impossible to remove all of the reeds, but getting some down gave the enemy less opportunity to hide. Still, it was a harry endeavor. At least one soldier in Delta Company was injured when a cache ignited during burning and at other times soldiers barely escaped injury when burning reeds initiated IEDs.

Thus far, Bravo and Charlie Companies had seen relative success, from a security and counter-logistics standpoint, in their areas of operations. Despite warnings from several people, the battalion had pushed into the ungoverned hinterland and established some form of control. There were signs of revitalization in Yusifiyah proper as 1st Platoon, Delta Company, continued to get positive reactions during patrols. More shops opened in the market and locals seemed comfortable talking to them. Locals reported receiving threats and the platoon would do its best to check on them.[39]

In mid–November, insurgents attempted to enter the house of a Rushdi Mullah resident with the intention of staging an attack on the base. The owner refused, so the insurgents shot his son in retaliation. Bravo treated the child and got him to the Ibn Sina Hospital in the International Zone. Bravo's work led to the locals opening up more to them and providing information.[40] Not to be overlooked is that the Iraqi man risked his family's life to deny safe haven for the terrorist. That was progress.

However, the greater Yusifiyah area was still fraught with peril and the baddest of the bad neighborhoods remained beyond reach. To this point, Delta Company had been securing the JSB and making limited forays into the dark denizens of Qarghuli Village. Route Malibu, the raised thoroughfare that cut a path straight through the sprawl was as dangerous as any the Polar Bears or previous units would see. Now, it beckoned. Now, it taunted. Now, it dared Delta Company to come. It was time for the smallest unit to get into a really big fight.

In the days following *Operation Polar Blizzard*, the battalion continued to conduct offensive operations in the form of security and counter-cache patrols. The companies began to establish contacts with locals and build their information network while holding onto the terrain they'd seized: BPs 148, 150, 155, Rushdi Mullah, and Al Taraq. While an imperfect comparison, the work is similar to the concept of community policing with elements of presence (precincts/bases), security (patrolling), intelligence, building of relationships, and disrupting of the enemy interspersed. There were resemblances between this approach and the marines' approach of a "Zip Code Offensive," but the Polar Bears were much more tied into the population with their new bases. It was now getting to be three months from the transfer of authority and the offense continued to dominate the counterinsurgency approach. That would not change as the battalion transferred to its next phase.

The enemy also had made some mistakes. One of those mistakes was spending so much time attacking FOB Yusifiyah, which may have had imperfect defenses, but offered a better chance to fend off an attack than the smaller bases. He wasted plenty of resources, especially mortars, to no avail. Similarly, the attack on BP 155 had required a fair amount of time and resources and the enemy botched it. The soldiers of Alpha Company had their say, of course. Chief of among his mistakes that enabled the success of the Polar Bears was his decision not to attack Bravo or Charlie in the first few days after the attack. Maybe the attack on BP 155 had been a test run and the others had been called off, but even in that attack, the enemy hadn't properly massed. The enemy hadn't made the position in Rushdi Mullah untenable by denying communications. Now the Polar Bears were entrenched and ready to take more ground, but the enemy was learning.

4

Into the Heart of Darkness

Appear at places to which he must hasten; move swiftly where he does not expect you.—Sun Tzu, *The Art of War*

"Karagol (Qarghuli Village) is an Al-Qaeda village. When the American patrols come through Karagol, they have no idea of this. They just drive through, and Al-Qaeda just watches them."[1] This is what an insurgent not affiliated with the group told journalist Dexter Filkins. Soon, they would do more than watch.

By November, the battalion had a somewhat secure and open line of communication from its base at FOB Yusifiyah to the power plant where a company from 2-14 IN occupied PB Dragon. While Bravo and Charlie worked to improve their areas of responsibility, the battalion needed to begin a new thrust to open a second line of communication and to block enemy traffic across the river. Without a force to stand watch in Qarghuli, insurgents were free to move across the Euphrates by boat and to hide among the sympathetic Qarghulis, the area tribe most likely to support Sunni insurgents. From there, they could stockpile weapons and supplies, plan, and then launch attacks. With Bravo and Charlie settling into a steady state, the time was right to turn the battalion's attention to the notorious environs to the south and west.

Delta Company began the process of moving up Route Malibu and into Qarghuli Village that month. Theirs would be an economy of force mission to block the flow of fighters, weapons, and material from the west side of the Euphrates River into the Baghdad area. This had the larger goal of denying the enemy a supply line to Baghdad and the more tactical objective of providing Companies B and C the ability to maximize the value of their operations. Delta Company was authorized about 80 personnel divided amongst four platoons designed for anti-tank operations and then a small company headquarters. The platoons were full strength if they had 18 soldiers and did not have the benefit of a forward observer team. The company did not have organic mortars. Infanti had task organized the battalion, providing the company with a rifle platoon from Alpha and taking an anti-armor platoon to be the battalion QRF. That still made the company small at around 90 soldiers compared to closer to 120 for Bravo and Charlie.

The first move into the heart of darkness was a multiday air assault to conduct reconnaissance in force and disrupt the enemy, thus setting conditions for a move up

Malibu. The mission kicked off on 14 November, 41 years to the day that the first air assault in U.S. history occurred at LZ X-Ray in the Ia Drang Valley of Vietnam. Helicopters from 3rd Battalion, 227th Aviation Regiment, 1st Air Cavalry Brigade, the same unit that air landed then-Lieutenant Colonel Hal Moore's 1st Squadron, 7th Cavalry Regiment 41 years earlier, put U.S. and Iraqi troops down into Qarghuli Village in the dead of the night. From there, the troops cleared houses and fields, getting an idea of what the terrain looked like on the ground. There were no major incidents in this foray.[2] By pushing into the village for a longer period than an average raid, Delta Company gained information and intelligence necessary to properly plan for a more sustained operation. The reconnaissance mission proved successful in allowing the battalion to plan an ambitious push along the Euphrates that had a multitude of moving pieces.

Following the mission, the battalion initiated a series of moves designed to free Delta Company to establish a permanent presence in the denizens of Qarghuli Village. They handed over the JSB and responsibility for the bridge to the 4/4/6 Iraqi Army Battalion and established a new base at an inoperable water treatment facility near the site of the June 2006 kidnapping. They also established an overwatch position on a curve along Route Malibu that provided them some ability to see up the road but more so the ability to control the curve. In general, this position, which would later become known as BP 154, had value but limited fields of vision. The base at the water treatment facility eventually took the name Bataan from the 31st Infantry's stand against the Japanese prior to internment in World War II.[3]

Shortly thereafter, in the third week of November, Delta Company began its march north up Route Malibu and the Euphrates. On the 25th of that month, the battalion launched *Operation Polar Black Diamond* with Delta Company in the lead and Iraqi soldiers in support. Landing early in the morning, the soldiers moved through canals and muddy fields clearing houses as they went. U.S. soldiers provided the cordon while Iraqi soldiers cleared the buildings. After seven hours of movement, the combined force arrived at their target house where they would establish Battle Position 151 along a major curve on Route Malibu. Iraqi soldiers detained ten people caught emplacing IEDs. One of the detainees led them to some weapons caches where the soldiers found spools of wire, a couple pressure plates, a few portable phones, and "a large metal object with wheels buried in the ground." The commander of Company D described the significant growth he saw in the Iraqi soldiers. "Two years ago (during his previous deployment) it was difficult to get Iraqi soldiers onto helicopters. Now it is second nature. The Iraqi soldiers have done an excellent job and are showing improvement in taking control of situations themselves."

The new position was in a building with a large front lawn allowing some standoff from the road. It sat approximately three kilometers north of the vehicle checkpoint that would eventually become BP 154. Soldiers could look out over the Euphrates and thus interdict movement in that area. They could now control a major part of Route Malibu where vehicles had to slow down and thus were vulnerable to IEDs. This operation "effectively install[ed] the first permanent U.S. presence in Karghouli (Qarghuli) Village."[4]

Unlike when Bravo and Charlie pushed into the northern portion of the battle

4. Into the Heart of Darkness

BP 151, the first foothold in the "veritable Heart of Darkness" that was Qarghuli Village.

space, the enemy did not provide Delta time to get its defenses built before it attacked. For the next few weeks, the insurgents assaulted the new position routinely with mortars, rockets, RPGs, and small arms. They would approach from multiple directions and often laid down the heaviest fire from the west bank of the Euphrates River where they knew the Polar Bears couldn't go. Possibly *Operation Polar Black Diamond* had tipped the battalion's hand giving the enemy time to prepare or perhaps the enemy learned from *Operation Polar Blizzard*. Regardless, the battalion was now in the heart of darkness, surrounded by Sunni insurgents and in for a fight.

The day after Delta Company established BP 151, a route clearance team proceeded up Route Malibu to the new position to clear the road. Behind them trailed a platoon en route to the new battle position. Further behind still was Infanti and his personal security detachment. The battalion commander was the tenth vehicle in the order of movement.

In front of Infanti was the security detachment's platoon leader. The platoon leader had laid back for an easy ride behind route clearance and an infantry platoon. Out of nowhere, he heard the boom of an IED that rattled his vehicle so hard he thought it was his vehicle that got hit. He quickly recovered his bearing, realizing the IED struck behind him. Looking back, he saw the door of a HMMWV flying through the air.

The detachment's medic reported over the radio that Infanti's truck had hit an IED, been knocked off the road, and flipped on its head. As the platoon leader exited the truck, debris was still flying through the air. Where Infanti's vehicle had been stood a fifteen-foot wide, five-foot deep hole in the road. The back half of the vehicle was gone, blown away in the strike. Diesel fuel spilled into the truck and onto the occupants.

The scene inside was even grimmer. Infanti's interpreter, who went by the *nom de guerre* Scarface, sat unconscious, upside down, blood everywhere. The back part of his head was gone. Infanti was bleeding from the ears and mouth. He was conscious, though in severe pain. The driver made it out by slipping from his body armor which caught on something in the vehicle. Despite the events, he had the presence of mind to assist in getting the others out. They got Scarface out and the platoon's medic made an earnest though ultimately futile attempt to save his life.

However, they had considerable trouble removing Infanti. His door had been "combat locked" meaning he had engaged an additional latch to keep it shut on impact or to prevent someone outside from getting in. Infanti was unable to undo the lock from the inside in his state and from his upside-down position. The platoon leader and Infanti's driver couldn't open it either. Fuel was everywhere and it seemed only a matter of time before something lit.

The platoon leader sprinted 200 meters to the rear of the convoy and, with much difficulty, got the back-hatch open. He grabbed a proto-type "rat claw" extraction tool and sprinted with the heavy piece of equipment. There, they hooked it to the door and had another vehicle pull the door off, hoping nothing would ignite the fuel. Nothing did and with great difficulty, they pulled Infanti out.

This was Infanti's third Purple Heart (second of the deployment) and the battalion's first introduction to a deep-buried IED. The raised nature of parts of Route Malibu enabled the enemy to get a heavy dose of explosives under the intended target. The IED was also command-wired. It had gone undetected by the route clearance team and seems to have been specifically targeted for Infanti, meaning the enemy knew his vehicle or had some system of identifying it.[5] Between the deep buried IED and the attacks attempting to drive Delta Company off of Malibu, it all portended a struggle over the next several months as the battalion continued up the Euphrates. Here in Qarghuli Village, things would be different from elsewhere.

In early December, Company D conducted its second operation to establish a position. Pushing further north, Delta grabbed a building that allowed it to see down a long stretch of the road and stare down a portion of the river. This new battle position, BP 152, was small and like BP 151 could accommodate a weapons platoon manned to its full strength. At times, BP 151 had a full rifle platoon housed there. However, the positions weren't built for comfort but for security and control. They provided some advantage to the Polar Bears and gave them some initiative. However, it did not give them the ability to patrol in force. For that, the company needed to lay down roots in Qarghuli Village.

On 4 December, 2-14 IN conducted what was believed to be the U.S. Army's first river-borne operation since Vietnam. Three days later, the Polar Bears conducted the second. This one would see soldiers arrive on the battlefield from three directions and as many domains. The operation, known as *Polar Valor*, was meant to establish a permanent headquarters for Delta Company on Route Malibu named BP 153. The date of the operation, 7 December, was chosen because it was assumed insurgents believed Americans wouldn't attack on one their holidays (to the extent that the anniversary of the Pearl Harbor attack is a holiday).[6]

The gist of the operation was that the battalion Scout Platoon and a battalion headquarters element consisting of the S3, one of his assistants, and the S2, would arrive on their objective via the Euphrates River, blocking any water borne escape.[7] Charlie Company would land via helicopter north of the objective area and clear south toward the Scouts. Delta Company would send HMMWV mounted forces north from BP 152 with an attached Iron Claw element. My platoon was Charlie Company's main effort. Along with about twenty of us there was a robust headquarters element of the commander, first sergeant, and about eight others and then about a squad of Iraqi Army soldiers and some trainers. The company headquarters element was too robust in my opinion. I could have brought another team along for increased combat power.

As we prepared for the mission, I issued the platoon an operations order, we conducted coordination with other units, and conducted a rehearsal in the form of a Rehearsal of Concept (ROC) drill. My platoons was split between a clearing force of 1st and 3rd Squads with me in overall command with my FO and a support by fire element of 2nd Squad reinforced by an M240B and M141 Shoulder-launched Multipurpose Assault Weapon-Disposables (SMAW-D), an anti-tank disposable rocket in the style of a bazooka. At 2100 on 6 December, Infanti saw us off from the Yusifiyah LZ as we headed for BIAP. There we did some training and briefings with the crews of the helicopters. Flying out of BIAP made it easier to mask our intentions. Had we flown straight from Yusifiyah, the enemy would be on high alert. In this case, it looked like a routine administrative flight from a small base to a large base. At 0030, we "cold" loaded the helicopters, getting on without the blades turning, and took off shortly thereafter.

The low that night was 44 degrees and we flew with the doors open for easy exit. Wind blasted us from four angles, coming in through both doors and both gunner's stations. My 2nd Squad Leader had his arms up trying to block the wind. I stared out in the night sky, trying to enjoy the view, but it was tough to ignore the chill. We crossed over the Euphrates River and landed on the far side, conducting a false insertion in an attempt to deceive the enemy as to our intent. The gunners were scanning into the distance and I couldn't wait to take off again feeling like a sitting duck. I was most comfortable on my feet, completely in control of myself. Minutes passed and we took off again en route to LZ Eagle, a patch of farmland north of the objective area on the east side of the river.

When the wheels touched the ground at 0130, we all rushed out, took two steps, and hit the dirt. We lay in the prone behind our assault packs, which were better for steadying weapons than providing useful cover. The night was brisk, but I was happy to be off the flying wind machine. I was also happy to find that the LZ was dry. As the birds flew off, I got to my knees and collected my bearings. The lead chalk turned their infrared strobe on and we all began to move out. We moved toward the northeast corner of the LZ. Here we reorganized into our movement formation. Before moving on, we confirmed that we had all of our soldiers and that they had all of their sensitive items. Then we pushed on to the objective.

It was not long before we came across a building and the point man reported we were at the first house on the objective. I didn't think we were. We should have moved much further and, even in the dark, it didn't seem right. All of the NCOs agreed with him that we were at the first house and I acquiesced, so we prepared to clear the house only to have the commander tell us it was not the right house and that we needed to bypass it. It was reminiscent of a mistake I had made in Ranger School that led to me failing a patrol. As platoon leader that day, the terrain didn't match the map, but everyone else thought we were right and I let it go. It's not a mistake I would make again.

This sequence of events had gotten our point man a little disoriented and probably me too. We had to pause and get things straightened out. Obviously, the commander was frustrated at me. We needed to make our hit time on the objective and time was ticking, but we had reached a canal and needed to find a way to cross. Averse to crossing at the road, the most likely location for an IED, I choose to cross at what looked like a shallow point. However, the water was waist deep and the first eight of us got soaked to the belly button. The commander waived the rest off and moved everyone up to the road, but it was no yet 0200 and eight of us were soaked with the temperature in the mid–40s.

When we reached the far side of the canal, we were in unfamiliar terrain and trying to assemble our force in the dark which is never a recipe for success. We had reached the objective, but with part of the force crossing the water and the other part bypassing, we were no longer in the proper configuration. I needed to get 2nd Squad into position to overwatch our movement. Once they were set, 1st and 3rd Squads moved forward toward the first house with my RTO, forward observer, and I trailing them. Once they cleared the house of enemy, the Iraqi Army soldiers would search. This allowed my soldiers, trained in clearing buildings under night vision devices, to do something they were particularly skilled at and the Iraqi soldiers, who were more familiar with their culture, architecture, and personal goods and thus knew where to look and how to search, to do something they were particularly good at. However, there was an issue in the very first house. After we determined it was clear and I reported it to my commander, my platoon, less 2nd Squad, moved on to the next building. While searching, the Iraqi Army soldiers found three men hiding in a closet, one claiming to be Egyptian. This demonstrates the importance of being clear in a task and to define what it means. My platoon saw clearing as a relatively dynamic task and did not look in every spot someone could be hiding. Additionally, very few urban operations training facilities have fully furnished buildings, meaning soldiers rarely encounter closets, beds, or other hiding places in training. It is not something I would have thought to clarify in rehearsals, but after years of personal and professional study, along with reflection, understand the need for everyone to define a task in the same manner.

Moving on, 1st Squad found a storehouse out back and we breached the door. There was nothing in it but foodstuffs. However, it was so warm in the building, it was hard to leave. I suggested we pause and move soldiers inside to wring out their socks, but the NCOs believed it was better to keep moving, so we pressed on. Sometimes it is better to just embrace the misery. It can be almost more uncomfortable trying to get comfortable. In training, we would have stopped and changed our socks and possibly put dry boots on, even in Ranger School. Sometimes in training, we would have halted the whole mission to get dry, but here you had to live with it and we lived with it. Only the sun was likely to bring us relief from the wet and cold. I believe it was the right call to cross the canal. Though the trail element didn't hit an IED, it was a potential location for one. Good or bad, seven of my soldiers lived with the ramifications of my decision.

We pushed on to the next house. Like many of the homes in the area it was massive. We were in the land of the Qarghulis, the one-time Saddam loyalists who had been given this area as a reward, but this house was different. It was missing a wall and there was a tree stump right in the middle of the house. It was very odd. The occupants tried to converse with me, but my limited Arabic and lack of an interpreter (the one with us moved with the commander and coordinated with the IA) made it useless. As the IA came up, we pushed on to the next house.

This one had a special grandeur to it to the point that I immediately called it the Great Pyramid upon laying eyes on it. The man inside informed us the 36 people lived inside, which is likely mind boggling to an American. It appeared to be two houses that were mirror images of the other connected by a door. It is quite possible the man had two wives. It seemed like each house we came upon had some memorable piece to it. In this one, a little boy was fascinated with us and would dart through the house as we cleared. He was so excited that we were there even though we were pulling out all the military aged men (roughly 18 to 45 year olds) in the house. In my notes, I wrote that he seemed to view us as his long-lost brothers. As bad as Qarghuli had been billed, we had yet to meet someone that wasn't willing to greet us warmly, even in the dead of the night.

At this point, one my team leaders, who seemed to never be fazed by the enemy or prospect of danger, began shivering pretty bad. There was little I could do so we pressed on. In the next house we found a warm (for that environment) room and put all the men in it with the team leader on guard. The house after that had a courtyard with a door locked from the inside. Thus, our breaching tools were useless, so we improvised by hoisting a soldier over the wall and he unlocked it. The opening of the gate wasn't quite as dramatic as Sean Connery's in *The Rock*, but it was well done.

Upstairs, as 1st Squad cleared, an older lady kept following another soldier, keeping her eyes on him. She made the soldier laugh and continued to follow him through the house. After he made it back down the stairs, she continued to call to him and invite him back up. It was surreal but ten years later, the soldier still remembered it when prompted. While he was being ogled, the rest of us who had crossed the canal stood around a candle taking every smidgen of heat we could. Standing there, my 1st Squad

Leader, who had gone in the canal, looked at me and said, "So, sir, this or Ranger School?" I had to say that in this moment, I was worse off than any single moment in Ranger School, but as an aggregate, the school was still harder. Nonetheless, I'm not sure I would have been an effective leader after crossing the canal if it weren't for the school teaching me to lead in adverse conditions.

After clearing the next house, we had to pause to switch over the security programming in our radios. My commander also wanted us to take a break and let the Iraqi Army clear some houses as the sky grew lighter; it was now easier for them since they didn't have night vision. I moved 2nd Squad up to the roof of the building we were in and had them establish overwatch of the area. 1st and 3rd set up a small guard position near the entrance and the rest of us took a break. I hadn't slept since the previous morning, so I found a candle laying in the foyer, placed my back against the wall, and closed my eyes long enough to get groggy but not rested.

When the sun was fully up, we pushed on and cleared the rest of our objective without incident and without any more interesting stories. After reaching our limit of advance and the IA completing their search of all the buildings, we moved down to a small hamlet on the river which had been the Scouts' objective. There, we linked up with the platoon, a host of Iraqi Army soldiers to include two who had stayed with my platoon in Al Taraq, and the battalion headquarters element serving as the forward command. The Delta Company element was still pushing up from BP 152.

It was now mid to late morning and the Scouts had secured a building that would be the base for the operation. Because it was secure, it gave our platoon the opportunity to rest. The sun had brought warmth and some dryness, but we were still over thirty hours without sleep and at least sixteen without a meal. I sat down and pulled out the stripped down MRE I had in my pack, just some crackers and a pouch of food, only to find that a mouse or rat had gotten into it while it sat in the tent back at Yusifiyah. I put it back in the bag and went on without food. Fortunately, we had come to a plush spot, and there were flushing toilets—truly a gem in Yusifiyah, something not even our own bases had—so we didn't have to urinate in the open, and there were plenty of blankets to use for warmth. Most of the soldiers took the time to get some deserved rest and food. However, before I bedded down, my RTO and I went to the roof to take in the view of the Euphrates River. Despite all the misery, it was worth it to behold something both biblical and historic.

I think there had been some thought to making the building the new patrol base, but it was too far off the road despite its otherwise suitability. It would require additional positions to secure it and the road and thus wasn't appropriate. Plus, from what I remember, the owner was an informant so kicking him out of his base wouldn't help the intelligence effort. My commander gave us the location of the chosen position, one of the building we had been in earlier, and we moved to it while the S3 negotiated with the owners. The owner received time to remove belongings and my heart sank as a I saw a tractor take off with a load of blankets. I had a wet poncho liner with me, but that was it.

While the Scouts and S3 secured the house and took care of mission priorities,

4. Into the Heart of Darkness

we went on patrol. We searched through some groves looking for caches and signs of the enemy before returning to the estate house that would become PB Inchon, named after MacArthur's famed landing in Korea. My platoon took a room to use as our sleeping area and we integrated with the Scouts and IA soldiers for guard duty. (The Delta Company unit was still moving up, making slow progress clearing the road in a fashion similar to *Polar Blizzard*.) I saw a kerosene lamp left behind by the owners and secured it for the platoon, placing it in the middle of the room and then positioning myself by the door so I could move in and out and be easily found. The concrete floors were freezing that night and the heater only provided marginal warmth, but it was better than nothing. We had packed extremely light by design, so soldiers had only a poncho liner to stay warm. To make it a little better, some soldiers wrapped up in shower curtains or clothing they'd found in the house. I found a bag of wool and made it into a bed and wrapped two potato sacks around myself for a blanket.

At some point in the night, I heard a friend's voice downstairs. Delta had arrived. They had some boxes of MREs so I rushed down to get some for the soldiers and ate my first meal in 36 hours. In the morning, the Charlie Company element went on an

Patrol Base Inchon after several months of buildup. The primitive base lacked most amenities but placed the Polar Bears in Qarghuli Village. The enemy could never dislodge them.

extended patrol around the area to disrupt the enemy while Delta Company built its defenses. We didn't uncover anything but we did have an opportunity to eat with a local. Delta got to work setting up HESCO barriers to be filled later and stringing concertina wire around the perimeter. Like Bravo, they didn't waste a second preparing for the enemy counterattack. By nightfall, we were in position to catch our birds and go home. We landed at Yusifiyah, tired, dirty, and hungry, but got a good meal and good night's sleep.[8]

When we got back to Al Taraq, there was work to be done. That night, the QRF, 1st Platoon, Delta Company, had been out near our base and engaged a mortar team. They believed they could see a body through their Tube-launched, Optically-tracked, Wire-guided (TOW) missile sites, but didn't have the manpower to move that far from their overwatch element. We received the mission to track down the body. It was difficult moving through the canal crossed and farm laden terrain while trying to adjust to the directions of someone looking through a site in the dark. Finally, the lieutenant told me I was standing right next to the body. I was actually standing right next to a very alive cow. Mission complete.[9]

While we returned to life on the Mullah Fayad Highway, Delta Company stayed. With the help of Charlie Company and the battalion Scouts, they had cleared the area. It was time to hold and build. Alpha Company, 2nd Battalion, 5th Cavalry Regiment (A/2–5 CAV), a mechanized unit from Fort Hood, Texas, took control of PB Bataan and BP 154 from Delta Company to allow them to focus on Qarghuli Village and Route Malibu. Not long before, A/2–5 CAV had replaced B/1–22 IN as the attached mechanized company. The new unit was a part of the 1st Cavalry Division, which now commanded Multi-National Division-Baghdad (MND-B). MND-B was the division headquarters for the Polar Bears and 2nd Brigade Combat Team.

Unlike what it was like after *Polar Blizzard*, the enemy would not give Delta time to get their feet under them. Delta had already seen that in establishing BPs 151 and 152. However, in establishing the other bases, Delta had generally faced direct fire assaults where they could identify and engage their assailants. At Inchon, things were different. Daily at dawn the base came under precise mortar fire. Patrols from the base began to encounter anti-personnel IEDs in addition to Route Malibu's cornucopia of anti-vehicle IEDs. The enemy also employed rockets and small arms to harass patrols. Reflecting on the early days at Inchon, First Lieutenant Doug Livermore, who at this point was serving as Delta's executive officer, wrote, "In many ways, we wished that the insurgents would come down and face us in the open, en masse, as they had in November and [early] December." Fortunately, the battalion snipers were able to locate and kill the spotters responsible for guiding the mortar attacks which reduced the precision and lightened the burden on Delta Company.[10]

The enemy may have preferred to fight from a distance against Inchon, but he still had no qualms attacking the smaller outposts in Qarghuli with a sizable force. On 13 December, 2nd Platoon, Delta Company, occupied BP 151 when 25 enemy armed with AK-47s began attacking the base from multiple sides. As the platoon rushed to the roof to reinforce the guards, a vehicle approached the river on the west bank with armed men looking to add an additional dimension to the fight. Fortunately, quick reaction by some of the soldiers reduced that threat and prevented the enemy from being able to attack from all sides. Darkness was descending on the land and the soldiers gained the upper hand with the ability to employ night vision and infrared lasers to engage the enemy while the insurgents had no such capability. As the light faded from the sky, the enemy withdrew having achieved little tangibly but demonstrated he was still able to attack in platoon-sized elements and coordinate attacks from both sides of the river. Still, as the fighting calmed down, in the distance a sniper cracked a round passed the battalion chaplain's head, as if to remind the soldiers he was there.[11]

The next day, in Rushdi Mullah, a Bravo Company patrol uncovered what appeared to be preparations for an insider attack. 1st Platoon discovered a cache in a 55-gallon drum that contained Iraqi Army uniforms and insignia as well as web gear for holding magazines and equipment. They found other empty 55-gallon drums as well, which could have been soon-to-be established caches or previously emptied ones.[12] It is hard to ascertain the intent of caching these uniforms. While insider attacks became a favorite tactic of the Taliban in Afghanistan in 2012, the various insurgent groups in Qarghuli had not tried one in such a manner, so it may have been to gain access to the base and then attack the soldiers—the insurgent that killed two NCOs in the 101st walked onto the TCP as a trusted agent (though not in uniform) and opened fire. Or, the insurgents may have intended to pose as Iraqi Army soldiers to harass or kill civilians and then drive a wedge between the government and populace and sew distrust. Either way, like many of the efforts of the enemy, the psychological value would be greater than the physical effect.

On the same day, members of Charlie Company and the IA participated in a brigade operation dubbed *Commando Vice*. The mission involved clearing suspected insurgent cells on the Euphrates. The mission along with a string of others to follow in the next four months was intended, among other reasons, to identify gaps and seems in the brigade's coverage and to develop plans for closing said gaps and seems.[13] Insurgents throughout the 20th century (and now in the 21st century) notoriously exploited the area around unit boundaries and spots where coverage of patrols and observation was deficient. It was important to find these areas and shore them up.

On 18 December, the Polar Bears kicked off *Operation Polar Warrior*. The operation saw the training teams of Alpha Company and their Iraqi partners air assault into Janabi Village with the aim of denying insurgents sanctuary in the area. Janabi Village was a part of the area of operations not covered by Bravo, Charlie, or Delta. It was in A/2–5 CAV's area of responsibility, but beyond their physical control. At 1000 and 1420, the coalition force came under fire from insurgents. Both times the enemy fled before the force could close with them. It would be several months before sustained operations in the area would kick off.

In a sign of progress for the Iraqi Army, a local tipped the group off and they were able to catch a high value target in the act of escaping. The operation further uncovered three caches. The first "contained a Belgian-made FAL (Fusil Automatique Léger) 7.62 mm rifle, two bolt-action Mauser rifles modified to accept Draganov telescopic sights, three rocket-propelled grenade launchers and one homemade RPG launcher." The second "contained two AK-47 magazine vests, two phone chargers, a cell phone, a 60 mm mortar system, six 60 mm (mortar) rounds, two 82 mm mortar rounds, a glue gun, a damaged PKM machine gun, a mortar sight, a box of rivets, two anti-tank rockets, four anti-personnel rockets, 100 rounds of 7.62 mm rounds [sic], 109 hand grenades, 100 feet of electrical cord, two spools of wire, batteries and propane tanks." The third, found specifically by the Iraqi soldiers, had two IEDs ready to be emplaced and some additional IED making material.[14]

While offensive actions, both large scale and patrolling, continued to be the hallmark of operations, the battalion remained mindful of the need for some stability operations, at least until they could build local governance capacity. On 22 December, Charlie Company took the lead on the battalion's first attempt to conduct a veterinary operation. Held at the Al Taraq school, the battalion brought in an MND-B staff veterinarian to assess and treat the village's animals. The number of people bringing animals was relatively low and it is hard to tell the effect the operation had on the people. In total, 95 sheep and 5 cows received treatment.[15] One thing I learned was that many of the locals did not own the land or livestock. I—and I believe others—assumed that the locals were subsistence farmers but in reality they were farm hands working for owners that didn't live in the immediate area. Thus, treating the animals didn't necessarily benefit the locals directly. Therefore, the operation had limited impact on the operational environment.

The success of *Polar Valor* notwithstanding and the actions that followed, December was not a safe month by any means. Despite mortars and direct fire attacks against the bases, the enemy's weapon of choice was the IED. An NCO in Bravo Company stepped on a pressure plate IED on 20 December losing three limbs.[16] On 23 December, a resupply convoy hit an IED on Route Malibu and killed Specialist Curtis Norris of Company F, 210th Brigade Support Company (F/210th BSB, sometimes referred to as Company F or Fox Company, 4-31 IN, 4-31 IN's forward support company) when his truck flipped. Norris, who was a vehicle commander in a convoy delivering an early Christmas dinner to Delta Company, was posthumously promoted to sergeant.[17]

The severe wounding of one soldier and the death of Norris certainly cast a pall over the season, but Christmas was not without some merriment in the Yusifiyah area. The men of Delta erected a Christmas tree at Inchon and decorated it with bands of machine gun ammunition, shot gun shells, and grenades with a claymore mine on top as the star. It may have had a certain dark sense of humor to it, but it was very much an "infan-tree" if there ever was one. There were also candy canes strung throughout and AT-4 anti-tank rocket launchers under the tree as presents. Charlie Company decorated their tree in a similar manner. In Rushdi Mullah, Bravo Company received a visit from Raad, the boy who had been shot when his father refused insurgents entry into his home. Medics changed his dressings and treated a rash on his brother's skin. Since the attack, their relationship with the boy and his family continued to strengthen.[18]

Down at Al Taraq, 1st Platoon, Charlie Company was without power as usual, thus in the dark and cold, but we had a small tree my saint of a mother sent us and someone

4. Into the Heart of Darkness

A shepherd herds his sheep while a gunner looks on near Al Taraq. The battalion held a veterinary clinic to assist the locals with little success.

else had sent the platoon a stocking and manger scene, so we probably lived closer in distance (only a few hundred miles to Jerusalem) and comfort to Mary, Joseph, and Jesus than any of us had before. We spent the day laying wire along the Mullah Fayad Highway. The day was not without incident as a route clearance operation with members of Alpha Company, detached to the engineers, hit an IED. However, none of the soldiers in vehicle were hurt.[19]

Ahead of the holiday, Kershaw sent a letter to the brigade's troops. In the letter he listed a set of accomplishments the soldiers had contributed to:

- We have eliminated the largest insurgent sanctuary—the notorious Shakariyah Triangle—as a source of attacks on Baghdad.
- We have found over 188 caches, removing improvised explosive device-making materials, heavy weapons and mortars from the hands of insurgent forces.
- We have forced terrorist cells to move, leading to their elimination by coalition and Iraqi forces.
- We have seen attacks drop in every category, particularly in our own casualties.

- We have fought side by side with the Jundis (Arabic for "soldiers") of 4th Brigade, 6th Iraqi Army Division "Baghdad Eagles," and watched their capabilities improve.[20]

This letter certainly strikes an optimistic tone and serves its purpose to tell the soldiers that their hard work and sacrifice was bearing fruit. However, the enemy was far from done and was still quite effective and savvy. Events would soon prove this.

In fact, it was only a couple days after Christmas that the enemy struck the battalion hard. On 26 December, Second Platoon, Delta Company, was out on patrol in Qarghuli Village searching for caches. On the patrol, the soldiers ignited a line of reeds to remove the obstruction. A cache hidden in the reeds caught fire making it impossible to remain in the immediate area. The platoon leader and platoon sergeant decided to pick up the patrol the next day. When they returned to the patrol, Sergeant Christopher Messer and Private First Class Nathaniel Given attempted to cross a canal when one of the two stepped on a pressure plate IED. In the resulting blast, Given was immediately killed. Messer had most of his lower half-amputated. Soldiers on site performed emergency medical care on Messer (the platoon medic was on leave) but he died before a MEDEVAC bird could load him. The battalion held a memorial for Norris, Messer, and Given on 30 December at Yusifiyah.[21]

As December rounded out, an old theme raised its head once more. Historians love to say that history does not repeat itself, but it does rhyme. Standing on the roof one evening I looked out into the night to the east to see a fire burning bright in the distance. Reminiscent of the fire that burned the living quarters on FOB Yusifiyah during a previous unit's tenure, a newly erected company command post building had gone up in flames. In the Triangle, everything burned. The cause was an electrical fire, like the previous blaze. It would take most of the rest of the deployment to clean up the ash and rubble and the building would never be rebuilt.

But there was still some good news to end the year. On 28 December Iraqi and U.S. forces (presumably special operations forces) combined to arrest an unnamed head of an Al Qaeda (or Islamic State) element in Yusifiyah who was implicated in and possibly led or supervised the kidnappings and murders of Specialist Babineau and Privates First Class Tucker and Menchaca from the 101st on 6 June 2006.[22] It had taken some time, but a small degree of justice was served.

To bridge the years, Charlie Company, A/2–5 CAV, and the IA combined for *Operation Polar Shield*, a mission meant to detain members of an insurgent IED cell. The operation occurred in Al Thobat, four kilometers south of Yusifiyah. The soldiers took six detainees, two whom were linked to the cell. The four others were vaguely detained "for their belligerence."[23] Contemporaneous to *Polar Shield* the battalion launched the QRF platoon, members of F/210th BSB, and the IA in a hasty operation. Styled *Operation Polar Pounce*, the combined force seized two Chinese-made S-60 57 mm anti-aircraft guns in Janabi Village. The F/210th element encountered an IED with a crush-wire initiator, but EOD cleared it without incident.[24]

At this time, it is important for the reader to get a good visual of what January

4. Into the Heart of Darkness

A MEDEVAC helicopter lands at Patrol Base Bataan to evacuate wounded Iraqi citizens to Baghdad. Helicopters were the fastest way to move casualties to expert care and could bypass the IED-laden routes.

and February in Iraq are like for a soldier. Despite its reputation as a hot, desert country, those months in Iraq are miserable due to their poor weather. It is a rainy, cold season and in the farm fields of Yusifiyah it is muddy and damp. In a letter home to my parents in January, I wrote, "[I'm] wearing my fleece [coat] and skull cap as I write this. Does that give you a good picture? ... It's muddy and rainy and dreary.... At worst, I have another month and a half before the weather improves and I'm just waiting for that time to come."[25] For all the hot of October, I found myself wanting that over the cold of January.

Despite the cold, we all pushed on; we were the Polar Bears from Fort Drum, New York. On 8 January, Charlie Company conducted a combined air and ground assault into the villages to the northwest of Al Taraq. The operation, *Polar Fire*, was intended to deny enemy sanctuary in the area beyond the company's immediate control. 1st Platoon left on foot from BP 147 and entered one of the hamlets while 2nd Platoon, the IA, and company headquarters landed further west via helicopters to clear another village. The two elements then linked up and cleared a third objective. The operation resulted in the detention of six suspected insurgents. Two of these terrorists were on coalition forces black lists, the Iraqi Army had two others on their watch list, and two were caught with IED making material. All of the detainees were linked to IED or mortar attacks.[26]

One incident that occurred during this operation is instructive of the need to streamline communications. Prior to the operation, my commander and I sat down and reviewed a list of suspects believed to be living on my platoon's objective and he gave me instructions on what to do if we came across any of these individuals. We found one, a suspected sniper, and my instructions had been to report and receive guidance with the intention of detaining. Officers often use their RTOs to communicate for them routine matters; my RTO and the commander's handled the exchange relaying information to their respective officer. In the exchange I received the message to not detain this individual without evidence. My commander later told me his order was to detain the man, period. Not long after, a soldier in the battalion died from a sniper's bullet. While we could not say it was this man I'd released, it is possible. Having been perplexed by the order, I should have asked to speak to my commander before proceeding. All leaders need to consider when it is time to "go direct" and talk straight to one another.

While I may have failed to detain a potential sniper, the Iraqi Army nabbed a much bigger catch. The day after *Polar Fire*, Iraqi soldiers detained the head of the 1920 Revolutionary Brigade, the largely Qarghuli organization of Saddam-loyalists.[27] The day after that, Kershaw helped continue to demonstrate the Iraqi Army's competence. The brigade commander and his Iraqi partner and counterpart Colonel Ali Jassim Muhammad Al Frejee (known as Colonel Ali) attended a meeting (known as a *Qaada*) in Mahmadiyah. Colonel Ali began the meeting by telling those gathered that kidnappings and killings were down, but then reminded them that there was much work to be done to fully secure the area. He then implored other Iraqis to do their duty and give information about enemy and criminals in the area. After his speech, the gathered citizens were able to bring up issues for discussion. Kershaw closed out the meeting telling the crowd he believed that they, the Iraqis themselves, could solve the problems some in their midst had mentioned.[28] Reading Colonel Ali's speech, his words are fiery whereas Kershaw's are empowering, which may have been an effective approach. The symbolism is clear: Colonel Ali, the Iraqi, is in charge; Kershaw, the American, is there to advise and assist.

Five days after Kershaw and Colonel Ali's meeting, on 15 January, the Iraqi Army would launch its largest recorded operation in the Yusifiyah area. A total force of over 600 Iraqi and American soldiers from the 4th Brigade, 6th Iraqi Army Division, 4–31 IN, and 2–15 FA, entered Janabi Village. Reports indicate that the entire Iraqi brigade participated in some way. A small force arrived by helicopter in advance of daylight while the bulk of the force drove to the attack position and walked in at first light. The troops detained 87 men, 12 of whom were on the Iraqi Army's terrorist watch list. The operation further netted several caches including RPGs and launchers, IEDs, and materials to make IEDs. One particular IED, described by one of the American participants as a catastrophic IED, was a 42 inches long pipe (6 inches in diameter) filled with homemade explosives. This operation, for which sources do not give a name, is notable due to the size of the Iraqi force and the sheer praise applied to them by their trainers relative to other reports. While most 10th Mountain Division produced news accounts offer rosy quotes, this one had a much higher number. Trainers indicated the Iraqi Army had a larger role in planning the operation, which is different than many of the previous American-led efforts.[29]

While the Iraqi Army was making progress, I was losing the battle of communication. My commander had to rely heavily on the initiative and decisions of his junior officers due to the nature of the area of operations. My platoon remained at Al Taraq most of the time while 3rd Platoon held a position east of the Alamo, by now renamed PB Siberia. With his force spread out, he couldn't direct every action and thus employed mission command. I often planned my own patrols and determined when and where things needed to happen in around the town. I feel I did a good job of fulfilling his intent, but realized that I was doing a poor job earning his trust because he didn't know what I was doing. To alleviate the frustration, I began providing him a weekly situation report that provided an overview of events in the Al Taraq area the previous week, my assessment of the area from an intelligence and operations standpoint, recommendations for the way ahead, all my patrol concepts for the next week, and the patrol debriefs from the previous week. I also included a maintenance status and an assessment of morale. These weekly reports significantly reduced the stress between my commander and I and allowed him to have a better understanding of the sector. While he circulated the battlefield, the company participated in a number of air assault operations that required his attention and planning, so he needed me to be on my game. The reports also helped to spur further thought about the area and the information and idea sharing became reciprocal.

At this time, I had begun a deep study of counterinsurgency led off by reading David Galula's *Counterinsurgency Warfare: Theory and Practice* and John Nagl's *Learning to Eat Soup with a Knife: Counterinsurgency Lessons from Malaya and Vietnam*. Both authors advocate small-level civic projects and that is what the battalion was up to on 23 January. Soldiers from the Polar Bears, the IA, and 210th Brigade Support Battalion combined on a project to check the water quality in Yusifiyah. At the request of the local water minister, the Polar Bears and IA pulled security for the support battalion soldiers, who drilled holes in the water pipes. The water minister noted the number of citizens who came out to watch the soldiers and indicated that was a sign of security.[30] He was not far off the mark. No American company had responsibility for patrolling Yusifiyah. The QRF patrolled it as an additional task and Alpha Company did as part of its partnership, but it was not like Al Taraq, Rushdi Mullah, or Qarghuli. The truth is, it wasn't safe, but it was safer than elsewhere in the area and the number of people gathered indicates a perception of security, which is more important than reality at times. (For example, it is extremely safe to fly, but many are more scared of it than the far more dangerous act of driving.)

But while 23 January may have given an indication of the safety of Yusifiyah, the next day would utterly demonstrate the lack thereof in Qarghuli. Only a month prior,

Kershaw told the brigade of their amazing progress in the Triangle of Death and fact that insurgents were on the run, but on 24 January they came together in force to conduct a complex attack against Delta Company. On that day, 4th Platoon was traveling south on Route Malibu away from Inchon when they were struck by a series of "daisy-chained" IEDs (seven or eight 155 mm shells in all.) To understand the sheer magnitude of the attack, the noise of the explosion came over loud and clear at Rushdi Mullah. All four of the platoon's HMMWVs were disabled in the attack and three soldiers were wounded. Similar to how American forces typically use some type of explosion—a claymore mine or anti-tank rocket—to initiate an ambush, the strike was the opening to a larger attack. Insurgents opened up on the patrol with RPGs and machine gun fire. Without the ability to move out of the kill zone in trucks, the platoon rallied in a house and fought back. Their hasty defensive position was in danger of being overrun as the enemy advanced on the position. However, the platoon leader and platoon sergeant were able to maintain order and defeat the enemy with a counterattack aided by helicopter gunships.

Certainly this could be seen as the most harrowing experience of any element during the deployment thus far. An entire platoon faced annihilation, but theirs was not Delta's only battle at the moment. Insurgents were able to isolate 4th Platoon because they also attacked Inchon creating multiple dilemmas for the company. While 4th Platoon fought for their lives out on Malibu, Inchon was under its own onslaught, receiving fire from RPGs and machine guns from three directions and taking indirect fire mortar rounds as well. If that wasn't bad enough insurgents attempted to breach the base's defenses by sending a suicide vehicle-borne IED toward the gate. Fortunately, fire from the base initiated the IED before it was close enough to blow a hole in the wall or kill soldiers. With their breach failed, the insurgents called off the attack after 30 minutes.[31]

The combined attack reveals the depth of organization insurgents in the Qarghuli area had. The sheer planning just to stage for the attack proves the enemy had a significant amount of military savvy. Some believed that the attack on 4th Platoon was an attempt to kidnap soldiers. However, it appears much more likely as an attempt to win a great propaganda victory. Destroying a U.S. weapons platoon and getting into the wire of a company base would not defeat U.S. forces by any stretch, but the effect on the populace back home would be great and the local populace would be less likely to support the Americans and their Iraqi partners. Regardless, if there was any doubt at this point that the enemy was alive, well, and feeling froggy on the east bank of the Euphrates, it had been erased.

While things were burning in Qarghuli Village, there were signs that flames were extinguishing elsewhere. Demonstrating the dichotomy in the area of operations, a large group of Yusifiyah sheiks met at BP 147 to talk to each other, the Iraqi Army, and the battalion's leadership. The S3, the Charlie Company Commander, and LTC Imam, the IA battalion commander, organized the meeting which focused mostly on security, tribal politics, and public works. Certainly this meeting did not suggest everything was great in the Yusifiyah/Al Taraq/Mullah Fayad area, but it was something no one could have imagined occurring in Qarghuli Village. The greatest positive of the meeting was that Sunni sheiks turned up at all and that they were engaged throughout. As the meeting broke, the sheiks signaled they were willing to continue working toward a better situation by saying there needed to be many more meetings. The S3 hit the nail on the head when he candidly told a reporter, "No matter how much the Iraqi Army and the coalition forces want to move ahead, the only ones who can make that happen are the civilian leaders, and here, the civilian leadership is the sheiks." Charlie's commander intimated in a March 2007 letter to families that it was the first time since the invasion that Sunni leaders in the area "open[ed] a dialogue with Coalition Forces and Iraqi Security Forces" in the area of Al Taraq.[32]

To end the month, the Polar Bears launched *Operation Polar Ice* in Qarghuli Village. Originally conceived of as an air assault, red air (conditions making it dangerous to fly) required soldiers to move in by vehicle, dismount, and walk. For troops from 1st Platoon, Bravo Company, that meant searching around BP 152. They had a group of Iraqi Army soldiers with them who, according to Philip Sharp, conducted all the searches. The next day these soldiers also conducted a cache search east of the village but turned up nothing. A/2–5 CAV also conducted a series of patrols in conjunction with the mission moving around Bataan.[33]

There were signs of progress and signs of much work to be done at the close of the month. Soon, a new commander would arrive and bring with him, according to popular belief, a new strategy to win it all.

The focus of the battalion continued to be offensive operations with defensive measures interspersed. The offensive operations gained the battalion ground and the defensive measures allowed them to hold on while they built the Iraqi Army and prepared them for eventual control. As the calendar shifted to February, the Iraqi Army was beginning to show progress. Delta, while bruised, was doing everything the battalion needed it to do. It clashed with the insurgents allowing Bravo and Charlie to keep building in their areas. Again, stability operations took a backseat to other means. The Polar Bears never attempted to be the governance, only to provide short term relief. From the start, the counterinsurgency approach centered on building the Iraqi Army and seizing and holding ground for transfer to the Iraqis.

Their approach of taking and holding land, an extreme interpretation of 1/502 PIR's method, would soon become vogue with the arrival of General David Petraeus, but while there were signs of progress all around, no objective observer could say that the Polar Bears had secured the area or that the Iraqi Army was ready to take the lead. The coming months would bring a maddening mix of hope and despair. The one thing that would remain constant was that the battalion would never waiver from its approach.

5

A New Strategy?

The more things change, the more they remain the same.
—Jean-Baptiste Alphonse Karr

General David Petraeus assumed command of MNF-I on 10 February 2007. Just two months previously, he had signed, along with Lieutenant General James Amos, the U.S. Marine Corps Deputy Commandant for Combat Development and Integration, Field Manual 3–24/Marine Corps Warfighting Publication 3–33.5, *Counterinsurgency*. The manual's release came with much fanfare. It had eight chapters focused on what insurgency and counterinsurgency are, the integration of civil and military activities, intelligence, designing campaigns and operations, executing counterinsurgency operations, development of host-nation forces, leadership and ethics, and finally sustainment. Emma Sky, serving as Lieutenant General Ray Odierno's political advisor (POLAD), later wrote that "[t]he new religion was Counter Insurgency [sic] … and its sacred text was FM 3–24…."[1] (Odierno was commander of Multi-National Corps-Iraq.)

But when Petraeus arrived, he didn't move from FOB to FOB and handing out autographed copies of the manual. In fact, it would be a while before he issued a campaign plan. What he did do was send a letter to the U.S. servicemembers providing initial guidance. After opening with an assessment that the Coalition was in a critical time, Petraeus turned to informing his troops of what they must provide: security. "Security is essential for Iraq to build its future. Only with security can the Iraqi government come to grips with the tough issues it confronts and develop the capacity to serve its citizens." In this he struck an offensive-minded tone. "We must strike them relentlessly. We and our Iraqi partners must set the terms of the struggle, not our enemies. And together we must prevail." And regarding the path to victory, "In the end, Iraqis will decide the outcome of this struggle. Our task is to help them gain the time they need to save their country." Petraeus also informed the troops that they would live and fight alongside the Iraqi security forces.[2] He did not mention anything about troops building governance or civil capacities.

As the reader has seen, the hallmark of the brigade and battalion approaches to this point was offense. The multiple offensive operations were designed to seize the initiative and take the fight to the enemy. The Polar Bears had established at least ten new bases in an effort to provide security throughout the battlespace. Most of the rest of the effort lay in the development of 4/4/6 IA, the partnered Iraqi Army battalion. When considering where the battalion exerted its precious energy—security, partnering, offensive operations—the Polar Bears were already in line with the new approach. However, they would benefit in other ways as I'll discuss later.

The week prior to Petraeus taking command, I had been thinking hard on the subject of what we were doing and whether or not it was effective. I had been caught up in a personal study of counterinsurgency—a subject I admittedly was not familiar with prior to deploying—and had entered into a personal review of all we had done since September. On 3 February, I submitted the following assessment to my commander as part of my weekly report:

> Are we (C/4-31 IN) winning? Yes. But, the answer isn't that straight forward. Many, inside the unit and out, think that it's easy to say we're winning due to lack of attacks by the enemy. They believe we are in a "quiet sector." Others, inside the unit and out, think we're losing, because we aren't killing terrorists. However, there are two reasons we are not killing terrorists. First, the preferred method of attacks by the enemy in this sector rely on stand off [sic]. The enemy will attack us (through mortars, sniper fire, and IEDs) knowing that there is a degree of distance between him and us, giving him safety. It is hard to kill a coward. Second, killing terrorists isn't an effective way of defeating them. (John Nagl points out that safety of an area is [a] better measure of success than body counts.) The triggermen and emplacers are easily replaced. Snipers and mortarmen are a little more specialized, but they can also work with greater stand off and better cover. Regardless, the organizers, financiers, leaders and planners of the cells are the ones we want to take out. But, even their death does not make our fight easier.
>
> Counterinsurgency victory relies more on the capture of known, high ranking terrorists and on the fear struck in the hearts of the pawns. A captured insurgent is denied the martyrdom that helps insinuate further attacks and glorifies the job, thereby causing others to want the power. Additionally, a captured insurgent has intelligence value and can lead to further arrests and additional dismantling of cells. The capture of terrorists and the due process that follows also brings a sense of justice to the populace and Arabs value justice highly. Moreover, fear is [a] strong deterrent for the pawns. The insurgents in our area do not wish to risk their lives (if they did, they would attack through direct fire and probe our defenses). Therefore, night time raids, disruption patrols and the heard, if not observed, presence of our trucks on the road at night, make them less likely to do something bold.
>
> We are winning because we have taken actions to effect (sic) both parts of the threat. The company uses intel effectively to develop targets and then conducts operations to detain those targets. The platoons plan and execute effective disruption patrols, both day and night, that make our presence in sector unpredictable. The wire (along the Mullah Fayad Highway) is an obstacle used by the company to aid in the defense, however, the wire is not the reason IEDs have been rare. Daily foot patrols and constant presence on the road have deterred the enemy.
>
> The problem with counterinsurgency is that there really aren't tangible results. It is frustrating for leaders and soldiers alike.... However, the biggest factor will be the character of the key leaders. We will become utterly frustrated an inordinate amount of times over the next half o[f] the deployment. Our men will crave results and want to knock down doors and shoot people, we must temper them. They will openly complain that we do not take enough action because they don't understand the big picture. We will be frustrated with our higher ups thinking they do not do enough or give us too many restrictions. We will get frustrated with higher ups because we think they want us to do too much. We will (the CO and PLs) disagree and fight [with] and annoy each other. But, we have but one option and that is to

build on our success. In my opinion, we will be the deciding factors. Can we take the discontent of our soldiers and the berating of our superiors? The progress will be slow and people may not understand, but we will be successful. Remember, institutional learning and tactical innovations at [the] lowest levels are keys to winning the counterinsurgency fight.[3]

My take on the situation is reflected in the above words. Ultimately, I believed we were doing the right things but as subsequent slides in the presentation indicated, there was still much to do. Charlie Company was the only one in the battalion to not have taken a significant casualty to this point (either an assigned or attached soldier). Certainly, some thought we were in a quiet sector and compared to Qarghuli Village and Rushdi Mullah, it was. However, the early work of finding the caches and the later work of using intelligence to arrest leaders in the middle of the night seemed to be paying off. Others before me had presented a rosy assessment of our success as a battalion or brigade. Mine was more tempered. I was also trying to demonstrate the utility in our approach, not so much to the commander as others who may read it.

Despite the complex attack against Delta Company, no soldiers had died in January. For nearly five weeks, the battalion was without a fatality when on 6 February a sniper's bullet struck Private First-Class Brian Browning. He had been on the roof down at Patrol Base Shanghai (Rushdi Mullah).[4] He was the second soldier killed on the rooftop of Shanghai. While the IED was the chief implementer of carnage, at least one sniper was able to reach out and touch us as well. Time would tell if he'd strike again.

Despite the threat, the gear we wore was a significant hindrance. Each of us wore a Kevlar helmet, eye protection, gloves, and Interceptor Body Army with front, back, and side plates, a throat guard, and groin protector. Along with the protective gear, we carried at least 180 rounds of ammo on our persons plus an M4 rifle with 30 rounds, water, night vision devices, and more to include radios and grenades. The experimental physical training program and months of walking made us strong, but we could only run so long in the gear and insurgents could escape easily. While my soldiers were more fit than the average enemy, the additional 60 pounds of gear slowed us considerably, so it was to our relative surprise that we caught two insurgents red-handed on 9 February. Intelligence indicated that hidden within a large patch of reeds was a "mother of all" caches. I led the platoon through a grove en route and one of my grenadiers spotted two men digging. He alerted the platoon and I sent his squad, 3rd, to apprehend the men. I felt it highly unlikely we would capture them. Amazingly, they hastily threw dirt over their hole and forfeited their chance to run before my guys could catch them.

We kicked away the loose dirt and discovered a sizeable cache, though not the one the battalion S2 thought we'd find in the reeds. The contents included mostly different materials for initiating IEDs remotely. We took the men into custody and I assigned soldiers to guard them while I recorded and photographed the contents. We found nothing at the grid we originally intended to search. Satisfied, I told the guards that the detainees were their responsibility. If we came under contact, they were to throw the men down, lay on top of them, and protect them. It was clear these men had every desire to kill us, but it was now our responsibility to protect them.

We exited the palm grove and headed back toward the battle position. As we cleared the first farm field we came across a small canal that slowed our movement. At that point, there was a hamlet and women were crying for us to release the men. (The coordinated wailing of women in an attempt to release their men was about as annoying a tactic as there could be and one we encountered often; it never worked to win their release.) While not a big canal, it required some time to negotiate. The first half of the element was across when my RTO and I made our crossing. At that moment, a sharp *crack* rang in my ear as a sniper's bullet flew between my RTO's and my head. We hit the deck and my RTO began to report the situation as I took quick stock.

Reacting to a sniper is a fairly nebulous drill and one I rarely practiced as a cadet or lieutenant. The general plan is to throw smoke and break away but that works much better in the woods where there is cover and limited sight lines. Attacking toward the enemy sniper would have been bold, but we had only a general idea of where he was and over 300 meters of open land to cross. I wanted to go into the village and occupy a building, however, the wailing women gave me pause to wonder what may await us in the houses. Also, I had taken a small force with me and now had three soldiers tied up with detainees and carrying the cache. Releasing the detainees and dropping the cache also would have been a win for the enemy. The greatest value was getting back with everything. Ultimately, I fell back on the limited training I had and initiated a break contact drill.[5]

When we got back to base, one of the detainees' faces was bloody. One of the escorts had taken my instructions and thrown the man down and jumped on him, incidentally thrusting his face into rocks on the canal's bank. His wounds were superficial but the lacerations were bleeding pretty good and he needed to be treated. My senior medic, always a dutiful soldier, refused to touch him. His blood was up. I had my junior medic clean him instead. I certainly could have ordered the senior medic to do it and some might say I shouldn't have let a soldier refuse to do his job. (To be clear, he never refused an order. He told me before I ever gave the word.) But when you've been in a frustrating situation for that long getting shot at from the shadows against an enemy unwilling to fight you straight up, emotions run high and everyone sometimes needs a break. I feel I did more good for the long-term health of the platoon not forcing the issue. Besides, if I hadn't been the platoon leader, I might have been right there with him.

There are a handful of decisions I think about a lot from my time in Iraq and the decision to break contact is one of them. It was not aggressive, but none of my guys died and we brought the cache and detainees home. We didn't strike fear into the heart of the insurgents but we did remove two of their members and some material from the battlefield. I fell back on what I knew, but I had considered other options. I have no idea what the right answer is even after ten years of thinking about it. What makes our ability to bring the detainees in all the better is that they turned out to be pretty bad dudes after one confessed to murder during questioning and the other's cell phone implicated him in terrorist attacks in Baghdad. These weren't two-bit players.

* * *

When Petraeus took the reigns of Multi-National Force-Iraq he also took control of implementing "the Surge." While the surge of U.S. troops—five Army brigade combat teams, two Marine battalions, and several enabling elements—was not something Petraeus had asked for, the timing of it linked him to the decision. There seemed to be two opposing national sentiments. One was that the change in leadership and surge of forces only represented that the situation was worse than advertised and the nation needed to "cut slingload" in Iraq. The other was more hopeful. Petraeus, the effective editor-in-chief of FM 3-24, buoyed by the additional forces, would breathe new life into the situation. But even then, some wondered if a surge was necessary.

At the same time, there was some indication that the Polar Bears and Commando Brigade were making noise. Lawrence Kaplan, a foreign policy expert and one-time Distinguished Visiting Professor at the U.S. Army War College, noted that officers at the Pentagon were recommending 2nd Brigade, 10th Mountain Division as one for others to study. Pondering the idea of a new strategy, Kaplan wrote, "What if there were one true path all along? If there were, historians will trace it back through the Triangle of Death in 2007, Ramadi in 2006, Tall Afar [sic] in 2005, and, finally, to Mosul in 2004. There, General Petraeus first previewed some of the techniques and methods of counterinsurgency employed by the brigade commanders [Kershaw, Colonel Sean MacFarland (Ramadi), and Colonel H.R. McMaster (Tel Afar)] but never promulgated as a countrywide policy—until now." He wondered if the whole strategy wasn't already in place and just not implemented far and wide. (Kaplan, it should be noted, argued that Iraq was a wash and the real surge should take place in Afghanistan.)[6] Interestingly, the actions of Petraeus, McMaster, and MacFarland have received a fair amount of recognition and study, while Kershaw's campaign has gone largely overlooked, until now.

For the Polar Bears, one of those units in Kaplan's lineage of counterinsurgency adherents, life went on as normal. Two days after Petraeus received the guidon, Bravo and Charlie Companies launched *Operation Polar Dagger*. A Bravo Company section searched an objective and established a traffic control point in the hopes of pushing any fleeing enemy toward another Charlie Company objective which lay south and west of Al Taraq. Other than a brief fire fight, the mission was uneventful, but Sharp's assessment of the operation is revealing that counterinsurgency techniques were effective:

> Missions like this one were common for us. We called them Cordon and Knock out of frustration in place of its proper name Cordon and Search. A Cordon and Search is a mission where you isolate an objective allowing nothing in or out and then clear and search the objective, usually for enemy personnel and/or equipment. For the longest time the Army had trained us to charge in hard during the search portion without much concern for collateral damage. The nature of the conflict in Iraq had changed this approach, and rightfully so. It was still irksome to now calmly knock, wait for an answer (!) and then calmly move inside and begin the search. At the time it felt like our wings were clipped.
>
> Looking back reveals the wisdom of this policy. Our searches were no longer the dreaded wave of destruction that brought the enmity of the civilian population. It didn't seem like it at the time, but our searches still managed to keep the opposition off balance and at times provided intelligence for future use.[7]

5. A New Strategy?

As I had noted in the assessment above, soldiers might find the method frustrating, but it was effective and it was on the leaders to keep faith with the process. Sharp's words are his reflection five years later and demonstrate that, with time, soldiers could see the value in a frustrating but important approach.

And continue on we did. On 13 February, I sent a patrol out from Al Taraq with my Weapons Squad Leader in charge of an element consisting mostly of 2nd Squad. Their task was to burn the reed line along a canal that ran parallel to Route Saliva, a road we never used that led to the hamlets west of Al Taraq. In the process, something exploded in the canal and we pulled the patrol in unsure if anything else might cook off. So we let the area cool down. That night we sent out a small unit ambush and the next day at noon, we went out to search the area where the explosion occurred. What we found was the start of a very nice Valentine's Day for the platoon. By the end, the enemy was thoughtful enough to hand us seven caches.

The first two were 100 meters apart along the canal. In one we found five Russian sabot rounds (used in tanks), a directional charge, and four tubes that could be used to make directional charges. In the other, we found two 60 mm mortar base plates, an AK-47, two magazines, and 300 rounds of 7.62 mm ammo, half of which had cooked off. Later that day, we took another patrol along the canal and found five more caches including five directional charge IEDs packed and prepared for employment. The brigade credited us with having removed 25 IEDs from the enemy's hands that day.[8]

Not everything we did panned out, even when sticking to our principles. Our proximately to the locals placed them in danger. Often times, this meant that insurgents used them to get to us either through coercing the locals into assisting or allowing their attacks or by bearing violence in the enemy's attempt to demonstrate they were not safe. Occasionally, they became collateral damage in our own earnest actions. In mid–February, one of my soldiers was shot at the entry control point of T147 while standing guard in the turret of a HMMWV. While he was ultimately unharmed (not even a bruise), I sent up a report and the decision was made to fire mortars at the enemy. (I provided a distance and direction based off the guard's report.) Ultimately, the battalion fired three 120 mm mortars and four civilians were injured in the exchange.

Out of contact, we moved quickly to care for the locals. My medics established a triage point providing instructions to the infantrymen of one of the squads. My senior medic had trained my soldiers well and they were able to perform well under the conditions (one lady had her entrails sticking out of her stomach). I requested a MEDEVAC and soon the casualties were on their way to Baghdad. Two would die; the other two we would continue to treat once released from the hospital. The company and battalion moved quickly to provide compensation for the dead. Our quick reaction and willingness to make amends in a manner acceptable to Arabs prevented the locals from blaming us or turning against us. They ultimately blamed the enemy. The take away for us was that being aggressive had its risks, but there were ways to mitigate those risks by being upfront.

The Polar Bears did their best to avoid civilian casualties and were generally good at providing medical care to anyone harmed in the course of war no matter which side was responsible. Counterinsurgency theorist John McCuen opined:

> The military should be very careful to avoid the shotgun approach: this is, accepting a few neutral civilian casualties to get a few rebels. It does not work this way because the few neutral casualties create ten-fold new rebels among the casualties' friends and relatives. The military should also avoid indiscriminate bombing, shelling, or killing of any kind. Everybody—including the population—understands that innocent people are going to get killed in war. On the other hand, the people immediately recognize and resent flagrant disregard of life and property. Wholesale killing and destruction must be avoided by the counterrevolutionary forces. More than this, government troops and police should immediately give the same care to civilian casualties that they give to their own casualties. Such humanitarian action will often turn an initial bad impression into a lasting good one.

The incidental deaths of two locals presented a situation where the populace could have turned their backs to the Polar Bears, but by doing all it could to save them and to reconcile, the battalion showed itself better than the enemy.

Between 16 and 17 February, the Warriors of A/2–5 CAV combined with the Polar Bears (possibly from Delta or just from Alpha) and Iraqi Army soldiers for *Operation Polar Iron*. The operation consisted of ground and air assaults into Qarghuli Village with the intent of disrupting insurgent activity. In total, the soldiers detained 49 individuals suspected of terrorist activity, including one believed to be an Al Qaeda cell leader and another on the black list for involvement with Sunni extremist activities. Despite some small arms fire and some IEDs found and cleared, no coalition soldiers were harmed.[9]

Small signs of progress popped up toward the end of the month. On 20 February the Iraqi Police at the Yusifiyah Joint Security Station received new equipment. General Abid Muhammad, chief of the Iraqi police district, distributed the gear himself. On 23 February, Iraqi Security Forces arrested five members of Al Qaeda (likely Islamic State) near the JSB and another two terrorists near Yusifiyah, one of which was the head of the Islamic Army in Yusifiyah, and without hyperbole, I reported to my parents on 24 February that "we've all but eliminated roadside bombs in our company's sector."[10] The triple stand concertina wire and roving patrols at night had left the stretch of the Mullah Fayad Highway within control of Charlie Company IED free.

During this time, the battalion employed a fair amount of soft power as part of its continuing counterinsurgency thrust. While Companies B, C, and D continued to fight throughout their areas, Yusifiyah persisted in its steady progress. On 23 February, Iraqi Police, Iraqi Army soldiers, and members of Alpha Company secured the reopening of a mosque in the largely-Shia town. The mosque had closed after an insurgent attack on it in October but now the locals finally felt comfortable opening it for worship. "This is a good day for the people of Iraq," said First Lieutenant Ali Kudair of the Iraqi Police. "There are a lot of mosques opening in the area and it shows that we are progressing as a nation." There were no attacks reported though there were apparently some fistfights. Still, the largely peaceful opening drew a large number of worshippers.[11]

Around this time, Charlie Company and members of the Brigade Support Battalion conducted a medical operation at the school in Al Taraq. 1st and 3rd Platoons provided security while the company commander oversaw the execution. My platoon had the inner security and assisted with operations at the school. 3rd Platoon patrolled the town. Both platoons had ambush positions north of the town in concealed terrain to block any enemy advance from that direction. The northern approach was the most likely for the enemy given the amount of concealment, so we sent our guys out in the dark to occupy hidden positions in case the enemy moved in on us. Truck mounted gunners from my platoon overwatched the fields to the east and west and soldiers back at the battle position and 3rd Platoon's patrol secured the south.

As my senior medic noted in the press release, it was nice to have some doctors in town since he and the junior medic were constantly flooded with people seeking medical care beyond the capacity of an Army medic. Our medics were amazing, but an aid bag and aid station can only provide so much. Planners chose the Al Taraq School hoping it would get people comfortable with the facility. Further, it was much easier to secure than to bring locals into the base and was a known area for locals to come to. In total, 75 residents received care. One teen receiving care stated that the Americans were his "friends." However, Iraqi doctors were not present and this highlighted a continuing weakness of these operations. It continued to be Americans providing for Iraqis, a potential path to dependence.

As the operation was underway, terrorists fired a series of RPG rounds and rifles at the school. The fire didn't last long and was wildly ineffective. Our ambushes did not return fire or report anything beyond hearing the noise indicating it was far off, probably north of the Janabi Run Canal. The battalion operations sergeant major grabbed me and asked why my soldiers weren't returning fire and I told him we weren't going to fire into our own guys. He was there with the personal security detachment, but they weren't tied into the defenses and thus weren't briefed on the security plan. If the ambushes couldn't engage, we couldn't.

Despite the attack, my commander made the decision to continue the operation. He wanted to show the enemy that they couldn't deter us. It would be a propaganda win for them and could only embolden the enemy if we closed shop early. It was the right call and I don't remember any dissenting voices among the Charlie leaders. The enemy had just proven himself almost impotent, unable to do anything but fire ineffective rounds in our general direction. Why provide him with a victory? Besides, the school was a pretty safe place for the locals to be. It had concrete walls and roofs. We had a very strong security apparatus there and around town. It would take a massive assault to deter us. Instead, we won that day.[12]

Back in Yusifiyah, the battalion's medics also went the extra mile in taking care of a severely sick seven-month-old baby. The child was the size of a two-month-old, severely dehydrated and unable to drink from a bottle. Despite their limited means—the aid station was not set up for inpatient or infant care—the medics took the baby in for four days until he was well enough for the father to take him home. They ensured the father knew how to care for the child moving forward.[13]

But it wasn't all soft power. On 24 February, *Operation Polar Thunder* saw two Bravo platoons, 1st (minus one squad in a screen line) and 3rd, air assault into objectives near Rushdi Mullah. The operation was intended to catch a large player in the Rushdi Mullah insurgent syndicate. The soldiers were looking for one of the "Clooneys," a group of brothers who resembled the actor George Clooney. Unfortunately, the target was not home.[14]

And as the month ended, the Polar Bears were reminded just how dangerous Iraq was. On 27 February, a group of route clearance soldiers acting as a combined element of a detached platoon from Company A and engineers from the Brigade Special Troops Battalion were clearing roads north of the Polar Bear area of operations in a place labeled Zone 310. A vehicle struck an IED and was badly mangled and on fire. Three of the engineers died. A staff sergeant from Alpha Company, badly burned, was able to open the door and get out. He survived with nearly 90 percent of his body burned.[15] The NCO would lose both of his hands and spend a long time in recovery. Eventually, he turned his adversity into inspiration. Medically retired, he does a lot of work in the veteran and Ranger communities, occasionally speaking at Ranger School graduations.

On the last day of February, I left 1st Platoon, Charlie Company, and became the platoon leader for 3rd Platoon, Delta Company. Prior to arriving at Yusifiyah, I had received word that my new platoon lacked discipline and needed someone to straighten them out. When I got there, I sat down with my new platoon sergeant. His assessment was the same. (He was also new to the platoon.) With this information and no time to assess the platoon, I gave a tough, "I'm not your friend" speech to the guys, who almost to a man had a look of dread on their face. I was following the principle that it is easier to get softer than harder as a leader and trying to establish a clear rank structure. The problem was, I didn't give the platoon time to demonstrate who they were before I told them who I thought they were. If there was one saving grace, I did pull aside my new RTO and talk to him personally. I felt we needed to develop rapport immediately. I told him I trusted him. Later, he told me that meant a lot to him even if I had bombed the introductory speech.

That morning, I attended an operations order brief with Alpha Company. There was a mission kicking off early the next day to establish a new position on Route Peggy further east of BP 155. The mission involved a wide assortment of personnel and formations. Alpha and its Iraqi partners would be the main effort, but along with my weapons platoon were a tank platoon from A/2-5 CAV, a platoon of the Task Force Iron Claw route clearance unit, and Air Force Joint Terminal Attack Controllers (JTAC) who were specialized in the coordination of air assets with ground elements. Our role was largely one of security. We would secure BP 155 and allow Alpha to maximize its forces. The route clearance team would clear the road and Alpha with the tanks and IA would clear the new area. Behind them, an engineer team would quickly build up a defensive position using HESCO barriers and dirt.

Alpha's executive officer, who was in charge of the operation and with whom I had served in Charlie before the deployment, asked me if I was ready to move out. At that point, I hadn't even had time to make my (poor) opening remarks to the platoon. He said I could move out early in the morning if necessary. I took the extension. Wars are full of stories of platoon leaders taking over platoons and leading them into battle without having met them, but I wanted at least a few hours to plan and figure out the capabilities of the platoon. A weapons platoon, unlike a rifle platoon, has 18 soldiers

5. A New Strategy?

when full up. There are supposed to be four NCOs, a platoon sergeant (for administration), a section sergeant (for tactics), and two squad leaders. The platoon has five vehicles and mounts an Improved Target Acquisition System (ITAS), the system used to fire TOW missiles, as a means of seeing further on the battlefield (we did not use TOW missiles during our time in Iraq). When the mission kicked off, things generally went according to plan. However, the hastily built position of HESCOs stacked on top of each other would slowly implode forcing Alpha to take over a hardstand building later on and use that position solely to control the road.

There continued to be signs of progress in the Triangle as March came about. On the first day of the month, the same day as the operation to establish a new battle position on Route Peggy, government officials hosted a conference to discuss the Law Enforcement Plan of Baghdad. Their goal was to get support from local leaders for the plan. Tribal chieftains pledged to "purge their areas of terrorist cliques."[16] While it's hard to tell what the chiefs planned on doing, the fact they were there engaging with government officials was a good sign.

More signs came during sensitive times. Shiites from Baghdad had to transit the Triangle of Death to get to holy sites in Karbala and other parts of Anbar province.

A HMMWV takes up a guard position in a field during an operation in the Yusifiyah area during an operation to build a new base on Route Peggy.

The fact that many did not make it in 2004 led to the reputation of the area as a place where everything burns leading to the bestowing of the grim, geometric moniker. But as the annual Shiite Arbaeen pilgrimage took place in 2007, there was no violence against those transiting the Triangle, largely through Mahmudiyah along Route Jackson. It was incredible to see buses barreling down the route with people literally sitting on the roof, fearless in an area where there was once a $1000 bounty on their head. Across the country, there were several instances of violence, but not here.[17]

Also, a Yusifiyah resident identified an IED to the soldiers at the Yusifiyah Joint Security Station and the Iraqi Army was able to disarm the device and get their own EOD to destroy it. A seemingly minor affair, the fact that the Iraqi Army could handle the situation internally demonstrated that they were at least somewhat weaned from dependence on the U.S. In another incident, a resident provided a tip that led to the discovery of a small cache (a single 122 mm artillery shell).[18] But while the battalion had been seeing signs of progress for months, Qarghuli Vilalge remained a relatively lawless land and Rushdi Mullah was still a dangerous place. Yusifiyah, Mullah Fayad, and Al Taraq were safe only in comparison. Thus, members of Odierno's staff still saw the Triangle of Death in early March as one of the most dangerous areas of Iraq and decided that that area around it needed more forces to pacify it.[19]

The effect of Odierno's decision was to send two of the Surge brigades into the belts around Baghdad, one to the north and the other to the south where it would butt up against 2nd Brigade Combat Team. Concomitant was the creation of a new division headquarters, Multi-National Division-Center, to oversee the southern belts. This divested 2nd Brigade from the Baghdad command. The Army tapped the 3rd Infantry Division out of Fort Stewart, Georgia, commanded by Major General Rick Lynch, to lead the new command. What this meant for the Polar Bears was that they no longer could retain the services of A/2–5 CAV, whose division headquarters served as the MND-B command. Thus, 3rd Infantry Division would have to provide an equivalent company. It did so in the form of Company B (Bayonet Company), 2nd Battalion, 69th Armor Regiment (B/2–69 AR) from the 3rd Infantry Division's lone brigade on Kelley Hill at Fort Benning, Georgia (the rest of 3rd Infantry Division's brigades were based out of Fort Stewart, minus its Combat Aviation Brigade, which staged out of Hunter Army Airfield in Savannah). As Peter Mansoor, Petreaus' executive officer noted, the creation of MND-C brought "greater concentration of effort to eliminating terrorist and militia sanctuaries south of Baghdad in the so-called triangle of death [sic]."[20]

On 29 March, my platoon drew the task of escorting B/2–69 AR in from Camp Stryker. Our mission was intimated to me as "If there are any IEDs out there, ensure they hit your [light armored] vehicles not theirs." We brought them in with no incident, but later that day when were on our way back to Stryker for the second load, my old platoon was on patrol in Al Taraq with the IA. Their mission was to distribute water to locals. As we were arriving into Stryker, reports came over the radio of an IED strike. I remember being surprised by an IED in the village. We had walked that terrain so often when I was there and never found an IED. We had taken contact in the village from time to time, but never a bomb. I wondered why. Was it due to some change in the way people operated there or just an opportunity attack? I asked the platoon sergeant about it later and he told me how proud he was reflecting on the way the guys responded after the blast and reacted to the casualties. That made me feel good. Still, an interpreter, *nom de guerre* "Zee," and an Iraqi soldier died in the explosion.[21] I did not feel good about the quick reaction force being an hour away.

That would be the last operation for Charlie Company in Al Taraq. Charlie's initial operations during and immediately following *Polar Blizzard* combined with relentless efforts had kept the enemy at bay along with the fortune of good geography. Open fields around Al Taraq made it harder for the enemy to mass as in other areas. Charlie was the first company to hand significant battle space to the Iraqi Army, handing over the entire sector from Mullah Fayad to beyond Al Taraq. Delta had previously given up the JSB, but not its battle space. With Charlie's departure, Bravo Company picked up the sector for partnership purposes extending their influence from Rushdi Mullah to Yusifiyah proper, where, for a time, one of its platoons manned the Joint Security Station with the Iraqi Police. Charlie's commander assessed the handover thusly:

1. We successfully turned our area over to a *trained* indigenous force that continues the forward momentum our unit set forth.
2. We received orders for yet another difficult mission which involved starting over in a completely new area and doing the same thing we had just accomplished over the course of the last 7 months in yet another troubled spot.[22]

The new mission he referred to was *Operation Commando Auger*. This was an air assault by Charlie into the Abu Haswa region of the Southern Belt. The area was located north of Yusifiyah. The operation, conducted on 5 April, established a combat outpost (COP) near the town of Haswah to be known as COP Corregidor. (The commander notes that this was the company's ninth move of the deployment.) With that operation, the Polar Bears were now stretched far and wide across the area of operations having gained significant terrain north and west of their original boundary.[23]

March was a month of progress. From the little signs like the IA being able to defuse a bomb or a local tipping off the unit to the big things like tribal chieftains cooperating with the government or the IA taking control of a sector, the approach appeared to be working. Freeing a company to be able to attack into ungoverned space was a major sign of progress. But Rushdi Mullah was far from quelled and Qarghuli Village was like Mogadishu on the Euphrates. There was still a lot of work to be done and a lot danger to endure.

Like the enemy was keen to do, on 8 April he reminded the battalion it had not won just yet and that this was still a land on fire. A/2-5 CAV and B/2-69 AR were still in the midst of their relief in place. The experienced soldiers were showing those new to the area how to operate. Two Bradleys, at the position known as BP 154, sat at the S curve on Route Malibu as usual. While the two vehicles scanned the palm tree and grass lined roads, a man rolled a tire with an IED in it up to one of the Bradleys, approaching at a perpendicular angle to how the vehicles faced. While children played nearby, he crawled under the vehicle, placed the bomb, and walked off casually. Not long after, an immense explosion went off setting the vehicle on fire and blowing a hole in the floorboard. The vehicle's ammunition stores were ablaze and cooking rounds off in a scene reminiscent of that September day on Route Earnhardt.

Private First Class Nick White was in the driver's hatch, somewhat detached from the main part of the Bradley. This provided him all the buffer he needed to survive the blast as he was able to climb out of the driver's hole. The others were not so lucky, Staff Sergeant Harrison "Ducky" Brown, Private First Class David Simmons, and Sergeant Todd Singleton died in the flames. A combined force of A/2-5 CAV and B/2-69 AR attempted to respond. (My platoon, still nominally the QRF, was on another mission to Stryker at the time.) However, due to the fire and exploding rounds, they could not rush into the vehicles. After escaping, White made an earnest yet futile attempt to put the flame out. He would be evacuated to Baghdad and return to duty in about a week.[24]

Shortly after the attack, one of my classmates took over the B/2-69 AR platoon that had been involved. He immediately took it upon himself to beef up BP 154. Whereas platoons previously had just sent out a section, he moved his platoon to the position and adjusted its location to put it at an intersection. He arranged for a connex to serve as sleeping quarters and built up obstacles and positions that provided 360 degree security and the ability to protect from attacks. It went from a battle position in name to one in being. He was determined never to let anything like that happen again, and it didn't. As on Route Earnhardt in late September, the enemy had taken advantage of a change in units to burn a vehicle down, but like Charlie Company after the Earnhardt incident, the company adapted and created a better way to not only protect his guys, but to accomplish the mission. The enemy had a lot of fight left in him, but so did we. It was a continuous cycle of react and adapt on both sides.

The attack on BP 154 may have been a stark reminder of the danger that lurked at every corner, but April also brought a nice reminder that the battalion was close to completing its tour, close in military terms. In less than sixty days, the battalion would begin the process of returning home. However, as men started to sniff the finish line, rumors began to swirl. In a letter to Charlie Company families, the commander tried to quell the rumors—which were likely worse back home than in Yusifiyah. He acknowledged the rumors and the fact that 3rd Brigade, 10th Mountain Division, our sister brigade in Afghanistan, had had its tour extended. There seemed to be an understanding that an extension may occur but hope that it would not. Charlie's commander noted that both Infanti and Kershaw, while realistic about the situation, believed the extension would not happen. In several letters to my family I was enthusiastic about going home slightly early, in July, as some rumors seemed to say. I sent a letter as early as Valentine's Day, saying, "I was emphatically told by our deputy brigade commander that we will not be extended."[25] And I remember the company executive officer telling me they had already had meetings about shipping containers home. It all was encouraging, including the rumor we would get home in less than a year.

In early April, 3rd Platoon happened to be up at Stryker as we often were. The men never complained because the food there was great, the internet was plentiful and fast, and we could go to the Post Exchange on Camp Victory. We were less the QRF platoon and more that all-everything platoon, but it kept us occupied and I always enjoyed any mission where it was just me and the guys. Whatever the reason, I was in the brigade tactical operations center on 9 April when Kershaw spotted me and asked me to come to his office.

After small talk he asked what the soldiers wanted to know ... other than when we were going home. I told him that was what we really wanted to know. He told me to tell him what I had heard and he would tell me what he thought, so I started with the rumor we would be going home early (on 13 November, I sent a letter to my parents reporting a rumor we'd be home in June). He said there was no way that was happening. I then said I heard we were going home on time. He said that might happen, which was not encouraging, so I told him there were rumors we would be extended three months. He responded more vigorously to this one saying it was possible. The 101st had been tapped to return to Iraq and one of their brigades would replace us, but if they did so on time, their dwell time, the time a unit or soldier is home between deployments, would be less than a year. It is incredibly tough to prepare a brigade for combat in one year, less is much harder and it would put additional strain on troops, some facing their third or fourth tour. What he didn't explain, and might not have completely known, was that the Surge put a huge strain on timelines across the Army. I appreciated the commander's candor but I hated the thought. I think I decided to focus on the chance the extension wouldn't happen more than the chance it would. We went on to talk about books and reading lists.

A day later, my platoon was down at Bataan, the Water Treatment Facility that the mechanized company used as a base of operations. We'd gone down there to secure one of the two battle positions cater-corner to it that provided the base security. When we did this, we'd rotate half the platoon to Bataan for an hour or two to get some snacks and drinks (Gatorade and soda) and to use the slow internet and phones. I was sitting there at a computer checking my e-mail when the soldier next to me opened a news website. "Hey, sir, do you see this?"

I looked over. There in bold letters were words telling me we were extended. Even though Kershaw had prepared me, finding out officially from the news was a gut punch. Worse, there seemed to be really no guarantee that this was the first of one. What if there were more? How long would we be here?

Secretary of Defense Robert Gates made the official military announcement on 11 April that all currently deployed and soon-to-deploy units in the Central Command area of responsibility, namely Iraq, Afghanistan, and the Horn of Africa, would be deployed fifteen months with a minimum of twelve months dwell time.[26] General Casey, now the Chief of Staff of the Army, and acting Secretary of the Army Pete Geren sent notice to soldiers on 13 April. By then, though, we all knew. By waiting on the announcement, they had allowed the information to leak. Casey's and Geren's communiqué said:

> To the soldiers and families of the U.S. Army, yesterday, we announced that active-duty Army units now in the Central Command area of responsibility and those headed there will deploy for not more than 15 months and will return to home stations for not less than 12 months. We made this difficult decision after careful thought, and owe you an explanation. We wanted to

tell you in advance, but events caused us to move faster than planned. Faced with the increased probability of sending units to combat with less than 12 months dwell time, the possibility of numerous late-breaking unit extensions, and understanding that we are in a long and difficult struggle that will require a steady deployment of ground forces, we had to change our current policy of 12 months deployed. We intend to return to the 12 month policy as soon as possible. Deployments of 15 months with a minimum of 12 months reset, retraining and recovery allows us to sustain a predictable flow of well-trained and well-equipped formations to the theater commanders. This also allows us to provide a more predictable and dependable deployment schedule for soldiers and families. Though there is nothing certain in war, this represents a solid commitment to 12 months of dwell time at home. This predictability is essential to the long term health of our service. This nation, led by its ground forces, has been at war for over five years fighting for America's freedom, America's security and America's future. The Army exists to field forces for victory. We are in this war to win, and you are making a difference every day. We know this decision asks even more from you and your family, but it is essential to our success. We are both personally and profoundly grateful for your service, your many continued sacrifices and your deep commitment to accomplishing our shared mission during this time of danger and uncertainty. You are the strength of our nation.[27]

I have kept my copy of that letter all these years for whatever reason. It may be that because the leadership lessons contained therein were important. On the positive side was taking the time to inform soldiers and lay out the clear reasons behind a tough decision. On the negative side was the fact that it took to the last minute to make the decision. More likely I kept it initially because it greatly impacted my soldiers and I and then held on to it in order to remind myself constantly of the human effect of military decisions. That doesn't cause me to not make a tough decision, but I always want to know what I am doing and whom I'm doing it to.

The problem with this policy is that it didn't really help soldiers get a year at home; it ensured that units did, but soldiers are fluid. Many soldiers in my unit would not be deploying ever again. A large number were stop-lossed and the tour extension added another three months on their additional time (cynics might say sentence). Others would leave the Army after the deployment, possibly in response to the policy. On the other side, though, many soldiers ended up returning home to receive orders to units in the pipeline for deployment, so in a matter of months, these guys were back to Iraq or on to Afghanistan for another 15-month stint. The policy didn't protect them from this, so 4–31 IN would return to Fort Drum in November 2007 and the unit would not be able to deploy again until November 2008, but the soldiers may well be overseas before then.

In *Duty: Memoirs of a Secretary at War*, Gates talks about efforts by Congress to force each soldier to spend 12 months at home and he demonstrates the impossibility of the task,[28] and he is right; it would be ridiculously time consuming for personnel officers to individually certify each soldier in the Army. It would be almost impossible for a unit to field a full complement of soldiers who had not deployed in a year. There were just too many units overseas and too many soldiers stop-lossed or exiting the service. The extension was the best they could do.

It was hard to see this at the time and my reaction as a young officer was not entirely professional. I wish I had been more stoic about it. Alpha Company's first sergeant, a veteran of Somalia in 1993, wrote to his friend and reporter Mark Bowden, "The boys and I are hanging tough over here, despite the latest news. I wish I could rant and rave about the extension, but in reality, I cannot. Sure, it sucks missing [my daughter's] birthday and the litany of big events, but we serve, bottom line. Kind of makes three months in Mogadishu seem like a cakewalk."[29] That is the reaction of a professional, experienced soldier. I had nothing to complain about.

Of course, even those that stayed in the unit didn't have it easy. In Gates' memoir, he takes responsibility for the negative effects of the extensions. He writes of a letter he received from a soldier's daughter telling him that in the twelve months her dad was "home" he wasn't really home. He was in the field getting ready to go. Further, Gates believes he may have contributed to the rash of Post Traumatic Stress Disorder (PTSD) diagnoses. It is admirable for him to take responsibility for this and other effects of the decision. Few senior leaders seem willing to do such things. I've been told often enough never to let your soldiers know you are wrong, which I find a useless yet too prolific leadership lesson.

Gates also relates that his senior military advisor, Lieutenant General Pete Chiarelli, who had been the commander of MNC-I as late as December 2006, told him that the soldiers were expecting the three-month extension and thought he was an "asshole" for not making the decision.[30] I do not remember a single soldier thinking that, so I'm not sure where Chiarelli, an officer I respect, got that impression. I can only surmise that he meant soldiers knew the decision would be made and thought Gates an asshole for not just making it then and getting it in motion.

Many writers and politicians were concerned this move would break the force (a decision many stated at the announcement of the Surge), but I think the decision to grow the Army, combined by the decision to draw down forces within a couple years helped stave that off. Of course, it is hard to measure when an army is "broken," the term being incredibly nebulous. Still, I think the real risk was just how little rest the "front line" units were getting as it was on a day to day basis. Placing an extra three months on that only exacerbated the risk. Fifteen months is a long time to face danger every day and deal with the ambiguity of Iraq. It is a long time to live in austere conditions away from loved ones or the pursuit of happiness. It is a long time to maintain a rigid standard. Rarely have leaders and soldiers received the credit they deserve for the relative paucity of immoral and unethical actions and atrocities. The handful that did occur were bad, like the rape and murders perpetrated by the 101st soldiers, and deserved swift action by the military, but it is amazing given the length in months and tours soldiers were deployed that so little actually occurred. Still, the high suicide rate is indicative of the toll this all took on the troops. (It should be noted that suicides in the military, at least since the turn of the century, are more likely to be committed by a first term, non-combat veteran soldier than one who had deployed.)

From a counterinsurgency stand point, the extension had one positive effect in that it provided continuity for over a year. The Polar Bears could continue to implement their campaign plan for a longer period and maintain their relationships. Continuity in counterinsurgency is always a struggle. Units on 12-month tour would generally have about 10 of those months to really implement those plans, maybe less. Then the next unit would come in with its own plan. Frankly, the Polar Bears could use the time to consolidate gains, hand over areas, train the Iraqis, and push further into the Triangle. The extension did not solve the problem of whole sale change out at the end of the 15 months. The Army still has not developed an effective policy, though units have begun embedding officers and NCOs into their predecessors early to ease the transition.

The counterinsurgency gain did come at the expense of soldiers exposed to the enemy for consecutive days over a period longer than nearly any combat unit in American military history. While not fighting a battle against a peer enemy that attacked daily, most Polar Bear soldiers had been under the threat of contact from the enemy from early September, broken only by leave. When considering just units, as the policy did, nearly 15 months of continual front-line duty by a unit like the Polar Bears that lived where it worked meant they were on the line longer than nearly any unit in American history. The effects of this are speculative at best, but may help explain some of the issues veterans have today.

In the wake of Gates' announcement and Casey's and Geren's letter to the troops, rumors began to swirl that the tours were going to increase to 18 months and that became quite disconcerting. The media began picking up on these rumors and reporting them. This led Odierno to send the following letter to all soldiers in his command:

> Tuesday [19 June] there were reports in the media about possible further extensions of tours of duty in Iraq, based on coverage of Acting Secretary of the Army Geren's Senate confirmation hearing.
> Let's be clear, no one extended here now to 15 months will be extended further.
> I ask leaders to move quickly to quell potential rumors. Inform your Soldiers and Family Readiness Groups without delay.[31]

Odierno was referring to statements Geren made in the hearing saying that it was possible the tours could lengthen if the Surge was extended and that planning was occurring at Army headquarters to be ahead of the curve.[32] Reading Geren's words, they are incongruent with Odierno's and it is hard to tell what was actually going on. A closer look at the MNC-I commander's words indicate though that his statement applies only to those units who were already in Iraq. Thus, it was still possible for tours for incoming units to go to 18 months.

Delta's company commander printed the letter out and distributed it to the company. I kept that letter (without a scratch, dog ear, or crease). I suppose I thought it would be a "get out of jail free" card if they tried to extend us as if I could hold it up like it were a contract. It never came to that.

Despite my or anyone else's feelings about it, the extension was a fact and life went on. Unfortunately, it would not go on much longer for Corporal Ryan Bishop. An automatic rifleman in Charlie Company, Bishop died from an IED strike while on a dismounted patrol near Route Starbucks in the sector north of Yusifiyah. He was Charlie's first casualty. The enemy had well prepared defenses when Charlie establish COP Corregidor during *Commando Auger*. At his memorial ceremony on 18 April, Charlie's commander said, "He wanted to do his part for his country, and I always remember him being the first one to clean his weapon after missions.... He would always make coffee in the morning over a wood fire.... The coffee wasn't for him; it was for everyone else.... Bishop had the kind of selfless service you could not learn. You either have it or you don't." Among other awards, Bishop had earned the Army Commendation Medal with a Valor Device prior to his death. He left behind a wife, Melanie.[33]

Bishop was the first soldier killed in the battalion whom I had really interacted with. His was the first memorial ceremony I attended and it was at once a great tribute to an awesome soldier and a terrible experience. The atmosphere was thick with sadness and sorrow and I'm sure some desire for vengeance. Bishop was one of those soldiers whom everyone in the company knows for good reasons.

* * *

Rivers throughout history have been obstacles to armies. Even today, crossing a river in combat can be an exceptionally hazardous operation requiring detailed planning and the coordination of artillery, aviation, engineers, smoke, and maneuver forces, among others, but the Euphrates was less an obstacle and more a highway for insurgents. It's great length and relatively small width made it easy to find ways across it. In April, the only American position to be able to see the river clearly was BP 151. (Later, BP 152 would be moved to the west side of Route Malibu and be able to see it as well.) With no American unit similarly positioned on the west bank as the Polar Bears were on the east bank, the far side of the biblical waterway was a nuisance. Ultimately, it was a sanctuary of sorts that provided the enemy a distinct advantage.

It was time the Polar Bears asserted some control over it. Odierno's decision to move a brigade into the southern belt hadn't yet produced the effect that it would which was to limit the freedom of maneuver outside of the Commando brigade's area of operations, but that move along with some control of the west bank would go a long way to denying the enemy sanctuary and disrupting his communications and logistics. Thus, the brigade launched an operation on 21 April named *Commando Dive*. The 4–31 IN portion of this, *Polar Dive*, involved a two-platoon air assault to the west side of the river. 4th Platoon, Delta Company, and 1st Platoon, Bravo Company, participated in the operation with the battalion executive officer providing the command and control. The battalion S2 and a contingent of Iraqi Army soldiers accompanied the force.

Day One of the operation went off well for those involved. However, 21 April was a grim day for the battalion. In separate incidents Staff Sergeant Steven Tudor from Fox Company and Corporal Ray Bevel from Charlie Company were killed. Tudor was a transportation NCO whom I had interacted with several times. He was exceptionally competent and extremely helpful. He died from wounds suffered during a mortar attack on PB Yusifiyah in which two other soldiers were wounded. Tudor had served in Desert Storm and Somali. He left behind a wife, two children, and a grandchild. I also knew Bevel and had interacted with him when I was in Charlie. He died from an IED blast while on patrol near Route Primus in his company's sector. Bevel was remembered for the ridiculous amount of mail he would get and give out to his fellow soldiers. These care packages became known as "Bevel Boxes." He was a good, competent soldier ready

The inside of the new BP 152 which was just large enough to house soldiers. The spartan conditions came with bunks stacked three high, a single wooden outhouse, and plenty of cabin fever.

to step up as a leader but he wouldn't get that chance. He was survived by his wife. The battalion held a memorial ceremony for both soldiers on 27 April. In a May letter to the families, Charlie's commander said of Bishop and Bevel, "There were no better men amongst our ranks, no finer Soldiers in our profession." He then thanked the families for their dedication to duty.[34]

Despite the heartbreaking loss of two stellar soldiers in other parts of the area of operations, the cross-river mission went on. For three days, the two platoons searched homes and the S2 maximized his opportunity to gather information face to face from the citizens on the far shore. One of the men the ad hoc unit talked to encouraged them to build a base on his side of the river to protect them from Syrians who entered the area. The fundamentalist group calling itself the Islamic State had already begun rising from Al Qaeda in Iraq, so it's possible this man was indicating the first inklings of a transnational movement to establish a caliphate.

It was almost inevitable that the element would turn up some sort of cache given how secure any insurgent operative on that side of the river would feel, so it is no surprise that they found a number of armor piercing rounds. However, it is interesting that the unit stumbled upon the house of a bomb maker. Sharp describes searching the bomb maker's office and being amazed at how human this guy was. In addition to the obligatory Quran, the man had books ranging in subjects from history and politics to science and chemistry. Some were in English. He had pictures of his family and friends. Far from an impressionable country bumpkin, this guy was intelligent and family-oriented. The contrast between terrorist and family man has all the trappings of a devious Hollywood villain.

The mission continued to bring surprises. On the second day, the combined element came upon a house with a sandbagged position on the roof. At night, one man from the village would man it to provide security from insurgents. Sharp also notes that they found a house with a picture of Ali Hussein, a revered figure for Shiites. However, the family who lived in the house was Sunni. Apparently, this was a tactic for protection against the largely Shia Iraqi Army. The picture was used to make the family appear of the other sect so the IA wouldn't harass them. Fear of the Iraqi Army continued to be a hindrance to progress in the Polar Bears area of operations. While this instance occurred outside of the area, it is indicative of the distrust that existed between Iraqi Sunnis (who largely inhabited the farmland around Yusifiyah) and the Iraqi Army.

On the first day of the operation when the patrol came across the bomb maker's house, they were unable to apprehend the man. However, since his two brothers lived there, they arrested those men for association. As the second day of the operation was winding down, the bomb maker's mother showed up with him in tow. She traded her allegedly guilty son to get her other two back in an episode made for reality TV or an episode of "The Jerry Springer Show." The bomb maker gave a lot of information while in the custody of the two platoons, but they were unable to arrest anyone further during the three-day operation. While he was ratting on everyone else, apparently the bomb maker was giving an allocution speech admitting to making more than 100 IEDs.

At 2130 on 23 April, National Guardsmen pulled up to the west bank of the Euphrates and loaded the provisional force into boats and extracted them back to Polar Bear lines. The end result of the operation was the capture of three suspects and a cache as well as some intelligence. The battalion also proved they could cross the river even if it was only in raider fashion. Further, the battalion learned that there was a need for security and at least some desire for the Americans to provide it. While it would be a while before the battalion could truly address the cross-river problem, *Commando Dive* was not an isolated incident. The battalion would be back.

In a supporting effort, my platoon had moved from south to north, roughly paralleling the movements of the force across the river, in Qarghuli registering every military aged male we could find in the biometrics system. We found three Sadaam Husseins. A final casualty of the operation was at least one boat which members of 4th Platoon, Delta Company, destroyed with gunfire. So much for the insurgent navy![35]

The brigade operation as a whole appeared successful in interrupting terrorist activities. On top of the Polar Bears' achievements, the Iraqi Army and 2–15 FA detained 33 in *Operation Eagle Dive*, their parallel mission. They also found a treasure trove of enemy material. "Caches found during the operation contained two machine guns, two shotguns, six AK-47s, two ski masks, 27 mortar rounds, 280 57 mm rockets, four

155 mm rockets, nine 12-volt batteries, multiple mortar fuses, three IEDs, 500 hand grenades, four 82 mm mortar tubes, a large rocket and six rocket-propelled grenade launcher sights. Additionally, numerous IED-initiation devices and 30 DVDs of Al-Qaeda propaganda were discovered."[36] 2-14 IN's parallel operation, *Trident IV*, conducted with the Iraqi Army, nabbed six detainees and a small cache.

Four days after the end of *Polar Dive*, Bravo Company was on a relatively routine patrol that merits reporting for its illustration of soldiers in combat in Iraq. 1st Platoon and a team of Psychological Operations (PsyOps) soldiers were out in sector, about two miles from Rushdi Mullah. The PsyOps team passed out fliers as part of the patrol. The mission went off without much of a hitch and soldiers began the trek back to PB Shanghai. The patrol came to a canal that had a single crossing point consisting of a small metal bridge about four inches in width, roughly the width of a soldier's boot. Obviously, this was a dangerous place, a chokepoint that ground movement to a halt. As one of the Bravo Company soldiers was crossing the bridge, the enemy opened fire hitting him in the buttocks, the "million dollar wound," and knocking him into the canal.

But he would have to survive the patrol first. He ended up submerged in the water and had to fight against the weight of his equipment to get his head back to fresh air. As his head came up, he became aware of the firefight occurring around him. However, his legs were in pain and he couldn't support any weight on them. It was only then that he realized what had happened. Unable to do much of anything but hold on to the edge of the canal, he remained in the water with rounds flying past him shouting profanities.

Braving the fire, his team leader and a teammate ran up and tried to pull him out by having him walk up the side of the canal. However, the wounded soldier still couldn't bear any weight. Weighed down by gear and soaking clothes, he was too much for the other two to drag out without some assistance. Without orders and still under fire, the teammate jumped into the canal, submerged himself, and got under the wounded. Then he hoisted his brother up on his shoulders enough to allow the team leader to pull the wounded servicemember out. The team leader then kicked the soldier down the reverse slope of the canal to shield him from bullets

Now somewhat protected from enemy fire, the team leader and squad leader began medical aid on the soldier, cutting away his pants legs and applying tourniquets. (The patrol had no medic with it due to him being on leave.) At one point, a tourniquet became loose and had to be retightened. Apparently, the team leader pulled so hard that the soldier's leg fat squished into the wound and stopped the bleeding. The platoon leader was able to get a helicopter MEDEVAC and the soldier went first to the CSH in Baghdad and then onto Germany, Fort Bragg, North Carolina, and finally back to Fort Dum. He would have to fight two medical evaluation boards—a process to determine if a soldier's physical health meets requirements for his job—to remain an infantryman, but he succeeded.

Reflecting on this incident five years later, the soldier wrote: "I have no regrets about the decisions that led up to me being shot. [Presumably, decisions to join the military and the infantry.] It (the incident) leaves a lot of anger though. I wasted 9 months of my life in a country on the far side of the world, fighting for people I don't even care about at the age of 19. I spilled my own blood on their soil to give them a better way of life. But no one will ever know or even care about that. I know that we did improve their way of life while we were there. There was a visible effect, and I'm just another statistic of another young American soldier wounded in a country most Americans know nothing about in a war that they don't care about."[37] Hopefully, this book changes some of that.

The soldier's outlook and indignation, no doubt shared by many veterans of 4–31 IN who served in Yusifiyah and its environs, is one reason I share this story, but I share it more because it shows some of the everyday heroics that occur and the care that soldiers have for each other. I don't know if any of those responding to their wounded comrade received awards for their actions—I suspect not—but they certainly deserve to be awarded, at least based on the soldier's testimony. However, I doubt either care about that. They weren't thinking about danger or awards, just about saving their brother.

The medical logistics of this story also outline one of the great advantages modern U.S. soldiers—along with their partners and, at times, indigenous civilians—enjoy. The soldier endured a lot to earn the million dollars that neither he nor Forest Gump would ever see a penny of, much of that just to get out of the canal, but once out his squadmates got to work quickly and the battalion got a helicopter in fast. He moved from Baghdad to the United States in less than a week where he was able to recover far away from the dangers of being in a war zone where the enemy could care less what the Geneva Conventions say about the sanctity of medical hospitals and medical transport units. That sort of strength helped keep the numbers of dead in one of our longest wars under that of the number of casualties for the Normandy landings on 6 June 1944.

The beginning of May was a hopeful time for the Polar Bears. Signs were pointing to success. On the first day of the month, the battalion went on the offensive, launching *Operation Polar Scrum*. Charlie Company conducted an air assault to clear 24 kilometers of their battlespace and to get to know the people of the area.[38] The other companies had smaller roles. The main effort, however, was Bayonet Company, as the mission was largely in response to the attack on BP 154 that had killed three soldiers. They conducted a ground assault with parallel forces clearing the village on either side of Janabi Road. Americans hadn't touched Janabi Road until after Bayonet Company arrived, so it still held a lot of mystery.

The 2nd Platoon, Bayonet Company would arrive on their own in their Bradley Fighting Vehicles and clear the buildings south of the road. My platoon, which was now attached to the company, would be the main effort and clear the north side of the road. We were chosen largely because of our experience in operations similar to this. However, if we were the right ones, we were also the wrong ones. Never full up at 18 souls, we needed at least eight to man our vehicles and normally a ninth to lead them if we strayed too far. Generally, when we were dismounted, I was a high-ranking squad leader moving with two 3-man teams, a machine gun, and my RTO. Clearing houses, especially as the platoon got further from the road, required more than that. To alleviate this problem Bayonet's commander, decided to provide us a section of Bradley Fighting Vehicles (two) to be manned by their normal crews. This allowed us to put twelve on the ground. Five stayed in two HMMWVs as support vehicles with my platoon sergeant providing leadership.

The M2 Bradley provides an awesome array of capabilities from TOW missiles to a 25-mm chain-driven automatic cannon. It is big and imposing and can survive direct and indirect fire that neither a HMMWV nor a foot soldier ever could, but to a light fighter such as us 10th Mountaineers were, it is a death trap; a big, steel coffin; a shield upon which to lay while your funeral pyre burns all around. Looking into the eyes of the men as I briefed them on the mission was a stark reminder of that. My two sergeants never seemed to care what mission I gave them, but if there was a pass to be used, one would have cashed it in right there. I looked at the men and said, "I know [what you are thinking], but you know me." I was telling them that I wouldn't let us do anything that was unnecessarily dangerous hoping that would reassure them.

After a walk-through rehearsal at Bataan, the men bedded down for a few hours. We awoke, checked our equipment and selves, and loaded into the hulking machines in the pre-dawn darkness. As the ramp closed tight, locking us in, the apprehension was palpable. It was not fear, nor foreboding. It was just a sense that between now and the next time that ramp opened, we were all reliant on someone else. There was nothing we could do to not hit an IED and nothing we could do to maintain situational awareness. We were literally and figuratively in the dark. There was a dim glow of panel lights that illuminated my RTO's face as he sat across from me. I'll never forget him hunched over, staring blankly forward, holding the antennae on his radio down.

We rode for somewhere between 10 and 20 minutes until the vehicles lurched to a stop. The soldiers exited the Bradleys and pulled security on either side of the road adjusting their night vision devices. I knelt at the end of the ramp and my RTO took his place beside me. The taillights of the vehicle we had ridden in were bright enough that I could make out my map. When we had exited, the area didn't look as I had expected, but it wouldn't be the first time that we expected something to look one way based on imagery study and arrived to see something else. However, instead of additional or missing buildings, the buildings were arranged differently than we had studied.

Looking around, I asked my RTO, "Does this look like the right place to you?"
"No."
"Do you want to get back in there [the Bradley]?"
"No."
"Ok, we'll start here."

My read of the ground was that we were one or two hundred meters beyond where we were supposed to be. Beyond the negative morale effect of getting back in, the practicality of doing so was complicated. My platoon sergeant and the other vehicle would have to back up in the dark without anyone to secure them. Then the Bradleys would have to do the same. On the other hand, we would have to move through an objective we hadn't cleared yet, in an unfamiliar area, right after two loud vehicles had alerted the neighborhood. Still, to me, starting from there was the most prudent choice.

Despite the noise of the Bradleys, few if any of the residents had been alerted to our arrival. Disembarking before the first call to prayer, most everyone was still asleep in their beds. Thus, we encountered a lot of military aged males who would usually flee if they got wind of an operation (they were more likely to be around during routine patrols). However, as the light came up and we pushed further east on the objective (a total of 55 houses) we began finding houses with no men in them. There we encountered a common theme: the men were all in Baghdad. The Yusifiyah area suffered from a common paradox: the men were always gone to Baghdad, but no one could go to Baghdad for medical services because they would all be killed. So it was during *Polar Scrum* as the women pleaded for health clinics because Baghdad was too dangerous while telling us that was where there men were.

We wrapped up our clearance in six hours. On the south side, 2nd Platoon took a bit longer. However, they took fire during their search and detained more than fifty individuals. We detained none. I believe this was the difference between an experienced and inexperienced platoon, but it could also have been the difference in our mentalities. Nearly everyone in Yusifiyah seemed shady and nearly all of them had something in their house (a wire, a rifle, etc.) that could be used loosely on which to base an arrest, but we couldn't arrest every man (or so I thought). At some point, there needed to be a level of discretion and the system could only properly handle so many detainees. Besides, the two detainees 1st Platoon, Charlie Company encountered in February were difficult enough to deal with under fire, but they were worth the risk. Fifty was way too many for a platoon to handle. The other platoon leader compared stats with me after the operation, but I saw no reason to indulge him. There will likely never be a hard metric that can possibly judge the success of an operation or patrol in counterinsurgency, but if there is, it won't be number of detainees. Of course, maybe all the bad guys lived on the south side of the road. Still, the other companies did some detaining as well. In total, the battalion arrested 85 suspects.[39]

In *Polar Scrum*, the battalion was able to push two platoons into a relatively untouched area with impunity. That was a sign of progress. The enemy hadn't prepared defenses or a means of resisting. Success seemed assured. The Polar Bears had made national news for their efforts with some U.S. military leaders crediting the company and platoon outposts and battle positions as helping to "rein in" the area. Journalist Zeke Minaya indicated that these leaders no longer saw the area as the "Triangle of Death." Alpha Company saw the outposts as the start of a larger solution to the troubles of the area. Holding the area allowed the battalion to fan out. Soldiers could gain the locals' trust and gather intelligence. "[T]hey begin to learn who is supposed to be there and they can tell when something is out of place," the commander said. A squad leader indicated that attacks were down. From his perspective, the Polar Bears were "gaining real estate, [and] taking away supply routes from the enemy." The S3, though, highlighted one of the major risks of the bases in that the enemy may try to overrun them.[40] Aside from the daisy-chain IED/ambush of 4th Platoon, Delta Company (which was part of a large attack) all of the major attacks from the enemy were against fixed sites. However, none had been successful.

Alpha Company's 3rd Platoon Leader, his platoon no longer being attached to the route clearance team but now attached to Delta Company, said that garrisoning troops in the hinterland in small bases provided forces freedom of maneuver and enabled greater speed and flexibility than would be gained by operating out of a large forward operating base. At the time, his platoon was engaged in the hunt for a sniper. The small outposts allowed his platoon to react quickly to leads. In this case, they didn't catch the sniper, but continued to exert pressure on him.[41] The outposts put them in the area and in a position to move quickly.

Those early May days were also filled with good news on the civil project front. While offensive and defensive actions—along with partnership efforts—characterized the battalion's efforts, civil action remained a strong, if somewhat under the radar, effort. Led by the battalion civil-military coordination officer (S5) and assisted by Civil Affairs Team 5 of Company A, 478th Civil Affairs Battalion, progress seemed apparent. The café and market in Yusifiyah were bustling with business. The sewage, water, and electric ministries had completed or made progress on several projects to include street cleaning, building trash collection points, and working to fix sewers, repair the drinking water pipes, and replace transformers. All rudimentary efforts to an average American reader, these seemed like great leaps for the Iraqi government in the area. There was even a 400 million dinar (roughly $272,000 in 2007) project to build a new administration building bringing jobs to the area.[42] Certainly none of this would be possible without the security that the Iraqi Army and Police provided. By this point, U.S. soldiers rarely patrolled the city; nearly all security came from indigenous national forces.

The S5 gave voice to the seeming hope after an early May Yusifiyah *nahia* (local council) meeting at the Joint Security Station. Where he had grown accustomed to taking the lead in these affairs, he noted that the members of the council took control of the meeting and discussed projects. Even with all the work listed above, there were still many issues to be resolved but it was looking more like the government officials could take the lead. One project in particular was installing street lights in the market along with improving electrical infrastructure. The S5 noted he had arranged for U.S. Army Corps of Engineers representatives to come to Yusifiyah to confer with Abbas Abbas Al Sakbari, the council's lead engineer.[43]

The battalion and the Iraqis had worked long and hard to turn Yusifiyah into a viable town and not a slum. Early May demonstrated that work was paying off and on 8 May the goal of handing over the town officially to the Iraqis was realized. The 4th Battalion, 4th Brigade, 6th Iraqi Army Division took control of Yusifiyah that day, relieving the Polar Bears of that area of responsibility.[44] The official designation was "in the lead" meaning the Polar Bears were still very much present if not visible in the picture. In theory, the Iraqis controlled all of the Polar Bears' area of operations. In practice, the Iraqis were in charge of the city and the surrounding parts, but the Polar Bears still had the lead along Route Malibu and the Mullah Fayad Highway from Rushdi Mullah on. Alpha Company would retain its role as partners, but this move would allow the battalion to start looking further west and contemplating a move to the power plant or across the river.

Those early days in May demonstrated that the battalion's methods were worthwhile. Soldiers had paid a high price in blood in April, but by the second week of May, the Iraqis controlled from Yusifiyah to Al Taraq. The local government was functioning quite well. Nothing that would happen after would change any of that, but the enemy, so hard pressed to regain an inch of ground lost, would not concede defeat in Qarghuli Village. An obscure sheik in Mahmudiyah had claimed a bounty of ten U.S. soldiers for the rape of Abeer Qassim Al Janabi the previous year. Al Qaeda had already taken two. Whether the sheikh was part of the insurgents or not, the enemy was out to exact the balance in the most loyal of its lands.

6

That Uncheremonious Pyre

*You smug-faced crowds with kindling eye
Who cheer when soldier lads march by,
Sneak home and pray you'll never know
The hell where youth and laughter go.*
—Siegfried Sassoon, "Suicide in the Trenches"

The road known as Route Malibu was as perilous as they come. The twin factors of a population supportive of the old regime (or at least pro–Sunni insurgent groups) and the road being a fill, elevated and easily dug under, were bad enough. Added to that were the large presence of former Al Qaeda terrorists and the sanctuary across the river. While IEDs were a problem in other parts of the sector, particularly portions of Route Sporster (which was primarily controlled by IA along most of the road) and the Mullah Fayad Highway, the road through Delta Company's area of operations was the land of the deep-buried, large IED. Other areas generally saw a series of artillery shells filled with explosives, but the enemy here placed hundreds of pounds of explosives under the road and had perfect hiding places to lie in wait. Delta had endured a rough month of April striking 17 IEDs and finding 31 more while coming under small arms fire 33 times.

So it was not unusual when a patrol on 3 May discovered an IED near the bend in the river along Route Malibu about 800 meters from Inchon and north of BP 152. The only thing the discovery seemed to portend was another long month and more business as unusual. However, when EOD arrived they placed an exploratory charge on the road to blast a small hole to get a better look at the bomb. Instead of cutting a small hole, the charge set off the actual IED leaving a deep crater in the road. This crater was a ready-made location for further IEDs and enemy IED emplacers put two more bombs in the crater overnight. The next day, a patrol discovered the new IEDs and when EOD destroyed them, the crater got so big that the road was nearly cut in half, risking the ability for vehicles to travel on it.

Route Malibu was the only lifeline to Delta Company's headquarters. Lines of communication—paths between two headquarters generally made of roads or waterways—have been major needs of fighting forces since recorded Western military history. Without a ground line of communication and without a strong fleet of river craft, the only way to reach Delta Company would be by air and air assets were extremely needed everywhere. The road had to remain open. Thus, someone would have to guard the crater to prevent any more IEDs. Even one found and cleared would likely result in the cutting of the road. 1st Platoon, Delta Company, drew the task of guarding the crater until a rapid road repair team could resurface the road. How long that would be was anyone's guess. The reader may recall that engineer assets were never in great enough supply to meet demand.

On 8 May, Delta Company attempted to fill the crater with sandbags. Delta's commander selected 3rd Platoon, Alpha Company, to accomplish the task. The soldiers drove to the site and established a chain gang to pass the sandbags down the line. At the end of the line was the platoon leader who was responsible for putting the sandbag in the hole. As the men went to work in the evening, they heard a boom and saw an explosion. The next thing the platoon leader knew he was waking up to the voice of the lieutenant hurt during *Polar Blizzard* and unable to see. He was at Walter Reed Army Medical Center with no idea how he got there. (He would eventually lose sight in one eye and leave the Army to go to law school.)[1]

From then on, there would be constant vigilance over the crater. At night, two HMMWVs would cover the largest of the holes. This left the platoon with only eight total soldiers on the site severely limiting the ability of the force to do much to protect itself. It could not patrol around the vehicles and gunners could only face in two directions. Those in the HMMWVs had extremely limited fields of view.

While the section of vehicles and soldiers guarded the crater, insurgents from Islamic State of Iraq watched from the dark recesses. They studied the patterns that the soldiers naturally set. They observed the soldiers' movements, their guard rotations, their security posture. For five nights, they observed and they built their plan. The group's leader briefed his men and they rehearsed their attack. On the night of 9 May going into the 10th, the assault force crept in the pitch-black environs east of the vehicles. They were ready to go, but as they approached, they heard the sound of a HMMWV engine and that indicated something wasn't right. The leader aborted the attack.

The insurgents regrouped and waited an extra night. On the morning of 12 May, still far from first light, 17 young Arab men gathered. Each had his own reason for being there, but here they were with the intentions of kidnapping eight American soldiers. Four men made up the command-and-control node for the attack (part of which likely was a videographer). There were also two 3-man assault teams and a 2-man sniper team (which may actually have just been an overwatch element). Rounding out the group were 2-man and 3-man IED emplacement teams.[2]

The insurgents began moving into position. Along the road lay a single strand of concertina wire, the only barrier between the insurgents and the Americans. The terrorists listened but they did not hear the steady drone of a diesel engine in idle as they had two nights previously. As the insurgents looked on in the dark, they likely could not see a gunner in either turret. It is possible that the Americans were not properly manning their positions and it is just as possible that the Americans were staying low and their heads did not peak above the shield. There is no one to attest either way. Regardless, the conditions were set and the attack was a go.

At 0444, the insurgents moved forward and cut the wire. To the north and south insurgents placed IEDs on the road to delay responders, as they had done in June 2006 at the AVLB site and the previous year to delay soldiers in response to a downed helicopter. Exploiting the roughly 50 meters between HMMWVs with no flank security, the insurgents rushed the vehicles from behind. Hoping to disorient the occupants, the assailants threw concussion grenades into the turrets. However, it appears their grenades were more powerful than expected.[3] Like everything else in that forsaken place, the HMMWVs became ablaze and now burned. Four soldiers likely never made it out of the burning hulks: Platoon sergeant Sergeant First Class James Connell and Private First Class Daniel Courneya in the north vehicle and Sergeant Anthony Schober and Iraqi *jundi* (soldier) Sabah Barak in the southern vehicle.

As the soldiers emerged from the vehicles to return fire, the insurgents purposely aimed low hoping to disable but not kill. It is believed that Specialist Alex Jimenez returned fire from the turret of his vehicle, engaging the enemy with an M2 .50 caliber machine gun. Three others, Private First Class Joseph Anzack and Privates Christopher Murphy and Byron Fouty began engaging with their rifles. However, in the dark, with the burning fire rendering the soldiers' eyes and night vision mostly worthless, the bullets likely never found their mark. In the ensuing melee, Murphy dropped his equipment and began running north. It is likely, though unconfirmed, that he was attempting to reach Inchon and alert the company and thus dropped his gear to increase speed. However, he would never make it; he was killed before he got too far. Jimenez and Fouty from the north vehicle and Anzack, originally in the southern truck, were unable to hold off the stronger enemy. All three were likely captured alive then drug east and placed on vehicles to be transported elsewhere.

Meanwhile, at Inchon soldiers were awoken by the explosions and sound of gunfire so close the base. 1st Platoon's other half, with the platoon leader in charge, mounted their vehicles and moved south running into a fake IED a few hundred meters north of the ambush site. The platoon leader dismounted his troops and proceeded on foot. It took the platoon about 20 minutes to arrive on scene. From the south, soldiers from 3rd Platoon, Alpha Company, manning BP 152, moved toward the scene also coming into contact with a fake but presumed real IED. As the two platoons linked up on the objective they came across a fiery, heart wrenching scene. They took in a grim view of HMMWVs "burning fiercely in the middle of the road while onboard ammunition exploded randomly from the heat." The scene likely looked similar to the one 1st Platoon, Charlie Company, had encountered in September 2006 with one key difference: dead American soldiers burning in those vehicles. The only evidence of what may have become of the three missing bodies, as yet unidentified, were two blood trails running to the east.[4]

Islamic State of Iraq quickly took responsibility claiming the attack was in retaliation for the rape of Abeer Qassim Al Janabi and the murder of her and her family. However, it is more likely that this was the justification the terrorist organization used to gain the tacit approval of the populace than any real motivation. Kidnapping U.S. soldiers was a propaganda coup and was an important objective of the insurgents in its own right.[5] Regardless of the reason, Islamic State warned the U.S. Army not to search for the soldiers if they wanted them to remain safe. The search would "lead to nothing but exhaustion."[6] Despite the warning, the Polar Bears, the Commando Brigade, and the coalition were ready to do all it could to locate its missing soldiers.[7]

At about 0520, an alert went out for all stations to go immediately to 100 percent security. My platoon, still nominally the Quick Reaction Force, was tied down guarding one of the two little outposts outside of Bataan. We turned the radio to the battalion net and listened, getting bits of information as it came in. When the order for 100 percent security came in, there was no accompanying context. As a platoon leader, my decisions on what to do may have changed. As it was, we added a guard to the rooftop position, got everyone in their boots and awake, and stood by. Eventually, I sent a patrol to Bataan to get a report on what was happening and we learned the depressing news.

Quickly, a massive manhunt materialized involving U.S. and Iraqi soldiers. Kershaw dubbed the search *Commando Razor* and the Polar Bears labeled all efforts within the battalion *Polar Charade*. Iraqi soldiers flooded the area around the ambush site within hours of the attack.[8] The battalion scouts flew into the Qarghuli Village area that morning kicking off the first of twelve air assault operations within the first 72 hours of the kidnapping. Most of the searching, however, occurred on foot with soldiers moving to jump off points in HMMWVs. The initial focus was within a 15-kilometer radius of the site.

Delta Company initiated a mass arrest of all military aged males. It was a tactic the commander had used in the past after a reed burning detail hit an IED. However, this was on a much grander scale. By the end of the search, Delta had arrested some 500 in all. I pleaded Bayonet's commander to let our platoon get into the search. I had scant knowledge of any of the soldiers, having briefly spoken to Connell and had to escort Anzack to Inchon when a rumor spread online that he was dead and the commander saw it fit that he contact his family. Aside from that, I knew none of them, but my men knew them well. They had lived in the barracks with them, trained with them, and in some cases fought alongside them. Sitting on a small guard position while soldiers from Baghdad searched seemed wrong. In the afternoon we were relieved and directed to BP 152 (now located a little south of the previous position and on the west side of the road) where I linked up with the platoon leader there and he told me the houses near the position hadn't been searched, so we took part in the mass round up.

As we searched, tensions were high and it is a credit to the platoon that nothing happened outside of the rules. One of my squad leaders, who had been in 1st Platoon to start the deployment, was especially angry and had the look in his eye that said he was just waiting for someone to give him an excuse. However, he did nothing but lead his squad with precision. Ultimately, the greatest excitement came when we heard shots in the field behind a house and I went rushing around the corner with my RTO and began hurrying the platoon forward to deploy only to find out an Iraqi soldier had

American and Iraqi soldiers prepare for a patrol in Qarghuli Village. Following the 12 May attack, the coalition partners grew closer searching for the missing Americans and the men responsible for the loss of soldiers from both nations.

indiscriminately fired his weapon. We arrested every male we deemed to be of military age (a rather arbitrary distinction) and moved them to BP 152 to await transport. We then went to Bataan to spend the night and await orders. That night, in the dark of the tent, I had the worst headache I'd ever experienced in my life. I could not shake it. I have always been overly stoic in emotional times and I think this was my body's way of reacting. I barely knew the men, but they were my brothers and the thought of them being tortured was difficult to bear.

At that time, 3rd Platoon, Delta Company was about sixteen men. All told, however, about 4000 Iraqi and American men flooded the area after the attack.[9] In the first week and a half, forces launched 37 operations involving 19 U.S. Army companies and 22 Iraqi companies.[10] Blackhawk and Comanche Companies (B and C) of 1st Battalion, 23rd Infantry Regiment (1–23 IN), Stryker units out of Fort Lewis, Washington, arrived. They were part of the MNC-I reserve. (By pure coincidence, I would go on to command Comanche Company three years later.) Sergeant Josh Apel, the Stryker vehicle commander for Comanche's commander noted the complex nature of the terrain with houses sparsely spread, orchards laced throughout, and canals everywhere and saw the difficulty in finding the soldiers. They could have been anywhere. "It was like finding a needle in a haystack," he wrote, "but we knew we had to do our best no matter what."[11]

Delta Company went to work destroying all of the bridges over the Caveman Canal that led away from Route Malibu, working in conjunction with the sappers from Company A, 2nd Brigade Special Troops Battalion.[12] The canal bifurcated the battle space with Company D on the west side and Company B and the IA on the east side. The purpose in destroying the bridges was to limit the ability of insurgents to move in and out of Qarghuli Village from the east. Most importantly, vehicular traffic had to move within the control of U.S. forces making it more difficult to move heavy material or kidnapped personnel in the sector.

While the search got underway, Fox Company, by nature of its organization, drew the unenviable task of recovering the remains of the HMMWVs. The soldiers loaded the bodies of the four Americans and one Iraqi soldier who died at the scene and transported them to Yusifiyah for movement back to the United States (or another specific area in the case of Sabah Barak). They also loaded the burnt-out hulks of the HMMWVs and any other debris they encountered, cleaning up the site after investigators had canvased it.[13]

Two days after the incident, 14 May, the search had been fruitless in its purpose but had succeeded in putting insurgents on the run. By that point, six insurgents involved in the attack had been captured and, according to an intelligence report, had revealed the names of all the attackers as well as the details of the plan. It seemed the master mind was a local Sunni insurgent leader named Muhammad Khalil Ibrahim Al Qarghuli, or MKI. Further information came from other detainees. Eventually, 20 men rounded up by Delta Company would be sent to Camp Cropper, the Army's detainee holding facility in Baghdad, for processing as official detainees. Islamic State warned, "Your soldiers are in our grip. If you want the safety of your soldiers, then do not search for them."[14]

MKI became the primary target of forces in Yusifiyah from then on, branded as the local leader of the Islamic State. As a Qarghuli he was from the area and had been a disciple of Zarqawi. MKI was implicated in the June 2006 kidnapping of Menchaca and Tucker, as well. Locals told of how he enforced rules that prevented tomatoes and cucumbers from being sold together because they resembled the sexual organs of females and males, respectively. This was a rule Al Qaeda in Iraq under Zarqawi had enforced as well.[15] Locals also told us that the reason there were no goats in the area was that MKI had told them they either needed to put pants on them to cover their genitalia or get rid of them. Whether these stories are true or not is inconsequential; they indicate the fear MKI and his men wrought and the level of extremism they subscribed to.

On the 14th, in his diary, Apel wrote, "I could only pray that these men were found soon because we were up against local enemy and we knew they had the advantage on us in these remote areas." He was writing after a day when his company—and his own Stryker—had come under fire several times and they had found IEDs. They found

Strykers of limited value in the canal-crossed terrain, but made use of them as support vehicles and mobile command posts. Still, Blackhawk helicopters proved better mounts on most occasions for these mounted soldiers.[16]

As the search wore into its second week, the strain began to weigh on the soldiers who were frustrated in their efforts. However hopeless the situation may seem, though, the soldiers, especially those in Delta, retained their determination. Associated Press photojournalist Maya Alleruzzo accompanied Delta Company's 2nd Platoon on one of its patrols. One of the photos she took shows three Delta soldiers sitting on fuel cans. The soldiers are trying to get a few moments rest in between missions. The soldier on the left of the photo has his head in his hand, eyes closed, with his squad automatic weapon across his lap; the one in the center has his arms crossed over his rifle, leaning into them trying to nap; to the right another soldier looks exhausted and somewhat dejected.[17] At the time of the photograph, information indicated that two of the three missing soldiers were still alive. However, it had not been corroborated nor did the information say which of the three may be deceased.[18]

Another one of Alleruzzo's photos was picked up by many news outlets. It depicts one of the soldiers in the foreground with other soldiers behind him in a staggered column formation. The soldier's look is both exhaustion and resolve. In an e-mail to the *Baltimore Sun*, Alleruzzo described the conditions of the search for Delta Company, "They were out on patrol before dawn every day, in 115-degree heat, on foot. Sometimes they got an hour break to eat and sleep and then they were back at it; … they were sweating out water faster than they could replace it."[19]

The attack had effectively destroyed 1st Platoon, Delta Company. With the company manning three bases and still needing to conduct patrols and missions, the platoon needed to be reconstituted quickly. The platoon leader would remain in charge for the time being. The platoon's section sergeant took over the role of platoon sergeant. The other Delta Company platoons did not contribute men to the platoon given how small they already were. Instead, each rifle company gave up two to three soldiers to fill the ranks.

As the second week wore on, Kershaw was clearly concerned about morale and morality as soldiers continued to be frustrated. He sent a letter to the troops, published in the brigade's internal magazine as well as the Fort Drum newspaper, *The Blizzard* (since renamed *The Mountaineer*). Along with the previously stated concerns, Kershaw wanted to keep soldiers focused on their counterinsurgency mission in addition to the search. The letter read, in part:

> At this time it would be easy and natural to forget our moral position—to return hate for the hate we have seen in the loss of our comrades.
>
> However, we must not forget our moral high ground, the fact that our country is founded on freedom and laws which protect us from torture, from groundless arrests and searches.
>
> Our mission dictates that we search homes and people here, but we are bound by the Geneva Conventions, Army regulations and our own moral fiber to be fair and just, to prohibit torture and shameful treatment. We cannot forget that "Iraqi" does not equal "terrorist," and that the loss of a comrade does not justify abuse of any sort.
>
> Defense of yourself, your fellow Soldiers or innocent civilians is always permitted, but in

the wake of a painful time for our brigade, do not let yourself be swayed from the mission which is to help the Iraqis.[20]

On 22 May, reports seemed to corroborate the idea that one of the three missing soldiers was dead. A Libyan and a Moroccan were captured on 20 May in a raid near Yusifiyah (likely by special operations forces). A high-ranking security source, speaking on condition of anonymity, stated "Preliminary investigations with the Libyan confirmed that the 'terrorist cell' which carried out the kidnapping executed one of the three soldiers in retaliation for the American and Iraqi forces' continued operations to search for the soldiers and to prove they were serious about carrying out their threats." The source also said that captured terrorists confirmed that the American and Iraqi units had flooded the area so quickly that the insurgents could not move the captured soldiers. To that point, 1,200 military aged males had been arrested.[21]

The information regarding the inability to move the soldiers is somewhat suspect considering the ultimate disposition of two of the captured soldiers. However, it at least lends some context to the discovery the next day. Iraqi Police fished Anzack's body out from the Euhprates on 23 May, 11 miles south of the ambush site near Al Iskandriyah. His body may have been in the river anywhere from two to eleven days and it was likely he had died within 24 hours of the attack. His head had been shot up with an automatic weapon and his torso had other severe wounds on it.[22]

On 25 May, the Stryker soldiers went away having exhausted their usefulness and being needed elsewhere. That day, Apel, a truly kind-hearted man who I came to know well years later when he served as one of my scouts, wrote in his diary, "I feel for the families of these men as the search will continue without us. So many days of searching without out [sic] much luck at all. I can't imagine what this unit is feeling knowing that that they have brothers out there somewhere. I hope and pray that they will be found and for the family and loved ones of the soldier that was found [Anzack] I hope that they realize their soldier died a hero."[23]

The battalion held a memorial ceremony on 28 May, fittingly Memorial Day in the United States, for the six fallen soldiers (including Anzack and Sabah Barak). It was a somber affair, for sure. Chaplain Bryan stated, "The men we now honor, the men we have regarded so sincerely as our own, have been shared with the free people of the world. I have stood with the soldiers of Company D's 1st Platoon many times and am always in awe of their steadfastness. Understandably, they mourn the tragic loss of their soldiers, but they have a stern momentum (that) the enemy will never overcome. They will not defeat our will to fight, and they certainly will not defeat us in spirit."[24]

The departure of the Stryker soldiers did not slow down the effort. *Polar Charade* continued into June with every company searching their areas thoroughly. In early June, Bravo Company and Iraqi soldiers patrolled as part of the operation and detained 19 suspects near Rushdi Mullah. On 3 June, the company detained two other men with known ties to insurgents, but not directly linked to the 12 May attacks.[25] To that point, Multi-National Division-Center had conducted 33 air assaults and 66 company-level operations, and flown 350 hours of unmanned surveillance missions. Tracking dogs had swept the area for clues and engineers drained the Caveman Canal. Almost all of the weapons and equipment used in the attack had been found, but not the soldiers themselves.[26]

The next day, Islamic State of Iraq released a video showing the identification cards of Jimenez and Fouty and also what appears to be contents of their wallets such as U.S. and Iraqi currency, credit cards, and a Christian cross. The audio in the video said the soldiers were dead. The video had a caption saying, "Bush is the reason for the loss of your prisoners." The video also included footage of what appears to be the perpetrators planning or briefing the attack on a diagram board along with footage of the attack.[27]

Five days later, soldiers from the 2nd Battalion, 505th Parachute Infantry Regiment, 82nd Airborne Division in Samarra found the identification cards and other personal effects of Jimenez and Fouty that had been shown on the video. (Samarra is a city at least 125 kilometers north of Yusifiyah somewhat close to Tikrit and arrayed on the Tigris River.) The soldiers had been participating in an operation when they got into a firefight with insurgents with two soldiers being wounded. The soldiers forced the insurgents to flee and in the ensuing search of the area discovered the effects along with video production equipment, rifles, and ammunition as well as documents, computers, and other equipment.[28]

Despite the location of the personal effects in Samarra, the battalion did not remain east of the Euphrates. It was unlikely the soldiers were able to be transported that far north alive and thus the insurgents were likely spreading evidence to throw off searchers. The battalion was now beginning its second excursion to the west bank which would be followed by a series of further operations. This mission, an air assault conducted at night between 13 and 14 June, entailed Charlie Company landing across the water and establishing blocking positions. The latest raid netted several detainees who were held for questioning as well as some intelligence, though it is unclear exactly what they found. Some of the men expressed frustration that they were not able to find their missing comrades nor detain any of the key players linked to the attack. Charlie Company's commander, who led the air assault, told a reporter, "All I know is that it's the first thing I think about when I wake up, and it's the last thing I think about when I got to sleep—finding these soldiers."[29]

While the search continued with vigor, the Polar Bears maintained focus on their purpose and stayed true to their plan, which included, among other things, training the Iraqis and building relationships with locals. Ultimately, this meant seizing the far end of the sector, the Yusifiyah Thermal Power Plant, and connecting the base in Yusifiyah to it via both Route Malibu and the Mullah Fayad Highway. In effort to facilitate this, Charlie Company handed COP Corregidor over to Troop B, 1st Squadron, 89th Cavalry Regiment from the same brigade in preparation for its final move onto Route Malibu. This occurred on 15 June, and, in the spirit of counterinsurgency, on the same day medics participated in a medical operation in Mullah Fayad where they treated eighty patients, mostly children.[30]

Despite the natural desire to distrust Iraqis and withdraw, it is a credit to the battalion leadership that they continued to push things like medical operations and local engagement. It was the right thing to do tactically as well as morally. However, there is no doubt there was at least some passive complicity of the population in the 12 May attack and enmity was high. That being said, the discipline of the Polar Bears shines as there were no reported incidents of abuse of detainees by U.S. soldiers or any other unethical actions. While we should all expect the upmost ethical conduct of our servicemembers, given the circumstances it reflects well on the troops that they were able to do the right thing despite the animosity.

Throughout the months of May and June, the Iraqi Army received a crash course in operations. The workload forced them to learn, adapt, and grow. To that end, when the 3rd Infantry Division, in command of MND-C, launched *Operation Marne Torch* on 19 June, the Polar Bear role was minimal. Alpha Company provided the bulk of the force in partnership with the Iraqis who provided a preponderance of the total force in the area. The operation in Yusifiyah led to nine detainees.[31]

The Polar Bears' dedication to its mission and the strengthening of the Iraqi Army would come together to finally create tangible progress that had seemed so close before the 12 May attacks. It would not remove the cloud of the missing soldiers but demonstrate in stark terms the effectiveness of the counterinsurgency approach that the battalion employed. However, it would take an unexpected twist to cement this progress and prepare the Yusifiyah area for a day when it didn't need U.S. troops to keep it secure.

Leading into 12 May 2007, there was plenty of reason for hope in Yusifiyah. The Iraqis were in control of Yusifiyah proper, nearly all of Route Sportster and a large swath of the Mullah Fayad Highway. Local civil officials were beginning to get on track to provide basic services. The Polar Bears seemingly held the initiative, but then, on 12 May, Islamic State struck with a vengeance, setting the area ablaze again.

The effect, though, was different. The Iraqi Army and Americans banded together to attack those who perpetrated the act. The mini-surge of troops into the area put the insurgents on the run and provided them no freedom of movement or maneuver. The populace began to grow tired of the extremism and became angry at having to bear the consequences for Islamic State's excesses. Though all of the rest of May and the beginning of June were largely dedicated to the search, the battalion's counterinsurgency objectives had been furthered. Rather than seeding the initiative to Islamic State, the attacks spurred action that firmly wrested the initiative for the Americans and their Iraqi partners.

The battalion's ability to maintain its moral and ethical standards underpinned their efforts. The attack brought a series of offensive actions and placed emotional men in and among the populace. One slip could have swayed the populace to the side of Islamic State and set back all of the hard work that the battalion had done to that point. While devastating, the 12 May attack enabled the battalion to increase the security of the region and its ethical conduct allowed them to solidify that progress. The search would continue, but the battalion was ready to press the offense.

7

A New Day

> *They* [a failed Jihadist movement] *destroyed themselves with their own hands, with their lack of reason. Delusions. Their ignoring of people. Their alienation of them through oppression, deviance and severity, coupled with a lack of kindness, sympathy and friendliness. Their enemies did not defeat them, but rather, they defeated themselves, and were consumed and fell.*—Atiyah Abd Al Rahman as reported by Joby Warrick in *Black Flags*

In mid–July, the British Broadcasting Corporation picked up a report from a London-based Arabic language newspaper detailing the tribal mosaic of the northern Babil Province area known as the Triangle of Death. This reporting highlighted the difficulties of forming a tribal council similar to what had occurred in Anbar Province the previous year when the Anbar Awakening brought Sunni tribes to bear against their erstwhile insurgent allies. Multiple Iraqi leaders pointed to the tribal differences, both by sect and culture, that contributed to a lack of a clear vision for the area. To them, this prevented the type of tribal cooperation needed to bring the community to bear against insurgents. Only one of those interviewed, an Iraqi general, expressed clear optimism that security could come to the area. One of the leaders noted that the area had experienced periods of security such as toward the end of the Marines' tour, but nothing ever stuck.[1] It was up to the Polar Bears and their Iraqi Army allies to try to establish a lasting peace.

Little good news came in June when one considers that for most soldiers and officers the primary thought on their minds was the safety of Jimenez and Fouty. (On 27 June, the Army officially changed their designation from DUSTWUN to MISCAP, missing, presumed captured, the modern-day MIA designation.[2]) However, there was a major event that demonstrated the people of the area were no longer afraid of the government and in fact endorsed it. The Polar Bears, in conjunction with the 4th Brigade, 6th Iraqi Army Division and the 23rd Military Police Company, 503rd Military Police Battalion, 16th Military Police Brigade, a unit out of Fort Bragg, North Carolina, that advised and partnered with the Iraqi Police at Yusifiyah's Joint Security Station, put on a highly successful Iraqi Police recruiting drive. Held at the security station, the drive sought 200 qualified applicants. That many lined the streets waiting their turn when the drive opened at 0800 on 23 June. By the end of the drive two days later, exactly 1,000 more had applied.

Recruits had to pass a basic literacy test and be an Iraqi citizen of 20 to 35 years of age who was not already in the Iraqi Army or a member of an extremist groups. (Preventing insurgents from infiltrating Iraqi security institutions was a never-ending concern.) They also needed to be willing to move at the will of the government and have their records checked. Remarkably, only 23 of the 1,200 failed the literacy test and had to be turned away. The bulk of the applicants came from Yusifiyah proper and Mullah Fayad, but three were from Qarghuli Village, and others came from the disparate towns of the greater Yusifyiah area. All of the major tribes were represented among the applicant pool. One applicant was a female, which is not insignificant even if it is not overly significant.[3]

Petraeus visited Yusifiyah on 23 June and toured the Yusifiyah Joint Security Station as the recruiting drive got underway. He walked among the troops, engaging them in conversation. The general praised the Polar Bears for having a vision and being able to increase security forces in the area without backing terrorism. Presumably he was talking about the battalion not enabling certain tribal groups at the expense of others, though it is unclear exactly what he meant. "You guys are doing very much the right thing," Petraeus said speaking to members of the battalion. "This is a unit that gets it."[4]

Late on the first night of the recruiting drive, in another sector, a man approached an Iraqi Army checkpoint. Arriving around 2330, the man claimed he had escaped from Al Qaeda (possibly Islamic State) operatives who had captured him and his brother two weeks previously for failing to pledge allegiance to the organization. He requested help rescuing his brother whom he had left in an orchard because his brother could not keep up. The Iraqi soldiers took the man, who still had his shackles on, to PB Shanghai. Then the Iraqis and an American contingent from Bravo Company launched a patrol to recover the brother, who was a local sheikh. Bravo Company provided medical attention to the men who had signs of torture and at least one dislocated shoulder. The men offered 40 names of the individuals involved in their capture and other insurgent activities.[5]

The turnout of the recruiting drive and the recovery of the sheikh, though not a recognizable tipping point, indicated a turning of the tide in the Yusifiyah area. The locals were beginning to trust the Iraqi Army and Police as well as the government in visible ways. They did not fear being associated with the government as demonstrated with the large number of applicants for police work. (However, Qarghulis still appeared apathetic to national service.) Rather than fearing for their lives at the hands of sectarian security forces, they turned to them in an hour of need to be saved from the insurgents.

Yusifiyah had seen signs of progress before. Prior to 12 May, things were moving in the right direction. Despite the attack that led to the capture of Anzack, Fouty, and Jimenez, parts of Yusifiyah were much more secure. However, no sign of progress, not even the Iraqi Army taking the lead in Yusifiyah, ever seemed to really change the course of events. Now, though, they were right on the precipice and every sign of progress was a tiny grain of sand beating on the pile waiting for the right one to come along and knock the whole thing over. It was coming, but not at the moment.

The grains kept falling as the Polar Bears seized on the momentum the flooding of troops provided them. It was time to finally plant the flag at the Yusifiyah Thermal Power Plant. In fact, there was no better way to let the insurgents know that they had gained nothing in seizing the three soldiers than to secure the symbolic location of previous evolutions of terrorists and to capture the last of Route Malibu. In the early hours of a late June morning, Charlie Company moved in to secure the wide perimeter around the main building where Company A, 2–14 IN was located (PB Dragon). Once the perimeter was secure, more soldiers arrived via helicopter and began to search and clear the sprawling complex. A fleet of support vehicles rushed in to rapidly build up positions and secure the newly gained ground.[6] Charlie Company established a final battle position north of Inchon but south of the power plant, and occupied that location as well as PB Dragon jointly with Company A, 2–14 IN. Shortly after the operation, the battalion moved its headquarters to Dragon and began building it up. A small rear detachment remained at Yusifiyah along with Alpha Company and the Iraqi Army battalion.

Looking back on nearly ten months of operations, the battalion's position had changed considerably. In mid–September, Charlie Company had been north of the Yusifiyah area and the battalion occupied Mahmudiyah. Bravo Company occupied some of the traffic control points on Route Sportster, but largely worked out of Yusifiyah with Alpha Company. Delta occupied the JSB and surrounding environs. Now, Charlie and the battalion headquarters (to include the headquarters company and F/210 BSB) were at the power plant; Delta lined Route Malibu; a mechanized company, B/2–69 AR, occupied the area south of Qarghulli Village; and Bravo Company had responsibility for a wide swath of the northern sector. The Iraqi Army was in control of a large portion of the battle space. Only Alpha Company held its original position, though it had expanded its holdings. With the battalion's flag planted in the same compound two soldiers had been tortured in, the initiative was squarely on the side of the Polar Bears and the Iraqi government.

All of this started getting local tribes interested in freeing themselves from Islamic State formally. The people were demonstrating a willingness to back the government and now the tribes considered doing the same. Just a couple weeks previously it seemed a long shot; now it seemed a matter of time. The tribes discussed forming neighborhood watch organizations. Before anything could be formalized or approved, some locals took it upon themselves to act now and seek forgiveness later. Phil Sharp describes in his book the first time Bravo Company became aware that locals had taken charge of their own security. They heard a firefight in the distance of Al Taraq and came to find out that a group of tribesmen were attacking an insurgent group.[7] I remember sitting in the Delta Company command post one day when 3rd Platoon, down at BP 152, called up about a lot of commotion and clanging south of their position. The clanging turned out to be a local signal for tribesmen to converge on and beat an IED emplacer.

After this, the watch groups seemed to spring up overnight like mushrooms after a rain. I was escorting Delta Company's commander down Route Malibu when we

7. *A New Day*

Dirt fields, palm trees, and mud brick houses ... a typical scene in Qarghuli Village.

came upon a building with sandbagged positions on the roof. Naturally we stopped in and found out that the locals had created their own local security station. We were not the only ones to see something like this. Up in Rushdi Mullah, Bravo Company's commander noticed it as well. "It was literally overnight," he recalled. "...the military aged males of the towns and villages stood up their own security forces and began to guard their villages. One morning we woke up and there they were, out guarding the streets." He would go on to say, "[W]hen we start[ed] talking to these guys who were doing it, it was just fabulous because this is exactly what we had always been saying they needed to do ever since we got there. They needed to step up and take charge of their own security and they did."[8]

The local watch group was an outgrowth of a movement begun on the other side of the river in Ramadi. Sheikh Sattar Abu Risha, leader of a small tribe and a man believed to be a mobster, met at his compound with U.S. Army Captain Travis Patriquin. The latter was a former Special Forces NCO who spoke Arabic. Sattar and his people had become weary of Al Qaeda's excesses and he offered his services as the leader of a militia. Patriquin's brigade commander, Colonel Sean MacFarland, asked for permission to pursue this and received the go ahead from Casey.[9] Prior to the Patriquin/MacFarland initiative, there had been at least four other attempts to start of tribal security group, but all had failed for various reasons. Thus, the success of the movement was far from assured. However, it grew into the Anbar Awakening.[10] One of the first things Petraeus did upon arrival in February 2007 was to fly to Anbar to see the Awakening for himself. (He was the first to attempt to create a movement like this back when he commanded the 101st Airborne Division in Mosul.)

It wasn't just the company commander who saw a difference in the Rushdi Mullah area. As June began to fade, violence had not ended, but the acrimony of the locals against U.S. troops and the IA seemed to lessen while the locals' enmity toward the insurgents increased. Around 20 June, 1st Platoon, Bravo Company, was out on a patrol with Iraqi soldiers. They noticed kids were out more and adults were more open to them. The unit came under fire. No one was hit, but in pursuit of the shooter, the patrol came upon a bystander who took a stray bullet through his cheeks, in the right side and out the left. They immediately provided medical treatment and evacuated the casualty by helicopter to Baghdad. Three days later the man returned and the population took notice. From then on, the population became very friendly with the platoon.[11]

This all had an effect on insurgents. They realized that Americans were here to stay and so were the Iraqi soldiers and even a horrific event like 12 May had failed to do anything but increase resolve. Thus, they shifted their attacks to civilians hoping to drive a wedge and incite fear. It is important in counterinsurgency for the government to gain the confidence of the people, thus the insurgent must demonstrate the government cannot protect the people. That was the goal now. However, the insurgents were sloppy. In capturing two sheikhs and subjecting them to torture, they ineptly allowed the men to escape. The sheiks came into contact with U.S. forces who provided medical treatment. Upon recovery, the sheikhs began to coordinate their tribes' actions with the Iraqi Army.[12] The insurgents had chosen to employ coercion and intimidation rather than persuasion to repair their rift with the Sunni tribes and it in effect made the gap wider. Islamic State of Iraq and others of their ilk were slowly becoming fish without water to swim in and fleas incapable of biting the dog. It appeared that the final grain of sand had toppled the mighty pile. Things really seemed to come together as locals became more involved and intelligence began to stream in.

Delta Company spent long hours stringing wire along Route Malibu to prevent IEDs, but topography made it much less effective than the Mullah Fayad Highway wire had been. There, the highway was flat and even with the ground, mostly, and few roads led onto the highway allowing U.S. forces to block access. Route Malibu was raised, as the reader knows, but strewn with access points that locals needed left open. At this point, locals were not allowed to drive the length of Route Malibu but they could cross the road to conduct business such as getting goods to market. Therefore, the enemy could still access the road easily. Delta Company, however, did what it could by stringing row upon row of wire, sometimes seven or eight rows across, making it nearly impossible for an insurgent to cut through the wire in time to plant an IED and be gone before a patrol came by. It was hot, backbreaking work as soldiers worked in the summer heat and it was not without risk. A soldier in 2nd Platoon was shot through the legs during one of the work details.[13]

As in Charlie Company, Delta Company patrols ran the routes, but Malibu was much longer than the two kilometers between Al Taraq and the Alamo. However, soon after the arrival of the neighborhood watch groups who came to be known as Concerned Local Citizens (CLC), IEDs became rare if not extinct on a road that had once seen some of the largest blasts in the country. Certainly, among the new allies were old enemies. But the safe roads not only prevented U.S. casualties, they enabled progress. In counterinsurgency, working today with the man that shot at you yesterday can be good policy.

The CLCs played their part in reducing the threats on the road by establishing checkpoints and ensuring that people not from the area were watched and at times denied entry. Another method that worked was the ability of the Polar Bears to provide financial support to the area while reducing the threat. As violence began to fall and Sunnis became more willing to engage legitimately with the government, there was room to pay locals for needed services. One problem in Iraq, at least in the Yusifiyah area, was the complete lack of waste management. Litter abounded, as the only method of reducing rubbish was to burn it and a stiff wind could push one's trash pile across town. This not only had a negative effect on aesthetics, it provided insurgents plenty of room to hide IEDs. Thus, Delta Company's commander employed a band of locals to move from one end of the company sector to the other cleaning up trash and doing other odd jobs.

It is my firm opinion that the majority of Iraqis preferred to live in peace and make a living and if they got that living legitimately, they had no need for the insurgency. It is in that vein that Delta Company went to work employing as many as they could. The battalion awarded a local man a contract to repair all the water pipes running parallel to Malibu bringing more work to the area as well as clean(er) water. Trash picking and water pipe laying were local projects ran and staffed by locals with a positive effect on the community.

Delta Company also began to offer money for weapons. Locals could turn in or point out a cache and receive payments on a scale. Platoon leaders carried Iraqi dinar on them (signed out and accounted for by the company fire support officer). However, it is unclear what effect this truly had. Charlie Company, now just north of Delta, did not employ this program. In speaking with their commander, he informed me the area was not ready and he was concerned he may be taking old equipment off the insurgents' hands and providing them with money to buy new weapons. This program was a balance of risk and opportunity.

While developments allowed Delta Company the ability to be close to the locals and do more non-lethal and civic-type operations, it remained steadfast in its pursuit of insurgents and search for Jimenez and Fouty. There was a sort of Jekyll and Hyde style to the company in that the company could extend an olive branch or a carrot but be prepared to use a sword or stick as needed. At all hours of the day, the company would react to tips. There were many times the company was within minutes of capturing insurgent leaders. By this time, my platoon had reverted to control of our parent company. I remember being yanked out of bed in the middle of the night, assembling

Soldiers patrol in Qarghuli Village. Foot patrols with small numbers were common and provided a degree of flexibility that vehicles could not.

my platoon, and moving out in a matter of minutes to cordon off an area while another platoon moved in. The success of the mission escapes me, likely because we moved so fast that I never fully woke before we returned to Inchon. Insurgents were hard pressed to get relief from our pursuit and rumors began to circulate, endorsed by Infanti, that insurgents had begun to dress as women to avoid capture. However, where before the Surge, the outskirts of our sector were a frontier, forces now surrounded the Yusifiyah area and leaving our sector led an insurgent into the teeth of another unit.

In early July, Delta Company was at its Jekyll self, leading a battalion effort in Qarghuli Village to provide medical support to the locals. The medical operation treated more than 200 people. One medic lamented that many of the health issues they saw came from poor drinking water. During the clinic, many locals indicated that the Polar Bears had removed terrorists with little to no mention of the Iraqi soldiers and volunteers (as captured by the reporter on scene, at least). "It's wonderful that the Americans are doing all the things they do," said one local resident. "The situation here has gotten much better since the arrests after those soldiers were kidnapped. We're free to walk around now, thanks to the Americans. And when people come to harass us, we kick them out." Another local added, "It's very, very good of the Americans to do this for us. Since the soldiers got rid of the terrorists, we've been able to start negotiations for power and water improvements."[14]

Even with the improvements, counterinsurgency was stressful and this was amped up by the constant lack of good news in the search for Jimenez and Fouty. Soldiers acted out in strange ways. The easiest reaction to predict and control was over aggression. Harder were those that simply refused to go on. Charlie Company had a squad leader that said he was done and in Delta, a platoon leader said he couldn't lead his platoon anymore. These occurred before the 12 May attack. Lower ranking soldiers also at points said they couldn't patrol anymore. It was difficult to determine who was really afflicted and who was just scared ... or lazy.

But in July an event occurred that I could never have foreseen and that made it clear to me that a soldier was at his breaking point. We were out in a market in the central part of Qarghuli Village. I was talking to a shop owner. Things were looking good. A barber shop was open and another stall sold satellite receivers for TVs. As I talked, I heard yelling behind me and looked back. I expected to see that some local had gotten into the middle of our cordon or that we were in danger. Instead, I saw the platoon sergeant's driver walking, without his gear, away from the patrol. My first instinct was he had the runs ... it was the only thing that could make me want to take my gear off in the open like that. But I heard my platoon sergeant yelling for him to get back here and I ascertained that the soldier was just going to walk off.

I moved quickly to intercept him. I was clueless as what to do so I just got real loud and told him to get in the vehicle. He responded forthwith and put his gear back on before entering the HMMWV. I was absolutely embarrassed, probably in a way I never have been. I was not embarrassed because I had failed, but because my platoon had done something to tarnish the prestige of the American military with the locals. Several locals watched this commotion go on and we looked far from a disciplined unit. We looked the essence of dysfunction. I had no choice but to pack the platoon up and leave until I could deal with the distraction.

I believe what happened was a long time coming, but that day it started when my platoon sergeant told the soldier to get out of the vehicle and pull security. It was a policy I had enacted earlier in reaction to the manpower shortages we had. I came across it while reading through obsolete anti-armor doctrine. When I dismounted the platoon on a vehicular patrol, I needed every troop with me. We always left the drivers and gunners behind, but the gunners were powerless to stop people from walking amongst the vehicles and the drivers were unable to see the sides and rear of the vehicle, so I ordered the drivers to get out and kneel down so they could secure the vehicle and gunner while the gunner maintained focus further out. (Later in the deployment, I passed the tactic on to an observer from the Joint Readiness Training Center. He dismissed it telling me that it might work in our "quiet" sector, but would never work in a more dangerous area.)

The driver refused to do his job that day. My platoon sergeant reacted like the majority of infantry platoon sergeants might and the soldier determined he didn't want to deal with my platoon sergeant anymore. Thus, the soldier acted in an incredibly irrational manner. We dropped the soldier off at the base and went back to patrolling while I considered what I needed to do. I do not remember there being a formal punishment for it. There were deeper issues at play. Upon our return from Iraq, the soldier demonstrated a will to commit suicide and was admitted to the hospital. After months of treatment, he reportedly left the Army under bad terms having attempted to steal drugs from Walter Reed. It turned out he was addicted to something, but I do not know when that occurred. I have talked to this soldier several times since he left the Army and his life is in order, but he went through some very dark days. I add this anecdote largely because it demonstrates the effects of counterinsurgency on some soldiers. It may not be a form of war with raging firefights and constant shelling, but it affects soldiers nonetheless. The constant threat of ambush and the inability to tell friend from foe weighs on everyone. I have often used this scenario in decision making exercising for subordinate who generally respond that it is an unrealistic situation.

In early July, information indicated that there may be something to find in regard to the whereabouts of Jimenez and Fouty on the west side of the Euphrates River. Thus, the battalion began a series of raids into the area that would culminate in the establishment of a permanent outpost on the far side of the water. On 6 July, *Operation Polar Schism* commenced as members of the battalion and Iraqi Army partners air assaulted into the village of Al Owesat roughly across from PB Dragon. Americans were largely in support of the main objective: two mosques believed to be connected to the kidnapping. Iraqi soldiers searched the mosques with U.S. troops providing a cordon. The other objective was a small number of Sunni insurgents known to frequent those parts. They detained six men but found no corroborative evidence.[15]

That same day, locals led soldiers in Charlie Company's area of operations to twelve weapons caches in Qarghuli Village and fingered the insurgents who were responsible for the caches. The caches were roughly a kilometer from the 12 May ambush site. They contained, among other things, mortar rounds, blasting caps, hand grenades, and a video camera, essentially material for making and exploiting IEDs. The soldiers detained two Iraqis.[16]

In less than a week, the Polar Bears and Iraqi Army were at it again crossing the river for a clearance of Al Owesat and Al Thobat. The mission, *Operation Polar Tempest*, was again related to the search from Jimenez and Fouty. During the operation, insurgents attacked the combined force leading to one dead insurgent. A local guide led the provisional element to a water pump directly across the river from where the 12 May attack occurred. At the location were two small boats that the soldiers elected to render inoperable. In retrospect, it seems unlikely the soldiers were transported to the other side of the river in the early days after the search, so the water pump (as a waypoint) likely had nothing to do with the operation, at least initially, but at the time, it was worth pursuing. In addition to destroying boats, the force detained twelve for questioning and recovered an SVD-63 Dragunov sniper rifle. These excursions also had the effect of putting insurgents on the west side of the river on their heels. It was no longer an uncontested sanctuary. Following the operation, the Polar Bear S3 opined that the operation showed "that we have a very capable Iraqi Army unit to take on these complex missions."[17]

Polar Tempest was but one of several events on a busy day for the battalion. That day, a local informant led members of Delta Company to two different caches in Qarghuli Village. The contents of the caches were small but represented the thirteenth and fourteenth caches Iraqis had pointed out to soldiers in less than 96 hours.[18] While money likely motivated this, it would not have been possible without security. Many times prior to the summer locals refused cash from Americans fearful that it would lead to their death or dismemberment if terrorists caught them with it. Now, they were not only willing to take it but to receive it for turning in insurgents or fingering their munitions.

Also on the 12th, members of the Iraqi Army conducted an operation in Al Taraq with their partners from Alpha Company. Dubbed *Operation Polar Alpha*, the mission was a search of the town. The Iraqis found a fairly large cache consisting of "an 82 mm mortar round, a six-inch-long pipe bomb, 120 rounds of 7.62 mm machine-gun [sic] ammunition, a pressure-plate [sic] initiator for an IED, two 57 mm mortar rounds, two rocket-propelled grenade launchers and a homemade RPG launcher, and one barrel for a Soviet-style DShKa [sic] heavy machine gun." The Iraqi soldiers also engaged three suspected terrorists who were able to escape.[19]

Around this time, the rotation of attached mechanized companies came to an end. The security situation had improved so much that leaders judged B/2–69 AR's services were needed elsewhere. They handed PB Bataan over to the IA and headed elsewhere.[20] In an indication of how secure the area was, the IA manned the once company-sized patrol based with little more than a squad. Despite this, military vehicles were still able to drive the roads around it with impunity.

Despite the enormous progress in improving security and now quality of life, the Triangle of Death remained a dangerous place for Americans and Iraqis alike. On 17 July, Charlie Company was conducting an air assault during daylight. As the helicopters went in for landing, they came under fire from the ground forcing one of the helicopters to pull away. Sergeant Nathan Barnes, one of the commander's RTOs, was shot and killed while sitting in his seat waiting to hop off.[21] Barnes, as I remember, was an incredibly technically competent, loyal soldier. What I remember more than anything is attending his memorial ceremony. One of his friends spoke and he said something that really stuck with me through all of these years. He said, "Nathan would want you to call him Nathan, not Sergeant Barnes." It has always seemed such a powerful statement, maybe because it is a reminder that who we are is more than our rank and authority. Barnes would be the last man to die in Task Force Polar Bear.

Iraqi citizens also continued to bear the brunt of insurgent attacks as the terrorists attempted to reestablish themselves. In mid–July, eight Iraqi citizens came to Patrol Base Yusifiyah with wounds sustained during a mortar attack. Seven of the victims were children under the age of 13. One six-year-old girl had to be evacuated to Baghdad, but recovered and continued receiving care from the Iraqi and American medics once she returned to her family.[22]

On 18 July, Iraqi soldiers and Polar Bears moved in around 2200 to detain a suspected member of Al Qaeda (few sources use the title Islamic State) for kidnapping the two brothers on 23 June as mentioned above.[23] The Iraqi Army was making some inroads with locals as the populace was increasingly becoming the target of insurgent violence. There were still significant trust issues, but things were better now than they had been.

However, more than anything, the locals wanted to work with the Americans whom they trusted more than the Shia national security forces. Part of this was the gulf in medical capabilities between the Americans and Iraqis, even the Iraqi security forces. Part of it was that no matter how much people said Iraqis were in the lead, Route Malibu was almost wholly an American and CLC operation. The Americans were there in force and the Iraqis were not, at least in Qarghuli Village. Thus, on 23 July when locals in Qarghuli Village chased a group of insurgents away after they caught the insurgents working at a cache site, the men reported it to the Americans. The Americans found locals guarding the site until soldiers from Delta Company could secure it.

The cache, located near a canal in the Qarghuli farm fields, "contained 210 57 mm rockets, 25 82 mm rockets (likely mortars), eight 120 mm mortars, a large rocket of uncertain type and a bag of homemade explosive [sic]." An EOD team destroyed the contents, which were not worthy of use in their manufactured purpose, but could have been used to make IEDs. Second Brigade's operations officer noted that many Qarghulis were beginning to turn in caches. Assessing the fact that Sunnis were turning against Islamic State, he opined, "Sunni alliances with al-Qaeda were a marriage of convenience against the emergence of Shia-dominated Iraqi government. But that marriage is going bad."[24] Certainly in July 2007 it appeared headed for an ugly divorce.

Kershaw held a video-teleconference with Watertown, New York, area media members on 31 July where he echoed his operations officer's assessment. He indicated that many locals across the brigade's area had begun identifying IEDs to soldiers before they detonated. IED attacks had gone from an average of 250 per month (roughly 60 per week) to less than 20 per week. That still left about 80 attacks in a month, but represented a sharp decrease. Kershaw does not state it explicitly, but it appears of those 20 per week, at least some were found by soldiers or pointed out by locals before they went off. Kershaw also noted that some locals had taken it upon themselves to grab one of the brigade's sought-after individuals and deliver him to U.S. forces.

Kershaw additionally took time to speak about the progress of the Iraqi Army, a recurring theme of his messages. He said that when the unit first arrived, the IA had control of about a third of the area of operations but now possessed half. Kershaw indicated that the IA would take more if they had more troops and that the concerned local citizens were helping to fill the gap. The commander opined that "[n]onindigenous soldiers are not good for counterinsurgency. If these tribesmen [concerned local citizens] are accepted into [the] legitimate security forces, as everyone hopes, that would help." He added that one of the greatest values of the Sunni tribesman was their ability to provide intelligence.[25]

It would be easy to take Kershaw's comments out of context and believe he was saying that his forces were not good at counterinsurgency. However, what Kershaw was indicating is that ultimately it takes indigenous forces to fully win in an area. His forces had worked hard to train the Iraqi army and set the conditions for long term stability and security, but at the end it required an Iraqi face. They were the ones that knew the area, the ones accountable to people, and the ones who would remain.

Relations in Rushdi Mullah had significantly improved and the IA, U.S. forces, and locals were getting along and helping each other out. Sharp relates a story of a canal getting clogged but the clog was within the U.S. perimeter. The people had no clean water and approached a patrol about clearing it. The platoon acted immediately and soon American and Iraqi soldiers assisted while locals brought their own labor and equipment and cleared the clog. After this event, more Iraqis were determined to develop relationships with the security forces.

Sharp's assessment, five years after the fact, was that it was a:

> major victory. It wasn't a victory that is easily measured by military means. There were no enemy causalities to add and compare, no major equipment destroyed or damaged, no strategic piece of terrain seized from an enemy's defenses. There was no major battle involving strategy and tactics nor the advantages and disadvantages of two armies battling it out. Nevertheless, it was a major victory.[26]

So it was that victory in this fight did not come from vanquishing an enemy so much as marginalizing him and stealing his base. Certainly, there was a heavy component of fighting the enemy, but one would never physically see his destruction as in a different type of war. If the canal in Rushdi Mullah counts as a major victory, an incredible victory was just around the corner.

On 3 August, the Sheiks in the greater Yusufiyah area had a meeting. Many had not seen each other since the invasion. They were coming together now, though. At the meeting, Sunni and Shia leaders embraced each other with hugs and tears.[27] This would be the first in a series of meetings that would bring tribal leaders together as the Polar Bears, Iraqi Army, and locals sought to cement the newfound security and economic development. The brigade as a whole had the strongest reconciliation in terms of concerned local citizens on record in the Multi-National Division-Center area of opperations.[28] Now the Polar Bears were working to bring locals together.

As such, the Polar Bears moved the last of their forces, save Alpha Company and a rear detachment, out of Yusifiyah for good and onto PB Dragon two days after the meeting.[29] The containers and equipment were gone and nearly all of the staff moved forward. The town and the surrounding area had become, in a good way, a local problem with the support of Iraqi national security forces.

It was good news, but while many in the company and battalion—no doubt across the country—longed for the day they could get out of the Army as they were now in the extra innings portions of their contract, they all wanted to go home with Jimenez and Fouty, and no amount of reconciliation or success would compare to not having those two in hand. In that vein, the Polar Bears and their Iraqi Army partners launched another excursion to the west side of the river on 11 August. In *Operation Polar Schism*

III, the combined unit air assaulted across the Euphrates to search a mosque where suspected insurgent cell leaders were anticipated to be hiding, much like in *Operation Polar Schism* on 6 July. The battalion believed that the cell leader had information on the whereabouts of Fouty and Jimenez. Four insurgents briefly engaged the soldiers and were detained along with 18 others for further questioning.[30]

In mid-August U.S. Representative Brian Baird (D-WA) returned from a visit to Iraq. He had previously been there in May. While he had voted before to reduce troop numbers in Iraq, he came away believing the Surge was working and troops needed to stay in place a little longer based largely on observations in the Triangle of Death. He walked through Yusifiyah's market, saying later, "In areas where previously patrols were going out every night and being hit with IEDs … all of those measures are better." Baird added, "Local Iraqis are standing up against the extremists on all sides. They are turning in the insurgents. They are fed up with al-Qaida [sic]."[31]

On 20 August, the Polar Bears' sister battalion, the 2-14 IN Golden Dragons, conducted their own air assault into Al Owesat. Infanti had been advancing the information that insurgents were dressing as women to evade capture and that proved true. However, the insurgent detained by the Golden Dragons must not have been too well disguised. This one even attempted to pass as pregnant.[32]

Though things had gone good in the summer months, many positive events were still unexpected. In the latter part of August, Bravo was patrolling in the small community of Dawoud near Al Taraq. Since the first time troops had entered the hamlet ten months previously, residents had always fled upon the approach of Polar Bear or Iraqi Army soldiers. This day, though, they were greeted and invited on a tour. One local man even fixed the soldiers breakfast and talked to them about the village, security concerns, and the civil operations taking place in Al Taraq. It was a windfall of nearly a year of earnest work without the slightest hint of progress. Now, here the locals had finally welcomed the Americans and were ready to join the growing chorus of collaboration.

Many of the residents had feared the reaction of Islamic State or Al Qaeda if they made contact with the Americans or Iraqi Army, seeing it as a potential death sentence, but with security and economic improvements apparent everywhere, even in Qarghuli Village, the residents felt secure and wanted to be part of it all. "Residents have realized that coalition forces can offer their area security and help provide essential services," offered Bravo company's new commander. "They have seen the improvements in quality of life that their brothers in Qarghuli Village are experiencing from working with our task force."

"Ten months of hard patrolling in this area was worth it to have the people greet us and invite us into their homes," said one of Bravo Company's platoon sergeants. "It's absolutely amazing to see how Dawoud Village has changed, and it means a tremendous amount to the soldiers to see how their actions have led to this. It makes the whole deployment worth it."[33]

Bravo company's previous commander who then served as an assistant operations officer, reflected on this time period and assessed the decline in violence.

> The indirect fire decreased over the course of the deployment. The direct fire contacts were pretty constant throughout. It was several times a week we went out on daytime patrols and would have some sort of direct fire contact. Maybe not every single day, but it was pretty often. There was a lot. But, it stopped instantly in that July timeframe when the "awakening" happened. Overnight, the Sons of Iraq (another name for the concerned local citizens), I think they called themselves, stood up and contact stopped. So in areas where we knew if we went there we were going to get into a gunfight, we were now being invited down to have breakfast with local leaders to inspect the bunkers they had built to protect their villages from the foreign al-Qaeda [sic] fighters who were coming in from all the different countries in the area to fight them.[34]

Dawoud Village seems to be the culmination of this sea change for Bravo Company.

Surprises and reconciliation continued into September. On the sixth anniversary of the 9/11 attacks, Infanti and the company commanders were to attend a meeting of sheikhs held in Qarghuli Village south of BP 151. It was not expected to be a large gathering and the Delta Company commander gave the security task to my platoon of 15 or 16 soldiers. We would integrate with a platoon of Iraqi Army soldiers. We laid out a rather simple plan for security and planned to tie into the battalion commander's personal security detachment while using the Iraqis to help search sheikhs and form part of the perimeter. Our plan had largely focused on the outside. My few dismounts and I would secure the inside and keep an eye on the commanders, but soon it became apparent that security would be much tougher than expected. As the commanders flowed in, so did sheikhs, from Qarghuli Village, Rushdi Mullah, and Yusifiyah, then from Mahmudiyah and Lutifiyah, and then Baghdad. They came from far and wide and in numbers. The best headcount we could get was over 200 sheikhs, some who had not spoken to each other in years.

The meeting was powerful in its symbolism. Nothing like this could have happened—not with these sheikhs, not in Qarghuli Village—in June or possibly even July. It was a statement on the security of the area and the desire to reconcile and truly make a difference. The numbers alone were amazing but the fact that these sheiks came from so far and traveled to Route Malibu and the foot of a place once known as the "Heart of Darkness" was truly remarkable. Sunnis were working with coalition forces while being guarded by the largely Shia Iraqi Army.

The next day, my platoon escorted the company commander to a smaller meeting near PB Inchon. Anderson Cooper, the reporter for CNN, was in the area and attended. He spent some time talking to locals and Kershaw and the report he filed is mostly an assessment of the concerned local citizens. Upon asking one of the locals why they oppose Sunni extremists, the man replied, "Killing people, stealing goats, everything, you name it," highlighting the overreaches of the groups.

Kershaw spoke of the effect of the local security groups. "I haven't had more than one IED destroy a vehicle in an area where concerned citizens were located … in the past two months." A cynic might note that the U.S. military was paying people to not plant IEDs. However, the brigade commander followed this saying, "In the three months since this has started, we have gathered more insurgents up, more terrorists, than we did in the preceding nine months. And that's because they have pointed out to us these people within their own ranks." While some of these arrests may have been due to blood feuds, it demonstrates that a common criticism of the concerned local citizens doesn't hold water. The United States did not just pay insurgents not to fight. Islamic State and Al Qaeda were not the recipients of cash, it was the locals who had allied themselves with these groups in response to disorder and the overreaches of the Shia dominated military force. There is a much-ballyhooed notion that in counterinsurgency (as if there is universal similarity in all situations) that the majority of the population are fence sitters with a few hard cores for the legitimate government and a few hard cores for the insurgent. The truth is, at least for that part of Iraq—and the awakening movements demonstrated this to be true for much of the country—there was a large part of the population "in play," but they often were on a side at a given time, either actively or passively. They may support one side or chose to actively not aid or abet the other, but they weren't on the fence.

Kershaw acknowledged this. "Were some of these people part of the insurgency? Sure they were…. Our job over here isn't to do what's comfortable for us, and it isn't to do what we want," he said. "Our job is to do the nation's bidding. If this gets our nation closer to a solution for this country … then that's what we're gonna [sic] do."[35]

As always though, these positive reconciliations, improved relations, and reduction in violent acts had the cloud cast over it that Jimenez and Fouty were still missing and presumed captured. The prospect of the battalion returning home without the two soldiers loomed large. Despite nearly four months of hard searching, following every lead, and seeking intelligence, the two remained missing as the prospective October return to Fort Drum inched closer. Summing up the feeling of most Polar Bear soldiers, one soldier who had known Fouty since basic training said, "You don't want to leave a buddy just out there. You feel like you left them behind."[36]

In honor of Prisoner of War/Missing in Action National Recognition Day, 21 September, Kershaw sent a letter to the troops. It read, in part:

> This day has special meaning to 2nd Brigade Combat Team, 10th Mountain Division (LI), as it brings a firsthand accounting to the 3,300 Soldiers deployed to southwest Baghdad.
>
> Somewhere out there, two of our own remain. Despite the tireless efforts, resources, analysis and searching, Spec. Alex Jimenez Jr., 25, and Pvt. Byron Fouty, 19, are still missing. Their official status changed from Duty Status, Whereabouts Unknown to Missing / Captured on July 1.
>
> As we strive to find them, I ask all of the Commandos to keep our missing comrades and their Families [sic] in your prayers. This day of remembrance may not relieve the pain they feel, but I hope that it can extend our sympathy and support to them in this time of need that has gone on for so long.
>
> The search for our two Commandos continues. We have resolved to find them, and that mission remains the No. 1 priority for this BCT. We continue to bring the full weight of our intelligence assets—signal, open source and human intelligence assets—to bear in the search for Jimenez and Fouty. Our patrols continue to search for any lead that will bring us closer or will connect the dots of other leads that will shed light on this mystery.
>
> To date, we have arrested more than a dozen al Qaeda affiliates involved in either the planning or the execution of the May 12 attack. We continue to question these detainees and the residents of Qarguli Village [sic], who until recently lived in the shadow of fear of the al Qaeda

tyranny. Locals are coming forth in droves, identifying the terrorists, often at great peril to themselves and their families. They are beginning to cast out the enemy and side with us.

The attack along Route Malibu not only resulted in the capture of Jimenez and Fouty, but also left five other Soldiers from D Company, 4th Battalion, 31st Infantry Regiment, 2nd BCT, and an Iraqi soldier killed in action. As we reflect on those missing, I ask that we also keep these Soldiers and their Families [sic] in our prayers as well.

To take risks is a matter of honor. These Soldiers risked everything to accomplish their mission. We can do no less on this day than to remember them. As we pause to reflect on their sacrifice, we can reaffirm ourselves to our Soldiers Creed, our mission here and our teammates.

This day is a way to remember the heroism and bravery that each of these service members displayed. I ask that you reflect on this aspect as well.

Remember each of these service members, particularly those closest to us. Take time on Sept. 21 to reflect upon their memories. As the slogan imprinted on serene black POW/MIA flag states—you are not forgotten![36]

Despite the uneasy feeling, the battalion had to prepare to redeploy.[37] Returning the unit after 15 months was the best of two bad options for the military. Going home meant the soldiers returned without closure and knowing that two of their buddies were still out there, somewhere. Maybe they were alive and being tortured and praying for their rescue. Maybe they were dead and their family was denied the ability to bury them with dignity. Leaving the unit in Iraq posed problems as well. While things were going well, people were burnt out and the longer one goes the more he is at risk of becoming complacent. Also, as the days wore on, the potential for someone to break his bearing increased, and the strain on the families and the soldiers would grow exponentially. I personally struggled reconciling being burnt out (I had returned from leave in early November and had been there nearly a year straight) and the pledge I made in the Ranger Creed, "I will never leave a fallen comrade to fall into the hands of the enemy...." In the end, I had no choice regardless, but it didn't feel right.

But for now, as I often played the Green Day song "Wake Me Up When September Ends" in my head (ironically, the video follows a marine in Iraq), things went on. What passed for exciting had changed. There was no longer the fear of death around every corner. However, life was not dull. On 26 September, Charlie Company raided a house based on intelligence and discovered, among other things, a book of propaganda praising the 9/11 attacks on the World Trade Center and Pentagon. One can only wonder the intended use for the propaganda. The troops also found a manual for constructing vehicle-borne IEDs, something that once originated with frequency from the Yusifiyah area but seemed extinct these days.[38]

And there were still new bases to build. At least, there was one to build. Toward the end of September the Polar Bears made one more excursion to the west side of the Euphrates. Except this time, they stayed. Delta Company with an attached Alpha Company platoon established a battle position there. This new outpost allowed the battalion to apply some pressure on insurgents and keep eyes on activity on that side.[39] The locals had asked for it, having shown Infanti a trench they had built to defend themselves against insurgents. While the battalion could not line the west bank as it had the east bank, it had taken its largest step to denying the enemy the river.

Soldiers rest on a rooftop during a patrol. Patrolling was never ending but it kept the enemy on his heels and brought enough security to the area to allow the locals to stand up to Islamic State.

September ended and October came which meant that soldiers from the 101st Airborne Division (Air Assault) were arriving to begin the process of replacing the Polar Bears. The unit, 3rd Battalion, 187th Infantry Regiment, the "Rakkasans," had not been part of the brigade that occupied the Triangle of Death prior to 2nd Brigade, 10th Mountain Division. However, the locals could only tell them by their patch which was the same. It was an issue apparent to us, but not to the Army. The 101st had done many great things in Iraq, but members of 1st Platoon, Bravo Company, 1st Battalion, 502nd Parachute Infantry Regiment, had done bad things and that was the reputation of the patch in those parts.

On 5 October, Kershaw spoke to the media and offered up two pieces of information that demonstrate the brigade's (and thereby the battalion's) success in improving the area. The first was they had enrolled 16,000 males into the concerned local citizens with 8,800 under contract and working (at $10 a day, which was a much heftier sum in Iraq than America). The other was that attacks in the area were significantly down, averaging five in a two-week period. There had been a significant increase in IEDs or caches turned in by locals. Roads that had been considered too dangerous to traverse six months previously were now safe and open.⁴⁰ The number of concerned local citizens at work portended a lasting effect ... if the Iraqi government fully accepted the program and budgeted for it.

Prior to the Polar Bears starting their journey home, one last piece of hope for the return of their missing comrades surfaced. On 9 October, the Golden Dragons of 2–14 IN followed some concerned local citizens to a cache site at a house in Fetoah Village, seven miles north of the ambush site. There they had found amongst explosives the M249 squad automatic weapon belonging to Alex Jimenez as well as Sergeant Schober's M4 rifle and M203 grenade launcher, and Corporal Anzack's M4. The soldiers detained nine men for questioning and sent the weapons to the Army's criminal investigation command.⁴² Soldiers were aflutter with hope, but it was not to be. November would come soon and with it would come the time to hand the reigns to the soldiers of 3rd Battalion, 187th Infantry Regiment.

Still, all the hard work came together on 18 October 2007 when 32 tribal sheiks gathered at the Al Rashid Hotel on the third day of a peace conference in Baghdad to sign a pioneering pledge aimed at curbing violence in the region. The sheiks were all from the Mahmudiyah political district (which included Yusifiyah) and the accord was an effort engineered by the United States Institute of Peace (USIP), an organization created by Congress, through the initiative of 2nd Brigade Combat Team. Kershaw's embedded providential reconstruction team put him in touch with the organization. For the commander, the institute brought unique capabilities to the region. He and his staff embraced the organization and they were able to reach the accord which called for prioritizing security, rule of law, local governance, social wellbeing, and the local economy. Kershaw saw this as the completion of Phase I of the reconciliation process, and it was all done for $1.5 million or roughly the cost of a single Tomahawk cruise missile.⁴³

While USIP and the leadership of 2nd Brigade Combat Team ultimately brought together the tribal leaders, it was the work of the Polar Bears, their sister battalions, and their Iraqi national and local partners that established the conditions to enable the accords. For fifteen months, soldiers had worked hard at a form of warfare far from what they likely envisioned when they enlisted or commissioned. It was a strange form of warfare, at times resembling the letter of the infantry manual and at times appearing like armed social work. The soldier had become the problem solver, the counselor, the city-planner, the county engineer, and the police chief. With the security and stability won with blood and sweat, the peace process was able to move forward culminating in a first of its kind peace accord. Most soldiers probably took little notice of the signing, but it is proof that it all meant something in the end.

On 2 November, the new battalion took charge and bid farewell to the Polar Bears. In a speech at the transition ceremony, Kershaw noted the hardships, but also his pride in his troops' accomplishments while maintaining their morality. He said, "Commandos, you have fought the good fight, you have kept the faith and never wavered. You have suffered, bled and yet reached out when others would have struck." He added, "But you have been able to see the fruits of your efforts in the faces of the children in

South Baghdad, and the lives whom [sic] you've helped to make better."[44] When the brigade returned home, it was the most deployed brigade in the United States Army with forty total months in combat since 2001.[45] Many of the soldiers in the battalion had seen every month of that, some having deployed under stop loss. It was a battle-hardened unit, well versed in the ways of counterinsurgency and small unit tactics. It was now home, but not everyone would leave.

It would take time to see whether or not all of this progress could hold. The next chapter will cover the decade following the Polar Bears' departure. The final chapter will explore what the Polar Bears did to lead to this landmark peace agreement and level of security, but it should be noted that the Polar Bears were in a relatively unique situation for counterinsurgency. Save for Vietnam that cannot be easily classified as an insurgency or a conventional war, most nation's fighting a counterinsurgency are a sovereign power of some sort. The most notable insurgencies of the 20th century, wars in places such as the Philippines, Algeria, and British Malaya, were generally fought by a powerful country that had international recognition as a sovereign and thus some sort of governance responsibility and authority. The United States was never a sovereign in Iraq.

Thus, this changed what they had to do to be successful and created a delicate situation. They could not do "too much" when it came to governance. But they needed to bring sustainable security to the region to enable reconciliation and progress within the governance. Thus, rather than reshaping the government, the Polar Bears and the Commando Brigade focused on setting the conditions for success. Therefore, offense ruled the day with local defense as a means of holding and controlling terrain. Stability operations occurred, but were never intended to provide civil services for sustained periods of time. The Polar Bears had gone all in on developing Iraqi security forces and fighting the enemy while holding terrain. The next decade would prove that either wise or foolish.

8

Going Home, Staying Behind

"Only the dead have seen the end of war."—George Santayana

On 27 October 2007, the sixteen soldiers of 3rd Platoon, Delta Company, 4th Battalion, 31st Infantry Regiment and several other soldiers set foot on American soil at Wheeler-Sack Army Airfield where Major General Michael Oates, commander of the 10th Mountain Division (Light), greeted us. We took a short bus ride to our company area, turned in our weapons and night vision devices, and practiced the 10th Mountain Division song one more time. Then we loaded up on buses again, rode to McGrath Gym, and stood in formation once more, listened to a speech we don't remember, sang our song, and then fell out to greet our families. It had been fifteen months since mid–August 2006 when most of us jumped on a plane full of excitement. Many of us were now weary. In the weeks to follow most of the rest of the battalion would flow in behind us and in mid–December we would all receive a well-deserved 30-day leave period. But two members still hadn't made it back and that weighed heavily on the minds of most.

Doug Livermore, the erstwhile battle captain and Delta Company executive officer, reflected on his thoughts at this time:

> I left Iraq with terribly mixed emotions. On the one hand, I had played my small part in a great undertaking, helping to bring peace and stability to a region that previously had been a den of insurgency and animosity.... I departed a country substantially more stable than I'd found it. Yet, on the other hand, I witnessed firsthand the awesome sacrifices made by our nation's precious sons and daughters in some of the most horrible conditions imaginable. Though memories of my days in Kargouli Village [sic] still haunt me, like many warriors before me thoughts of my fallen brothers are far more troublesome. The horrible randomness of war inevitably leaves the survivors wondering why they were allowed to live while others, perhaps more worthy, were taken.[1]

It was good to be home, but some never came home alive and some hadn't come home at all. Some never came home the same.

For me, being home felt great. Fifteen months seemed way too long to be gone. It was good to see family and get my life started again, but my feelings were similar to those of Livermore's. My platoons had fought hard and we saw real progress, but when you look at how many people were killed or wounded, I was often left to wonder: why none of my men? Across fifteen months and two platoons and a total of about 65 subordinates, only four earned Purple Hearts and only three while I was their platoon leader. None of the four were seriously wounded to the point of leaving theater, though the one who had been injured prior to me taking over 3rd Platoon, Delta Company, had to recover long term. We drove the same roads and walked in the same fields as others. While I'd like to claim that we were more aggressive in our patrolling and posture and more respectful in our interactions with the locals, I have no way of proving that. I never experienced survivor's guilt, though I know some have.

On 19 November, the brigade officially uncased its colors. At the ceremony, Oates said, "The Commandos inherited an area of constant conflict and enormous anger, an Iraqi population that was both hostile and distrusting, and an Iraqi security force that was untrained and unreliable. In the span of the next 15 months, the battalions of 2nd Brigade Combat Team effectively targeted al-Qaeda terrorists, they partnered with the Iraqi Army to conduct operations to secure the noncombatant population and they took an enormous risk to reconcile the Sunni tribes to a position of cooperation.

"The results speak for themselves. While the area remains dangerous, the level of violence is a fraction of when they arrived, al-Qaeda is disrupted, the Iraqi security forces are greatly improved and local citizenry has returned to a more normal daily life—free from the insidious violence a year ago."

Oates closed his remarks, saying, "The loss of our young soldiers, the wounds suffered by so many and the personal challenges of the long repetitive tours can appear overwhelming at times—and many in our society may question the sacrifice. But to those of you who have stepped forward when your country needed you, to those of you who risked everything to help those who live in absolute fear and unspeakable conditions, and to those of you who stood by your soldier in good times and bad—your sacrifice is the noblest of all American endeavors and is honored by all. Never doubt it."[2]

While most soldiers were happy to be home, almost all still had an uneasy feeling about the missing two. The brigade and battalion did their best to keep the soldiers at the forefront of their minds as well as honor the sacrifice of the many soldiers killed during the deployment. The unit brought Jimenez's and Fouty's families to Fort Drum. On 20 November, Kershaw and his command sergeant major sat down with Hillary and Gordon Dibler, Fouty's mother and stepfather who raised him from a young age, as well as Andy Jimenez, Alex's father. Kershaw assured them that the 101st had vowed to continue the search. Infanti also met with the families, telling them, "They're missed, and there's no proof (of their status). That's why I didn't send a letter, like I did to the families of soldiers killed. We'll keep looking."[3]

On 7 December, the battalion hosted many of the families of the fallen soldiers at a ceremony to unveil a shadow box honoring the soldiers and interpreters killed during the deployment. Infanti said the intent was both for the families to meet soldiers and see that their loved ones had not been forgotten and for soldiers to have the chance to interact with families. Additionally, Infanti said, "My soldiers have a fear that people will forget their buddies (who) have died. The memorial was for remembrance. I want

8. Going Home, Staying Behind

my soldiers to know that their buddies will not be forgotten and that they didn't die for nothing. They made a difference."[4]

I escorted Anzack's father and Anzack's father's wife that week. I didn't know the younger Anzack, but I got to know him very well that week despite him being deceased. His father, more than anything, wanted to talk to soldiers and hear stories of his son. At first, soldiers were hesitant, not sure what to talk about but as they realized that any small anecdote lit the man's face, it started flowing. It was cathartic for both the soldiers and Anzack's father. In February, I went with several Delta Company NCOs and soldiers to Boston. The Bruins asked us to provide a color guard and to receive jerseys with the names of Fouty and Jimenez on them. The former was from Detroit and the Red Wings, visiting that day, presented his jersey while the Bruins honored Jimenez, from Massachusetts, and provided his jersey. 1st Platoon, Delta Company's platoon sergeant and I received the jerseys from the team captains and then handed them over to the parents.

Soon after, the long-awaited leave period began. Infanti left command for a position at the Pentagon and Kershaw moved on from the brigade. Soon, most of the companies would receive new commanders and executive officers. The S3 would depart the battalion. Many of the officers moved on to their career courses. A large swath of soldiers departed the Army. Others left for new assignments, some going back to combat shortly after returning to fill short units. Inevitably, the band broke up never to be put back together again. What was Task Force Polar Bear of 2006–2007 was now a new unit with the same name and lineage.

The Polar Bears under a new commander would go on to train United States Military Academy cadets in the summer of 2008. It was there that they would learn that two Polar Bears, Alex Jimenez and Byron Fouty, were coming home at last. On 9 July 2008, soldiers discovered the remains of the two missing soldiers and the next day a medical examiner in Dover, Delaware, verified they belonged to Fouty and Jimenez. Jimenez's remains were held for viewing in Massachusetts and then buried on Long Island. Fouty was laid to rest at Fort Sam Houston in San Antonio, Texas.[5] By that point, the Polar Bears' successor in Yusifiyah had lost one soldier, Second Lieutenant Tracy Alger, killed on Route Sporster on 1 November 2007 during the transition. She would be the only 3rd Battalion, 187th Infantry Regiment casualty in the area. Eventually, the brigade covering the entire triangle would be reduced to a 650-man battalion.[6]

Despite the Polar Bears' success, the Yusifiyah area did not retire into lasting peace. Over the next ten years the area would go through highs and lows, but it would never reach the dangerous levels of violence and instability that existed from 2004 to 2007. When the Polar Bears left, there was a strong presence of national and local indigenous forces. Early indications were positive. Shortly after the unit returned home, national security forces entered the Yusifiyah area and killed 14 terrorists while arresting 25 and seizing a large amount of war material.[7] And while U.S. forces had still faced some sort of attack on a near daily basis—ineffectual as it may have been—following the November transfer of authority, on 30 May 2008, author Jim Frederick reported that there hadn't been a single attack on U.S. forces that month.[8]

But in response to the increased security of the area, terrorist groups changed their tactics finding gaps and ways to exploit them. On 14 May, a teenage girl (Iraqi sources estimated her as being 8 to 12 years old while U.S. forces estimated her between 16 and 18) waited outside an Iraqi Army position (possibly the patrol base at Yusifiyah) for hours saying she needed to speak to the company commander. When he returned, the girl blew herself up killing the captain.[9] Terrorists had taken advantage of a cultural sensitivity to males searching females.

Earlier in May, the MP platoon at the Yusifiyah Joint Security Station experimented with the first "Daughters of Iraq" unit recruiting women to train as local security forces with the goal of getting some in the national security forces. (Marines had attempted to start a "Sisters of Fallujah" program in December 2007.) After the suicide bombing, the need for trained females in the security forces became apparent and the numbers increased steadily in just a couple of weeks. The women were largely used to search other women and were not allowed to carry guns or man checkpoints alongside men.[10] The ability of Yusifiyah to build a pan-denominational female security group demonstrates just how far it had come. However, it is unclear what ever came of the group as reporting drops off after early June of 2008.

Despite the suicide bombing, security continued to improve in an around the belts. This led to medical personnel employed by Baghdad's Al Karkh Health Department to begin returning to work, ending a labor shortage. As such, the government was able to begin building additional medical facilities and in the summer of 2008 construction began on a 50-bed hospital in Yusifiyah.[11] This would reduce the need for residents of the area to travel the hour plus trip to Baghdad for medical care.

Terrorists proved at the beginning of 2009, though, that it is not the number of attacks but the effect that counts. While U.S. forces and Iraqi national and local security forces had been successful in reducing overall violence and returning normalcy to the area, they could not stop everything. On 2 January 2009, several tribal leaders of both Sunni and Shia sects gathered at the home of Yusifiyah-area Sheikh Mohammed Abdullah Salih for a national reconciliation meeting. While they were congregating, a man named Amin Al Qarghuli entered wearing an explosives-laden belt and blew himself up, killing at least 23 and wounding 110. Al Qarghuli was attacking his own people, Qarghuli sheikhs, for participating in the peace process.

Only days after the attack, though, residents were undeterred by the bombing. They noted how much more vibrant Yusifiyah was compared to the same time two years previously. An Iraqi Army officer acknowledged there were still bad actors in the area, but noted there were much less than there had been. Shiite pilgrims moved through unabated. Yusifiyah was proving resilient.[12] At this point, the insurgents in Yusifiyah can only truly be seen as terrorists given that they were primarily using suicide bombings against the populace to drive a wedge that wouldn't go.

From that point until the summer of 2013, a span of 54 months, only one more violent act was worthy of English speaking news. That was when a gunman executed seven people in a mass shooting at a mosque in August of 2011.[13] During this time, the Russian company responsible for the Yusifiyah Thermal Power Plant began plans to complete the project.[14] The idea that a company which had ceased work for nearly a decade was ready to come back provides some indication of how international businesses viewed the security of the area in particular and Iraq in general. The fact that something once known as the Triangle of Death could fade into international obscurity for four and half years demonstrates not that the fires of Yusifiyah had been extinguished, but that the area was now manageable.

In 2011, President Barak Obama enacted the final measure of the U.S. troop withdrawal from Iraq. The process, which started under President George W. Bush, was complete by December of that year. Though there were actually U.S. military forces present—such as special operations units—in effect, the U.S. military had handed the Iraq security problem squarely to the country. As such, Islamic State of Iraq, which had been beaten out of their operating grounds and lost the majority of their leadership, saw an opportunity to go back on the offensive. In July 2012, Abu Bakr Al Baghdadi, the leader of Islamic State of Iraq since 2010, declared a new phase to his group's operations called "Breaking the Wall." This phase included operations to free prisoners and assassinate court officials. He called on the men of Iraq to join the fight.[15]

As the group gained momentum in its new offensive, it sets its sights on its old stomping grounds which maintained their strategic significance. In July 2013, Islamic State of Iraq and its allies launched an offensive called the Rumayian Liberation Battle. By the middle of the month the coalition of insurgent organizations claimed to have brought Yusifiyah, among other towns, under its control.[16] It is hard to corroborate this claim if for no other reason than the ambiguity of what it meant to have a town under the control of a terrorist organization. However, clearly Yusifiyah was important to them both for the large number of Sunnis that lived around the city and for its location as a staging area for attacks in Baghdad with access to the smuggling routes in the desert.

Later in the year, Islamic State of Iraq and Syria (ISIS) forces, as they were now called, revived an old Al Qaeda tactic in the Yusifiyah area, the car bomb. On 16 December, two car bombs exploded near a funeral tent in the town killing 24 Shiite pilgrims preparing for the Arbaeen ritual.[17] This was a significant means of asserting their resurgence. In 2007, Sunni terrorist were unable to pull off a single act of violence against Shiite pilgrims traveling through the Triangle of Death for Arbaeen. In 2013, a single act of violence killed 24.

Still, it does not appear that ISIS ever took firm control of Yusifiyah, only that it placed added pressure on the area. A report in the *Long War Journal* in 2014 noted that across Iraq, ISIS was using the 2006 Al Qaeda in Iraq/Islamic State of Iraq plan to gain control of the belts around Baghdad and place pressure on the capital.[18] When the report appeared, ISIS had gained control of the town of Jurf As Sakhar, south of the JSB. The report only noted an "uptick" of attacks in Yusifiyah. When ISIS gained control of Jurf As-Sukr, they did so using 400 fighters and 200 mortar rounds.[19] The once potent combination of concerned local citizens, Iraqi Army units, and U.S. soldiers that had sent Islamic State running in 2007 was gone and replaced by an unprepared Iraqi Army and ineffective home guard.

Jurf As-Sukr was the target because Saddam Hussein had built tunnels there that aided in the smuggling of material. Yusifiyah and its environs were once again becoming a support zone and staging area for attacks in Baghdad. Insurgents were slowly building up their men, weapons, and equipment for an eventual assault on the town. It was happening rather quietly, while Iraqi security forces battled ISIS elsewhere. The lush farm fields and canals with their reeds along with the rugged terrain provided ample cover for their movement. To fight back, the IA began using barrel bombs to clear reeds and vegetation. In Yusifiyah, Iraqi forces were dealing with ISIS sleeper cells. The terrorist group was exploiting deep distrust between the Sunnis in the area and the Shiite government forces. The government had failed to fully take advantage of the Sunni tribes' discontent with Islamic State, especially after the Americans left, and now the tribes were fighting in conjunction with their erstwhile enemies that had been their erstwhile allies. Local tribal leader Abu Shakir explained, "Tribes started to form armed groups to fight the government forces and all groups have one objective: marching toward Baghdad to bring down Maliki's government."[20] Seven years after the Polar Bears left, things were seeming to break apart not because of the military, but because of the sectarian policies of Iraqi prime minister Nouri al Maliki. And so the story of Iraq played out in Yusifiyah; no amount of military victory could save it from political discord.

Of course, that was 2014, and in 2017 ISIS was on its heels in Iraq, beaten back. Yusifiyah and its surrounding hamlets have fallen back into obscurity in the English-speaking world. What the region's ultimate fate will be is anyone's guess, but the Polar Bears proved that the area at least has the capacity for peace and prosperity, something the region largely enjoyed for more than half of a decade before Islamic State returned, and as of May 2017, the peace accord tribal sheiks signed on 18 October 2007 still stood as a recognized document setting priorities and creating a means for cooperation amongst the tribes.[21]

Late in the deployment, as the search continued with little hope, a soldier who had been in 1st Platoon, Delta Company throughout the deployment, sat down smoking a cigarette while talking to a reporter. Thinking about how much Route Malibu had changed, he said, "We gained a little more support in being able to work with this village…." From his viewpoint, the shift was not as dramatic. "They're a little more open with us. But we paid for this road in blood."[22] His observation is poignant and something to consider. The battalion paid dearly for everything it gained. What were the costs? And, given those costs, was it worth it?

With the discovery of the bodies of Jimenez and Fouty the total killed in action came to fifteen from 4th Battalion, 31st Infantry alone. This does not include the losses from Fox Company of 210th BSB or those attached to the battalion from other units at the time of their death. Nor does it include the loss of Callahan to a non-battle accident. The battalion had lost only one soldier, First Lieutenant Adam Malson, during their previous tour and none at any other point of time in Iraq.[23]

The actual number of those killed in action is hard to ascertain. Chaplain Jeff Bryan lists 30 casualties in his memoir plus three interpreters and one Iraqi soldier (Sabah Barak whom Bryan lists as Shahatay Barak).[24] However, some of these were sol-

8. Going Home, Staying Behind

diers from attached units who died elsewhere in Iraq that Bryan or his assistants had ministered to. Other sources list various numbers. The most reliable number of U.S. casualties I can come up with is 22: Corporal Joseph Anzack, Jr. (D/4-31 IN), Sergeant Nathaniel Barnes (C/4-31 IN), Corporal Ray Bevel (C/4-31 IN), Corporal Ryan Bishop (C/4-31 IN), Staff Sergeant Harrison "Ducky" Brown (B/2-69 AR), Specialist Brian Browning (B/4-31 IN), Sergeant First Class James Connell, Jr. (D/4-31 IN), Corporal Daniel Courneya (D/4-31 IN), Second Lieutenant Johnny Craver (B/1-22 IN), Specialist Byron Fouty (D/4-31 IN), Private First Class Nathaniel Given (D/4-31 IN), Private First Class Thomas Hewett, (B/1-89 CAV), Private First Class Statieon Greenlee (A/4-31 IN), Sergeant Alex Jimenez (D/4-31 IN), Sergeant Christopher Messer (D/4-31 IN), Corporal Christopher Murphy (D/4-31 IN), Sergeant Curtis Norris (F/210 BSB), Specialist Nicholas Rogers (B/4-31 IN), Sergeant Anthony Schober (D/4-31 IN), Private First Class David Simmons (B/2-69 AR), Sergeant Todd Singleton (A/2-5 CAV), and Staff Sergeant Steven Tudor (F/210 BSB).[25] The battalion shadow box memorial to the fallen has 26 pictures, three are interpreters, and one is Callahan.

Of the 22, 13 occurred on Route Malibu alone with Delta Company bearing nine of those killed. The soldiers killed in Task Force Polar Bear represented roughly 40 percent of the fatalities across the entire Triangle of Death during 2nd Brigade's deployment. In total, the brigade suffered between 52 and 54 killed (depending on the source) and 270 wounded, with some estimating the Polar Bears at 119 wounded.[26]

In the coming years more would die of invisible wounds. In late April of 2010, I was sitting at home when my phone rang. It was one of my squad leaders. He had gotten out and was working his way toward a degree in elementary education. We had kept in touch largely through social media. When I picked up the phone, he gave me startling news: one of my former Delta Company RTOs was dead. He had been my RTO for several months and we had gotten to know each other well. I endeavor to say we were friends no matter how improper some would say that was. I cared for him and we had kept in touch. He had earned his stripes and moved on to another post and gone back to Iraq. All my interactions with him were light and some of the other guys and I had just been joking with him that week, but what I didn't know was that he was on anti-depressants and had recently decided to stop taking them. Then he pulled a gun out and shot himself.

I didn't want to believe it at first. He seemed too happy, too unaffected by it all. I called his mother and stepfather and made arrangements to attend his funeral. I had so many emotions. I had lost a friend and soldier and was sad, but I was also mad at him. It took me several years to truly understand suicide in the military and I held onto beliefs I'd developed in adolescence. I ended up attending the wake but had a commitment to another military brother I could not break. Those two opposing emotions made it difficult during that time. Fortunately, that commitment was the David E. Grange, Jr. Best Ranger Competition and I spent the next week with a lot occupying my mind and body.

I eventually got over any negative emotions toward him and realized that if it could happen to him, it could happen to anyone. I also realized there are not always a lot of signs. I came to wonder if the process of breaking up units after deployment had anything to do with it. Delta Company has lost at least two more soldiers to their demons. Likely others in the battalion have committed suicide as well. I once saw this as a sign of weakness but have learned that soldiers have hidden wounds. It is my sincerest hope that this work encourages those that have served in the Triangle of Death. Shortly, I will turn to the gain. But there is still some cost to speak of.

Beyond suicide, death, and injury (of which there were over 100), there were other costs to U.S. soldiers. Some soldiers experienced marital issues. I remember one soldier sitting in my office crying telling me how he couldn't compel himself to spend time with his family. He just wanted to withdrawal. Others suffered behavioral health issues. Sharp reports of one soldier arrested for stalking Miley Cyrus and another, in a domestic dispute, breaching the door to where his wife was with a shotgun as we would in Iraq.[27] And one of my old gunners, who moved on to Alaska and became an NCO in the 1st Brigade Combat Team, 25th Infantry Division, was charged with involuntary manslaughter, negligent homicide, and assault consummated by battery in connection to the hazing-induced suicide of Private Danny Chen.[28] He had been Chen's squad leader. Ultimately, a court martial convicted him of dereliction of duty, hazing, and maltreatment of a subordinate and sentenced him to 60 days of hard labor and demoted him two ranks.

Some soldiers have struggled to hold down steady employment and no doubt others have dealt with substance abuse issues. A number of soldiers likely take a large amount of prescription drugs to deal with the multitude of things they brought back. This is to say nothing about the effects on families. It should be noted that not every soldier left Iraq a broken man or that even most soldiers did. Most soldiers have thrived since returning, but there were many that have suffered greatly from their experience.

Lastly, there was the cost to the Iraqis. Reflecting on this, Staff Sergeant Philip Sharp wrote:

> …I want to mention the human cost where it hits the most though gets the least amount of coverage of all. I am speaking about the Iraqi people themselves…. I have watched the nation of Iraq and its people struggle and make great strides in doing so [over three deployments].
>
> To them must go the greatest of consideration and respect. The price they paid is by far much higher than we have paid with regard to human cost. The lion's share and brunt of the suffering was indeed upon their shoulders. Many Americans know that the Iraqis have suffered. It is through the sterilized lens of a screen that this is made known to them, one that can be turned off when its presentation becomes too much to care for. It is by far more vivid and etched in your mind to see it firsthand.[29]

The Iraqis stayed behind when we came home. They had started to fight Islamic State and Al Qaeda and now they were there with a new unit. Eventually, there would be no Americans around. The tyranny of geography would continue to make the Yusifiyah area important for irregular challengers to the legitimate Iraqi government. They have proven resilient, but they have paid a high price.

So what was the gain for all that cost? This gets back to the question that started this entire project. Were we really successful or did it just appear that way? Sitting at

8. Going Home, Staying Behind

dinner one night with Anzack's dad, I told him that the death of his son as part of the 12 May attack meant something. I always saw it as a turning point. The flooding of the area with troops and the mass arrests led to the citizens turning on the insurgents and coming to our side. Undeniably, the Yusifiyah area became dramatically safer in the wake of the attack and kidnappings. I sincerely felt that was true when I told him that, but I could not know beyond my own feelings that we were successful.

The early returns from outside observers, especially recognized counterinsurgency experts, were positive. Bing West, a former Assistant Secretary of Defense for International Security Affairs who wrote a well-regarded book about Marine counterinsurgency in Vietnam and then several others about Iraq and who had played a bit role in the formation of Field Manual 3–24, *Counterinsurgency*, wrote that the 2nd Brigade Combat Team, 10th Mountain Division "had lost sixty-nine killed [actually 52 or 54], but had done such a thorough job that [their replacement brigade] had lost only one soldier since taking over in November 2007." He notes that there were no known insurgents operating in the town of Oweset where the Polar Bears had emplaced their last battle position. Concerns among the new commanders in the area were not of the enemy but getting the concerned local citizens paid and getting micro-grants approved.[30] West, a war critic, was not one to heap praise unnecessarily. David Kilcullen, an Australian who served on Petraeus' staff and has written extensively on modern counterinsurgency, assessed that the brigade had performed "extremely well throughout the Surge."[31]

Perhaps the most ringing endorsement came from Petraeus himself. The commander of Multi-National Force-Iraq and counterinsurgency golden boy renamed the area the "circle of life" (or "love" depending on the source) following the summer of 2007.[32] Petraeus had previously noted that the brigade understood counterinsurgency in his visit to Yusifiyah in June 2007, and there was Lawrence Kaplan, who noted before the sea change in security that Kershaw and the brigade were doing great things.

In April 2009 the Congressional Research Service released a report titled "Operation Iraqi Freedom: Strategies, Approaches, Results, and Issues for Congress" looking at key policy issues the new Obama administration may pursue. The report noted:

> While unit partnering became much more widely institutionalized in 2008, the practice had been used by some U.S. units in the past. In 2007, for example, in the turbulent area of Mahmudiyah and Yusufiyah south of Baghdad, Colonel Mike Kershaw, Commander of the 2nd Brigade of 10th Mountain Division, tasked his entire field artillery battalion to embed with the 4th Brigade of the 6th Iraqi Army Division and its battalions. The de facto transition team—350 soldiers, staff, and all of their enablers—was far more robust than a MiTT [Military Transition Team], and had the added value of providing a visible example of how a U.S. battalion is organized and functions. The results in terms of Iraqi operational capabilities were apparently positive. Near the end of the brigade's tour, COL Kershaw reported, "We really conduct almost no operations where we do not have Iraqi forces either embedded with us, or where they are in the lead."[33]

In late June of 2017, the United States Institute of Peace honored the 2nd Brigade Combat Team, 10th Mountain Division (Light), for its work in Mahmudiyah district from August 2006 to November 2007, that led to the ground-breaking peace accord.

Kershaw, Command Sergeant Major (Retired) Anthony Mahoney, and Colonel (Retired) John Laganelli, the brigade's deputy commander, were on hand with Kershaw to accept a plaque from Stephen Hadley, the chairman of USIP's board who served as George W. Bush's National Security Advisor when the Polar Bears were deployed. Hadley said the accord was "an example of the inestimable value that is offered when the disparate instruments of American foreign policy work together for a common objective.…" He added, "The relative stability of the Mahmudiyah region following the accord is a step toward the broader peace in Iraq that will serve the interests of Iraqis, Americans and people worldwide." Lieutenant Colonel (Retired) William Zemp, who was part of the brigade that followed the Polar Bears, noted that the area had passed four major tests of the peace accord to include rejection of Al Qaeda and Islamic State of Iraq and then resistance to the renewed ISIS offensive.[34]

This honor came nearly ten years after the Polar Bears exited stage right. In the aftermath of 2/24 Marines' experience in the Triangle of Death, the battalion commander had been all too ready to pronounce the area stabilized, but within only a matter of months, the area began to devolve again. It is possible to blame that on the unit's successors, however, there is no evidence to suggest either the 2nd Battalion, 70th Armor Regiment or Company E, 1st Battalion, 108th Armor Regiment of the Georgia National Guard performed poorly. All we can say for certain is that the 1st Battalion, 502nd Parachute Infantry Regiment discovered a hornet's nest. When they left, there were no such pronouncements of success. However, when one divorces the actions of 1st Platoon, Bravo Company, from the overall performance of the unit, that unit took great strides to set conditions for the Polar Bears.

In fact, while the Polar Bears inherited a dangerous piece of real estate in September 2006, it is undeniable that their task was made easier by the work of their predecessors. The 2/24 Marines established a foothold, E/1–108 AR set up shop at FOB/PB Yusifiyah, and B/1/502 PIR established positions along Route Sporster and at the JSB. Had the Polar Bears needed to fight all the way in, their gains would not have been so great.

Still, this does not diminish the incredible accomplishments the Polar Bears achieved with their local and national Iraqi partners. Yusifiyah attained a degree of normalcy during their tenure—normalcy for Iraq, at least. Citizens threw off their shackles and were able to defend themselves. The economy began to show gains. The government demonstrated degrees of effectiveness not previously seen, and it lasted. Only one other U.S. soldier died in the area and despite numerous challenges to its security and stability, the agreement signed in October 2007 stands today.

Understanding the success of the Polar Bears requires understanding the depth of the problem. How dangerous was the area? Was Yusifiyah the most dangerous place in the Iraq? It is a dubious claim if for no other reason than the ambiguity of the statement. What makes something dangerous and, by extension, more dangerous than something else? At times, Yusifiyah was surely one of the most dangerous areas for U.S. troops and certainty it was at times for Shite pilgrims. While the Polar Bears were there, they had significant casualties vice the country at large. In December 2006, 3 of

115 servicemembers killed in Iraq came from Yusifiyah, or 2.6 percent of all deaths in Iraq. In April 2007, 6 of the 117 troops who died did so in Yusifiyah, or 5.1 percent. Finally, with the deaths of Jimenez and Fouty included, 7 of 131 servicemembers who lost their lives in action in May 2007, or 5.3 percent, died in Yusifiyah. Excepting Fouty and Jimenez, as their exact date of death is unknown, brings that to 3.8 percent.[35] (It is unclear where Jimenez and Fouty fall in the aggregate numbers.) For an area not much larger than 20 square miles, those numbers are significant.

It is easy to claim that any area in Iraq was dangerous and killed in action doesn't tell the whole story, but one can reasonably conclude that Yusifiyah was a deadly area for U.S. troops before the Polar Bears arrived and that by pushing forward it became even deadlier. It was an area that was worse for a soldier's health than most other areas in Iraq, but by the time the Polar Bears left, the area's fortunes had been reversed. That is something all survivors should be proud of; not only did they make a difference then, they established conditions for security that have withstood major crises.

What the Polar Bears did was bring security to an area that could be sustained beyond the departure of American troops and set the conditions for long term stability. Ultimately, in a counterinsurgency environment, neither foreign troops nor military force will be the decisive aspect. Some may point to examples of brutally repressed insurgencies, but a Western democracy like the United States cannot in the present age do such things, so success was creating a situation where the host nation had a chance. The Polar Bears did that and the local government ran with it to the point that today the government is still sufficient.

Certainly, the Polar Bears' work is worthy of note when considering counterinsurgency. However, little attention was ultimately paid to the Triangle of Death when it wasn't a hotbed of killing. While the southern belt was strategically important, it was not a major city like Tel Afar or Ramadi. Therefore, it has remained an obscure instance beyond the major incidents such as the rape and killings and the kidnappings, but it deserves to be studied. There are a few well-known examples of success in urban environments such as Mosul and the two cities mentioned above. The Triangle of Death offers an example of a successful rural counterinsurgency approach.

My thesis for the Command and General Staff Officer Course Art of War Scholars program was a case study of the battalion before and after the arrival of Petraeus. I concluded that Petraeus had been important to the battalion's ability to provide stability to the region, but not for the reasons most would think. The battalion was executing Petraeus' operational approach long before he published it. However, the creation of Multi-National Division-Center provided more air assets and placed units on the periphery of the brigade forcing insurgents to move into U.S.–occupied territory wherever they went. Because the battalion had already done the work before hand, once everything was set, which coincided with the 12 May attacks, they were ready to take advantage of it. It was often frustrating, but often fruitful.[36]

Reflecting on his tour, a platoon sergeant said, "It was a nasty place.... The feeling [of danger] was there as soon as you hit the ground." He reflected on the danger to civilians and soldiers nearly everywhere, but then he said that Yusifiyah had been "cleared out." "Some of the things my guys did, and the other soldiers did, are beyond the scope of what people normally do." Then he added, "There's a part of us still there."[37]

The platoon sergeant's words are undeniably true. I have never completely left Yusifiyah. It has shaped me as an officer greatly and I have been drawn to it. I never thought that would be the case; I hated the place, but it is part of me. I think many soldiers feel the same way. Polar Bear soldiers saw some terrible things and endured deplorable conditions for 15 months. Friends died and were horribly wounded, so we circle back to those fundamental questions: Were we successful? What does it mean?

Firmly, we were successful if imperfectly. All of the evidence points to that when one defines success as establishing the level of security needed to build governmental institutions and enable long term stability. In fact, writing this book has made me even more proud to have had a small part in all of this, but what's the so what? Ultimately, I'm not sure, but the final chapter will attempt to answer that question in part.

9

What It All Means: Theory of Small Unit Counterinsurgency

The techniques must be chosen and tailored to fit the local requirements and environment, which must be completely understood. Look upon the former revolutionary wars as shopping lists of techniques that have worked and can work in similar situations.—John McCuen, *The Art of Counter-Revolutionary War*

"What good is an experience if we do not record it and attempt to learn from it, to build off it?" I scrawled those words on the inside cover a notebook in the summer of 2007. I had gone into Iraq with little understanding of counterinsurgency. After reading about it and living it, I figured I had learned some things. Also, I realized that there really aren't any counterinsurgency books out there that provide a good perspective on what the platoon leader, the company commander, or the battalion operations officer should be thinking about and doing. (Two articles, one by Craig Coppock titled "The Counterinsurgency Cliff Notes," the other by David Kilcullen called "Twenty-Eight Articles," have explored small unit counterinsurgency.) The Army responded to criticism that FM 3-24 was too high level by releasing FM 3-24.2, *Tactics in Counterinsurgency*. That manual explores many of the concepts the Polar Bears employed, but it is still a manual which brings it strength as well as limitations. A quick look at its enclosed reading list indicates that that the writers were inspired by large-scale counterinsurgent actions while interweaving themes from Iraq.

Still, many counterinsurgency practitioners from Iraq and Afghanistan have failed to write books like past generations (especially mid-20th century) and those books that do exist largely focus on the operational and theater levels. While in Iraq, I read, among others, Galula's *Counterinsurgency Warfare*, Nagl's *Learning to East Soup with a Knife*, Alistair Horne's *Savage War of Peace*, Robert Taber's *War of the Flea*, and even John Poole's *Tactics of the Crescent Moon*. I certainly learned a lot, but I had to read between the lines to learn lessons for my level. The books provoked thought more than served as something to guide me. Thus, it is my intent to synthesize Task Force 4-31 IN's deployment and leave something for future generations to use.

In developing the following, I have consulted my notes to include the aforementioned notebook and classes I taught at the Infantry Basic Officer Leader Course that have survived. There will be actions I'll mention that don't show up in the previous chapters. This is because the actions may not have worked with the flow of the narrative, but they are important to know about to understand the Polar Bears' counterinsurgency approach. I hope the reader will forgive me for not mentioning these areas sooner.

The intent here is not to produce a series of immutable principles, but to describe what the Polar Bears did and comment on it. It is useless to search for a blueprint for counterinsurgency. Every situation is different. However, by understanding the things the Polar Bears did that made them successful, a future practitioner may be better prepared when analyzing the unique situation they find themselves in.

Analyzing the Polar Bear' deployment, the following actions, in order of emphasis, demonstrate their long-term game plan: 1. Clear and hold terrain, 2. Conduct offensive operations to keep insurgents on their toes and increase security, 3. Train and enable the indigenous force, 4. Conduct civil/stability operations. Some may not agree with this list, but this is how I analyze how the battalion spent its time and resources.

Research and Prepare

Counterinsurgency is a bit like a puzzle where you build the frame before touching anything in the middle. There has to be a clear goal and endstate that all actions revolve around. In the case of the Polar Bears, they had that. From the start, the end state was a government and an Iraqi Army capable of securing and administering the area as well as the vision of owning all of the greater Yusifiyah area with two lines of communication open between the town and the power plant. Without a vision of the desired end state, it is unlikely the Polar Bears would have achieved the level of success they did. Certainly no one was considering that a ground-breaking peace agreement would be reached and few likely considered having local citizens form armed watch groups. That was all stuff for the middle of the puzzle, but they needed to know where they were going to make a coherent plan to get there. John McCuen, a largely forgotten mid–20th century counterinsurgency theorist, admonished, "When the enemy knows what he is doing, trial and error is a most dangerous way to fight a war."[1]

The Polar Bears under Infanti and their brigade commander Kershaw clearly understood the fight they were getting into. They put into place measures that would ensure that at least the platoon sergeants and platoon leaders, and those above them, understood the complexity of the situation. This included required readings, presentations, and discussions to instill an understanding of Iraq, the Arab culture, and counterinsurgency. However, it also combined training on urban warfare tactics such as room clearing and standard infantry tactics such as patrolling. All of these aspects were important to the battalion.

By understanding the end state, the leaders were able to develop a plan from the start. With Kershaw and Infanti understanding that the Iraqi Army was one of the keys to success, both developed plans to provide training, advising, assisting, and partnering to that organization. Kershaw designated the majority of his field artillery battalion as advisors. While there was not a need for a full battalion of guns, the opportunity cost was additional infantry manpower. Many commanders in this time period converted their artillerymen into infantrymen to increase their forces. Making them trainers reduced the forces Kershaw could place into sector in the short term. There was a gamble that the Iraqi Army would be able to take over territory; it paid off. In the transaction, the Polar Bears lost capable officers who had trained with the battalion and had deployed before as Infanti sent some of his senior-most lieutenants to assist in the field artillery battalion's mission. Of course, Infanti also gave up an entire company headquarters to this task. As noted previously, the 4/4/6 IA was not well regarded but turned into a capable unit. Both commanders took a fair amount of risk but did so because they knew, from their research and preparation, how important it was.

It is also clear that the leaders and their staffs employed operational art by arranging tactical actions in time, space, and purpose in the pursuit of strategic aims. The campaign to open up the two lines of communication to the Yusifiyah Thermal Power Plant and to divide the insurgency amongst those on one side of the river and those on the other reminds me of the campaign to open up the Mississippi and bifurcate the Confederacy. The Union seized forts along the Mississippi River slowly gaining more territory from the Confederacy. It was a slow, painstaking process not without its struggles such as Major General Ulysses Grant's expeditions attempting to get around Vicksburg, but the idea of gaining and holding ground was the same. Similar to Grant, the battalion laid out a plan before moving out and understood how they wanted to attack even if not completely sure what that would look like, and there were unintended results; Charlie was not originally supposed to stay in Al Taraq, but the plan helped guide the action.

Lastly comes personal study. Infanti had a reading system in place where all officers had to have a book checked out of the battalion library. From time to time, he would send out articles for all of his officers and senior NCOs to read such as Kilcullen's "Twenty-Eight Articles," but, ultimately, self-development is on the officer or NCO. Prior to deploying to Iraq, I largely failed at this. After dedicating myself to the subject, I began to not only understand the fight we were in but to be able to contribute with ideas of what more we could be doing.

Recent years have brought debate about how much the Army should focus on maneuver warfare and how much it should focus on small war. Without a large presence in environments such as Iraq and Afghanistan, the focus has shifted largely to renewed emphasis of fighting the big war against a near-peer. This is understandable given the environment. However, units would be wise to continue to train their leaders for counterinsurgency through academic means. Whether that happens or not, leaders should dedicate time to self-development.

Shocking the System: Clearing and Holding

The battalion did not sit around. Shortly after taking control of Yusifiyah, they established a new foothold on the Mullah Fayad Highway called the Alamo. In and of itself, that was a good initial action, but more importantly, within two weeks of taking the reins the battalion conducted a massive offensive operation involving four companies and assaulting the enemy in three places. The boldness of the action so shocked the enemy that it was several weeks before he could respond. The history of 1/502 PIR in Rushdi Mullah indicates that the enemy was capable of attacking at will.

The weaknesses in the plan are also instructive. Unfamiliar with the terrain, the planners developed an unrealistic timeline. There was no blocking force to prevent the enemy from fleeing. Units ran out of or came close to running out of fuel and water. There were no engineer assets planned to actually build the base at Rushdi Mullah leaving Bravo to construct it with shovels and picks like a World War I trench. Finally, what to do with Al Taraq beyond the first 48 hours had been left to anyone's guess. These are significant weaknesses. The battalion got away with the lack of engineers but came close to paying for it in one attempted suicide vehicle-borne IED on Rushdi Mullah. The battalion lost a great opportunity by not having isolated its objectives. There are resource limitations to consider here, but planners need to be aware of tradeoffs and do their best to mitigate the risk they accepted.

While there were significant weaknesses with the plan, the battalion was poised to exploit success. When information led to the discovery of a cache along the Janabi Run Canal, Charlie Company learned how to search for caches and went to work finding them. Charlie Company had the good fortune of being in an area so lucrative with supplies but had to combine that with the good sense to exploit that fortune. Further, the battalion quickly saw the successes in Al Taraq and decided to exploit that by permanently setting up shop there. What this demonstrates is a degree of flexibility. No plan should be rigidly followed, and certainly not one in such a fluid environment as counterinsurgency.

Operation Polar Blizzard was not the only shock to the system. The battalion also shocked the system in Qarghuli Village. Rather than a single, grand offensive operation, the battalion used a series of quick succession operations to seize a foothold in the village. Rather than slowly move up Route Malibu, the battalion went in aggressively. It built a series of bases over a matter of weeks to establish its presence, then it spent the next several months fighting to secure the area and retain it against frequent enemy attempts to dislodge the Polar Bears.

Ultimately, the Polar Bears stayed behind and never gave up ground it had fought for in Yusifiyah (though it did conduct raids across the river). They put down roots in the areas they pushed into and eschewed comfort to be close to the people. No shocking of the system would have been meaningful without staying behind. As British veteran of Afghanistan and counterinsurgency theorist Emile Simpson notes of his time in Central Helmand in 2010, "we found that the single greatest shift in popular perceptions of us came when we started to live among people. This meant getting out of our forward operating bases and actually permanently living in the villages in much smaller fortified compounds."[2]

As a unit enters a new area, it will need to seize a foothold. This is true of both physical and human terrain. Not only does the unit need a base within its area of opera-

9. What It All Means

A patrol of HMMWVs passing Battle Position (BP) 152 heading south on Route Malibu. Nearly a third of all soldiers killed in 2nd Brigade died on this road, but it went quiet in the late summer of 2007.

tions to operate out of, it needs contacts that can pass information. Finding those people willing to talk to you early on is important. More important is discovering the right way to do it. In Iraq, few people wanted to be seen talking to Americans. Some would approach us when they were far away from observation. Some wanted to be "arrested" so that no one could observe them. They could be detained, brought to the base for interviews, and then released with deniability. However one wants to interact, once they come to your side, particularly the early contacts, you have to have a plan to protect them or you'll set back your efforts considerably.

Holding an area requires security. Before the Polar Bears could ever hope to change the tide in the area, they had to convince the locals they were there to stay. Only in the case of cross-river excursions did the battalion ever display a raider mentality, and even then the eventual outcome was to establish a permanent presence. When the battalion faced its most difficult moment—the 12 May attack—it never wavered from its desire to clear and hold all of the terrain in greater Yusifiyah. It pressed on and took the last bit of Route Malibu. That was important. The insurgents were doing what they could to deny terrain to the Polar Bears. Repelling them was one thing; but showing the commitment to stay by increasing their footprint was even better. Likely one of the most important things the battalion did was stay and never abandon a base without giving it to an Iraqi unit.

Holding generally placed soldiers in spartan conditions that are maybe hard to imagine. There were stretches of days where I slept outside on a cot under a camouflage net. Many bases were just big enough to house the soldiers and provide guard positions. While many bases lacked amenities, so long as soldiers could eat, sleep, and have some shelter, the most important part of any base was the ability to protect the force. Soldiers needed the ability to stay where they were. Defenses were often rudimentary to begin with—Al Taraq initially had a vehicle and a strand of wire—but the rule of the defense is to never stop improving. The principles of the defense are thoroughly laid out in Army manuals open to the public. I will not belabor them here.

A fair amount of manpower went into guarding positions once they were established. In fact, for long stretches my platoon could do nothing but hold its position. This happened at times in Al Taraq and was always true of BP 152, but like Grant, Admiral David Porter, and others opening up the Mississippi, any terrain we took had to be held even if it was only a garrison. While soldiers mostly ate packaged food, slept on cots, showered and did laundry with water bottles, and went long stretches without TV, internet, or phone service, this kept bases down to their intended purpose and prevented even more soldiers being needed for security.

Defenses were one of two things that allowed the Polar Bears to secure themselves. The other was aggressive patrolling. In October, there were times that so many Charlie Company patrols were out that my element looked more like the make-up of Captain Miller's small group in *Saving Private Ryan* than an infantry platoon, but the aggressive patrolling prevented the enemy from attacking the base directly with the added benefit of increasing our awareness and increasing the locals' understanding that we were there to stay. We would conduct patrols day and night sometimes showing up in unexpected places after marching through the dark. At times, the only intent of the patrol was to stir the dogs at 0200 to let people know we came through.

In the early stages, much of the patrolling will come from squads and platoons as units saturate the area. However, leaders at the company and battalion level (and the brigade, to some degree) along with staff officers, need to get out and walk the terrain so they understand it. The battalion commander and S3 circulated often, and the S3 went on a number of operations as the leader of a command element. When the S3 went, he usually brought staff officers along as his radio operators so they could gain an appreciation for the terrain and people. Not all staff officers need to walk the ground, but members of the intelligence and operations shops do. The S2 went as often as he could. Without this knowledge, plans for operations can be unrealistic or even useless. Leaders need to be out there for the same reasons.

As patrols begin to go out, there is a need to track where they are, where they are going, and where hasn't been touched. This will help to avoid setting patterns and ensure there are no gaps in coverage. Two tools can be extremely effective. First, the "horse blanket" is a map cut up into sections with a corresponding designation. This creates a regional address and helps simplify orders and reporting. At times, my commander would want to know more about a particular area, say R7, and direct us to patrol there with specific intelligence requirements to answer. At other times, he may look at a map and tell us to patrol through R15, R18, and R9 to look for caches. Later, when I took over the base at Al Taraq and became responsible for my own patrol schedule, I used these sectors to determine where I needed to patrol. Some weeks I may look to hit R5 three or four times and other times I may look at the map and realize R20 hadn't been touched in two weeks. We could also break down intelligence requirements by sector. What we may want to know about a populated sector might not be true about an unpopulated sector. In unpopulated sectors we were looking for signs of enemy infiltration routes, caches, and activity. In populated sectors, we were focused on a wider array of things.

The flip side of this is the honesty trace. An honesty trace is a report from the patrol leader that shows the exact route of the patrol and notes key events along the way. This allows the commander to see the difference between planned and executed patrols for decisional purposes and provides a common understanding of the patrol. Patrols deviated routinely in Iraq due to civilians, tough terrain, or contact with the enemy, among other reasons. As a commander analyzes his battlespace, the more information, the better.

The honesty trace should be filed with a patrol debrief. At my best, I would conduct a post-patrol after action review with the members of the patrol where we'd discuss what we saw and did and how we could get better. The value of this is that eventually

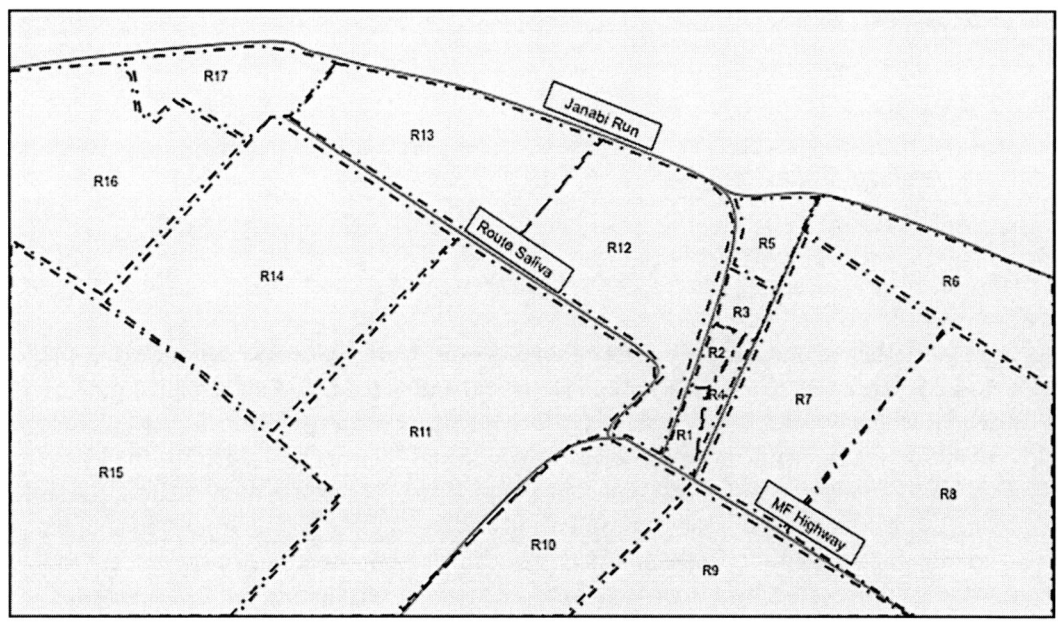

Example Horseblanket

lower ranking soldiers feel they have a voice and report things they saw that leaders may not have noticed. One of the key purposes of patrolling is to gather information and soldiers are taught that they are sensors. It is important to get the information they gain. While it could be uncomfortable having a young soldier or NCO provide constructive criticism of my decisions and actions on a patrol, it made us better and let the soldiers know I valued their opinion.

From the after-action review, I would type a patrol debrief and submit it to the company commander. The debrief looked for a myriad of information: start and end times of the patrol, size and composition of the patrol, task and purpose, route trafficability, where the patrol went, who the patrol talked to, what the patrol found, what enemy contact did the patrol make, and what information requirements did the patrol answer. Often the debrief also included a narrative description of the patrol from start to finish. Here is an example of the format:

DATE TIME GROUP:
TYPE OF OPERATION:
UNIT:
PATROL LEADER:
PATROL START TIME/RETURN TIME:
TASK:
PURPOSE:
LOCATION:
PATROL TYPE:
INTELLEGENCE REQUIREMENTS:
NUMBER PERSONNEL:
NUMBER VEHICLES:
ROUTE TRAFFICABILITY:
ENEMY CONTACT:
PERSONS TALKED TO:
BUSINESSES ENCOUNTERED:
SUMMARY/NARRATIVE:

Another important early action is the census. Unlike a census conducted in the United States, this census is less about statistical understanding than actually knowing who is where. We didn't have a standard format, but a census usually included a picture of all the teenage and above males in the home and their names, a grid to the house (since there were no addresses) or a contrived address (based on a numbering convention), and a list of the number of women and children in the house. Other information may include a picture of cars and licenses plates, the occupations of the males, and whether they were Sunni or Shia. We would lay this information out in a slide presentation that allowed us to quickly pull up data based on intelligence or in preparation prior to a patrol or operation. The census was incredibly helpful when source reporting

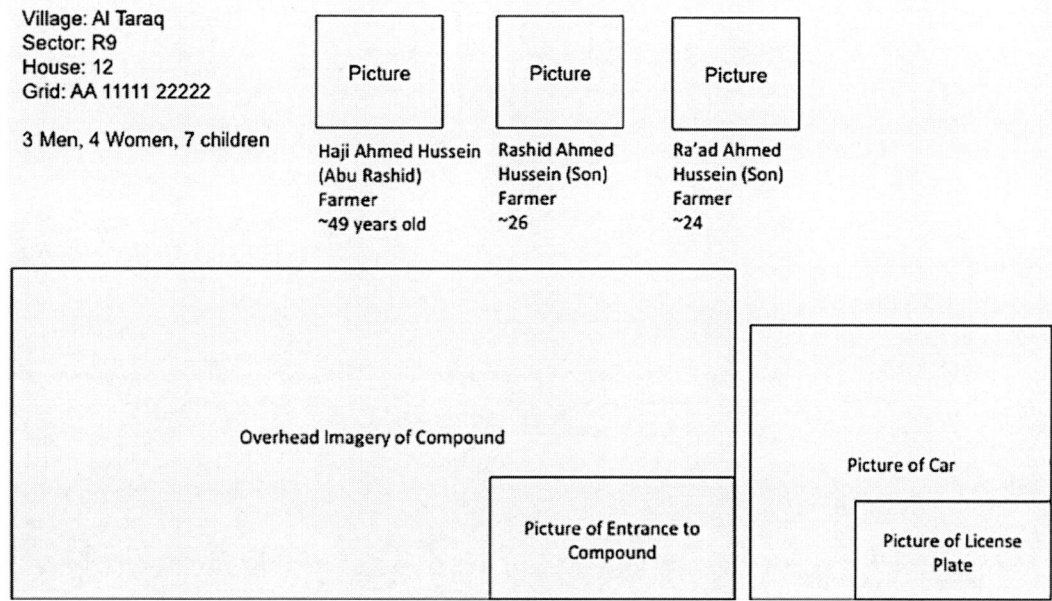

Example Census Sheet

came in both about enemy activity and potential persons who could assist. As we got further in the build phase, knowing who had what skills was vital.

The census was a never-ending project. At least once we returned to a home and found a completely new family in there. (The new family claimed vociferously that they had always lived there.) Some hamlets were remote and we rarely got to them. Often times, not everyone was home when we arrived, either by design or accident. It was important to re-verify census data every time we went into a house.

As the census develops, the unit will learn how people are related. Who interacts with who and what kind of interaction is it? Building a wire-link diagram will help to understand the levers. Additionally, white, grey, and black lists are useful. White lists are untouchables. These are important people you don't arrest unless they are caught in the act of doing something really egregious. Individuals on grey lists are those you want to keep an eye on, interview, and gather more intelligence on. They are persons of interest not directly implicated. Black lists are for those individuals you want to detain on sight.

One of the things that I look back on and regret is never building a terrain model at Al Taraq that laid out the area of operations. Often times I would brief and debrief patrols on a black and white imagery map that did not have great detail. I think a better collective understanding would have come from having a three-dimensional model to use where we could move icons and rehearse things.

Finally, when it comes to the initial holding of an area, it is okay to restrict some freedoms. Units may have a good reason to prevent movement on certain roads or to enact curfews, to force peaceful crowds to disperse, or to make other restrictions. Secu-

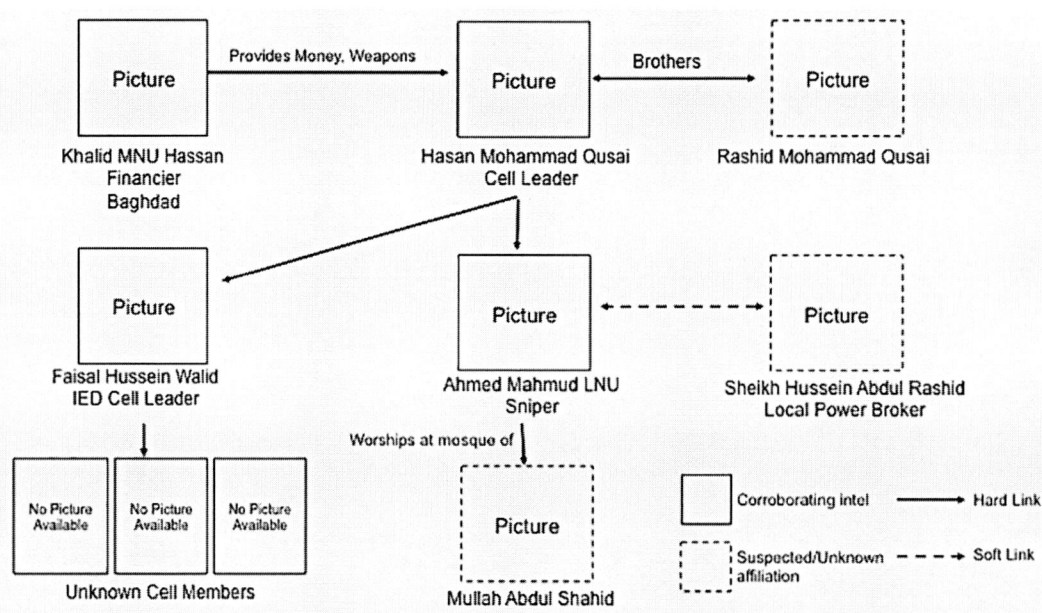

Example Wire Link Diagram

rity is important and it is the basic need that must be established before other things can happen, but there must be a plan to release the rights back to the people and this plan must be communicated clearly to the locals. As McCuen states, "The pressure against the population must be the absolute minimum demanded by the situation, but they must be sufficient to destroy or neutralize the revolutionary organization and its influence. Without this first step, there can be no effective mobilization of the population."[3] By the end of 4–31 IN's time in Iraq, all roads were open to foot and vehicle traffic. There was concern about vehicles moving through battle positions so the commanders and locals developed a solution: bypasses around the positions. This prevented farmers from having their produce searched in brass tacks detail and allowed soldiers to identify potential threats vice innocuous activity. However one does it, locals need to know that the goal is to return to a normal, though more secure and stable, life with the help of the indigenous government. Finally, as McCuen states, it important to impose all of the restrictions upfront rather than slowly implementing constraints.

Insurgents will seek to cause mistrust between the foreign belligerent (and possibly indigenous security forces) and the local populace. As long as there is mistrust, progress will be stunted. For example, the coalition may severely restrict freedoms in the beginning and then start providing freedoms as time goes on. The insurgents will seek to destroy those freedoms. What better than blowing up an American checkpoint to resume mistrust and lack of freedom, especially when the Americans let you in? What better to make the locals hate the Americans than to trick Americans into firing on locals? Therefore, the release of restrictions should be slow and methodical and any event to occur in the face of it requires a measured reaction rather than an emotional one.

The Offensive

The battalion certainly put the weight of their effort clearing and holding terrain. *Operation Polar Blizzard* was the first major operation and the consolidation thereafter lasted the better part of two months. Then the battalion began its march up Route Malibu. However, beyond these operations, and at times concomitant with them, the battalion focused heavily on other offensive operations. While a popular notion of counterinsurgency is one of delivering government services and talking to locals, the Polar Bears put a larger part of their weight against the most dynamic element of tactical operations. This isn't to say stability-type tasks were not important, but that the unit spent less on them than going on the offensive. The battalion conducted at least 24 offensive operations (not including company level operations not planned by the battalion) to seven stability operations (this does not include routine stability actions by the Civil Affairs team or the S5). While another common myth is that Petraeus used more classical counterinsurgency tactics that his predecessor, the Polar Bears conducted six more offensive operations under Petraeus than under Casey and only one more recorded stability operation.

The Polar Bears used offensive operations for three main purposes: clearing an area (as discussed in the previous section), maintaining pressure on the enemy, and extending reach (such as the river raids across the Euphrates). Many of the offensive operations had a secondary purpose of enhancing the capability of the Iraqi Army.

The Polar Bears' ability to maintain pressure on the enemy forced Islamic State and other insurgent groups to confront them rather than work toward their own objectives. When the insurgents had freedom of maneuver in Yusifiyah, they had the ability to significantly effect Baghdad. They also maintained control of the populace. Counterinsurgency theorist David Galula notes, "As long as the population remains under his control, the insurgent retains his liberty to refuse battle except on his own terms."[4] The offensive reduced the enemy's control of the populace. When he lost the freedom of maneuver, the only way to regain it was to confront the Americans and the Iraqi Army. The Polar Bears and their partners put the enemy on the run and forced him into a fight that disrupted the insurgents' plans. So, while the first nine months of the deployment were a bloody affair, they were also setting the conditions for long term security. In essence, the battalion bought its partnership efforts time with its offensive operations.

Most offensive operations occurred in areas the Polar Bears were looking to control or within the boundaries of controlled territory. However, the battalion also used offensive operations to extend influence in areas it otherwise could not control. The eventual placement of a position on the west bank of the Euphrates was an emergent aspect to this operational approach. The initial excursions grew out of a need to disrupt the enemy's flow of arms and men across the river. With nearly all of its forces committed to controlling the major lines of communication, there was little hope the battalion could control the west side of the river in force. Therefore, it used these operations to notify the enemy that it had the ability to operate over there and that it could stay for a matter of days. They later seized on the opportunity to stay when the locals proved amenable.

One offensive operation, *Commando Vice*, occurred to discover gaps and seams. Gaps are areas where there is no coverage from a force and seams are areas along the boundaries of two units that the enemy can exploit to his advantage. Covering internal gaps is relatively easy and the use of horse blankets and honesty traces assists in this along with well-defined boundaries. Seams can be trickier. They generally develop because they are on the outskirts of a unit's area of operations and units cannot cross boundaries without permission. Insurgents learn where the borders are and figure out they can generally operate in these areas with impunity. As Galula notes, "By moving from one side of the border to the other, the insurgent is often able to escape pressure or, at least, to complicate operations for his opponent."[5]

There are a couple methods of dealing with this. One is to have fluid borders that essentially create space for both units to operate in. This requires coordination to ensure that units are aware of other units in the area and to ensure that both units don't just assume the other is covering the area. The other is to maintain rigid borders but provide a buffer, say 400 meters, that allows a unit to cross during routine operations with prior coordination or at any time in pursuit of an enemy. This includes the ability to fire into the other unit's sector with indirect and air delivered munitions. Again, this requires control measures to prevent fratricide or a unit from killing civilians in another unit's area and leaving the latter to clean up the fall out.

The battalion maximized its use of helicopter assets to conduct operations. This enabled them to get into areas quickly before the insurgents could move and to bypass the insurgents' main defense, the IED. Clearly, helicopters were not perfect as it could place the unit a long way from sustainment, but it kept forces off the road and enabled surprise. Similarly, use of river boats, though the Polar Bears employed these much less than helicopters, enabled the battalion to approach from unexpected angles and to block enemy egress routes.

Training the Iraqis

A cardinal sin of counterinsurgency is not using indigenous security forces. No lasting effect can come from just using imported forces. As shown, a recurring theme of Kershaw's communications to his soldiers and to the outside world was that building the Iraqi Army was imperative. His decision to provide a 350-man advisory and partnership force was risky as it prevented him from using that force in another capacity, but ultimately, these efforts allowed him to posture the Iraqi Army to take over battlespace and free his forces for other operations. Similarly, Infanti dedicated a company headquarters to this mission and placed many senior lieutenants and junior captains into advisor roles. These moves dramatically increased the pace of development and ultimately provided a much larger force for both commanders. The other aspect of this is that the partnership enabled sustainability. Both commanders could reasonably plan for the indigenous force to take over because they were in lockstep with their counterparts.

In terms of the training, you must have the stamina to make these soldiers capable. Cultural differences can be extremely frustrating. It is easier often to conduct operations yourself. However, this will lead nowhere. Plus, the indigenous soldiers are likely better at many tasks due to their cultural and language advantage. Focusing specific attention on officer and NCO development will pay off in the long run. The Commando Brigade developed an NCO Academy to train its partners. Despite cultural differences, effective armies employ officers and NCOs well. Officers need to be able to plan, communicate, and make decisions under stress. NCOs need to be well versed in tactics, able to lead under fire, and able to train their subordinates.

While I assess that training and enabling the Iraqi forces was 3rd in priority for the Polar Bears, this isn't to say it was not something they cared about. They dedicated an entire company headquarters to it, but clearly partnership was part of the long game. Infanti did not try to rush the Iraqi Army into the deeper fight in the hinterlands. While Iraqi soldiers were part of nearly every operation and quickly took up residence alongside Bravo Company, the Polar Bears would provide the brunt of the force early on. In many ways, the Iraqi Army was able to learn to crawl and walk in environs around Yusifiyah proper and along Route Sportster and then run in other areas as it got up to speed.

When conditions were set, the Polar Bears embraced and enabled the development of local security forces as well. These concerned local citizens had a vested interest in their area and a knowledge of the physical and human terrain that not even the Iraqi Army could claim. While the idea of the locals taking control of their own security was one that permeated the Polar Bears, it was not a featured aspect of their plan. Rather, like the position on the west bank of the Euphrates, it was emergent. As in other places, the battalion maintained the flexibility to capitalize on opportunities.

The battalion was not as effective as it could have been. Often times Charlie and Delta had little contact with the Iraqi Army outside of a large offensive operation. Once or twice when I was at Al Taraq I had a small number with me. There were occasions when we had IA soldiers but no interpreter. The battalion could have partnered a team or squad at every base. These small groups of Iraqi soldiers would have significantly enhanced the capabilities of the platoons and the partnership would have served as an immersive training environment for the Iraqis.

There will be unique aspects to the organization, culture, and quality of any indigenous force as well as a certain level of ability. Indications are that the 4/4/6 IA battalion was not a very well-trained or led unit in September 2006 when the Polar Bears assumed responsibility. So it took time and patience, but in the end the dedication paid off. In fact, some could conclude that even though the battalion focused more energy on other actions, its development of the Iraqi Army and embracing of the concerned local citizens was decisive as it was the means to a sustainable victory.

Intel

Intelligence in counterinsurgency operations is much more bottom up driven than in a more conventional, maneuver warfare fight. Rather than orders of battle, insurgents generally have loose organizational structures tailored by region. Further, a local element is less a subordinate in many ways than a franchisee or a contractor. National intelligence assets in Iraq were not focused on developing information relevant to the battalions and the enemy had a very fluid structure that could adapt as needed. Therefore, the small unit must have its own plan to collect, analyze, and operationalize information. For the Polar Bears, every company received one all-source intelligence analyst to assist in this process and at times they received human intelligence soldiers as well.

It is important to understand that intelligence is a two-way game. The enemy is collecting on you and they often get it straight from you. They watch you constantly. They use others to spy on you, sometimes unwittingly. For example, shepherds would pass our patrol bases daily and look in. Some may be spying. Others may be stopped and asked for information from local insurgents such as: Do the soldiers wear their body armor in the base? Do they carry their weapons? Where are the guards posted? The best defense against this is an aggressive stance, but deception is also important if underutilized. Building false positions can really help. Using screens, camouflage nets, or covers to prevent observation are also useful methods. Randomly changing guard mounts can also help significantly in this area.

In gathering your own intelligence, partnered indigenous forces will beat you hands down in most situations. An exception may be where the security force is not as well respected amongst the locals as you. This happened outside of Yusifiyah proper in the early stages, but once the local indigenous forces came about, they were way better. In this case, it is best to let them gather intelligence on their own and report back to you. Your presence could hinder collection. Regardless of how it's collected, "intelligence has to come from the population, but the population will not talk unless it feels safe, and it does not feel safe until the insurgent's power has been broken."[6] It will not talk openly or in spades, at least. Thus, the elements of offensive operations, security, and talking to locals must all come together.

Biometrics became very important while we were in Iraq. The reader may remember that my platoon's entire job during a three-day operation was to enroll people in the Army's biometric database. This allowed us to keep track of people and reporting and to identify anyone whose finger prints may pop up on a weapon or bomb. The use of biometrics has increased significantly and it is used to ensure indigenous partners are not tied to anti-government organizations or crimes. Units should embrace this as an important measure of intelligence.

As a company leader in a counterinsurgency fight, do not abdicate intelligence

A shepherd boy passes by the entry control point at T147. Was he spying or just doing his job?

responsibilities to the S2 and his shop. You must do the thinking yourself with the help of the intel guys. They have access to a wider array of information, but you are deeper in the area. You must work together and complement each other. Additionally, it became vogue to have a company intelligence support team largely centered on the company's fire support officer and NCO. These makeshift cells can enhance your capabilities but have to work for you. Years later, as a commander training at the National Training Center, our observer-coach-trainer constantly hammered me because my intelligence team wasn't producing the types of reports the training center expected. However, the reports they expected didn't help me to understand the battlefield and I didn't waste my soldiers time on needless work.

Prior to entering a new area, it is important to conduct intelligence preparation of the battlefield (IPB). U.S. Army manuals cover what this means in depth. For the purposes of this book, I will talk more broadly. Officers need to define the battlefield by determining the limits of their operating area, describe the battlefield effects considering the effects of terrain, weather, and the populace on friendly and enemy forces, evaluate the threat by considering the enemy's composition, disposition, and strength, as well as his capabilities answering the questions, "How can he hurt me?" "How can

I keep him from hurting me?," and "How can I hurt him?," and finally determine the likely and most dangerous courses of action the enemy will take. Once IPB ends, it is time to enter into the area (normally this is a clearance operation if it is completely new), then update the IPB.

While IPB calls for an assessment of composition, disposition, and strength, this will be hard to do initially. Unlike when the United States fights an enemy acting in a conventional capacity, there is no standard organization and no amount of overhead surveillance will reveal an order of battle. Therefore, it is imperative that the unit continue to update as information becomes available. It is okay to make educated guesses and refine as you go. An officer waiting for perfect information will never find it in any situation, least of all against a non-uniformed enemy. Patrols should seek to confirm guess work as much as possible and commanders can develop priority intelligence requirements to get after specific areas.

The weekly reports I developed as a platoon leader were also a good way to update the collective understanding of the enemy. I prepared an initial assessment of the enemy situation and then could update that based on information gathered throughout the week. At times, I would determine a certain enemy cell was dormant. At other times, I would report the enemy operating in new areas. The company and battalion intelligence teams could take these snippets and build them into a more complete picture and feed that back down the line for refinement.

Mobile and Static Forces

Clear, Hold, Build. Those are the tenets of many counterinsurgency approaches. But another tenet is having mobile and static forces. The idea is that one unit holds and builds bases, establishes contacts with locals, creates inroads, etc., while another unit is available for sweeps and major operations. This also allows the employment of a sort of "good cop, bad cop" approach. If the mobile force does something to upset the locals, the static force can always claim it wasn't them.

This is good in theory, but hard in practice. Even at the height of the Surge, there were few forces to go around that weren't owners of some battlespace. However, Kershaw found a way to make this work with some innovation. Due to his career bouncing between the regular army and the 75th Ranger Regiment, he had extensive contacts in the special operations forces. He leveraged these to employ a mobile counterterrorism force to come in and eliminate targets. For larger operations, his advisors in 2–15 FA and their Iraqi partners could form a large group for sweeps or to beef up the local force. The Polar Bears had a smaller, but similarly constructed force with their Alpha Company partnered with an Iraqi battalion. Nearly always, the static force, being the four-battle space owning companies, participated in operations as well. The Iraqis provided an increase in numbers. During the aftermath of the 12 May 2007 attack and kidnapping, many of the extra forces that flooded into the area were Iraqis.

This also allowed the Iraqis to train and validate their capabilities as they prepared to eventually take over a sector. When the Polar Bears left, the Iraqis hadn't taken over the area themselves and weren't conducting all their operations alone, but they were much better off than they had been. Ultimately, it was the Iraqis who would carry the counterinsurgency fight into its final stages.

With each operation designed to hold more terrain, the Polar Bears lost mobility with their own soldiers. On 2 October 2006, seven platoons mobilized to conduct an operation. After that, the battalion never mustered more than three to conduct an operation outside of a unit's battle space. In fact, often times one company could not spare more than a single platoon leading to provisional units created for the operation alone. Thus, it was highly important that some type of mobile force remain whether it was a platoon held in reserve, an Iraqi Army unit, or some type of special operations force.

Mission Command

Counterinsurgency as a form of warfare naturally lends itself to mission command, the U.S. Army command philosophy that seeks for leaders to employ disciplined initiative in accomplishing the mission. Under mission command, leaders provide their subordinates intent, a mission, and parameters and the subordinates determine the best way to approach the problem and have latitude to make adjustments as the situation on the ground changes. It is a flexible form of command that requires such things as the ability to accept prudent risk and create common understanding. While mission command is the Army's philosophy, it takes trust for commanders to employ. I've never heard of a commander relieved from not using mission command, but if, in the employment of the philosophy, things go awry, that will fall squarely on the shoulders of the commander.

The reader may recall that I wrote a letter to my parents very early on that I would become very independent. This was the first indication that mission command was alive and well in 4-31 IN. Whether my commander believed in it or not, I didn't know, but circumstances forced him to employ it nonetheless. The battalion commander and S3 managed the campaign from Mahmudiyah then Yusifiyah and then the power plant and developed plans and orders, but Infanti generally allowed his commanders to plan and execute operations within their battlespace. He could redirect priorities and apportion assets, but he did not direct all of the actions. Similarly, the company commanders, especially in Charlie and Delta where platoons were not co-located with the command, allowed a degree of flexibility to their subordinates. When I controlled T147 at Al Taraq, I planned my own patrols and could adjust them on the fly if I needed to. Obviously, I had to report things up the chain, but unless I had a specific mission, I could conduct operations as my resources allowed and my imagination enabled.

This was a highly effective method for managing the battlespace in Yusifiyah. Even such a small sector had a diverse range of conditions. The terrain, people, and threat in Yusifiyah proper were different than those in Al Taraq which were different than those in Qarghuli Village. Thus, different leaders needed flexibility to adapt to the situation. As Kilcullen writes, "…we have a tendency to template ideas that succeed in one area and transplant them into another ... this is usually a mistake—often programs succeed because of specific local conditions of which we are unaware...."[7] Further, employing mission command brought creativity into the picture. Commanders and platoon leaders could experiment with different initiatives to see how they worked and apply different programs as they saw fit. In one case, the Delta Company commander offered rewards for caches while the Charlie Company commander, just north of him, determined his area wasn't ready for that system. Having the capability to do this ensured that the person on the ground with the most knowledge of the area was employing the best practices for the situation he was in.

Implementing mission command also allowed the commanders to truly "own" their battlespace, something Infanti had admonished all of his soldiers about from the start. While certain decisions remained in the hands of the battalion commander, local leaders could make decisions that affected the populace. This provided them strength and credibility when dealing with the populace. If the locals brought a concern to a commander, he could respond to it rather than continuously saying, "I'll have to check with higher." Commanders were responsible for their area in all aspects, not just implementing battalion orders. It was a truly effective way to lead.

Mission command primarily involves leadership and one of the most difficult parts of leadership in COIN is getting soldiers to fight and die for something they see no tangible results in. Most soldiers may never have the information needed to grasp the complexity of the situation and many may never grasp the complexity of COIN. In fact, it took me several months of study before I could appreciate what the battalion was up to. Many times it will seem useless. Insurgents will have a tactical advantage. When killed, their bodies rarely remain long enough to be counted and thus confirmed dead, so soldiers don't see the importance of their sacrifice of a friend or limb. They want body counts. There is an external need to understand the balance even when there is an understanding that body counts were improperly used in Vietnam. (Many of those lectures I sat in way back that made me question the Polar Bears' success highlighted dead insurgents.) While body counts can be a fine metric if it is one of a host of factors, it can never become the be all end all. Safety and self-governance are true measures. Leaders can try to explain this or they can leave it alone, but they have to get the soldiers to fight.

In the early goings, this won't be tough. Infantrymen especially are ready to do their jobs, but when the dog realizes he is fighting a tick and not another dog, when the fight seems unfair, when the enemy turns out to be a ghost, things will get frustrating. Casualties will mount with no tangible trade off. At this point, the leader must ensure ethics and morality remain intact and must keep soldiers motivated to fight. The best way, in my opinion, is to push information relentlessly. Let soldiers know who they've captured, what intelligence came from it, how many locals are coming to the government, etc. Soldiers are often left in an information-less environment and this leads to being bitter.

Ultimately, morality rests on the platoon leader, the officer closest to the men. This does not absolve the responsibility from the commanders, but there are a handful of distinct reasons a young, inexperienced officer is placed in charge of a platoon. Among those reasons are the need to be the dispassionate outsider who can assess things differently and to be the moral beacon. All soldiers are required to be ethical in their conduct, but, as an officer, the platoon leader has a special responsibility. When emotions run high, say after an ambush that leaves five dead and three missing, the platoon leader must temper passions. As the enemy continues to play by a set of rules outside of Western morality and convention and soldiers question the restriction of the Law of Land Warfare and the rules of engagement, it is the officer that reminds them of the higher calling of soldiers to represent the best of their nation's values.

In the end, mission command cannot be implemented without ethical conduct. Breaches in ethics completely tear apart missions. American society has clearly stated that it wants its soldiers to uphold values to a standard much higher than the average citizen and that it won't accept less. Locals will respond to excesses in ways that hamper the mission. The actions of four soldiers in 1/502 PIR likely set the mission back significantly from a local level to a strategic level. Further, when the enemy resorts to excesses as it did against the Sunni populace in Qarghuli, a unit that has not conducted itself ethically will not be poised to bring the populace in. Thus, complete trust that officers are operating and enforcing the highest ethical standards is a primary key to implementing mission command and accomplishing the mission.

Civic Projects

Civic projects were not a major feature of the Polar Bear plan. The S5 and the Civil Affairs teams worked hard in Yusifiyah proper to build governance, but there are only seven recorded actual operations (planned by the battalion) that were civic in nature. It is fair to say that civic projects were an economy of force mission. For a unit so successful, this is counterintuitive to counterinsurgency theory, but it worked.

Why did it work? It worked because the battalion sought to affect a hierarchy of needs that first meant the establishment of security. Until that occurred, nothing else would be paramount, so when the battalion did conduct civil projects, it appears almost exclusively to have been in stop-gap fashion. The message was clear that the battalion was not going to begin providing a service it was not prepared to handover at some point, so it would assist in providing medical care from time to time, but was not going to become a permanent provider of services.

Thus, initial civil projects, such as medical clinics, may be run entirely by the United States. It is okay to get out and assess the needs of the populace and use soft power as an act of good faith. However, until the government can provide for its people, nothing you do is truly sustainable. You have to beware of making the locals dependent on something their nation cannot provide. The Polar Bears were always willing to provide medical assistance, but the evidence demonstrates the locals were never confident in Iraqi care. It was rare during a medical operation to find an Iraqi medical professional. It would not be for a while after the battalion rotated home that a medical clinic of any sort stood up in the area. Ultimately, it is fair to criticize the Polar Bears for not placing more emphasis on getting Iraqi medical professionals to the people.

It is okay to conduct a civic project that turns out to be a failure or useless, so long as it is not a grand or expensive one. The veterinary clinic the battalion hosted in Al Taraq did little to advance the cause, but it didn't cost the battalion much. Further, the presence in the town and the opportunity to interact with locals provided some benefit. Too often in counterinsurgency, the counterinsurgent attempts to bring a grand project to the people who either don't want it or can't sustain it. When those fail, it can be catastrophic. The failure of the veterinary operation to advance the Iraqi government or boost security in the area did not set the Polar Bears back.

The Polar Bears ultimately pushed the civic projects to the company commanders, thus implementing this aspect of the plan through mission command. Once conditions began to improve, Delta Company employed locals in a host of projects. The commander was keen to find local power brokers or people who could bring together the right team and then employ them. Thus, he found people to help repair the electrical transformers in the area, emplace new water pipes, and reduce the litter strewn everywhere. Charlie Company spent time with locals in the northern part of Qarghuli Village to help rebuild their market area. Ultimately, the company commanders were better positioned to implement civic actions than the battalion due to the distinctive needs of their areas, so the lesson is not that the Polar Bears eschewed it so much as that they ensured the projects that did occur made sense and were bottom up driven.

There may be no formal governance in an area. There will, though, likely be informal governance. In Iraq, the Polar Bears sometimes could find a sheikh who ran the local area or acted as its leader. In Al Taraq, no one wanted to take charge—at least in front of the Americans—and it took time and patience to find the power players who could be the go betweens. If you can find those people willing to be the leader or who have the capacity, foster it. Eventually, you'll want to coopt them into formal governance if they are willing. Listening to the needs of the locals and working toward that end will greatly help. It is important to deliver what they think they need, not what you think they need. I would commend anyone in this situation to read *The Ugly American* by Eugene Burdick and William Lederer. The term has come to mean the opposite of what the Ugly American is in the book. He goes into the village, learns from the people, earns their trust, and then helps them help themselves.

One word of caution: be careful when establishing contacts, as the person may demand an inordinate amount of your time. Ensure the person has the power to deliver. We faced this somewhat frequently where an initial helping hand became more burden than ally. One of my commanders wanted us to respond to any tip from an "informant" who had once led us to a cache of 50 rounds of ammunition. She rarely provided anything of value but commanded my time considerably.

Thoughts on Hearts and Minds

The phrase "hearts and minds" has become so ubiquitous and overused as to render it nearly meaningless. Kilcullen states that the term "hearts" refers to "persuading people their best interests are served by your success" and that "minds" refers to "convincing them that you can protect them, and that resisting you is pointless."[8] He goes on to note that the population doesn't have to like you. Kilcullen's statements are true and thus I personally believe the phrase "hearts and minds" should be retired. Ultimately, the counterinsurgent is attempting to gain support in the manner a politician might—some supporters are enthusiastic, some back them out of self-interest, and some as the best of bad options—while denying the enemy support from the populace. The counterinsurgent is also trying to demonstrate security and convince the populace they are or will be more secure by supporting the counterinsurgent or their indigenous partners. Thus, the best way to look at it is as "support and security."

The aforementioned Simpson published a book titled *War from the Ground Up* in 2013 where he posits that war has a language. Sides are advancing competing narratives and the people are the audience. Under this theory, sides are essentially wrestling to convince the people that they are "better off" with them rather than in an optimal position. Simpson hedges this by stating that "[t]he application of counter-insurgency [sic] doctrine can be compared to that of a sales technique. One may be the best salesman, and apply the technique, but if the product is poor, one will still struggle to make the technique work."[9] Thus, in the end, it is about both support *and* security—setting conditions—and then, ultimately, about the indigenous government following through by actually being better.

Final Word

There are two other cardinal sins I have yet to point out: trying to make progress too fast and reading too much into relative peace. Counterinsurgency requires a methodical approach, even when there are shocks to the system. It is a long game and units should not expect to complete the task in their time. The Polar Bears were set up by the units before them and their work was solidified by those after them. However, within two months of 12 May 2007, commanders above brigade were considering if it made sense to have an entire battalion in Yusifiyah. It had become seemingly peaceful. However, pulling the Polar Bears out would have created a vacuum. There were still places exclusively in the hands of Americans. Fortunately, patience prevailed and there was time to ensure that security remained.

The Polar Bears prepared for their deployment through study and then seized the initiative with a bold operation. From there, they placed a heavy emphasis on security by using offensive operations, remaining in the area, and patrolling aggressively. They developed the Iraqi Army into a capable fighting force that could retain terrain. They responded to emergent events by embracing opportunities. The principles listed above are what worked for the battalion. Some of these are common throughout most counterinsurgencies; others are unique. It is up to future Army leaders to apply what makes sense to the unique environment they find themselves in, just like the Polar Bears did.

Conclusion

The 31st Infantry Regiment Memorial at the National Infantry Museum at Fort Benning, Georgia, is a small rectangular base of black stone supporting a larger, vertically facing black stone, with a small white polar bear, "George," sitting on top. On the obverse side is a small plaque barely bigger than a sheet of letter paper with the regiment's distinguished unit insignia and a short narrative of how the regiment got its nickname. On the reverse side, another plaque lists the conflicts the regiment has fought in and from what years. For Afghanistan (2001–) and Iraq (2003–), the dates are left open ended. There is no other ornamentation, no sign that alerts a passerby that it is the 31st Infantry Regiment Memorial, no list of donors. Save for the Polar Bear on top, there is nothing that would cause one to take notice of it among the grand, well-appointed monuments that surround it. Nothing could be a more fitting tribute to the unit. The Polar Bears have fought everywhere the nation needed them and made major contributions, but they remain obscure, just a blue-collar unit that gets the mission done with little fanfare.

Like the rear panel on the monument indicates, the story of the Polar Bears is unfinished, and this narrative, which encapsulates barely more than a year of the 31st Infantry's distinguished history, is unfinished as well. I have endeavored here to provide the reader with a look at how the battalion approached counterinsurgency and a glimpse into the life of soldiers in the war. I have sought to determine whether the unit was successful and what it all means, to figure out if all the blood was worth it. This story is not the be all end all history of the 2006–07 deployment to Iraq. This book, combined with Jeff Bryan's *Memoirs from Babylon* and Philip Sharp's *Not in the Wind, Earthquake, or Fire*, contributes to the history, but that history is far from complete. With time, more information will come out that will enhance our understanding of this time, and there is still much to be written about the men who went into the blazing fire in 2006.

The Triangle of Death rose from an obscure patch of farmland of moderate interest to archeologists to a strategically important area of operations where insurgents and coalition forces clashed, but just as quickly, it returned to obscurity. Of the four books that have come out focused on the area, only one, *Black Hearts*, has captured national attention and this is largely for its ethical lessons. There is still a large part of the story to be told. A deeper look at the Marine Corps' time in Yusifiyah and their counterinsurgency approach would contribute considerably to our understanding. Also, there is a considerable gap in our understanding of eras of 2nd Battalion, 70th Armor Regiment, and the Georgia Army National Guard. These gaps, though, are for someone else to take on.

Like the unit that served there, Yusifiyah is of high military importance but of low profile. Today, the area can be seen as the ashen embers of a bon fire, capable of reigniting in a grand fashion if properly fueled, but not at risk of sparking in the moment. I suspect that as long as groups compete for power with the Baghdad sovereign, Yusifiyah and the surrounding area will remain like this.

The story of small unit counterinsurgency in Iraq has also received little attention. Petraeus has received a fair amount of study with books like Fred Kaplan's *The Insurgents*, Thomas Ricks' *The Gamble*, Linda Robinson's *Tell Me How This Ends*, and Peter Mansoor's *Surge*, among others, providing an in depth look into counterinsurgency under Petraeus. Of course, these were all written contemporaneous to Petraeus' command. (Pre-ISIS Iraq has commanded little attention on the bestseller list in recent years.) While commanders like H.R. McMaster and Sean MacFarland have received plenty of attention for their counterinsurgency successes, their approaches have received little study. While my monograph for the School of Advanced Military Studies, "Adapting Short of Doctrine," explored both officers' approaches, it is less than 50 pages and also looked at three other officers. This book addresses the gap in writing on small unit counterinsurgency in Iraq, but it is far from the definitive authority. There is much left to be explored and a deeper look into this subject will benefit future generations.

Certainly there is much left for others to explore and write about, but I feel this work has done a fair job of presenting what we currently know. If I can set the record straight, as I sought to do earlier in the book, I want to emphasize that the 1st Battalion, 502nd Parachute Infantry Regiment, of the 101st Airborne Division (Air Assault) performed admirably minus the actions of 1st Platoon, Bravo Company. In fact, without their work, it is unlikely the Polar Bears would have found as much success. Establishing the positions on Route Sportster provided the battalion with a start. Their forbearers contributed as well. Just like the story of Iraq in general is not as simple as: things were bad, Petraeus arrived, things were good, so too is the story of Yusifiyah not: things were on fire, the Polar Bears arrived, things were not on fire.

The 4-31 IN received a fighting chance and ran with it. It went in bold, struck fast, and kept the pressure on the enemy from the start. It had a vision, but adjusted its plan as opportunities emerged, embracing the concerned local citizens and taking the opportunity to limit insurgent influence on the west bank of the Euphrates. It made mistakes. Among others, the battalion failed to learn from the attack on BP 154 and left eight men and two vehicles with limited sight lines guarded by a single strand of concertina wire at a crater. Those men are all dead today. It failed to isolate its objectives until *Operation Polar Valor* limiting the success of operations. Generally, though not covered here, the battalion failed to communicate its vision, approach, and logic to its squads and platoons which could cause resentment, confusion, and mistakes among those executing the plan.

The Polar Bears were not perfect by any stretch, but ultimately, they understood the fight they were in, had a plan, and worked toward an understood end state. They succeeded in setting the conditions for a stable and secure Yusifiyah. There will never be a peaceful Yusifiyah so long as the state of Iraq does not possess a monopoly on violence, but it remains a place able to secure its populace by the standards of its nation. The Polar Bears paid a high price as had the soldiers and marines before them. The Iraqis paid an even higher price, but in the end, the sacrifice was worth it. It was not a temporary victory, but one that has lasted over a decade as of this writing.

This is the story of a group of common men and women who came together to achieve an uncommon end state, a story of leaders who studied their problem and developed a workable solution, and a story of a unit that adapted to its threat and environment. It is the story of a burning fire, beaten back, and reduced to charred remains that occasionally caught again. It is a story of anonymous Americans and Iraqis achieving something remarkable. It is the story of war without glory, of a battle won in war of uncertain finality.

Acronyms and Abbreviations

AVLB	Armored Vehicle Assault Bridge
BIAP	Baghdad International Airport
BMNT	Before Morning Nautical Twilight
BP	Battle Position
CALDOL	Center for the Advancement of Leader Development & Organizational Learning
CASEVAC	Casualty Evacuation
CLC	Concerned Local Citizens
COIN	Counterinsurgency
CROWS	Combat Remotely Operated Weapon Station
CSH	Combat Support Hospital
DUSTWUN	Duty Status-Whereabouts Unknown
ECP	Entry Control Point
EIB	Expert Infantryman Badge
FM	Field Manual
FO	Forward Observer
FOB	Forward Operating Base
FRAGO	Fragmentary Order
GPS	Global Positioning System
HESCO	Hercules Engineering Solution Consortium
HHC	Headquarters and Headquarters Company
HMMWV	High-Mobility Multi-Purpose Wheeled Vehicle
IED	Improvised Explosive Device
IPB	Intelligence Preparation of the Battlefield
ISIS	Islamic State of Iraq and Syria
ITAS	Improved Target Acquisition System
JSB	Jurf As Sukr

Acronyms and Abbreviations

MEDEVAC	Medical Evacuation
MKI	Muhammed Khalil Ibrahim
MiTT	Military Transition Team
MND-B	Multi-National Division-Baghdad
MND-C	Multi-National Division-Center
MNC-I	Multi-National Corps-Iraq
MNF-I	Multi-National Forces-Iraq
MP	Military Police
MRE	Meals Ready to Eat
NCO	Non-Commissioned Officer
POLAD	Political Advisor
PB	Patrol Base
PsyOps	Psychological Operations
PTSD	Post Traumatic Stress Disorder
ROC	Rehearsal of Concept
ROTC	Reserve Officer Training Corps
RSOI	Reception, Staging, Integration, and Onward Movement
RTO	Radio Telephone Operator
RPG	Rocket Propelled Grenade
TCP	Traffic Control Point
TF	Task Force
USIP	United States Institute of Peace
VBIED	Vehicle-borne Improvised Explosive Device
YTPP	Yuifiyah Thermal Power Plant

Chapter Notes

Introduction

1. Tina Susman, "Search for U.S. soldiers, answers after May attack," *Los Angeles Times* (Los Angeles, CA), 19 July 2007, accessed 24 January 2017, http://articles.latimes.com/2007/jul/19/world/fg-search19; Thomas Frank, "Search continues for two missing U.S. soldiers," *USA Today*, 7 August 2007, accessed 3 July 2017, https://usatoday30.usatoday.com/news/world/iraq/2007-08-07-mia-cover_n.htm.

Chapter 1

1. Lawrence Kaplan, "The Wrong Surge," *The New Republic*, 18 February 2007, https://newrepublic.com/article/62655/iraq-surge-petraeus-coin; Sean Smith, "Life in the 'triangle of death,'" *The Guardian* (11 May 2007), accessed 26 March 2017, https://www.theguardian.com/world/2007/may/11/iraq.iraqtimeline; Sean Alfano, "'Triangle of Death' is a U.S. Nightmare," (18 May 2007), accessed 26 Match 2017, http://www.cbsnews.com/news/triangle-of-death-is-a-us-nightmare/; Nicholas Ziemba, "Gripping Hands from the Shadows: Remembering Garrison Avery," in *The Strong Gray Line: War-Time Reflections from the West Point Class of 2004*, Cory Wallace, ed. (New York: Rowman & Littlefield, 2015), 30.
2. Doug Livermore, "Economy of Force," in *The Strong Gray Line: War-Time Reflections from the West Point Class of 2004*, Cory Wallace, ed. (New York: Rowman & Littlefield, 2015), 187.
3. Jim Frederick, *Black Hearts: One Platoon's Descent into Madness in Iraq's Triangle of Death* (New York: Crown, 2011), 3.
4. "Iraq's Nuclear, Biological and Chemical Facilities," *Federation of American Scientists* website, accessed 13 November 2014, fas.org/nuke/guide/Iraq/facility/inc-wmd.htm; "Iraq's Nuclear, Biological and Chemical Facilities (Detailed List)," *Free Republic*, last modified 6 February 2003, accessed 13 May 2017, http://www.freerepublic.com/focus/news/837079/posts; "Sites Visited by U.N. Weapons Inspectors," Fox News.com, last modified 18 March 2003, accessed 13 May 2017, http://www.foxnews.com/story/2003/03/18/sites-visited-by-un-weapons-inspectors/; Rick Atkinson, *In the Company of Soldiers: A Chronicle of Combat* (New York: H. Holt, 2004).
5. Kim Sengupta, "U.S. Troops Refused Requests to Protect Explosives Store," *The Independent* (UK) (28 October 2004), accessed 13 May 2017, http://www.independent.co.uk/news/world/middle-east/us-troops-refused-requests-to-protect-explosives-store-545385.html; William J. Broad and David E. Sanger, "Video Shows G.I.s' at Weapons Caches," *New York Times* (26 October 2004), accessed 13 May 2017, http://www.nytimes.com/2004/10/29/politics/video-shows-gis-at-weapon-cache.html?_r=0; Charles Duelfer, "Comprehensive Reports of the Special Advisor to the DCI on Iraq's WMDs," 30 September 2004, 2.
6. Ben Brown, "Iraq Contrasts: Candy and Kicks," *BBC News* (4 February 2004), accessed 13 May 2017, http://news.bbc.co.uk/2/hi/middle_east/3459703.stm.
7. Pete Connors, "Interview with SPC Stephen Rockhold," interview by U.S. Army Combat Studies Institute, Fort Leavenworth, KS, 25 January 2006.
8. Frederick, *Black Hearts*, 48; "Howard Seeks Reasons for Moving Iraq Troops," *The London Evening Standard* (19 October 2004); Anthony Shadid, "Iraq's Forbidding 'Triangle of Death,'" *The Washington Post* (23 November 2004), accessed 13 May 2017, http://www.washingtonpost.com/wp-dyn/articles/A5710-2004Nov22.html; Bill Roggio, "Stirring the Hornet's Nest," *The Long War Journal* (23 November 2004), accessed 13 May 2017, http://www.longwarjournal.org/archives/2004/11/stirring_the_ho.php.
9. "Iraqi Governing Council Member Reportedly Escapes Assassination Attempt," *BBC Monitoring Middle East* (May 27, 2004), 1, accessed 14 May 2017 through ProQuest; "Body of Iraqi Council Member's Son found in River," *BBC Monitoring Newsfile* (28 May 2004), 1, accessed 14 May 2017, https://lumen.cgsccarl.com/login?url=http://search.proquest.com.lumen.cgsccarl.com/docview/452812025?accountid=28992; "(Update) Dead Bodies of 2 Japanese found in Suburb of Baghdad," *Jiji Press English News Service* (29 May 2004), 1, accessed 14 May 2017 through ProQuest; Mariam Fam, "Iraqi Gunmen Destroy another Police Station; "Prominent Sunni Cleric Calls for U.S. to Leave," *The Record* (12 June 2004), A08, accessed 14

May 2017 through ProQuest; "Many Gunmen Arrested, Six Iraqis Killed in Large-Scale Raid in Al-Yusufiyah," *BBC Monitoring Newsfile* (10 October 2004), 1, accessed 15 May 2017 through ProQuest.

10. David T. Watters, *Marine Forces Reserve Operational History: Global War on Terrorism (2004–2007)*, http://www.marforres.marines.mil/Portals/116/Docs/CmdDeck/GWOT%202004–2007.pdf, 16.

11. James Hider, "Triangle of Death that Awaits British Troops," *The Times* (19 October 2004. 1, accessed 14 May 2017 through ProQuest; John F. Burns, "With 25 Citizen Warriors in an Improvised War," *The New York Times* (12 December 2004), accessed 13 May 2017, http://www.nytimes.com/2004/12/12/weekinreview/with-25-citizen-warriors-in-an-improvised-war.html; David Galula, *Counterinsurgency Warfare: Theory and Practice* (Westport, CT: Praeger Security International, 2006), 62.

12. Burns, "With 25 Citizen Warriors in an Improvised War."

13. James Hider, "A Free-for-all Criminal Zone Far from Basra," *The Times* (23 October 2004), accessed 14 May 2017 through ProQuest.

14. Watters, *Marine Force Reserve Operational History*, 18.

15. Frederick, *Black Hearts*, 48.

16. Ahmed Hashim, *Insurgency and Counter-Insurgency in Iraq* (Ithaca, NY: Cornell University Press, 2006), 46; Burns, "With 25 Citizen Warriors in an Improvised War."

17. Kim Sengupta, "'This is Now the Most Dangerous Place in Iraq. We are Coming Up Against Zarqawi's People.'" *Belfast Telegraph* (22 November 2004), accessed 14 May 2017 through ProQuest.

18. Jackie Spinner, "Marines Widen their Net South of Baghdad; Troops Say Offensive is Vastly Different from Urban Warfare in Fallujah," *The Washington Post* (28 November 2004), accessed 14 May 2017 through ProQuest.

19. Watters, *Marine Force Reserve Operational History*, 19.

20. "Eleven Said Killed, 23 Injured in Car Bomb Attack South of Baghdad," *BBC Monitoring Newsfile* (9 January 2005), accessed 14 May 2017 through ProQuest; "Iraqi/U.S. Casualties Rise in Blasts, Clashes Across Iraq," *BBC Monitoring Newsfile* (11 January 2005), accessed 14 May 2017 through ProQuest; "More than Ten' Said Killed in Wedding Blast South of Baghdad," *BBC Monitoring Newsfile* (11 January 2005), accessed 14 May 2017 through ProQuest.

21. Watters, *Marine Force Reserve Operational History*, 19; Chuck Connon, "Mad Ghosts in the Triangle of Death," *Soldier of Fortune*, 10 March 2016, accessed 5 July 2017, https://www.sofmag.com/mad-ghosts-in-the-triangle-of-death/.

22. Darrell Fawley, "Polar Bears in the Desert: 4–31 IN and Counterinsurgency Operations in Iraq" (Term Paper, Ohio University, 2014), 10.

23. Connon, "Mad Ghosts in the Triangle of Death."

24. Liz Sly, "7 U.S. Servicemen Killed in Attacks; Insurgent Captured, Military Says," *Knight Ridder Tribune News Service* (8 May 2005), accessed 14 May 2017 through ProQuest.

25. Frederick, *Black Hearts*, 55.

26. Jeremy Redmon, "Blog: The 48th Goes to War: Latest Dispatches from Iraq: All Quiet at Radio Relay Point 5," *The Atlanta Journal-Constitution* (Feb 27, 2006), accessed 14 May 2017, through ProQuest; Moni Basu, "Georgia's Guard: The 48th in Iraq: Best Man, Best Friend Mourned Series: Georgia's Guard: The 48th," *The Atlanta Journal-Constitution* (20 August 2005), accessed 15 May 2017 through ProQuest; Tracy Smith, "U.S. Unit Helps Bring Water to Iraqi Farmers," *U.S. Fed News Service, Including U.S. State News* (10 July 2005), accessed 15 May 2017 through ProQuest.

27. Thomas Ricks, *Fiasco: The American Military Adventure in Iraq* (New York: The Penguin Press, 2006), 427.

28. Frederick, *Black Hearts*, 60.

29. Ibid., 78.

30. Ibid., 81–2.

31. Jerry Eidson, "In God I Trust," in *The Strong Gray Line: War-Time Reflections from the West Point Class of 2004*, Cory Wallace, ed. (New York: Rowman & Littlefield, 2015), 162–3; Frederick, *Black Hearts*, 64.

32. Frederick, *Black Hearts*, 83.

33. Eidson, "In God I Trust," 162; Frederick, *Black Hearts*, 85–7.

34. Frederick, *Black Hearts*, 93–4.

35. Ibid.

36. Eidson, "In God I Trust," 162; Frederick, *Black Hearts*, 98–101; "Iraq Coalition Casualty Count," iCasualties.org.

37. Fredrick, *Black Hearts*, 102–7.

38. Eidson, "In God I Trust," 163–5.

39. Ibid., 165; Frederick, *Black Hearts*, 139.

40. Eidson, "In God I Trust," 166–70.

41. Frederick, *Black Hearts*, 161–9.

42. Brett Walker, "First Lieutenant Benjamin T. Britt, KIA in Baghdad, Iraq, on December 22, 2005," in *The Strong Gray Line: War-Time Reflections from the West Point Class of 2004*, Cory Wallace, ed. (New York: Rowman & Littlefield, 2015), 25.

43. Frederick, *Black Hearts,* 206–222.

44. Ibid., 223.

45. Ibid., 234–6; Sue Diaz, *Minefields of the Heart: A Mother's Stories of a Son at War* (Washington: Potomac Books, 2010), 109–10.

46. "Iraqi Army Soldiers Secure Sadr-Yusufiyah," *U.S. Fed News Service, Including U.S. State News* (9 March 2006), accessed 15 May 2017 through ProQuest; Frederick, *Black Hearts*, 248–250.

47. Frederick, *Black Hearts*, 258–270.

48. John Ward Anderson, "Video Claims to show U.S. Pilot on Fire, Dragged," *Journal-Gazette* (6 April 2006), accessed 15 May 2017 through ProQuest; Joby Warrick, *Black Flags: The Rise of ISIS* (New York: Anchor Books, 2015), 209–10, 215.

49. Ibid.

50. Khalid al-Ansary and John O'Neil, "Bomb Kills 9 Iraqis at Marriage Registry Blood and Wedding Candies Dot Street," *International Herald Tribune* (5 May 2006), accessed 15 May 2017 through ProQuest; "Jordanian Paper Reports on Start of Military Operation to Arrest Zarqawi," *BBC Monitoring Middle East* (7 May 2006), accessed 16 May 2017 through ProQuest.

51. Nelson Hernandez and Hassan Shammari, "Scores Are Killed in Heavy Fighting South of Bagh-

dad," *The Washington Post* (16 May 2006), accessed 16 May 2017, http://www.washingtonpost.com/wp-dyn/content/article/2006/05/15/AR2006051500171.html; Dexter Filkins, "Bodies of G.I.'s Show Signs of Torture, Iraqi General Says," *New York Times* (20 June 2006), accessed 16 May 2017, http://www.nytimes.com/2006/06/20/world/20cnd-iraq.html; "Iraqi Al-Qa'Idah Group Claims Downing of Four Helicopters." *BBC Monitoring Middle East* (15 May 2006), accessed 16 May 2017 through ProQuest.

52. "Guess whose morale is down?" *The Augusta Chronicle* (17 May 2006), accessed 16 May 2017 through ProQuest.

53. Frederick, *Black Hearts*, 298.

54. "Iraqi Deputy PM for Security on Security Policy, Militias, Basra, Prisoners," *BBC Monitoring Middle East* (29 May 2006) accessed 16 May 2017 through ProQuest.

55. Joel Roberts, "Mistakes Led to Grisly GI Deaths Last June," *CBS News* (17 May 2007), accessed 16 May 2017, http://www.cbsnews.com/news/mistakes-led-to-grisly-gi-deaths-last-june/; Lolita Baldor, "Report Says Soldiers Were Not Protected," *The Washington Post* (17 May 2007), accessed 16 May 2017, http://www.washingtonpost.com/wp-dyn/content/article/2007/05/17/AR2007051700493_pf.html.

56. Frederick, *Black Hearts*, 301–9.

57. Akeel Hussein and Colin Freeman, "Two dead soldiers, eight more to go, vow avengers of Iraqi girl's rape," *The Sunday Telegraph* (9 July 2006), accessed 16 May 2017, http://www.telegraph.co.uk/news/worldnews/middleeast/iraq/1523465/Two-dead-soldiers-eight-more-to-go-vow-avengers-of-Iraqi-girls-rape.html; Dexter Filkins, "U.S. Says 2 Bodies Retrieved in Iraq Were Brutalized," *The New York Times* (21 June 2006) accessed 16 May 2017, http://www.nytimes.com/2006/06/21/world/middleeast/21iraq.html.

58. Filkins, "U.S. Says 2 Bodies Retrieved in Iraq Were Brutalized."

59. Frederick, *Black Hearts*, 337.

60. Ricks, *Fiasco*, 427.

Chapter 2

1. David Cloud and Greg Jaffe, *The Fourth Star: Four Generals and the Epic Struggle for the Future of the United States Army* (New York: Crown Publishers, 2009), 231–2.

2. All casualty figures come from the database at iCasualties.org.

3. George Bush, *Decision Points* (New York: Crown Publishers, 2010), 355.

4. Ricks, *Fiasco*, 430.

5. Warrick, *Black Flags*, 126–7.

6. Thomas Ricks, *The Gamble: General David Petraeus and the American Military Adventure in Iraq, 2006–2008* (New York: The Penguin Press, 2009), 13; Bing West, *The Strongest Tribe: War, Politics and the Endgame in Iraq* (New York: Random House, 2008), 106.

7. George W. Casey, Jr., *Strategic Reflections: Operation Iraqi Freedom, July 2004-February 2007* (Washington, DC: National Defense University Press, 2012), 66, 92, 94, 96.

8. Darrell Fawley, "Adapting Short of Doctrine: Counterinsurgency in Iraq March 2004 to December 2006," Monograph, School of Advanced Military Studies, 2017.

9. Fred Kaplan, *The Insurgents: David Petraeus and the Plot to Change the American Way of War* (New York: Simon & Schuster, 2013) 104–5; Kalev Sepp, "Best Practices in Counterinsurgency," *Military Review*, LXXXV, no. 3 (May-June 2005), 8–12; Carter Malkasian, "Counterinsurgency in Iraq: May 2003–January 2007," in *Counterinsurgency in Modern Warfare*, eds. Daniel Marston and Carter Malkasian (New York: Osprey Publishing, 2008), 250–252; Casey, *Strategic Reflections*, 47, 73.

10. Walter Kretchik, *U.S. Army Doctrine: From the American Revolution to the War on Terror* (Lawrence, KS: University of Kansas Press, 2011), 264.

11. "Short History of the 31st U.S. Infantry Regiment—The Polar Bears 'America's Foreign Legion,'" The 31st Infantry Regiment Association, accessed 16 May 2017, http://www.31stinfantry.org/wp-content/uploads/2016/06/A-History-of-The-Polar-Bears-June-2016.pdf; "31st Infantry Regiment—'America's Foreign Legion,'" The 31st Infantry Regiment Association, accessed 16 May 2017, http://www.31stinfantry.org/wp-content/uploads/2016/06/31st-U.S.-Infantry-Short_History-June-2016.pdf; "10th Mountain Division leaves 'boot' print on history," *The Mountaineer*, 8 September 2011, accessed 17 May 2017, http://www.drum.army.mil/mountaineer/Article.aspx?ID=5724; *The 31st Infantry Regiment: A History of "America's Foreign Legion" in Peace and War* (Jefferson, NC: McFarland, 2018).

12. Mao Tse-tung, *On Guerrilla Warfare*, trans. Samuel Griffith (Chicago, University of Illinois Press, 2000), 93. The actual quote is, "Many people think it impossible for guerillas to exist for long in the enemy's rear. Such a belief reveals lack of comprehension of the relationship that should exist between the people and the troops. The former may be likened to water and the latter to the fish who inhabit it. How may it be said that these two cannot exist together?"

13. "DoD News Briefing with Col. Kershaw from the Pentagon, Arlington, Va.," 5 October 2007, accessed 16 May 2017, http://archive.defense.gov/Transcripts/Transcript.aspx?TranscriptID=4053, 2.

14. John Sloan Brown, *Kevlar Legions: The Transformation of the United States Army 1989–2005* (Washington, DC: U.S. Army Center of Military History, 2012), 414; Chris McCann and Angela McKinzie, "2nd BCT Soldiers train on trauma lanes at NTC," *The Mountaineer*, 13 April 2006, accessed 16 May 2017, http://www.drum.army.mil/mountaineer/Article.aspx?ID=2200.

15. Chris McCann and Angela McKinzie, "2nd BCT Soldiers train on trauma lanes at NTC," *The Mountaineer*, 13 April 2006, accessed 16 May 2017, http://www.drum.army.mil/mountaineer/Article.aspx?ID=2200.

16. Angela McKinzie, "Polar Bears establish village at National Training Center," *The Mountaineer*, 13 April 2006, accessed 16 May 2017, http://www.drum.army.mil/mountaineer/Article.aspx?ID=2201.

17. Chris McCann, "2nd BCT Soldiers practices house-to-house searches," *The Mountaineer*, 11 May

2006, accessed 16 May 2017, http://www.drum.army.mil/mountaineer/Article.aspx?ID=1803.

18. "2nd BCT Soldiers earn coveted Expert Infantryman Badge," *The Mountaineer*, 22 June 2006, accessed 16 May 2017, http://www.drum.army.mil/mountaineer/Article.aspx?ID=1290.

19. Jamie Mial, "Fort Drum tests new PT program," *The Mountaineer*, 6 July 2006, accessed 16 May 2017, http://www.drum.army.mil/mountaineer/Article.aspx?ID=800.

20. Sharp, *Not in the Wind, Earthquake, or Fire*, 4–7; Jason Cutshaw, "Commando Brigade Soldiers deploy in defense of freedom," *The Mountaineer*, 24 August 2006, accessed 17 May 2017, http://www.drum.army.mil/mountaineer/Article.aspx?ID=575.

21. Steve Liewer, "Camp is renamed to honor victim of hotel rocket attack," *Stars and Stripes*, 14 May 2004, accessed 16 May 2017, https://www.stripes.com/news/camp-is-renamed-to-honor-victim-of-hotel-rocket-attack-1.19897#.WRuknhPysdU.

22. Sharp, *Not in the Wind, Earthquake, or Fire*, 6–7.

23. Bryan, *Memoirs from Babylon*, 77.

24. Sharp, *Not in the Wind, Earthquake, or Fire*, 11.

25. Ricks, *Fiasco*, 427.

26. Darrell Fawley, III, "Letter to Darrell Jr., and Annie Fawley," 13 September 2006.

27. Part of this section comes from a log I kept titled, "Chronical." I updated the entry from 17 August 2006 to 20 September 2006.

28. Ricks, *Fiasco*, 427.

Chapter 3

1. "Commando Brigade takes lead in southern Baghdad," *The Mountaineer*, 28 September 2006, accessed 17 May 2017, http://www.drum.army.mil/mountaineer/Article.aspx?ID=121.

2. Bryan, *Memoirs from Babylon*, 88–9.

3. Michael Kershaw, "Commander's Comments 3," *The Sandstorm*, 1 (3), n.d.

4. Anita Powell, "Tall task for 10th Mountain in Mahmudiyah," *Stars and Stripes*, 8 October 2006, accessed 17 May 2017, https://www.stripes.com/news/tall-task-for-10th-mountain-in-mahmudiyah-1.55134#.WRxvKxPysdU.

5. Sharp, *Not in the Wind, Earthquake, or Fire*, 16–7; Angela McKinzie, "2nd BCT Soldiers assist local nationals," *The Mountaineer*, 28 September 2006, accessed 17 May 2017, http://www.drum.army.mil/mountaineer/Article.aspx?ID=124.

6. Chris McCann, "2nd BCT Soldiers honor memory of fallen comrade," *The Mountaineer*, 28 September 2006, accessed 17 May 2017, http://www.drum.army.mil/mountaineer/Article.aspx?ID=123.

7. Sharp, *Not in the Wind, Earthquake, or Fire*, 14–22.

8. *Ibid.*, 21–2. There is some discrepancy to this as Bryan, on page 83, claims to have been at the Alamo on the Mulah Fayad Highway on 15 September. However, he may have been referring to TCP 5 where the operation launched from. Sharp's information comes straight from a dated journal entry, and thus that is the date I use here.

9. "4-31 Commander Receives Purple Heart," *Charlie 'Rock' Chat*.

10. Kimberly Kagan, *The Surge: A Military History* (New York; Encounter Books, 2009), 100.

11. Livermore, "Economy of Force," 187; "DoD News Briefing with Col. Kershaw from the Pentagon, Arlington, Va.," 3.

12. Ziemba, "Gripping Hands from the Shadows," 30; Dexter Filkins, *The Forever War* (New York: Vintage Books, 2008), 274–5; Webster Wright, "4–31 Soldiers Discover More Than 50 Weapons Caches," 2–10 MTN Public Affairs Office, 13 October 2006, accessed 17 May 2017, http://commandosof2bct.blogspot.com/2006/10/4-31-soldiers-discover-more-than-50.html.

13. Livermore, "Economy of Force," 188; Bryan, *Memoirs from Babylon*, 82–4.

14. The following narrative of *Operation Polar Blizzard* comes from multiple sources, primarily Lisa Beckenbaugh, "Interview with MAJ Chris Vitale," interview by U.S. Army Combat Studies Institute, Fort Leavenworth, KS, 4 October 2012; Sharp, *Not in the Wind, Earthquake, or Fire*, 29–33; Bryan, *Memoirs from Babylon*, 94–97; and an unpublished document labeled "al Taraq" that I wrote in the aftermath. Direct quotes and additional sources are cited separately.

15. "Iraqi Official Holds News Conference, shows Video of Al-Qa'Idah Leader," *BBC Monitoring Middle East*, 11 October 2006, accessed 20 May 2017 through ProQuest.

16. Bryan, *Memoirs from Babylon*, 98; based on Bryan's writing it likely this drive happened on 4 October or after.

17. Sharp, *Not in the Wind, Earthquake, or Fire*, 37.

18. Bryan, *Memoirs from Babylon*, 100. Bryan says the vehicle was one of Company C's, but my notes indicate it was a mortar platoon vehicle. It was certainly not from Charlie Company. My notes from that time say that one of the soldiers in the IED strike was killed, but there is no reporting to corroborate this.

19. *Ibid.*, 100–1; Sean Kirst. "Soldier returns home, thankfully," *The Post-Standard*, 21 November 2007, accessed 20 May 2017 through ProQuest.

20. Powell, "Tall task for 10th Mountain in Mahmudiyah."

21. "DoD News Briefing with Col. Kershaw from the Pentagon, Arlington, Va.," 5 October 2007, 2.

22. *The Bible*, New International Version, Biblica, Inc, 2011; Sharp, *Not in the Wind, Earthquake, or Fire*, 35–6.

23. Arwa Damon, "Troops 'roll the dice' with push into Triangle of Death," *CNN*, 17 October 2006, accessed 20 May 2017, http://www.cnn.com/2006/WORLD/meast/10/16/damon.btsc/index.html.

24. *Ibid.*

25. This list is based off of my notes. It is not all encompassing and is the closest approximation I can make with available data.

26. Susman, "Search for U.S. soldiers, answers after May attack."

27. Platoon Leaders, *A Platoon Leader's Tour* (West Point, NY: Center for the Advancement of Leader Development & Organizational Learning, 2010), 50–55.

28. Hannah Hayner, "Commander updates community on Iraq," *The Mountaineer*, 19 October 2006,

accessed 22 May 2017, http://www.drum.army.mil/mountaineer/Article.aspx?ID=3960.

29. Chris McCann, "Soldiers lend helping hand to Iraqi people," *The Mountaineer*, 26 October 2006, accessed 22 May 2017, http://www.drum.army.mil/mountaineer/Article.aspx?ID=3846.

30. Sharp, *Not in the Wind, Earthquake, or Fire*, 45.

31. 30. Chris McCann, "2nd BCT Soldiers honor fallen comrade," *The Mountaineer*, 2 November 2006, accessed 22 May 2017, http://www.drum.army.mil/mountaineer/Article.aspx?ID=3525; Andrade, *Surging South of Baghdad*, 58.

32. Beckenbaugh, "Interview with MAJ Chris Vitale." It is possible an error in typing out a recorded interview led to "patrol base" becoming "control base."

33. Josh White, "Troops Fortify Hold On Plant That Once Housed Insurgents," *Washington Post*, 25 October 2006, accessed 22 May 2017, http://www.washingtonpost.com/wp-dyn/content/article/2006/10/24/AR2006102401165.html.

34. *Ibid.*

35. *Ibid.*

36. Chris Sanchez, "Troops build bond with Yusufiyah citizens," *The Mountaineer*, 9 November 2006, accessed 22 May 2017, http://www.drum.army.mil/mountaineer/Article.aspx?ID=3293.

37. Shane Finn, "Letter to Rock Families and Friends, 1 December 2006," *Charlie Rock FRG Newsletter*, 1 December 2006; Chris McCann, "Iraqi villagers welcome U.S. help," *The Mountaineer*, 16 November 2006, accessed 22 May 2017, http://www.drum.army.mil/mountaineer/Article.aspx?ID=3575.

38. Chris McCann, "Iraqi villagers welcome U.S. help."

39. Angela McKinzie "QRF Soldiers make Yusufiyah a safer place," 4 December 2006, accessed 23 May 2017, http://commandosof2bct.blogspot.com/2006/12/qrf-soldiers-make-yusufiyah-safer-place.html.

40. Chris Sanchez, "4-31 Soldiers Help Rushdi Mullah Children," 2 January 2007, accessed 23 May 2017, http://commandosof2bct.blogspot.com/2007/01/4-31-soldiers-help-rushdi-mullah.html.

Chapter 4

1. Filkins, *The Forever War*, 275.

2. Nathan Hoskins, "1st ACB repeats history with air assault mission," Defense Video Imagery Distribution System, 4 December 2006, accessed 23 May 2017, https://www.dvidshub.net/news/8473/1st-acb-repeats-history-with-air-assault-mission; Livermore, "Economy of Force," 189.

3. Livermore, "Economy of Force," 189–190.

4. *Ibid.*, 190; Angela McKinzie, "Polar Bears air assault into terrorist safe haven," *The Mountaineer*, 7 December 2006, accessed 23 May 2017, http://www.drum.army.mil/mountaineer/Article.aspx?ID=3019.

5. "4-31 Commander Receives Purple Heart."; Platoon Leaders, *A Platoon Leader's Tour*, 141–7.

6. Angela McKinzie, "Polar Bears storm Iraqi village by air, land, water," *The Mountaineer*, 14 December 2006, accessed 23 May 2017, http://www.drum.army.mil/mountaineer/Article.aspx?ID=3196.

7. *Ibid.*

8. The narrative of *Operation Polar Valor*, comes from a document titled "Polar Valor" I have in digital form. I wrote the narrative in the document on 6 January 2007. It also comes from a letter I sent to my parents regarding the operation, Darrell Fawley, "Letter to Darrell Jr., and Annie Fawley," 11 December 2006.

9. Fawley, "Letter to Darrell Jr., and Annie Fawley," 11 December 2006.

10. Livermore, "Economy of Force," 190–1.

11. Bryan, *Memoirs from Babylon*, 1–5.

12. Sharp, *Not in the Wind, Earthquake, or Fire*, 64.

13. Andrade, *Surging South of Baghdad*, 60–1.

14. Chris McCann, "Polar Bears conduct cache-finding, detainment operations," *The Mountaineer*, 18 January 2007, accessed 5 June 2017, http://www.drum.army.mil/mountaineer/Article.aspx?ID=4356.

15. Chris McCann, "Veterinary care in Yusufiyah gets hairy," 27 December 2006, accessed 5 June 2017, http://commandosof2bct.blogspot.com/2006/12/veterinary-care-in-yusufiyah-gets-hairy.html.

16. Sharp, *Not in the Wind, Earthquake, or Fire*, 67.

17. Livermore, "Economy of Force," 191; Chris McCann, "Fallen Soldiers memorialized in Yusufiyah," 7 January 2002 [sic], accessed 5 June 2017, https://www.dvidshub.net/news/8760/fallen-soldiers-memorialized-yusufiyah." Fox Company was attached to the battalion for training and throughout the deployment, however, it's actual battalion headquarters was 210th Brigade Support Battalion. Thus, the correct designation is F/210th BSB although sources, including the McCann piece cited here, called it F/4-31 IN. McCann's article lists 26 December as the date of Norris's death, but Livermore says its 23 December. iCasualties.org, which aggregates casualties from the war, agrees with Livermore.

18. Chris Sanchez, "4-31 Soldiers help Rushdi Mullah children."

19. David Borowicz, "What a Way to Spend Christmas Day," 26 December 2006, accessed 5 June 2017, http://commandosof2bct.blogspot.com/2006/12/what-way-to-spend-christmas-day.html.

20. Michael Kershaw, "2nd BCT commander sends holiday letter," *The Mountaineer*, 21 December 2006, accessed 5 June 2017, http://www.drum.army.mil/mountaineer/Article.aspx?ID=3098.

21. Livermore, "Economy of Force," 191; Bryan, *Memoirs from Babylon*, 124; Chris McCann, "Fallen Soldiers memorialized in Yusufiyah." Bryan and Livermore disagree on whether Messer was alive by the time the MEDEVAC helicopter arrived. I have chosen Livermore's version due to his position as company executive officer.

22. "Iraqi TV Says 10 Killed in Blasts, Al-Qa'Idah Suspect Arrested, 51 Bodies found," *BBC Monitoring Middle East*, Dec 28, 2006, 1, accessed 20 May 2017 through ProQuest.

23. "Operation Polar Shield nabs six terrorists," 6 January 2007, accessed 5 June 2017, http://commandosof2bct.blogspot.com/2007/01/operation-polar-shield-nabs-six.html.

24. Chris Sanchez, "Polar Bears seize weapons in Janabi Village," 6 January 2007, accessed 5 June 2017, http://commandosof2bct.blogspot.com/2007/01/

polar-bears-seize-weapons-in-janabi.html; "Troops seize anti-aircraft weapons, find IED," *U.S. Fed News Service, Including U.S. State News*, 4 January 2007, accessed 20 May 2017 through ProQuest.

25. Darrell Fawley, "Letter to Darrell and Annie Fawley, 13 January 2007."

26. "Battalion detains six suspects in Operation Polar Fire," 18 January 2007, accessed 5 June 2017, http://commandosof2bct.blogspot.com/2007/01/battalion-detains-six-suspects-in.html.

27. "Iraqi Militant Leader Reportedly Arrested; Eight Abductees Freed," *BBC Monitoring Middle East*, 9 January 2007, 1, accessed 20 May 2017 through ProQuest.

28. Angela McKinzie, "Iraqis discuss future during Qaada meeting," *The Mountaineer*, 25 January 2007, accessed 5 June 2017, http://www.drum.army.mil/mountaineer/Article.aspx?ID=4261.

29. "Iraqi, U.S. Soldiers clear village, find caches," *The Mountaineer*, 25 January 2007, accessed 5 June 2017, http://www.drum.army.mil/mountaineer/Article.aspx?ID=4252.

30. Angela McKinzie, "Yusufiyah citizens get potable water in their community," *The Mountaineer*, 1 February 2007, accessed 6 June 2017, http://www.drum.army.mil/mountaineer/Article.aspx?ID=2999.

31. Livermore, "Economy of Force," 191; Sharp, *Not in the Wind, Earthquake, or Fire*, 96; Bryan, *Memoirs from Babylon*, 164–5.

32. Chris McCann, "Sheiks attends council meeting at Ahmed Suhel," *The Mountaineer*, 1 February 2007, accessed 6 June 2017, http://www.drum.army.mil/mountaineer/Article.aspx?ID=3000; Shane Finn, "Letter to Rock Families and Friends," *Charlie "Rock" Chat*, Volume 1, Issue 10, March 2007, 1.

33. Sharp, *Not in the Wind, Earthquake, or Fire*, 100–2; "A/2-5 CAV on the Move at SP Bataan," *Polar Bear Tracks*, Edition 7, Mid February 2007, 2.

Chapter 5

1. Field Manual 3-24/Marine Corps Warfighting Publication 3-33.5, *Counterinsurgency* (Washington, DC: Government Printing Office, 2006); Emma Sky, *The Unraveling: High Hopes and Missed Opportunities in Iraq* (New York, Public Affairs, 2015), 160.

2. David Petraeus, "Letter to Soldiers, Sailors, Airmen, Marines, and Civilians of Multi-National Forces-Iraq," 10 February 2007.

3. Darrell Fawley, "1/C/4-31 IN Weekly Brief, 21-27 Jan 07, 28 Jan-3 Feb 07," 3 February 2007.

4. Sharp, *Not in the Wind, Earthquake, or Fire*, 103.

5. Darrell Fawley, "1/C/4-31 IN Weekly Brief, 11-17 February 07," 18 February 2007.

6. Kaplan, "The Wrong Surge."

7. Sharp, *Not in the Wind, Earthquake, or Fire*, 105–9.

8. Chris McCann, "'Polar Bears' nab caches in expected finds," *The Mountaineer*, 22 February 2007, accessed 7 June 2017, http://www.drum.army.mil/mountaineer/Article.aspx?ID=2819; Fawley, "1/C/4-31 IN Weekly Brief, 11-17 February 07."

9. "Operation nets 49 suspects, uncovers three roadside bombs," *U.S. Fed News Service, Including U.S. State News*, 19 February 2007, accessed 20 May 2017 through ProQuest; "Polar Bears detain AIF leader, high value target and 47 others during mission," 25 February 2007, accessed 7 June 2017, http://commandosof2bct.blogspot.com/2007/02/polar-bears-detain-aif-leader-high.html.

10. "Iraqi Police receive new gear from IP general," 25 February 2007, accessed 7 June 2017, http://commandosof2bct.blogspot.com/2007/02/iraqi-police-receive-new-gear-from-ip.html; "Iraqi TV Reports Five Al-Qa'idah Members Arrested, Other Incidents," *BBC Monitoring Middle East*, 23 February 2007, accessed 7 June 2017 through ProQuest, Darrell Fawley, "Letter to Darrell and Annie Fawley, 24 February 2017."

11. Angela McKinzie, "Mosque opens for first time since terrorist attack," *The Mountaineer*, 1 March 2007, accessed 7 June 2017, http://www.drum.army.mil/mountaineer/Article.aspx?ID=2656.

12. Angela McKinzie, "Gunmen attempt to stop operation," *The Mountaineer*, 1 March 2007, accessed 7 June 2017, http://www.drum.army.mil/mountaineer/Article.aspx?ID=2653.

13. Angela McKinzie, "Providers, Polar Bears give 'life' to Iraqi baby," *The Mountaineer*, 1 March 2007, accessed 7 June 2017, http://www.drum.army.mil/mountaineer/Article.aspx?ID=2651.

14. Sharp, *Not in the Wind, Earthquake, or Fire*, 113–5.

15. Bryan, *Memoirs from Babylon*, 157–8.

16. "Al-Iraqiyah Reports Iraq Developments," *BBC Monitoring Middle East*, 1 March 2007, accessed 20 May 2017 through ProQuest.

17. Monte Morin, "'Triangle of Death' now a safe passage for pilgrims," *Stars and Stripes*, 11 March 2007, accessed 8 June 2017, https://www.stripes.com/news/triangle-of-death-now-a-safe-passage-for-pilgrims-1.61362#.WTmU0RPyvOQ.

18. "Iraqi citizen leads Polar Bears to IED," 12 March 2007, accessed 8 June 207, http://commandosof2bct.blogspot.com/2007/03/iraqi-citizen-leads-polar-bears-to-ied.html; "Polar Bears find bomb, unexploded ordnance," 15 March 2007, accessed 8 June 2017, http://commandosof2bct.blogspot.com/2007/03/polar-bears-find-bomb-unexploded.html.

19. Kaplan, *The Insurgents*, 258.

20. Peter Mansoor, *Surge: My Journey with General David Petraeus and the Remaking of the Iraq War* (New Haven, CT: Yale University Press, 2013), 76.

21. Sharp, *Not in the Wind, Earthquake, or Fire*, 125.

22. Shane Finn, "Letter to Rock Families and Friends, May 2007," *Charlie "Rock" Chat*, Volume 1, Issue 12, May 2007, 2.

23. Andrade, *Surging South of Baghdad*, 61.

24. Bryan, *Memoirs from Babylon*, 138–9.

25. Finn, "Letter to Rock Families and Friends, March 2007."; Darrell Fawley, "Letter to Darrell and Annie Fawley, 14 February 2007."

26. "DoD News Briefing with Secretary Gates and Gen. Pace from the Pentagon," 11 April 2007, accessed 9 June 2017, http://archive.defense.gov/transcripts/transcript.aspx?transcriptid=3928.

27. All Army Activities (ALARACT) 071/07, "Change

in Active-Duty Deployment Policy, DTG 13240Z APR 07," 13 April 2007. Original in all capital letters.

28. Robert Gates, *Duty: Memoirs of a Secretary at War* (New York: Vintage, 2014), 57–8.

29. Mark Bowden, "Soldier's commitment can't be deterred, or full repaid," 7 May 2007, accessed 9 June 2017, http://commandosof2bct.blogspot.com/2007/05/point-soldiers-commitment-cant-be.html.

30. Gates, *Duty*, 57–60.

31. Raymond Odierno, "Letter to the Soldiers of Multi-National Corps-Iraq," 21 June 2007.

32. Simon Tisdall, "U.S. to increase Iraq tours despite trauma warnings," *The Guardian*, 20 June 2007, accessed 9 June 2017, https://www.theguardian.com/world/2007/jun/20/usa.iraq1.

33. Angela McKinzie, "Polar Bears mourn loss of fallen comrade," *The Mountaineer*, 19 April 2007, accessed 9 June 2017, http://www.drum.army.mil/mountaineer/Article.aspx?ID=2105.

34. Chris McCann, "2nd BCT Soldiers mourn fellow troops," *The Mountaineer*, 10 May 2007, accessed 9 June 2017, http://www.drum.army.mil/mountaineer/Article.aspx?ID=1817; Finn, "Letter to Rock Families and Friends, May 2007."

35. Sharp, *Not in the Wind, Earthquake, or Fire*, 144–154; Andrade, *Surging South of Baghdad*, 60; "Operation Commando Dive leads to detentions, cache finds," *The Mountaineer*, 26 April 2007, accessed 10 June 2017, http://www.drum.army.mil/mountaineer/Article.aspx?ID=4519. Sharp lists the operation as *Polar Deliverance* instead of *Polar Dive*. This may have been his name for it based on the river and the strange nature of the place they were in, a reference to the 1972 film *Deliverance*.

36. "Operation Commando Dive leads to detentions, cache finds."

37. Sharp, *Not in the Wind, Earthquake, or Fire*, 154–159. The quote and details in the narrative for this section are the words of Specialist Crume who provided them to Sharp for his book. Sharp does not provide Crume's first name.

38. Finn, "Letter to Rock Families and Friends, May 2007."

39. "Operation Polar Scrum helps get suspected terrorists, IEDs of the street," 6 May 2007, accessed 11 June 2017, http://commandosof2bct.blogspot.com/2007/05/operation-polar-scrum-helps-get.html.

40. Zeke Minaya, "Bases are smaller, not the threat," *Stars and Stripes*, 10 May 2007, accessed 11 June 2017, https://www.stripes.com/news/bases-are-smaller-not-the-threat-1.63789#.WT2BVRPysdU.

41. Zeke Minaya, "'Polar Bears' Close in on Sniper," *Stars and Stripes*, 4 May 2007, accessed 13 June 2017, https://www.stripes.com/news/polar-bears-close-in-on-sniper-1.63559#.WUCQgBPysdU.

42. "Yusufiyah infrastructure, hope improving," 6 May 2007, accessed 13 June 2017, http://commandosof2bct.blogspot.com/2007/05/yusufiyah-infrastructure-hope-improving.html.

43. Chris McCann, "Yusufiyah Joint Security Station opens, hosts major projects meeting," 6 May 2007, accessed 13 June 2017, http://commandosof2bct.blogspot.com/2007/05/yusufiyah-joint-security-station-opens.html.

44. Chris McCann, "Baghdad Eagle battalion takes lead in counterinsurgency fight," *The Mountaineer*, 17 May 2007, accessed 13 June 2017, http://www.drum.army.mil/mountaineer/Article.aspx?ID=1710.

Chapter 6

1. Michael Hastings, "Before and after," *Los Angeles Times*, 12 May 2008, accessed 7 July 2017, http://articles.latimes.com/2008/may/12/opinion/oe-hastings12.

2. Andrade, *Surging South of Baghdad*, 94–5.

3. Susman, "Search for U.S. soldiers, answers after May attack."

4. Andrade, *Surging South of Baghdad*, 88–93; Livermore, "Economy of Force," 193.

5. Andrade, *Surging South of Baghdad*, 94

6. "U.S. warned to stop searching for missing soldiers," *The Chicago Tribune*, 15 May 2007, accessed 20 June 2017, http://articles.chicagotribune.com/2007-05-15/news/0705150300_1_highly-credible-intelligence-information-al-qaeda-five-soldiers.

7. The basic outline for this section comes from Andrade, *Surging South of Baghdad*, 88–92.

8. Bryan, *Memoirs from Babylon*, 173–4.

9. Angela McKinzie, "U.S., Iraqi troops search for comrades," *The Mountaineer*, 17 May 2007, accessed 22 June 2017, http://www.drum.army.mil/mountaineer/Article.aspx?ID=1706. This article incorrectly identifies Major General William Caldwell as the commander of Multi-National Forces-Iraq. As the Deputy Chief of Staff for Strategic Effects he served as MNF-I's spokesman.

10. Joseph Giordono, "Soldiers remain hopeful during 'frustrating' search for comrades," *Stars and Stripes*, 24 May 2007, accessed 20 June 2017, https://www.stripes.com/news/soldiers-remain-hopeful-during-frustrating-search-for-comrades-1.64465#.WUndWRPysdU.

11. Joshua Apel, *My Life in War: Did We Ever Really Leave?* (Middletown, DE: Self-Published, 2016), 110.

12. John Cano, "Tearing down bridges," 3 July 2007, accessed 22 June 2017, http://www.drum.army.mil/mountaineer/Article.aspx?ID=1078.

13. Bryan, *Memoirs from Babylon*, 174–5.

14. Livermore, "Economy of Force," 194; McKinzie, "U.S., Iraqi troops search for comrades." In the article, the word "soldiers" is capitalized both times. It is Army policy to capitalize "soldiers." However, it is not consistent with how Islamic State would have written it if their warning was in English at all. Arabic has no distinction between lower and upper case.

15. Warrick, *Black Flags*, 167.

16. Apel, *My Life in War*, 109–110.

17. Maya Alleruzzo, "10th Mountain Division soldiers rest after searching for three of their comrades missing days after a complex attack that left four U.S. soldiers and an Iraqi soldier dead in a village south of Baghdad on May 18, 2007," 18 May 2007, accessed 21 June 2017, https://www.mayaalleruzzo.net/americass-long-shadow/.

18. "2 of 3 Missing U.S. Soldiers May Be Alive," *ABC News*, 19 May 2007, accessed 21 June 2017, http://abcnews.go.com/International/story?id=3192089&page=1.

19. Laura McCandlish, "For a Detour family, somber photo of their loved one paints picture of soldier's 'fatigue and despair' in Iraq," *The Baltimore Sun*, 6 June 2007, accessed 21 June 2017, http://articles.baltimoresun.com/2007-06-06/news/0706060097_1_detour-merchant-family-photos.

20. Michael Kershaw, "Commander's Comments 11," *The Sandstorm*, 1 (11), n.d.

21. "Iraq Security Source Confirms One of Kidnapped U.S. Soldiers Killed," *BBC Monitoring Newsfile*, 22 May 2007, accessed 20 May 2017 through ProQuest.

22. "DoD confirms recovered body as Soldier missing after attack," *The Mountaineer*, 31 May 2007, accessed 22 June 2017, http://www.drum.army.mil/mountaineer/Article.aspx?ID=1507; 1507, 1370.

23. Apel, *My Life in War*, 111.

24. Chris McCann, "Infantry Soldiers pay respects to fallen comrades," *The Mountaineer*, 7 June 2007, accessed 22 June 2017, http://www.drum.army.mil/mountaineer/Article.aspx?ID=1132.

25. "Search continues for missing Soldiers," *The Mountaineer*, 7 June 2007, accessed 22 June 2017, http://www.drum.army.mil/mountaineer/Article.aspx?ID=1128.; "Patrol detains two suspects," 7 June 2007, accessed 22 June 2007, http://commandosof2bct.blogspot.com/2007/06/patrol-detains-two-suspects.html.

26. Andrade, *Surging South of Baghdad*, 97.

27. "ID cards of missing soldiers shown on insurgent website," *Cable News Network*, 4 June 2007, accessed 22 June 2017, http://edition.cnn.com/2007/WORLD/meast/06/04/missing.soldiers/index.html; Andrade, *Surging South of Baghdad*, 97.

28. "Troops find missing U.S. soldiers' ID cards," *Cable News Network*, 7 June 2007, accessed 22 June 2017, http://edition.cnn.com/2007/WORLD/meast/06/16/iraq.main/index.html.

29. Susman, "Search for U.S. soldiers, answers after May attack."

30. Angela McKinzie, "From infantry to cavalry, Soldiers establish command post," *The Mountaineer*, 14 June 2007, accessed 22 June 2017, http://www.drum.army.mil/mountaineer/Article.aspx?ID=1375.; Joe Caron, "Polar Bears lend helping hand to Iraqis," *The Mountaineer*, 21 June 2007, accessed 22 June 2017, http://www.drum.army.mil/mountaineer/Article.aspx?ID=1297.

31. "Commando Eagle starts off strong," 25 June 2007, accessed 22 June 2017, http://commandosof2bct.blogspot.com/2007/06/commando-eagle-starts-off-strong.html.

Chapter 7

1. "UK-Arabic Paper Explores Issues Relating to Iraq's Tribal Differences," *BBC Monitoring Middle East*, 13 July 2007, 1, accessed 20 May 2017, https://lumen.cgsccarl.com/login?url=http://search.proquest.com.lumen.cgsccarl.com/docview/459112039?accountid=28992.

2. Andrade, *Surging South of Baghdad*, 98.

3. "Yusufiyah-area men flock to IP recruitment drive," *The Mountaineer*, 12 July 2007, accessed 23 June 2017, http://www.drum.army.mil/mountaineer/Article.aspx?ID=1077.

4. Chris McCann, "Top commander in Iraq visits Commandos," *The Mountaineer*, 28 June 2007, accessed 23 June 2017, http://www.drum.army.mil/mountaineer/Article.aspx?ID=1224.

5. "Iraqi Army Soldiers rescue local sheikh," 26 June 2007, accessed 23 June 2017, http://commandosof2bct.blogspot.com/2007/06/iraqi-army-soldiers-rescue-local-sheik.html.

6. Bryan, *Memoirs from Babylon*, 188–192.

7. Sharp, *Not in the Wind, Earthquake, or Fire*, 180.

8. Beckenbaugh, "Interview with MAJ Chris Vitale," 8.

9. William Doyle, *A Soldier's Dream: Captain Travis Patriquin and the Awakening of Iraq* (New York: New American Library, 2011), 3–16.

10. Stephen Biddle, Jeffrey A. Friedmen, and Jacob N. Shapiro, "Testing the Surge: Why Did Violence Decline in Iraq in 2007?," *International Security*, Vol. 37, No. 1 (Summer 2012), 9.

11. Sharp, *Not in the Wind, Earthquake, or Fire*, 183–4.

12. *Ibid.*, 185.

13. Bryan, *Memoirs from Babylon*, 159.

14. Chris McCann, "Troops aid local residents, build friendships," *The Mountaineer*, 12 July 2007, accessed 24 June 2017, http://www.drum.army.mil/mountaineer/Article.aspx?ID=1076.

15. "Operation Polar Schism detains six in Owesat," 8 July 2007, accessed 25 June 2017, http://commandosof2bct.blogspot.com/2007/07/al-owesat-iraq-coalition-operation.html.; Andrade, *Surging South of Baghdad*, 98.

16. "Qarghuli Village Residents Lead Troops to Caches," *Charlie Rock Chat*, Volume 2, unnumbered issue, August 2007, 1.

17. "Operation Polar Tempest detains 12, recovers weapons," *The Mountaineer*, 19 July 2007, accessed 25 June 2017, http://www.drum.army.mil/mountaineer/Article.aspx?ID=1003.

18. "Iraqi citizen leads Soldiers to caches in known terrorists safe haven," 13 July 2007, accessed 25 June 2017, http://commandosof2bct.blogspot.com/2007/07/iraqi-citizen-leads-soldiers-to-caches.html.

19. "Soldiers aid Iraqi troops with Operation Polar Alpha," *The Mountaineer*, 19 July 2007, accessed 25 June 2017, http://www.drum.army.mil/mountaineer/Article.aspx?ID=1006.

20. Chris McCann, "Tanker troops move north, transfer patrol base to Iraqis," Defense Video and Imagery Distribution Center (31 July 2007), accessed 19 April 2016 from www.dvidshub.net/news.

21. Bryan, *Memoirs from Babylon*, 195.

22. Elizabeth Lopez, "Combat medic cares for child," *The Mountaineer*, 26 July 2007, accessed 25 June 2017, http://www.drum.army.mil/mountaineer/Article.aspx?ID=909.

23. "Iraqi man arrested in role for kidnapping brothers," *The Mountaineer*, 26 July 2007, accessed 25 June 2017, http://www.drum.army.mil/mountaineer/Article.aspx?ID=910.

24. "Informants lead Soldiers to huge weapons cache," *The Mountaineer*, 2 August 2007, accessed 25

June 2017, http://www.drum.army.mil/mountaineer/Article.aspx?ID=639.

25. Chris McCann, "2nd BCT commander updates local communities," *The Mountaineer*, 9 August 2007, accessed 26 June 2017, http://www.drum.army.mil/mountaineer/Article.aspx?ID=399.

26. Sharp, *Not in the Wind, Earthquake, or Fire*, 203.

27. Robert Griggs, "Sheik Meeting with COL Aman," e-mail message, 3 August 2007.

28. Andrade, *Surging South of Baghdad*, 227.

29. Liz Lopez, "Deployed Soldiers do what it takes to accomplish mission," *The Mountaineer*, 16 August 2007, accessed 26 June 2017, http://www.drum.army.mil/mountaineer/Article.aspx?ID=685.

30. "Operation Polar Schism III detains 22 in search for missing Soldiers," *The Mountaineer*, 16 August 2007, accessed 26 June 2017, http://www.drum.army.mil/mountaineer/Article.aspx?ID=689; "22 arrested during search for missing soldiers," *Stars and Stripes*, 14 August 2007, accessed 26 June 2017, https://www.stripes.com/news/22-arrested-during-search-for-missing-soldiers-1.67649#.WVHGUxPysdU. I could find no reference to an *Operation Polar Schism II*.

31. Kathie Durbin, "Baird: Early departure from war bad for Iraq (WA)," *The Columbian*, 17 August 2007, accessed 7 July 2017, http://www.freerepublic.com/focus/f-news/1882679/posts.

32. "Commando air assault detains suspected insurgent disguised as pregnant woman," 24 August 2007, accessed 26 June 2017, http://commandosof2bct.blogspot.com/2007/08/commando-air-assault-detains-suspected.html.

33. "2nd BCT soldiers receive unexpected invitation," *The Mountaineer*, 23 August 2007, accessed 28 June 2017, http://www.drum.army.mil/mountaineer/Article.aspx?ID=592.

34. Beckenbaugh, "Interview with MAJ Chris Vitale," 9.

35. Anderson Cooper and Pierre Bairin, "Former enemies kiss in 'triangle of death,'" *Cable News Network*, 12 September 2017, accessed 28 June 2017, http://www.cnn.com/2007/WORLD/meast/09/11/sunni.partners/index.html.

36. Chris McCann, "Search honors missing troops," *The Mountaineer*, 20 September 2007, accessed 28 June 2017, http://www.drum.army.mil/mountaineer/Article.aspx?ID=237.

37. Michael Kershaw, "Commentary: Let us not forget," *The Mountaineer*, 20 September 2007, accessed 28 June 2017, http://www.drum.army.mil/mountaineer/Article.aspx?ID=249.

38. Angela McKinzie, "Commandos start prepping to redeploy," *The Mountaineer*, 20 September 2007, accessed 28 June 2017, http://www.drum.army.mil/mountaineer/Article.aspx?ID=239.

39. "Polar Bears discovered 9-11 propaganda in Iraqi home," 30 September 2007, accessed 28 June 2017, http://commandosof2bct.blogspot.com/2007/09/polar-bears-discover-9-11-propaganda-in.html.

40. "DoD News Briefing with Col. Kershaw from the Pentagon, Arlington, Va.," 2.

41. "DoD News Briefing with Col. Kershaw from the Pentagon, Arlington, Va.," 3–4.

42. Angela McKinzie, "Missing weapons recovered near Iraqi home," *The Mountaineer*, 18 October 2007, accessed 28 June 2017, http://www.drum.army.mil/mountaineer/Article.aspx?ID=3978.

43. Darrin Mortenson, "A Local Peace Accord: Cause for Hope?" *Time*, 19 October 2007, accessed 4 July 2017, http://content.time.com/time/world/article/0,8599,1673698,00.html; Zach Abels, "Will the COINdinistas Rise Again?" *The National Interest*, 3 May 2017, accessed 4 July 2017, http://nationalinterest.org/feature/will-the-coindinistas-rise-again-20463?page=show.

44. Kerensa Hardy, "Rakkasans officially take reins from Commandos," 5 November 2007, accessed 28 June 2017, http://www.freerepublic.com/focus/f-news/1921188/posts.

45. Pauline Jelinek, "Army's most-deployed brigade coming home," *USA Today*, 5 October 2007, accessed 28 June 2017, https://usatoday30.usatoday.com/news/washington/2007-10-05-2639313229_x.htm.

Chapter 8

1. Livermore, "Economy of Force," 196–7.

2. Jason Cutshaw, "2BCT marks official return from Iraq," *The Mountaineer*, 21 November 2007, accessed 29 June 2017, http://www.drum.army.mil/mountaineer/Article.aspx?ID=3490.

3. Chris McCann, "2nd Brigade leaders reach out to Families of missing Soldiers," *The Mountaineer*, 29 November 2007, accessed 29 June 2017, http://www.drum.army.mil/mountaineer/Article.aspx?ID=3390.

4. Jennie Burrett, "4–31 Infantry holds memorial breakfast for fallen," *The Mountaineer*, 13 December 2007, accessed 29 June 2017, http://www.drum.army.mil/mountaineer/Article.aspx?ID=3215.

5. Alan Feuer, "With Final Word of Soldiers' Deaths, More Tears, More Sorrow, Some Relief," *New York Times*, 12 July 2008, accessed 29 June 2017, http://www.nytimes.com/2008/07/12/us/12soldiers.html.

6. Abels, "Will the COINdinistas Rise Again?"

7. "Iraqi Clerics Call for National Unity in Mecca; Update 15 December," *BBC Monitoring Middle East*, 16 December 2007, 1, accessed 20 May 2017, https://lumen.cgsccarl.com/login?url=http://search.proquest.com.lumen.cgsccarl.com/docview/458632226?accountid=28992.

8. Jim Frederick, "A Female Security Force in Iraq," *Time*, 30 May 2008, accessed 2 July 2017, http://content.time.com/time/world/article/0,8599,1810592,00.html.

9. Alissa Rubin, "Teen Suicide Bombers Kill 11 in Iraq," *Deseret News*, 15 May 2008, accessed 20 May 2017 through ProQuest.

10. Laura Arenschield, "Women of Iraq Sign Up to Fight Back," *McClatchy–Tribune Business News*, 10 May 2008, accessed 20 May 2017 through ProQuest; Alexandra Zavis, "Daughters of Iraq: Women take on a security role," *Los Angeles Times*, 4 June 2008, accessed 2 July 2017, http://www.latimes.com/world/la-fg-daughters4-2008jun04-story.html; Frederick, "A Female Security Force in Iraq."

11. "Council in Iraqi Capital Allocates Funds for Health Sector," *BBC Monitoring Middle East*, 13 August 2008, accessed 20 May 2017 through ProQuest.

12. "1st LD: 30 People Killed in Suicide Attack South of Baghdad," *Xinhua News Agency–CEIS*, 2 January 2009, accessed 20 May 2017 through ProQuest; Tom Peters, "As U.S. withdraws, will Al Qaeda in Iraq find new openings?" *Christian Science Monitor*, 13 January 2009, accessed 7 July 2017, https://www.csmonitor.com/World/Middle-East/2009/0113/p01s01-wome.html.

13. "Seven Shot Dead at Iraq Mosque." *Belfast Telegraph*, 17 August 2011, accessed 20 May 2017 through ProQuest.

14. "Tekhnopromexport Eyes 2 Tenders for Generation-Unit Building in Russia," *Interfax : Russia & CIS Business and Financial Newswire*, 20 July 2011, accessed 20 May 2017 through ProQuest.

15. Maamoun Youssef, "Al-Qaida: We're returning to old Iraq strongholds," *Associated Press*, 22 July 2012, accessed 3 July 2017, https://www.yahoo.com/news/al-qaida-were-returning-old-iraq-strongholds-131645698.html.

16. "Syria: Clashes Reported between Al-Nusrah Front, Kurdish 'Fighters,'" *BBC Monitoring Middle East*, 19 July 2013, accessed 20 May 2017 through ProQuest.

17. Ghazwan Hassan, "Scores Die in Iraq Ahead of Holy Day," *Chicago Tribune*, 17 December 2013, accessed 20 May 2017 through ProQuest.

18. Bill Roggio, "Analysis: ISIS, allies reviving 'Baghdad belts' battle plan," *Long War Journal*, 14 June 2014, accessed 3 July 2017, http://www.longwarjournal.org/archives/2014/06/analysis_isis_allies.php.

19. Michael Georgy and Ahmed Rasheed, "Tunneling through triangle of death, Islamic State aims at Baghdad from south," *Reuters*, 4 August 2014, accessed 3 July 2017, http://www.reuters.com/article/us-iraq-security-south-insight-idUSKBN0G41CO20140804.

20. *Ibid.*

21. Abels, "Will the COINdinistas Rise Again?"

22. Frank, "Search continues for two missing U.S. soldiers."

23. These figures come from the iCasualties.org Operation Iraqi Freedom database.

24. Bryan, *Memoirs from Babylon*, 231–2.

25. The ranks listed here do not necessarily reflect their rank at death due to posthumous promotions.

26. Jelinek, "Army's most-deployed brigade coming home."

27. Sharp, *Not in the Wind, Earthquake, or Fire*, 219.

28. Kirk Semple, "Army Charges 8 in Wake of Death of a Fellow G.I.," *The New York Times*, 21 December 2011, accessed 30 June 2017, http://www.nytimes.com/2011/12/22/us/8-charged-in-death-of-fellow-soldier-us-army-says.html.

29. Sharp, *Not in the Wind, Earthquake, or Fire*, 222.

30. West, *The Strongest Tribe*, 337–8.

31. David Kilcullen, *The Accidental Guerilla: Fighting Small Wars in the Midst of a Big One* (New York: Oxford University Press, 2009), 162.

32. John Nagl and Adam Scher, "How to smooth the transition in Iraq," *The Christian Science Monitor*, 6 October 2008; Mansour, *Surge*, 156. Mansour misplaces the Triangle of Death on the Tigris at this point in his book though correctly places it elsewhere.

33. Catherine Dale, "Operation Iraqi Freedom: Strategies, Approaches, Results, and Issues for Congress," *Congressional Research Service*, 2 April 2009.

34. United States Institute of Peace. "USIP Honors Army 10th. Mtn. Division Unit for Iraq Peacemaking," 28 June 2017, accessed 6 July 2017, https://www.usip.org/press/2017/06/usip-honors-army-10th-mtn-division-unit-iraq-peacemaking.

35. All numbers come from iCasualties.org.

36. Fawley, "Polar Bears in the Desert."

37. Kirst, "Soldier returns home, thankfully."

Chapter 9

1. John McCuen, *The Art of Counter-Revolutionary War: A Psycho-Politico-Military Strategy of Counter-Insurgency* (Bath, England: Pittman Books, 1966), 19.

2. Emile Simpson, *War from the Ground Up: Twenty-First-Century Combat as Politics* (Oxford: Oxford University Press, 2013), 212.

3. McCuen, *The Art of Counter-Revolutionary War*, 57.

4. Galula, *Counterinsurgency Warfare*, 9.

5. *Ibid.*, 23.

6. *Ibid.*, 50.

7. David Kilcullen, *Counterinsurgency* (New York, Oxford University Press, 2010), 44.

8. *Ibid.*, 37.

9. Simpson, *War from the Ground Up*, 155.

Bibliography

Books and Chapters

Alexander, Matthew, with John R. Bruning. *How to Break a Terrorist: The U.S. Interrogators Who Used Brains, Not Brutality, to Take Down the Deadliest Man in Iraq*. New York: Free Press, 2008.

Andradé, Dale. *Surging South of Baghdad: The 3d Infantry Division and Task Force Marne in Iraq, 2007-2008*. Washington, D.C.: Center of Military History, United States Army, 2010.

Apel, Joshua. *My Life in War: Did We Ever Really Leave*, Middletown, DE: Self-Published, 2016.

Atkinson, Rick. *In the Company of Soldiers: A Chronicle of Combat*. New York: H. Holt, 2004.

Brown, John Sloan. *Kevlar Legions: The Transformation of the U.S. Army, 1989-2005*. Washington, D.C.: Center for Military History, 2011.

Bryan, Jeff. *Memoirs from Babylon: A Combat Chaplain's Life in Iraq's Triangle of Death*. La Vergne, TN: Combat Chaplain Ministries, 2011.

Bush, George. *Decision Points*. New York: Crown Publishers, 2010.

Cloud, David, and Greg Jaffe. *The Fourth Star: Four Generals and the Epic Struggle for the Future of the United States Army*. New York: Crown Publishers, 2009.

Diaz, Sue. *Minefields of the Heart: A Mother's Stories of a Son at War*. Washington: Potomac Books, 2010.

Doyle, William. *A Soldier's Dream: Captain Travis Patriquin and the Awakening of Iraq*. New York: New American Library, 2011.

Eidson, Jerry. "In God I Trust." In *The Strong Grey Line: War-Time Reflections from the West Point Class of 2004*, edited by Cory Wallace, 161-171. New York: Rowman and Littlefield, 2015.

Engel, Richard. *War Journal: My Five Years in Iraq*. New York: Simon & Schuster, 2008.

Field Manual 3-24/Marine Corps Warfighting Publication 3-33.5, *Counterinsurgency*. Washington, D.C.: Government Printing Office, 2006.

Filkins, Dexter. *The Forever War*. New York: Vintage Books, 2008.

Frederick, Jim. *Black Hearts: One Platoon's Descent into Madness in Iraq's Triangle of Death*. New York: Crown, 2011.

Galula, David. *Counterinsurgency Warfare: Theory and Practice*. Westport, CT: Praeger Security International, 2006.

Gates, Robert. *Duty: Memoirs of a Secretary at War*. New York: Vintage, 2014.

Hashim, Ahmed. *Insurgency and Counter-Insurgency in Iraq*. Ithaca, NY: Cornell University Press, 2006.

Herbst, Jeffrey. *States and Power in Africa: Comparative Lessons in Authority and Control*. Princeton: Princeton University Press, 2014.

Kagan, Kimberly. *The Surge: A Military History*. New York: Encounter Books, 2009.

Kaplan, Fred. *The Insurgents: David Petraeus and the Plot to Change the American Way of War*. New York: Simon & Schuster, 2013.

Kilcullen, David. *The Accidental Guerrilla: Fighting Small Wars in the Midst of a Big One*. New York: Oxford University Press, 2009.

Kilcullen, David. *Counterinsurgency*. New York: Oxford University Press, 2010.

Kretchick, Walter. *U.S. Army Doctrine: From the American Revolution to the War on Terror*. Lawrence: University Press of Kansas, 2011.

Livermore, Doug. "Economy of Force." In *The Strong Grey Line: War-Time Reflections from the West Point Class of 2004*, edited by Cory Wallace, 187-197. New York: Rowman and Littlefield, 2015.

Malkasian, Carter. "Counterinsurgency in Iraq." In *Counterinsurgency in Modern Warfare*. Edited by Daniel Marston and Carter Malkasian, 241-259. New York: Osprey Publishing Ltd., 2008.

Mansoor, Peter. *Surge: My Journey with General David Petraeus and the Remaking of the Iraq War*. New Haven, CT: Yale University Press, 2013.

McCuen, John, J. *The Art of Counter-Revolutionary War: A Psycho-Politico-Military Strategy of Counter-Insurgency*. Bath, England: Pittman Books, 1966.

Platoon Leaders. *A Platoon Leader's Tour*. West Point, NY: Center for the Advancement of Leader Development & Organizational Learning, 2010.

Ricks, Thomas. *Fiasco: The American Military Adventure in Iraq*. New York: Penguin Press, 2006.

Ricks, Thomas. *The Gamble: General David Petraeus and the American Military Adventure in Iraq, 2006-2008*. New York: Penguin Press, 2009.

Robinson, Linda. *Tell Me How This Ends: General David Petraeus and the Search for a Way Out of Iraq*. New York: Public Affairs, 2008.

Sasser, Charles. *None Left Behind: The 10th Mountain Division and the Triangle of Death*. New York: St. Martin's Press, 2009.

Sharp, Philip. *Not in the Wind, Earthquake, or Fire*. No city provided. Philip Sharp Publisher, 2012.

Simpson, Emile. *War from the Ground Up: Twenty-First-Century Combat as Politics*. Oxford: Oxford University Press, 2013.

Sky, Emma. *The Unraveling: High Hopes and Missed Opportunities in Iraq*. New York: Public Affairs, 2015.

The 31st Infantry Regiment: A History of "America's Foreign Legion" in Peace and War. Jefferson, NC: McFarland, 2018.

Walker, Brett. "First Lieutenant Benjamin T. Britt, KIA in Baghdad, Iraq, on December 22, 2005." In *The Strong Gray Line: War-Time Reflections from the West Point Class of 2004*, edited by Cory Wallace, 21–26. New York: Rowman & Littlefield, 2015.

Wallace, Cory, editor. *The Strong Gray Line: War-Time Reflections from the West Point Class of 2004*. New York: Rowman & Littlefield, 2015.

Warrick, Joby. *Black Flags: The Rise of ISIS*. New York: Anchor Books, 2015.

Watters, David T. *Marine Forces Reserve Operational History: Global War on Terrorism (2004–2007)*. http://www.marforres.marines.mil/Portals/116/Docs/CmdDeck/GWOT%202004-2007.pdf.

West, Bing. *The Strongest Tribe: War, Politics, and the Endgame in Iraq*. New York: Random House, 2008.

Ziemba, Nicholas. "Gripping Hands from the Shadows: Remembering Garrison Avery." In *The Strong Gray Line: War-Time Reflections from the West Point Class of 2004*, edited by Cory Wallace, 27–34. New York: Rowman & Littlefield, 2015.

Journal Articles

Biddle, Stephen, Jeffrey A. Friedman, and Jacob N. Shapiro. "Testing the Surge: Why Did Violence Decline in Iraq in 2007?" *International Security*, Vol. 37, No. 1 (Summer 2012), 7–40.

Phonexayphova, Saythala Lay. "Lessons from Yusufiyah: From Black Hearts to Moral Education." *Military Review* (January-February 2016): 102–107.

Sepp, Kalev. "Best Practices in Counterinsurgency." *Military Review*, LXXXV, no. 3 (May-June 2005): 8–12.

Articles

Abels, Zach. "Will the COINdinistas Rise Again?" *The National Interest*, 3 May 2017. Accessed 4 July 2017, http://nationalinterest.org/feature/will-the-coindinistas-rise-again-20463?page=show.

Al-Ansary, Khalid, and John O'Neil. "Bomb Kills 9 Iraqis at Marriage Registry Blood and Wedding Candies Dot Street." *International Herald Tribune*, 5 May 2006. Accessed 15 May 2017 through ProQuest.

"Al-Iraqiyah Reports Iraq Developments." *BBC Monitoring Middle East*, 1 March 2007. Accessed 20 May 2017 through ProQuest.

Alfano, Sean. "'Triangle of Death' Is a U.S. Nightmare." 18 May 2007. Accessed 26 Match 2017, http://www.cbsnews.com/news/triangle-of-death-is-a-us-nightmare/.

Anderson, John Ward. "Video Claims to Show U.S. Pilot on Fire, Dragged." *Journal-Gazette*, 6 April 2006. 2A, accessed 15 May 2017 through ProQuest.

Arenschield, Laura. "Women of Iraq Sign Up to Fight Back." *McClatchy–Tribune Business News*, 10 May 2008. Accessed 20 May 2017 through ProQuest.

Baldor, Lolita. "Report Says Soldiers Were Not Protected." *The Washington Post*, 17 May 2007. Accessed 16 May 2017, http://www.washingtonpost.com/wp-dyn/content/article/2007/05/17/AR2007051700493_pf.html.

Basu, Moni. "Georgia's Guard: The 48th in Iraq: Best Man, Best Friend Mourned Series: Georgia's Guard: The 48th in Iraq." *The Atlanta Journal-Constitution*, 20 August 2005. Accessed 15 May 2017 through ProQuest.

"Body of Iraqi Council Member's Son found in River." *BBC Monitoring Newsfile*, May 28, 2004. 1. Accessed 14 May 2017 through ProQuest.

Bowden, Mark. "Soldier's commitment can't be deterred, or full repaid." 7 May 2007. Accessed 9 June 2017, http://commandosof2bct.blogspot.com/2007/05/point-soldiers-commitment-cant-be.html.

Broad, William J., and David E. Sanger. "Video Shows G.I.s' at Weapons Caches." *New York Times*. 26 October 2004. Accessed 13 May 2017, http://www.nytimes.com/2004/10/29/politics/video-shows-gis-at-weapon-cache.html?_r=0.

Brown, Ben. "Iraq Contrasts: Candy and Kicks." *BBC News*. 4 February 2004. Accessed 13 May 2017, http://news.bbc.co.uk/2/hi/middle_east/3459703.stm.

Burns, John F. "With 25 Citizen Warriors in an Improvised War," *The New York Times*. 12 December 2004. Accessed 13 May 2017, http://www.nytimes.com/2004/12/12/weekinreview/with-25-citizen-warriors-in-an-improvised-war.html.

Connon, Chuck. "Mad Ghosts in the Triangle of Death." *Soldier of Fortune*, 10 March 2016. Accessed 5 July 2017, https://www.sofmag.com/mad-ghosts-in-the-triangle-of-death/.

Cooper, Anderson and Pierre Bairin. "Former enemies kiss in 'triangle of death.'" *Cable News Network*, 12 September 2017. Accessed 28 June 2017, http://www.cnn.com/2007/WORLD/meast/09/11/sunni.partners/index.html.

"Council in Iraqi Capital Allocates Funds for Health Sector." *BBC Monitoring Middle East*, 13 August 2008. Accessed 20 May 2017 through ProQuest.

Damon, Arwa. "Troops 'roll the dice' with push into Triangle of Death." *CNN*, 17 October 2006. Accessed 20 May 2017, http://www.cnn.com/2006/WORLD/meast/10/16/damon.btsc/index.html.

"(Update) Dead Bodies of 2 Japanese found in Suburb of Baghdad." *Jiji Press English News Service*, May 29, 2004. 1. Accessed 14 May 2017 through ProQuest.

Durbin, Kathie. "Baird: Early departure from war bad for Iraq (WA)." *The Columbian*, 17 August 2007. Accessed 7 July 2017, http://www.freerepublic.com/focus/f-news/1882679/posts.

"Eleven Said Killed, 23 Injured in Car Bomb Attack

South of Baghdad," *BBC Monitoring Newsfile,* 9 January 2005. Accessed 14 May 2017 through ProQuest.

Fam, Mariam. "Iraqi Gunmen Destroy Another Police Station; Prominent Sunni Cleric Calls for U.S. to Leave." *The Record,* Jun 12, 2004. Accessed 14 May 2017 through ProQuest.

Feuer, Alan. "With Final Word of Soldiers' Deaths, More Tears, More Sorrow, Some Relief." *New York Times,* 12 July 2008. Accessed 29 June 2017, http://www.nytimes.com/2008/07/12/us/12soldiers.html.

Filkins, Dexter. "Bodies of G.I.'s Show Signs of Torture, Iraqi General Says." *New York Times,* 20 June 2006. Accessed 16 May 2017, http://www.nytimes.com/2006/06/20/world/20cnd-iraq.html.

Filkins, Dexter. "U.S. Says 2 Bodies Retrieved in Iraq Were Brutalized." *New York Times,* 21 June 2006. Accessed 16 May 2017, http://www.nytimes.com/2006/06/21/world/middleeast/21iraq.html.

"1st LD: 30 People Killed in Suicide Attack South of Baghdad." *Xinhua News Agency–CEIS,* 2 January 2009. Accessed 20 May 2017 through ProQuest.

Frank, Thomas. "Search continues for two missing U.S. soldiers." *USA Today,* 7 August 2007. Accessed 3 July 2017, https://usatoday30.usatoday.com/news/world/iraq/2007-08-07-mia-cover_n.htm.

Frederick, Jim. "A Female Security Force in Iraq." *Time,* 30 May 2008. Accessed 2 July 2017, http://content.time.com/time/world/article/0,8599,1810592,00.html.

Georgy, Michael, and Ahmed Rasheed. "Tunneling through triangle of death, Islamic State aims at Baghdad from south." *Reuters,* 4 August 2014. Accessed 3 July 2017, http://www.reuters.com/article/us-iraq-security-south-insight-idUSKBN0G41CO20140804.

Giordono, Joseph. "Soldiers remain hopeful during 'frustrating' search for comrades." *Stars and Stripes,* 24 May 2007. Accessed 20 June 2017, https://www.stripes.com/news/soldiers-remain-hopeful-during-frustrating-search-for-comrades-1.64465#.WUndWRPysdU.

"Guess whose morale is down?" *The Augusta Chronicle,* 17 May 2006. A04, accessed 16 May 2017 through ProQuest.

Hassan, Ghazwan. "Scores Die in Iraq Ahead of Holy Day." *Chicago Tribune,* 17 December 2013. Accessed 20 May 2017 through ProQuest.

Hastings, Michael. "Before and After." *Los Angeles Times,* 12 May 2008. Accessed 7 July 2017, http://articles.latimes.com/2008/may/12/opinion/oe-hastings12.

Hernandez, Nelson, and Hassan Shammari, "Scores Are Killed in Heavy Fighting South of Baghdad." *The Washington Post,* 16 May 2006. Accessed 16 May 2017, http://www.washingtonpost.com/wp-dyn/content/article/2006/05/15/AR2006051500171.html

Hider, James. "A Free-for-all Criminal Zone Far from Basra." *The Times* (23 October 2004. 5, accessed 14 May 2017 through ProQuest.

Hider, James. "Triangle of Death That Awaits British Troops." *The Times,* 19 October 2004. 1, accessed 14 May 2017 through ProQuest.

"Howard Seeks Reasons for Moving Iraq Troops." *The London Evening Standard.* 19 October 2004.

Hussein, Akeel, and Colin Freeman. "Two dead soldiers, eight more to go, vow avengers of Iraqi girl's rape." *The Sunday Telegraph,* 9 July 2006. Accessed 16 May 2017, http://www.telegraph.co.uk/news/worldnews/middleeast/iraq/1523465/Two-dead-soldiers-eight-more-to-go-vow-avengers-of-Iraqi-girls-rape.html.

"ID cards of missing soldiers shown on insurgent website." *Cable News Network,* 4 June 2007. Accessed 22 June 2017, http://edition.cnn.com/2007/WORLD/meast/06/04/missing.soldiers/index.html.

"Iraq Security Source Confirms One of Kidnapped US Soldiers Killed." *BBC Monitoring Newsfile,* 22 May 2007. Accessed 20 May 2017 through ProQuest.

"Iraqi Al-Qa'Idah Group Claims Downing of Four Helicopters," *BBC Monitoring Middle East,* 15 May 2006. Accessed 16 May 2017 through ProQuest.

"Iraqi Army Soldiers Secure Sadr-Yusufiyah." *US Fed News Service, Including US State News.* 9 March 2006. Accessed 15 May 2017 through ProQuest.

"Iraqi Clerics Call for National Unity in Mecca; Update 15 December." *BBC Monitoring Middle East,* 16 December 2007. Accessed 20 May 2017 through ProQuest.

"Iraqi Deputy PM for Security on Security Policy, Militias, Basra, Prisoners." *BBC Monitoring Middle East,* 29 May 2006. Accessed 16 May 2017 through ProQuest.

"Iraqi Governing Council Member Reportedly Escapes Assassination Attempt." *BBC Monitoring Middle East,* 27 May 2004. Accessed 14 May 2017 through ProQuest.

"Iraqi Militant Leader Reportedly Arrested; Eight Abductees Freed." *BBC Monitoring Middle East,* 9 January 2007. Accessed 20 May 2017 through ProQuest.

"Iraqi Official Holds News Conference, shows Video of Al-Qa'Idah Leader." *BBC Monitoring Middle East,* 11 October 2006. Accessed 20 May 2017 through ProQuest.

"Iraqi TV Reports Five Al-Qa'Idah Members Arrested, Other Incidents." *BBC Monitoring Middle East,* 23 February 2007. Accessed 7 June 2017 through ProQuest.

"Iraqi TV Says 10 Killed in Blasts, Al-Qa'Idah Suspect Arrested, 51 Bodies found." *BBC Monitoring Middle East,* Dec 28, 2006. Accessed 20 May 2017 through ProQuest.

"Iraqi/US Casualties Rise in Blasts, Clashes Across Iraq." *BBC Monitoring Newsfile,* 11 January 2005. Accessed 14 May 2017 through ProQuest.

Jelinek, Pauline. "Army's most-deployed brigade coming home." *USA Today,* 5 October 2007. Accessed 28 June 2017, https://usatoday30.usatoday.com/news/washington/2007-10-05-2639313229_x.htm.

"Jordanian Paper Reports on Start of Military Operation to Arrest Zarqawi." *BBC Monitoring Middle East,* 7 May 2006. 1, accessed 16 May 2017 through ProQuest.

Kaplan, Lawrence. "The Wrong Surge." *The New Republic,* 18 February 2007. https://newrepublic.com/article/62655/iraq-surge-petraeus-coin.

Kirst, Sean. "Soldier returns home, thankfully." *The Post–Standard,* 21 November 2007. Accessed 20 May 2017 through ProQuest.

Liewer, Steve. "Camp is renamed to honor victim of

hotel rocket attack." *Stars and Stripes,* 14 May 2004. Accessed 16 May 2017, https://www.stripes.com/news/camp-is-renamed-to-honor-victim-of-hotel-rocket-attack-1.19897#.WRuknhPysdU.

"Many Gunmen Arrested, Six Iraqis Killed in Large-Scale Raid in Al- Yusufiyah." *BBC Monitoring Newsfile,* 10 October 2004. Accessed 15 May 2017 through ProQuest.

McCandlish, Laura. "For a Detour family, somber photo of their loved one paints picture of soldier's 'fatigue and despair' in Iraq." *The Baltimore Sun,* 6 June 2007. Accessed 21 June 2017, http://articles.baltimoresun.com/2007-06-06/news/0706060097_1_detour-merchant-family-photos.

Minaya, Zeke. "Bases are smaller, not the threat." *Stars and Stripes,* 10 May 2007. Accessed 11 June 2017, https://www.stripes.com/news/bases-are-smaller-not-the-threat-1.63789#.WT2BVRPysdU.

Minaya, Zeke. "'Polar Bears' Close in on Sniper." *Stars and Stripes,* 4 May 2007. Accessed 13 June 2017, https://www.stripes.com/news/polar-bears-close-in-on-sniper-1.63559#.WUCQgBPysdU.

"'More than Ten' Said Killed in Wedding Blast South of Baghdad." *BBC Monitoring Newsfile,* 21 January 2005. Accessed 14 May 2017, through ProQuest.

Morin, Monte. "'Triangle of Death' now a safe passage for pilgrims." *Stars and Stripes,* 11 March 2007. Accessed 8 June 2017, https://www.stripes.com/news/triangle-of-death-now-a-safe-passage-for-pilgrims-1.61362#.WTmU0RPyvOQ.

Mortenson, Darrin. "A Local Peace Accord: Cause for Hope?" *Time,* 19 October 2007. Accessed 4 July 2017, http://content.time.com/time/world/article/0,8599,1673698,00.html.

Nagl, John, and Adam Scher. "How to smooth the transition in Iraq." *The Christian Science Monitor,* 6 October 2008.

"Operation nets 49 suspects, uncovers three roadside bombs." *US Fed News Service, Including US State News,* 19 February 2007. Accessed 20 May 2017 through ProQuest.

Peters, Tom. "As US withdraws, will Al Qaeda in Iraq find new openings?" *Christian Science Monitor,* 13 January 2009. Accessed 7 July 2017, https://www.csmonitor.com/World/Middle-East/2009/0113/p01s01-wome.html.

Powell, Anita. "Tall Task for 10th Mountain in Mahmudiyah." *Stars and Stripes,* 8 October 2006. Accessed 17 May 2017, https://www.stripes.com/news/tall-task-for-10th-mountain-in-mahmudiyah-1.55134#.WRxvKxPysdU.

Redmon, Jeremy. "Blog: The 48th Goes to War: Latest Dispatches from Iraq: All Quiet at Radio Relay Point 5." *The Atlanta Journal-Constitution,* Feb 27, 2006. Accessed 14 May 2017 through ProQuest.

Roberts, Joel. "Mistakes Led to Grisly GI Deaths Last June." *CBS News,* 17 May 2007. Accessed 16 May 2017, http://www.cbsnews.com/news/mistakes-led-to-grisly-gi-deaths-last-june/.

Roggio, Bill. "Analysis: ISIS, allies reviving 'Baghdad belts' battle plan." *Long War Journal,* 14 June 2014. Accessed 3 July 2017, http://www.longwarjournal.org/archives/2014/06/analysis_isis_allies.php.

Roggio, Bill. "Stirring the Hornet's Nest." *The Long War Journal.* 23 November 2004. Accessed 13 May 2017, http://www.longwarjournal.org/archives/2004/11/stirring_the_ho.php.

Rubin, Alissa. "Teen Suicide Bombers Kill 11 in Iraq." *Deseret News,* 15 May 2008. Accessed 20 May 2017 through ProQuest.

Semple, Kirk. "Army Charges 8 in Wake of Death of a Fellow G.I." *The New York Times,* 21 December 2011. Accessed 30 June 2017, http://www.nytimes.com/2011/12/22/us/8-charged-in-death-of-fellow-soldier-us-army-says.html.

Sengupta, Kim. "'This is Now the most Dangerous Place in Iraq. We are Coming Up Against Zarqawi's People.'" *Belfast Telegraph,* 11 November 2004. 1, accessed 14 May 2017 through ProQuest.

Sengupta, Kim. "US Troops Refused Requests to Protect Explosives Store." *The Independent* (UK). 28 October 2004. Accessed 13 May 2017, http://www.independent.co.uk/news/world/middle-east/us-troops-refused-requests-to-protect-explosives-store-545385.html.

"Seven Shot Dead at Iraq Mosque." *Belfast Telegraph,* 17 August 2011. Accessed 20 May 2017 through ProQuest.

Shadid, Anthony. "Iraq's Forbidding 'Triangle of Death.'" *The Washington Post.* 23 November 2004. Accessed 13 May 2017, http://www.washingtonpost.com/wp-dyn/articles/A5710-2004Nov22.html.

"Sites Visited by U.N. Weapons Inspectors." FoxNews.com. Last modified 18 March 2003. Accessed 13 May 2017, http://www.foxnews.com/story/2003/03/18/sites-visited-by-un-weapons-inspectors/.

Sly, Liz. "7 U.S. Servicemen Killed in Attacks; Insurgent Captured, Military Says." *Knight Ridder Tribune News Service,* 28 May 2005. 1, accessed 14 May 2017 through ProQuest.

Smith, Sean. "Life in the 'triangle of death.'" *The Guardian.* 11 May 2007. Accessed 26 March 2017, https://www.theguardian.com/world/2007/may/11/iraq.iraqtimeline.

Smith, Tracy. "U.S. Unit Helps Bring Water to Iraqi Farmers." *US Fed News Service, Including US State News.* 10 July 2005. Accessed 15 May 2017 through ProQuest.

Spinner, Jackie. "Marines Widen their Net South of Baghdad; Troops Say Offensive is Vastly Different from Urban Warfare in Fallujah." *The Washington Post,* 28 November 2004. Accessed 14 May 2017 through ProQuest.

Susman, Tina. "Search for U.S. soldiers, answers after May attack." *Los Angeles Times* (Los Angeles, CA), 19 July 2007. Accessed 24 January 2017. http://articles.latimes.com/2007/jul/19/world/fg-search19.

"Syria: Clashes Reported between Al-Nusrah Front, Kurdish 'Fighters.'" *BBC Monitoring Middle East,* 19 July 2013. Accessed 20 May 2017 through ProQuest.

"Tekhnopromexport Eyes 2 Tenders for Generation-Unit Building in Russia." *Interfax : Russia & CIS Business and Financial Newswire,* 20 July 2011. Accessed 20 May 2017 through ProQuest.

Tisdall, Simon. "US to increase Iraq tours despite trauma warnings." *The Guardian,* 20 June 2007. Accessed 9 June 2017, https://www.theguardian.com/world/2007/jun/20/usa.iraql.

"Troops find missing U.S. soldiers' ID cards." *Cable News Network,* 7 June 2007. Accessed 22 June 2017, http://edition.cnn.com/2007/WORLD/meast/06/16/iraq.main/index.html.

"Troops seize anti-aircraft weapons, find IED." *US Fed News Service, Including US State News,* 4 January 2007. Accessed 20 May 2017 through ProQuest.

"22 arrested during search for missing soldiers." *Stars and Stripes,* 14 August 2007. Accessed 26 June 2017, https://www.stripes.com/news/22-arrested-during-search-for-missing-soldiers-1.67649#.WVHGUxPysdU.

"2 of 3 Missing U.S. Soldiers May Be Alive." *ABC News,* 19 May 2007. Accessed 21 June 2017, http://abcnews.go.com/International/story?id=3192089&page=1.

"UK-Arabic Paper Explores Issues Relating to Iraq's Tribal Differences." *BBC Monitoring Middle East,* 13 July 2007. Accessed 20 May 2017 through ProQuest.

United States Institute of Peace. "USIP Honors Army 10th. Mtn. Division Unit for Iraq Peacemaking." 28 June 2017. Accessed 6 July 2017, https://www.usip.org/press/2017/06/usip-honors-army-10th-mtn-division-unit-iraq-peacemaking.

"U.S. warned to stop searching for missing soldiers." *The Chicago Tribune,* 15 May 2007. Accessed 20 June 2017, http://articles.chicagotribune.com/2007-05-15/news/0705150300_1_highly-credible-intelligence-information-al-qaeda-five-soldiers.

White, Josh. "Troops Fortify Hold On Plant That Once Housed Insurgents." *Washington Post,* 25 October 2006. Accessed 22 May 2017, http://www.washingtonpost.com/wp-dyn/content/article/2006/10/24/AR2006102401165.html.

Youssef, Maamoun. "Al-Qaida: We're returning to old Iraq strongholds." *Associated Press,* 22 July 2012. Accessed 3 July 2017, https://www.yahoo.com/news/al-qaida-were-returning-old-iraq-strongholds-131645698.html.

Zavis, Alexandra. "Daughters of Iraq: Women take on a security role." *Los Angeles Times,* 4 June 2008. Accessed 2 July 2017, http://www.latimes.com/world/la-fg-daughters4-2008jun04-story.html.

Unit Articles, Press Releases, Blog Posts and Newsletters

"A/2-5 CAV on the Move at SP Bataan." *Polar Bear Tracks,* Edition 7, Mid February 2007, 2.

"Battalion detains six suspects in Operation Polar Fire." 18 January 2007. Accessed 5 June 2017, http://commandosof2bct.blogspot.com/2007/01/battalion-detains-six-suspects-in.html.

Borowicz, David. "What a Way to Spend Christmas Day." 26 December 2006. Accessed 5 June 2017, http://commandosof2bct.blogspot.com/2006/12/what-way-to-spend-christmas-day.html.

Burrett, Jennie. "4-31 Infantry holds memorial breakfast for fallen." *The Mountaineer,* 13 December 2007. Accessed 29 June 2017, http://www.drum.army.mil/mountaineer/Article.aspx?ID=3215.

Caron, Joe. "Polar Bears lend helping hand to Iraqis." *The Mountaineer,* 21 June 2007. Accessed 22 June 2017, http://www.drum.army.mil/mountaineer/Article.aspx?ID=1297.

"Commando air assault detains suspected insurgent disguised as pregnant woman." 24 August 2007. Accessed 26 June 2017, http://commandosof2bct.blogspot.com/2007/08/commando-air-assault-detains-suspected.html.

"Commando Eagle starts off strong." 25 June 2007. Accessed 22 June 2017, http://commandosof2bct.blogspot.com/2007/06/commando-eagle-starts-off-strong.html.

Cutshaw, Jason. "Commando Brigade Soldiers deploy in defense of freedom." *The Mountaineer,* 24 August 2006. Accessed 17 May 2017, http://www.drum.army.mil/mountaineer/Article.aspx?ID=575.

Cutshaw, Jason. "2BCT marks official return from Iraq." *The Mountaineer,* 21 November 2007. Accessed 29 June 2017, http://www.drum.army.mil/mountaineer/Article.aspx?ID=3490.

"DoD confirms recovered body as Soldier missing after attack." *The Mountaineer,* 31 May 2007. Accessed 22 June 2017, http://www.drum.army.mil/mountaineer/Article.aspx?ID=1507.s

Finn, Shane. "Letter to Rock Families and Friends, 1 December 2006." *Charlie Rock FRG Newsletter,* 1 December 2006.

Finn, Shane. "Letter to Rock Families and Friends, May 2007." *Charlie "Rock" Chat,* Volume 1, Issue 12, May 2007.

Finn, Shane. "Letter to Rock Families and Friends." *Charlie "Rock" Chat,* Volume 1, Issue 10, March 2007.

"4-31 Commander Receives Purple Heart," *Charlie 'Rock' Chat.*

Hardy, Kerensa. "Rakkasans officially take reins from Commandos." 5 November 2007. Accessed 28 June 2017, http://www.freerepublic.com/focus/f-news/1921188/posts.

Hayner, Hannah. "Commander updates community on Iraq." *The Mountaineer,* 19 October 2006. Accessed 22 May 2017, http://www.drum.army.mil/mountaineer/Article.aspx?ID=3960.

"Informants lead Soldiers to huge weapons cache." *The Mountaineer,* 2 August 2007. Accessed 25 June 2017, http://www.drum.army.mil/mountaineer/Article.aspx?ID=639.

"Iraqi Army Soldiers rescue local sheikh,." 26 June 2007. Accessed 23 June 2017, http://commandosof2bct.blogspot.com/2007/06/iraqi-army-soldiers-rescue-local-sheik.html.

"Iraqi citizen leads Polar Bears to IED." 12 March 2007. Accessed 8 June 207, http://commandosof2bct.blogspot.com/2007/03/iraqi-citizen-leads-polar-bears-to-ied.html.

"Iraqi citizen leads Soldiers to caches in known terrorists safe haven." 13 July 2007. Accessed 25 June 2017, http://commandosof2bct.blogspot.com/2007/07/iraqi-citizen-leads-soldiers-to-caches.html.

"Iraqi, U.S. Soldiers clear village, find caches." *The Mountaineer,* 25 January 2007. Accessed 5 June 2017, http://www.drum.army.mil/mountaineer/Article.aspx?ID=4252.

Kershaw, Michael. "Commander's Comments 11." *The Sandstorm,* 1 (11), n.d.

Bibliography

Kershaw, Michael. "Commander's Comments 3." *The Sandstorm*, 1 (3), n.d.

Kershaw, Michael. "Commentary: Let us not forget." *The Mountaineer*, 20 September 2007. Accessed 28 June 2017, http://www.drum.army.mil/mountaineer/Article.aspx?ID=249.

Kershaw, Michael. "2nd BCT commander sends holiday letter." *The Mountaineer*, 21 December 2006. Accessed 5 June 2017, http://www.drum.army.mil/mountaineer/Article.aspx?ID=3098.

Lopez, Elizabeth. "Combat medic cares for child." *The Mountaineer*, 26 July 2007. Accessed 25 June 2017, http://www.drum.army.mil/mountaineer/Article.aspx?ID=909.

Lopez, Liz. "Deployed Soldiers do what it takes to accomplish mission." *The Mountaineer*, 16 August 2007. Accessed 26 June 2017, http://www.drum.army.mil/mountaineer/Article.aspx?ID=685.

McCann, Chris. "Baghdad Eagle battalion takes lead in counterinsurgency fight." *The Mountaineer*, 17 May 2007. Accessed 13 June 2017, http://www.drum.army.mil/mountaineer/Article.aspx?ID=1710.

McCann, Chris. "Fallen Soldiers memorialized in Yusufiyah." 7 January 2002 [sic]. Accessed 5 June 2017, https://www.dvidshub.net/news/8760/fallen-soldiers-memorialized-yusufiyah.

McCann, Chris. "Infantry Soldiers pay respects to fallen comrades." *The Mountaineer*, 7 June 2007. Accessed 22 June 2017, http://www.drum.army.mil/mountaineer/Article.aspx?ID=1132.

McCann, Chris. "Iraqi villagers welcome U.S. help." *The Mountaineer*, 16 November 2006. Accessed 22 May 2017, http://www.drum.army.mil/mountaineer/Article.aspx?ID=3575.

McCann, Chris. "Polar Bears conduct cache-finding, detainment operations." *The Mountaineer*, 18 January 2007. Accessed 5 June 2017, http://www.drum.army.mil/mountaineer/Article.aspx?ID=4356.

McCann, Chris. "'Polar Bears' nab caches in expected finds." *The Mountaineer*, 22 February 2007. Accessed 7 June 2017, http://www.drum.army.mil/mountaineer/Article.aspx?ID=2819.

McCann, Chris. "Search honors missing troops." *The Mountaineer*, 20 September 2007. Accessed 28 June 2017, http://www.drum.army.mil/mountaineer/Article.aspx?ID=237.

McCann, Chris. "Sheiks attends council meeting at Ahmed Suhel." *The Mountaineer*, 1 February 2007. Accessed 6 June 2017, http://www.drum.army.mil/mountaineer/Article.aspx?ID=3000.

McCann, Chris. "Soldiers lend helping hand to Iraqi people." *The Mountaineer*, 26 October 2006. Accessed 22 May 2017, http://www.drum.army.mil/mountaineer/Article.aspx?ID=3846.

McCann, Chris. "Tanker troops move north, transfer patrol base to Iraqis." Defense Video and Imagery Distribution Center (31 July 2007). Accessed 19 April 2016 from www.dvidshub.net/news.

McCann, Chris. "Top commander in Iraq visits Commandos." *The Mountaineer*, 28 June 2007. Accessed 23 June 2017, http://www.drum.army.mil/mountaineer/Article.aspx?ID=1224.

McCann, Chris. "Troops aid local residents, build friendships." *The Mountaineer*, 12 July 2007. Accessed 24 June 2017, http://www.drum.army.mil/mountaineer/Article.aspx?ID=1076.

McCann, Chris. "2nd BCT commander updates local communities." *The Mountaineer*, 9 August 2017. Accessed 26 June 2017, http://www.drum.army.mil/mountaineer/Article.aspx?ID=399.

McCann, Chris. "2nd BCT Soldiers honor fallen comrade." *The Mountaineer*, 2 November 2006. Accessed 22 May 2017, http://www.drum.army.mil/mountaineer/Article.aspx?ID=3525.

McCann, Chris. "2nd BCT Soldiers honor memory of fallen comrade." *The Mountaineer*, 28 September 2006. Accessed 17 May 2017, http://www.drum.army.mil/mountaineer/Article.aspx?ID=123.

McCann, Chris. "2nd BCT Soldiers mourn fellow troops." *The Mountaineer*, 10 May 2007. Accessed 9 June 2017, http://www.drum.army.mil/mountaineer/Article.aspx?ID=1817.

McCann, Chris. "2nd BCT Soldiers practices house-to-house searches." *The Mountaineer*, 11 May 2006. Accessed 16 May 2017, http://www.drum.army.mil/mountaineer/Article.aspx?ID=1803.

McCann, Chris. "2nd Brigade leaders reach out to Families of missing Soldiers." *The Mountaineer*, 29 November 2007. Accessed 29 June 2017, http://www.drum.army.mil/mountaineer/Article.aspx?ID=3390.

McCann, Chris. "Veterinary care in Yusufiyah gets hairy." 27 December 2006. Accessed 5 June 2017, http://commandosof2bct.blogspot.com/2006/12/veterinary-care-in-yusufiyah-gets-hairy.html.

McCann, Chris. "Yusufiyah Joint Security Station opens, hosts major projects meeting." 6 May 2007. Accessed 13 June 2017, http://commandosof2bct.blogspot.com/2007/05/yusufiyah-joint-security-station-opens.html.

McCann, Chris, and Angela McKinzie. "2nd BCT Soldiers train on trauma lanes at NTC." *The Mountaineer*, 13 April 2006. Accessed 16 May 2017, http://www.drum.army.mil/mountaineer/Article.aspx?ID=2200.

McKinzie, Angela. "Commandos start prepping to redeploy." *The Mountaineer*, 20 September 2007. Accessed 28 June 2017, http://www.drum.army.mil/mountaineer/Article.aspx?ID=239.

McKinzie, Angela. "From infantry to cavalry, Soldiers establish command post." *The Mountaineer*, 14 June 2007. Accessed 22 June 2017, http://www.drum.army.mil/mountaineer/Article.aspx?ID=1375.

McKinzie, Angela. "Gunmen attempt to stop operation." *The Mountaineer*, 1 March 2007. Accessed 7 June 2017, http://www.drum.army.mil/mountaineer/Article.aspx?ID=2653.

McKinzie, Angela. "Iraqis discuss future during Qaada meeting." *The Mountaineer*, 25 January 2007. Accessed 5 June 2017, http://www.drum.army.mil/mountaineer/Article.aspx?ID=4261.

McKinzie, Angela. "Missing weapons recovered near Iraqi home." *The Mountaineer*, 18 October 2007. Accessed 28 June 2017, http://www.drum.army.mil/mountaineer/Article.aspx?ID=3978.

McKinzie, Angela. "Mosque opens for first time since terrorist attack." *The Mountaineer*, 1 March 2007. Accessed 7 June 2017, http://www.drum.army.mil/mountaineer/Article.aspx?ID=2656.

McKinzie, Angela. "Polar Bears air assault into terrorist safe haven." *The Mountaineer*, 7 December 2006. Accessed 23 May 2017, http://www.drum.army.mil/mountaineer/Article.aspx?ID=3019.

McKinzie, Angela. "Polar Bears establish village at National Training Center." *The Mountaineer*, 13 April 2006. Accessed 16 May 2017, http://www.drum.army.mil/mountaineer/Article.aspx?ID=2201.

McKinzie, Angela. "Polar Bears mourn loss of fallen comrade." *The Mountaineer*, 19 April 2007. Accessed 9 June 2017, http://www.drum.army.mil/mountaineer/Article.aspx?ID=2105.

McKinzie, Angela. "Polar Bears storm Iraqi village by air, land, water." *The Mountaineer*, 14 December 2006. Accessed 23 May 2017, http://www.drum.army.mil/mountaineer/Article.aspx?ID=3196.

McKinzie, Angela. "Providers, Polar Bears give 'life' to Iraqi baby." *The Mountaineer*, 1 March 2007. Accessed 7 June 2017, http://www.drum.army.mil/mountaineer/Article.aspx?ID=2651.

McKinzie, Angela. "QRF Soldiers make Yusufiyah a safer place." 4 December 2006. Accessed 23 May 2017, http://commandosof2bct.blogspot.com/2006/12/qrf-soldiers-make-yusufiyah-safer-place.html.

McKinzie, Angela. "2nd BCT Soldiers assist local nationals." *The Mountaineer*, 28 September 2006. Accessed 17 May 2017, http://www.drum.army.mil/mountaineer/Article.aspx?ID=124.

McKinzie, Angela. "U.S., Iraqi troops search for comrades." *The Mountaineer*, 17 May 2007. Accessed 22 June 2017, http://www.drum.army.mil/mountaineer/Article.aspx?ID=1706.

McKinzie, Angela. "Yusufiyah Citizens get potable water in their community." *The Mountaineer*, 1 February 2007. Accessed 6 June 2017, http://www.drum.army.mil/mountaineer/Article.aspx?ID=2999.

Mial, Jamie. "Fort Drum tests new PT program." *The Mountaineer*, 6 July 2006. Accessed 16 May 2017, http://www.drum.army.mil/mountaineer/Article.aspx?ID=800.

"Operation Commando Dive leads to detentions, cache finds." *The Mountaineer*, 26 April 2007. Accessed 10 June 2017, http://www.drum.army.mil/mountaineer/Article.aspx?ID=4519.

"Operation Polar Schism detains six in Owesat." 8 July 2007. Accessed 25 June 2017, http://commandosof2bct.blogspot.com/2007/07/al-owesat-iraq-coalition-operation.html.

"Operation Polar Schism III detains 22 in search for missing Soldiers." *The Mountaineer*, 16 August 2007. Accessed 26 June 2017, http://www.drum.army.mil/mountaineer/Article.aspx?ID=689.

"Operation Polar Scrum helps get suspected terrorists, IEDs of the street." 6 May 2007. Accessed 11 June 2017, http://commandosof2bct.blogspot.com/2007/05/operation-polar-scrum-helps-get.html.

"Operation Polar Shield nabs six terrorists." 6 January 2007. Accessed 5 June 2017, http://commandosof2bct.blogspot.com/2007/01/operation-polar-shield-nabs-six.html.

"Patrol detains two suspects." 7 June 2007. Accessed 22 June 2017, http://commandosof2bct.blogspot.com/2007/06/patrol-detains-two-suspects.html.

"Polar Bears detain AIF leader, high value target and 47 others during mission." 25 February 2007. Accessed 7 June 2017, http://commandosof2bct.blogspot.com/2007/02/polar-bears-detain-aif-leader-high.html.

"Polar Bears discovered 9-11 propaganda in Iraqi home." 30 September 2007. Accessed 28 June 2017, http://commandosof2bct.blogspot.com/2007/09/polar-bears-discover-9-11-propaganda-in.html.

"Polar Bears find bomb, unexploded ordnance." 15 March 2007. Accessed 8 June 2017, http://commandosof2bct.blogspot.com/2007/03/polar-bears-find-bomb-unexploded.html.

"Qarghuli Village Residents Lead Troops to Caches." *Charlie Rock Chat*, Volume 2, unnumbered issue, August 2007.

Sanchez, Chris. "4–31 Soldiers Help Rushdi Mullah Children." 2 January 2007. Accessed 23 May 2017, http://commandosof2bct.blogspot.com/2007/01/4-31-soldiers-help-rushdi-mullah.html.

Sanchez, Chris. "Polar Bears Seize Weapons in Janabi Village." 6 January 2007 Accessed 5 June 2017, http://commandosof2bct.blogspot.com/2007/01/polar-bears-seize-weapons-in-janabi.html

Sanchez, Chris. "Troops build bond with Yusufiyah citizens." *The Mountaineer*, 9 November 2006. Accessed 22 May 2017, http://www.drum.army.mil/mountaineer/Article.aspx?ID=3293.

"Search continues for missing Soldiers." *The Mountaineer*, 7 June 2007. Accessed 22 June 2017, http://www.drum.army.mil/mountaineer/Article.aspx?ID=1128.

"2nd BCT Soldiers earn coveted Expert Infantryman Badge." *The Mountaineer*, 22 June 2006. Accessed 16 May 2017, http://www.drum.army.mil/mountaineer/Article.aspx?ID=1290.

"2nd BCT soldiers receive unexpected invitation." *The Mountaineer*, 23 August 2007. Accessed 28 June 2017, http://www.drum.army.mil/mountaineer/Article.aspx?ID=592.

"Soldiers aid Iraqi troops with Operation Polar Alpha." *The Mountaineer*, 19 July 2007. Accessed 25 June 2017, http://www.drum.army.mil/mountaineer/Article.aspx?ID=1006.

"10th Mountain Division leaves 'boot' print on history." *The Mountaineer*, 8 September 2011. Accessed 17 May 2017, http://www.drum.army.mil/mountaineer/Article.aspx?ID=5724.

Wright, Webster. "4–31 Soldiers Discover More Than 50 Weapons Caches." 2–10 MTN Public Affairs Office, 13 October 2006. Accessed 17 May 2017, http://commandosof2bct.blogspot.com/2006/10/4-31-soldiers-discover-more-than-50.html.

"Yusufiyah infrastructure, hope improving." 6 May 200z7. Accessed 13 June 2017, http://commandosof2bct.blogspot.com/2007/05/yusufiyah-infrastructure-hope-improving.html.

"Yusufiyah-area men flock to IP recruitment drive." *The Mountaineer*, 12 July 2007. Accessed 23 June 2017, http://www.drum.army.mil/mountaineer/Article.aspx?ID=1077.

Papers

Fawley, Darrell. "Adapting Short of Doctrine: US Military Counterinsurgency in Iraq March 2004 to December 2006." Monograph, School of Advanced Military Studies, 2017.

Fawley, Darrell. "Polar Bears in the Desert: 4-31 IN and Counterinsurgency Operations in Iraq." Term Paper, Ohio University, 2014.

Fawley, Darrell. "Polar Bears in the Desert: A Case Study of the Operational and Strategic Impacts of the Iraq Surge on Tactical Units." Thesis, Command and General Staff College, 2016.

Reports

Dale, Catherine. "Operation Iraqi Freedom: Strategies, Approaches, Results, and Issues for Congress." *Congressional Research Service*, 2 April 2009.

Duelfer, Charles. "Comprehensive Reports of the Special Advisor to the DCI on Iraq's WMDs." 30 September 2004.

Webpages

"Iraq's Nuclear, Biological and Chemical Facilities." *Federation of American Scientists* website. Accessed 13 November 2014, fas.org/nuke/guide/Iraq/facility/inc-wmd.htm.

"Iraq's Nuclear, Biological and Chemical Facilities (Detailed List)." *Free Republic*, last modified 6 February 2003. Accessed 13 May 2017, http://www.freerepublic.com/focus/news/837079/posts.

Unit Histories

"31st Infantry Regiment—'America's Foreign Legion.'" The 31st Infantry Regiment Association. Accessed 16 May 2017, http://www.31stinfantry.org/wp-content/uploads/2016/06/31st-US-Infantry-Short_History-June-2016.pdf.

"Short History of the 31st US Infantry Regiment—The Polar Bears. 'America's Foreign Legion.'" The 31st Infantry Regiment Association. Accessed 16 May 2017, http://www.31stinfantry.org/wp-content/uploads/2016/06/A-History-of-The-Polar-Bears-June-2016.pdf.

Briefings and Presentations

"DoD News Briefing with Col. Kershaw from the Pentagon, Arlington, Va." 5 October 2007. Accessed 16 May 2017, http://archive.defense.gov/Transcripts/Transcript.aspx?TranscriptID=4053.\.

Fawley, Darrell. "1/C/4-31 IN Weekly Brief, 21-27 Jan 07, 28 Jan-3 Feb 07." 3 February 2007.

Fawley, Darrell. "1/C/4-31 IN Weekly Brief, 11-17 February 07." 18 February 2007.

Interviews

Beckenbaugh, Lisa. "Interview with MAJ Chris Vitale." Interview by U.S. Army Combat Studies Institute. Fort Leavenworth, KS. 4 October 2012.

Connors, Pete. "Interview with SPC Stephen Rockhold." Interview by U.S. Army Combat Studies Institute. Fort Leavenworth, KS. 25 January 2006.

Photographs

Alleruzzo, Maya. "10th Mountain Division soldiers rest after searching for three of their comrades missing days after a complex attack that left four U.S. soldiers and an Iraqi soldier dead in a village south of Baghdad on May 18, 2007." 18 May 2007. Accessed 21 June 2017, https://www.mayaalleruzzo.net/americass-long-shadow/.

Cano, John. "Tearing down bridges." 3 July 2007. Accessed 22 June 2017, http://www.drum.army.mil/mountaineer/Article.aspx?ID=1078.

Documents

All Army Activities (ALARACT) 071/07. "Change in Active-Duty Deployment Policy, DTG 13240Z APR 07." 13 April 2007.

Odierno, Raymond. "Letter to the Soldiers of Multi-National Corps-Iraq." 21 June 2007.

Petraeus, David. "Letter to Soldiers, Sailors, Airmen, Marines, and Civilians of Multi-National Forces-Iraq." 10 February 2007.

Index

Abizaid, John 32
Abrams tank 15, 65, 112
Abu Habe, Iraq 77
Abu Haswa, Iraq 115
Abu Risha, Sattar 143
Abu Shakir 164
adviser *see* partnership with indigenous forces
Aeisha Brigade 26–27, 72, 75
Afghanistan, war in 1, 17, 35–36, 40, 95, 108, 116–118, 173–174, 192
Ahmed Suhel, Iraq *see* Al Taraq, Iraq
air assault operations 24, 56–57, 73, 85–86, 89, 95, 99–101, 103, 110–111, 115, 121, 133, 137–138, 148–149, 152
air support 102, 112
The Alamo: position at the AVLB 19–20, 22, 28, 42, 53, 132; position on the Mullah Fayad Highway 53, 55–58, 67, 69, 82, 101, 145, 173; *see also* Patrol Base Siberia
Alexander the Great 12
Alger, Tracy 161
Algeria 158
Ali Al Saleem Air Base, Kuwait 42
Al Iskandriyah 11, 137
Al Jazeera 14
Al Karkh Health Department 162
Al Najaf 15
Al Owesat 148, 152, 167
Al Qaeda in Iraq (AQIZ) 17, 24, 27–29, 32, 37, 54, 73, 85, 98, 110, 122, 124, 129–130, 135, 141, 143, 150, 152, 154, 160, 163, 166, 168
Al Qaqaa Weapons Facility 14, 22

Al Rashid Hotel 157
Al Taraq, Iraq 5, 56–62, 66–69, 72, 74–77, 81–83, 92, 94, 96–97, 99, 102–103, 108–110, 111, 114–115, 129, 142, 145, 149, 152–153, 173–174, 177, 179, 183, 187, 190
Al Thobat, Iraq 98, 148
Amos, James 104
Anbar Awakening 140, 144, 153–154; *see also* Sons of Iraq
Anbar Province, Iraq 11, 13, 15, 17, 113, 140, 144
Anderson, Joseph 14
Anzack, Joseph 132–133, 137, 141, 157, 161, 165, 167
Apel, Josh 134–135, 137
Arbaeen ritual 114, 163
AVLB *see* The Alamo, position at the AVLB

Baathist 12–13, 43
Babil Provence, Iraq 140
Babineau, David 28, 98
Baghdad, Iraq 11, 15, 17, 19–20, 26, 31–32, 35, 40, 42, 54, 56, 73, 89, 97, 99, 107, 109, 113, 116, 124–126, 133, 135, 144, 149, 153–154, 157–158, 162–163, 167, 181, 193; smuggling into 43, 85, 164
Baghdad Belts 114, 162–163; Southern Belts 115, 121, 169
Baghdad International Airport (BIAP) 42, 57, 89
Al Baghdadi, Abu Bakr 163
Baird, Brian 152
Barak, Sabah 132, 135, 137, 164
Barker, James 25, 28–29
Barnes, Nathan 149, 165
Bataan Death March 34
Beurhing, Charles 40
Bevel, Ray 121–122

bin Laden, Osama 17
biometrics 123, 184
Bishop, Ryan 120–122
body counts 188
Bowden, Mark 119
Bradley Fighting Vehicle 15, 115, 125–126
"Breaking the Wall" 163
British Malaya 158
Brown, Harrison "Ducky" 115, 165
Browning, Brian 106, 165
Bryan, Chaplain Jeff 2, 42, 55, 67, 69, 80, 137, 164–165, 192
Bush, George W. 31–32, 138, 163, 168

cache 17, 24, 67, 69–75, 77, 83, 86, 95, 97–98, 100, 103, 106–107, 109, 114, 122–124, 145, 148–149, 150, 156–157, 174, 177, 188
Callahan, Bobby 53, 164–165
Cambodia 35
Camp Beuhring, Kuwait 40–41
Camp Cropper, Iraq 135
Camp Liberty, Iraq 42
Camp Stryker, Iraq 44–46, 49, 53, 114, 116
Camp Udari, Kuwait 40
Camp Victory, Iraq 116; *see also* Victory Base Complex
car bomb *see* vehicle-borne IED (VBIED)
Carghuli Village, Iraq *see* Qarghuli Village, Iraq
Carolina Maneuvers 36
Casey, George: chief of staff of the U.S. Army 117, 120; commander of MNF-I 32–33, 37, 41, 143, 181
Caveman Canal 22, 135, 137; *see also* Route Caveman

census 178–179
Chen, Danny 166
Chiareilli, Peter 31–32, 119
Chinese forces in Korean War 34
Chosin Reservoir 34
civic engagements and projects 68, 101, 104, 128, 145, 158, 172, 189–190
Civil Affairs 128, 181, 189
civilian casualties 15, 27, 109–110; U.S. treatment of 29, 61, 83, 109, 144, 149
COIN *see* counterinsurgency
COIN Academy 33, 41
Cold War 37
combat engineers *see* Iron Claw route clearance team
Combat Outpost (COP) Corregidor 115, 120, 138
combat support hospital (CSH) 58, 124
community policing *see* Zip Code Offensive
Company A, 2nd Battalion, 5th Cavalry Regiment (A/2-5 CAV) 94–95, 98, 103, 110, 112, 114–116
Company A, 478th Civil Affairs Battalion 128
Company B, 1st Battalion, 22nd Infantry Regiment (B/1-22 IN) 65, 94
Company B, 2nd Battalion, 69th Armor Regiment (B/2-69 AR) 114–116, 125, 133, 142, 149
Company C, 210th Brigade Support Battalion 79
Company F, 2nd Battalion, 24th Marine Regiment (F/2/24) 15–16, 18, 29–30; *see also* Marines
Concerned Local Citizens 145, 150–151, 153, 156–157, 163, 167, 183–184, 193
Congressional Research Service 167
Connell, James 132–133, 165
Coppock, Craig 171
cordon and search 27, 38, 86, 108, 146–148
Cortez, Paul 25–26, 28–29
counterinsurgency 16–17, 31–33, 36–38, 43, 105–106, 108, 110, 119–120, 127, 136, 138, 144–145, 147, 150–151, 154, 158, 167, 169, 171–191; approach 2–4, 6, 9, 30, 33, 79, 84, 103, 139, 169; ethics in 104, 148, 188–189, 193; theory 10, 16, 109, 101

Courneya, Daniel 132, 165
Craver, Johnny 165

Daughters of Iraq 162
Dawoud Village, Iraq 152–153
Desert Storm 37, 121
Diem, John 28
Djibouti 35
Drum, Hugh 36
Duelfer, Charles 14
DUSTWUN 47, 140

82nd Airborne Division 14, 138
11 September 2001 terrorist attacks 35, 155
Euphrates River 1, 7, 9, 11–13, 15, 17, 20, 54, 85–89, 92, 95, 102, 115, 121, 123, 137–138, 148, 152, 155, 181, 183, 193
Expert Infantryman Badge 38, 42
explosive ordnance disposal (EOD) 22–23, 43, 57–58, 65, 67, 70, 74, 98, 114, 130, 150

Fallujah, Iraq 14, 17, 54, 68
Fetoah Village, Iraq 157
Field Manual 3-24, *Counterinsurgency* 33, 104, 167, 171
Field Manual 3-24.2, *Tactics in Counterinsurgency* 171
5th Armored Division 36
1st Air Cavalry Brigade 76
1st Battalion, 7th Cavalry Regiment 86
1st Battalion, 23rd Infantry Regiment (1-23 IN) 134
1st Battalion, 75th Ranger Regiment (1-75) 36
1st Battalion, 108th Armor Regiment (1-108 AR) 19, 30, 168
1st Battalion, 502nd Parachute Infantry Regiment (1/502 PIR) 19, 24, 32–33, 42–43, 47, 50, 52, 60, 103, 156, 168, 174, 189, 193
1st Brigade Combat Team, 1st Armored Division (1/1 AD) 32
1st Stryker Brigade Combat Team, 25th Infantry Division 166
1st Cavalry Division 94
1st Squadron, 1st Cavalry Regiment (1-1 CAV), 1st Armored Division 14
The Fiyahs 15, 17
FM 3-24 *see* Field Manual 3-24, *Counterinsurgency*
foreign fighters 19–20, 122, 153

Fort Irwin, CA 37
45th Infantry Division 36
48th Infantry Brigade 16, 19, 29–30, 168, 193; *see also* 1st Battalion, 108th Armor Regiment
Forward Operating Base (FOB) Mahmudiyah 21, 28, 52–53, 55–56
Forward Operating Base (FOB) Saint Michael *see* Forward Operating Base Mahmudiyah
Forward Operating Base (FOB) Yusifiyah: 19–20, 22, 30, 42, 56–57, 61, 67–69, 77–78, 83, 85, 89, 92, 94, 98, 121, 162, 168; establishment 16; catching fire 24; attack on 53
4th Armored Division 36
4th Battalion, 4th Brigade, 6th Division (Iraqi Army) 20, 61, 86, 98, 100, 105, 173, 183
Fouty, Byron 132, 138, 140–141, 145, 147–148, 151–152, 154–155, 160–161, 164–165, 169
Al Frejee, Ali Jassim Muhammad 100

Gallula, David 16, 101, 171, 181–182
Gates, Robert 117–120
Geneva Conventions 125, 136
Georgia Army National Guard *see* 48th Infantry Brigade
Geren, Pete 117, 120
Given, Nathaniel 98, 165
Global War on Terrorism 3–4
Grant, Frederick Dent 35
Grant, Ulysses 35, 173, 176
Green, Steven 25–26, 28–29
Greenlee, Statieon 61, 165

Hadley, Stephen 168
Haswah 115
Heartbreak Ridge 34
hearts and minds approach to counterinsurgency 14, 38, 190–191
Helmand, Afghanistan 174
Herbst, Jeffrey 30
Hewett, Thomas 165
Hiep Duc, Vietnam 35
Hittite ruins 12
Hittites 12
homemade explosives 77, 101, 150
Horn of Africa 117
Horne, Alistair 171
Houssen, Mouayad 52
Hussein, Ali 123

216

Index

Hussein, Saddam 12–13, 91, 100, 164; other people named 123

Ia Drang Valley, Vietnam 86
Ibn Sina Hospital 83
Ibrahim, Muhammad Khalil 135
improvised explosive device (IED) 7–8, 16–17, 19–24, 26–28, 37, 43, 51, 53–58, 61, 63–70, 74–75, 82–83, 86–88, 96–100, 105–106, 110, 112, 114–115, 120–121, 123–124, 126–127, 130–133, 135, 142, 144–145, 148–150, 152–153, 156, 182; command wire initiation device 58–60, 64–65, 88, 90–91, 94; crush wire initiation device 98; daisy chained 102; deep buried 88, 130; directional charge 109; pressure plate initiation device 69–70, 96, 98
Inchon landing 34, 93
Infanti, Michael 36–37, 52–53, 67, 72–73, 81, 85, 87–89, 116, 146, 152–153, 155, 1601–161, 172–173, 182–183, 187–188
insider attack 22, 95
intelligence preparation of the battlefield 185–186
Interim Governing Council 15
International Zone 83
interpreter 15, 22, 28, 88, 91, 183; casualties 115, 160, 164–165
invasion of Iraq 8, 12–14, 18–19, 24, 151
invasion of Normandy 125
Iraq coalition 40
Iraqi Ministry of Support 80
Iron Claw route clearance team 22, 43, 56–61, 63, 65–66, 69, 87, 89, 97, 112
ISIS *see* Islamic State
Islamic Army 110
Islamic State 8–9, 54, 98, 110, 122, 131–133, 135, 138–139, 141–142, 144, 150, 152, 154, 156, 163–164, 166, 168, 181, 193

Al Janabi, Abdullah 17
Janabi Road 125
Janabi Run Canal 43, 50–51, 67, 70, 72, 111, 174
Janabi tribe 13
Janabi Village 95, 98, 100
Japan 34
Japanese invasion and occupation of the Philippines 34

Jaysh-al-Islami 54
Jimenez, Alex 132, 138, 140–141, 145, 147–148, 151–152, 154–155, 157, 160–161, 164–165, 169
The Joint Readiness Training Center 147
joint terminal attack controller (JTAC) 112
Jurf As Sukr Bridge (JSB) 12–13, 19, 21–22, 28–30, 42, 83, 86, 110, 115, 142, 163, 168
Jurf As Sukr, Iraq 163–164

Kaplan, Lawrence 11, 108, 167
Karbala, Iraq 113
Karghouli Village, Iraq *see* Qarghuli Village, Iraq
Kershaw, Michael 36–37, 40, 52, 73–74, 79–81, 97, 100, 102, 116–117, 133, 136, 150–151, 153–154, 156–157, 160–161, 167–168, 172–173, 182, 186
Kilcullen, David 167, 171, 173, 187, 190–191
King, Edward 34
Kudair, Ali 110
Kuwait 40–42

Laganelli, John 168
Landing Zone X-Ray, Vietnam 86
Law Enforcement Plan of Baghdad 113
Law of Land Warfare 41, 189
Livermore, Doug 55, 94, 159
Lutifiyah, Iraq 11, 29, 42, 52, 68, 153
Lynch, Rick 114

MacArthur, Douglas 34, 93
MacFarland, Sean 32–33, 68, 108, 143, 193
Mahmudiyah, Iraq 5, 11, 13, 15, 18, 20, 29, 43, 52–53, 68, 81, 100, 114, 129, 142, 153, 157, 167–168, 187
Mahmudiyah Kidnapping 5
Mahmudiyah Rape and Killings *see* Rape of Abeer Qassim Al Janabi
Mahoney, Anthony 168
Al Maliki, Nouri 164
Mansoor, Peter 2, 114, 193
Mao Tse-tung 37
Marine Corps Warfighting Publication 3-33.5, *Counterinsurgency* 33; *see also* Field Manual 3-24
Marines 5, 15–16, 18, 29–30, 104, 108, 140, 155, 162, 167, 193–194; in Korea 34; *see also* Company F, 2nd Battalion, 24th Marine Regiment
Al Masri, Abu Ayyab 63
McConnell, Mitch 32
McCrystal, Stanley 26
McCuen, John 109, 171–172, 180
McMaster, H.R. 18, 32–33, 68, 108, 193
mechanized infantry 65, 117; *see also* Bradley Fighting Vehicles
medical evacuation (MEDEVAC) 58, 77–78, 98–99, 109, 124–125, 144
medical operation (MEDOP) 79, 81, 110, 138, 146
Mekong Delta, Vietnam 35
Menchaca, Kristian 28–29, 47, 98, 135
Messer, Christopher 98, 165
MIA 140
military transition team 8, 167
MISCAP 140
mission command 44, 101, 187–190
Mississippi River, Union operations on 173, 176
Mogadishu, Somalia 115, 119
Molson, Adam 164
Moore, Hal 86
Mosul, Iraq 108, 144, 169
MRE bomb 66; *see also* improved explosive device
Muhammad, Abid 110
Mujahadeen Shura Council 28
Mullah Fayad, Iraq 13, 56, 81, 102, 114–115, 138, 141
Mullah Fayad Highway 13, 42, 53, 55–58, 61, 64, 66, 72, 82, 94, 97, 105, 110, 128, 130, 138–139, 144, 173
Mullah Rushdi *see* Rushdi Mullah
Multi-National Corps-Iraq (MNC-I) 31, 104, 119–120, 134
Multi-National Division-Baghdad 94, 96, 114
Multi-National Division-Center 114, 137, 139, 151, 169
Multi-National Force-Iraq 9, 32–33, 104, 108, 167
Murphy, Christopher 132, 165

Nagl, John 101, 105, 171
National Guard 15, 19, 29–30, 123, 168, 193

Index

National Infantry Museum 192
The National Training Center (NTC) 37–38
Natonski, Richard 68
1920 Revolutionary Brigade 54, 100
9th Infantry Division 35
Norris, Curtis 96, 98, 165
North Hargawi, Iraq *see* Al Taraq, Iraq

Oates, Michael 159–160
Obama, Barrack 163, 167
Odierno, Raymond 104, 114, 120–121
Old Baldy 34
101st Airborne Division (Air Assault) 13–4, 19, 22, 24, 45–47, 51, 55–56, 95, 117, 119, 144, 156, 193
172nd Stryker Brigade Combat Team 31
196th Infantry Brigade 35
OP Dale 34
Operation Anaconda 35
Operation Commando Auger 115, 120
Operation Commando Dive 121, 123
Operation Commando Hunter 56, 68, 79
Operation Commando Razor 133
Operation Commando Vice 95, 182
Operation Eagle Dive 123
Operation Glory Light 24
Operation Marne Torch 139
Operation Phantom Fury 17, 68
Operation Plymouth Rock 17
Operation Polar Alpha 149
Operation Polar Black Diamond 86–87
Operation Polar Blizzard 9, 56–68, 70, 72, 79–80, 83, 87, 93, 115, 131, 174, 181
Operation Polar Charade 133, 137
Operation Polar Dagger 108
Operation Polar Dive 121, 124
Operation Polar Fire 99–100
Operation Polar Harpoon 35
Operation Polar Ice 103
Operation Polar Iron 110
Operation Polar Pounce 98
Operation Polar Schism 148
Operation Polar Schism III 151–152
Operation Polar Scrum 125–126
Operation Polar Shield 98
Operation Polar Tempest 148–149
Operation Polar Thunder 110
Operation Polar Valor 89, 96, 193
Operation Polar Warrior 95
Operation Restoring Rights 68
Operation River Walk 17
Operation Trident IV 124

partnership with indigenous forces 20, 37, 53, 56–5, 79, 95, 100–102, 104–105, 112, 115, 125, 128, 134, 139, 140, 148–149, 151, 157, 160, 167–169, 172, 181–184, 186, 191
Patriquin, Travis 143
Patrol Base Bataan 86, 99, 103, 117, 126, 133–134, 149
Patrol Base Dragon 80, 85, 142, 148
Patrol Base Gator Swamp 43, 45, 51
Patrol Base Inchon 93–94, 96, 102, 130, 132, 142, 146, 153
Patrol Base Shanghai 106, 124, 141
Patrol Base Siberia 82, 101; *see also* The Alamo, position on the Mullah Fayad Highway
Patrol Base Yusifiyah *see* Forward Operating Base Yusifiyah
Pearl Harbor attack 89
Persian Gulf War 13
Petraeus, Gen. David 2, 193; commander of Multi-National Force-Iraq 9, 33, 103–105, 108, 114, 141, 144, 167, 181; commander of 101st Airborne Division (Air Assault) 108, 144, 169; development of Field Manual 3-24 33, 108
Philippines 34; insurgency in 158
Phoenix Academy 33
Plain of Reeds, Vietnam 35
political advisor (POLAD) 104
Poole, John 171
Pork Chop Hill 34
Porter, David Dixon 176
post traumatic stress disorder (PTSD) 119
presence patrols 16, 149
providential reconstruction team 157
Psychological Operations 124

Al Qarghuli, Amin 162
Qarghuli tribe 13, 54, 85, 91, 135, 141, 150, 162
Qarghuli Village, Iraq 5, 7, 9, 17, 29, 55, 81, 83, 85–88, 91, 93–95, 98, 100–103, 106, 110, 114–115, 123, 129, 133–135, 141–143, 146–149, 150, 152–154, 159, 174, 187, 189–190
quick reaction force 20, 22, 81, 85, 94, 98, 101, 115–116, 133
Quintas, Leopoldo 18

Al Rahman, Atiyah Abd 140
Ramadi, Iraq 33, 68, 108, 143, 169
Ranger School 43, 90–91, 112; importance of for officers 63, 92
rape of Abeer Qassim Al Janabi 5, 9, 25–26, 28, 119, 129, 132, 169
rapid road repair team 131
rescue of Jessica Lynch 36
river-borne operations 88–89
roadside bomb 110
Rogers, Nicholas 80, 165
Route Caveman 22; *see also* Caveman Canal
route clearance *see* Iron Claw route clearance team
Route Earnhardt 43–44, 47, 116
Route Fat Boys 22, 51
Route Jackson 114
Route Malibu 7, 9, 83, 86–89, 94, 96, 102, 115, 121, 128, 130, 135, 142, 144–145, 151, 153, 155, 164–165, 174–175, 181
Route Peggy 21, 56, 70, 112–113
Route Primus 121
Route Saliva 109
Route Slipknot 43, 46
Route Sporster 21, 25–26, 29, 42, 57, 130, 139, 142, 161, 168, 183, 193
Route Starbucks 120
Rumayian Liberation Battle 163
Rumsfeld 31–32
Rushdi Mullah 12, 23–26, 29, 32, 56, 63–66, 68–69, 73, 77, 79–82, 84–85, 95–96, 101–102, 106, 111, 114, 124, 128, 137–138, 143–144, 151, 153, 174; first patrol base at 26–28

Sack, Carl 40
Sadr Al Yusifiyah 54
Saigon, Vietnam 35

Index

Al Sakbari, Abbas Abbas 128
Samarra, Iraq 138
sanctuary 17, 56, 73, 95, 97, 99, 114, 121, 130, 148,
sappers *see* Iron Claw route clearance team
Schober, Anthony 132, 157, 165
2nd Armored Division 36
Second Battle of Fallujah *see* Operation Phantom Fury
2nd Battalion, 14th Infantry Regiment (2-14 IN) 43, 49, 51, 80, 85, 88, 124, 142, 152, 157
2nd Battalion, 15th Field Artillery Regiment (2-15 FA) 37, 53, 100, 123, 186
2nd Battalion, 24th Marine Regiment 15-18, 30, 168
2nd Battalion, 70th Armor Regiment (2-70 AR) 18-19, 30, 168, 193
2nd Battalion, 502nd Parachute Infantry Regiment (2/502 PIR) 43, 51, 55
2nd Battalion, 505th Parachute Infantry Regiment (2/505 PIR) 138
2nd Brigade Special Troops Battalion 51, 112, 135
sectarian violence 15
Seminole Raid 35
Sepp, Kalev 33
7th Infantry Division 34
Shah-i-Koht Valley, Afghanistan 35
Shakariyah Triangle 12-13, 97
Sharp, Philip 3, 40-4, 73, 103, 108-109, 122-123, 142, 151, 166, 192
Sheridan, Phil 36
Sherman, William 36
Siege of Vicksburg 173
Simmons, David 116, 165
Simpson, Emile 174, 191
Singleton, Todd 116, 165
Sisters of Fallujah 162
6 June 2006 Kidnapping 28-29, 86, 98, 135
Sky, Emma 104
Smith, Mark 15, 17-18
smuggling 20, 26, 37, 70, 85, 163-164
Somalia, U.S. operations in 119, 121
Sons of Iraq 9, 153
Soviet Union 37
Special forces *see* special operations

special operations 26-27, 67, 98, 137, 143, 163, 186-187
Spielman, Jessee 25-26, 28-29
stop loss 118, 151, 157
suicide bombers 11, 19, 23, 26-27, 63, 162
suicide wagons 16
The Surge 2, 10, 108, 114, 119-120, 146, 152, 167, 186
Syria 20

Tabor, Robert 171
Taji, Iraq 33
Taliban 95
Task Force 6-26 26
Tel Afar, Iraq 32, 68, 108, 169
Tet Offensive 35
3rd Armored Cavalry Regiment (3rd ACR) 18
3rd Battalion, 14th Infantry Regiment (3-14 IN) 35
3rd Battalion, 187th Airborne Infantry Regiment (3/187 AIR) 156-157, 161
3rd Battalion, 227th Aviation Regiment 86
3rd Brigade, 10th Mountain Division (Light) 116
3rd Infantry Division 3, 22, 114, 139
Tigris River 19, 54, 138
Tikrit, Iraq 138
tour extension 116-118; 172nd Stryker Brigade Combat Team 31
Triangle Hill 34
Troop B, 1st Squadron, 89th Cavalry Regiment 138
Tucker, Michael 28-29, 47, 98, 135
Tudor, Steven 121, 165
12 May 2007 Attack and Kidnapping 7-8, 131, 134, 137, 139, 141, 144, 147-148, 167, 169, 175, 186, 191
23rd Infantry Division (Americal Division) 35
23rd Military Police Company 140
24th Marine Expeditionary Unit 17; *see also* Marines

The Ugly American 190
United States Army War College 108
United States Central Command (CENTCOM) 32, 117
United States Civil War 36

United States Congress 31-32, 118, 157
United States Institute of Peace 157, 167
United States Military Academy 35, 43, 161
United States troop surge *see* The Surge
United States troop withdrawal 163
Upper Mesopotamia 12
urban operations training 90
Uzbekistan 35

vehicle borne IED (VBIED) 18, 27-28, 52-53, 63, 80, 102, 155, 163, 174; *see also* improvised explosive device
vertical and horizontal construction engineers 69, 80
veterinarian operation (VETOP) 96-97, 190
Victory Base Complex 42; *see also* Camp Victory, Iraq
Vietnam 31, 33, 35-37, 86, 88, 167, 188

Walter Reed Army Medical Center 131, 148
War Zone D, Vietnam 35
Watt, Justin 28
West, Bing 167
West Point *see* United States Military Academy
Wheeler, Curtis 40
Wheeler-Sack Army Airfield 40, 159
White, Nick 116
World War II 34, 36, 43, 86

Yribe, Tony 25-26, 28-29
Yusifiyah Joint Security Station 110, 114, 115, 128, 140-141, 162
Yusifiyah Thermal Power Plant (YTPP) 13, 22, 24, 28, 42, 72-73, 80, 85, 129, 138, 142, 162, 173, 187

Zaedi tribe 43
Al Zarqawi, Abu Musab 17, 26, 32, 135
Zemp, William 168
Ziemba, Nicholas 11, 54
Zip Code Offensive 15-17, 30, 83-84
Zobai tribe 13
Zone 310 112
Al Zubaydi, Amar Adnan Muhammad Hamzah 18